ATARI ST INTERNALS
The authoritative insider's guide

By K. Gerits, L. Englisch, R. Bruckmann

A Data Becker Book
Published by
Abacus Software

Third Edition, Seventh Printing   December 1988
Printed in U.S.A.
Copyright © 1985,1986,1987, 1988   Data Becker GmbH
                                    Merowingerstraße 30
                                    4000 Düsseldorf, West Germany
Copyright © 1985,1986,1987, 1988   Abacus Software, Inc.
                                    5370 52nd Street, S.E.
                                    Grand Rapids, MI 49508

This book is copyrighted. No part of this book may be reproduced, stored in a retrieval system, or transmitted in any form or by any means, electronic, mechanical, photocopying, recording or otherwise without the prior written permission of Abacus Software or Data Becker, GmbH.

Every effort has been made to ensure complete and accurate information concerning the material presented in this book. However, Abacus Software can neither guarantee nor be held legally responsible for any mistakes in printing or faulty instructions contained in this book. The authors will always appreciate receiving notice of subsequent mistakes.

ATARI, 520ST, ST, TOS, ST BASIC and ST LOGO are trademarks or registered trademarks of Atari Corp.

GEM, GEM Draw and GEM Write are trademarks or registered trademarks of Digital Research Inc.

IBM is a registered trademark of International Business Machines.

ISBN   0-916439-46-1

Table of Contents

1	**The Integrated Circuits**	1
1.1	The 68000 Processor	3
1.1.1	The 68000 Registers	4
1.1.2	Exceptions on the 68000	7
1.1.3	The 68000 Connections	7
1.2	The Custom Chips	13
1.3	The WD 1772 Floppy Disk Controller	20
1.3.1	1772 Pins	20
1.3.2	1772 Registers	24
1.3.3	Programming the FDC	25
1.4	The MFP 68901	28
1.4.1	68901 Connections	28
1.4.2	The MFP Registers	32
1.5	The 6850 ACIAs	41
1.5.1	The Pins of the 6850	41
1.5.2	The Registers of the 6850	44
1.6	The YM-2149 Sound Generator	48
1.6.1	Sound Chip Pins	50
1.6.2	The 2149 Registers and their Functions	52
1.7	I/O Register Layout of the ST	55
2	**The Interfaces**	65
2.1	The Keyboard	67
2.1.1	The Mouse	71
2.1.2	Keyboard commands	74
2.2	The Video Connection	85
2.3	The Centronics Interface	88
2.4	The RS-232 Interface	90
2.5	The MIDI Connections	93
2.6	The Cartridge Slot	96
2.6.1	ROM Cartridges	97
2.7	The Floppy Disk Interface	99
2.8	The DMA Interface	101
3	**The ST Operating System**	103
3.1	The GEMDOS	106
3.1.1	Memory, files and processes	145
3.2	The BIOS Functions	152
3.3	The XBIOS	164

3.4	The Graphics	206
3.4.1	An overview of the line-A variables	227
3.4.2	Examples for using the line-A opcodes	230
3.5	The Exception Vectors	235
3.5.1	The line-F emulator	238
3.5.2	The interrupt structure of theST	240
3.6	The ST VT52 Emulator	245
3.7	The ST System Variables	250
3.8	The 68000 Instruction Set	258
3.8.1	Addressing modes	259
3.8.2	The instructions	263
3.9	The BIOS Listing	271
4	**Appendix**	463
4.1	The System Fonts	465
4.2	Alphabetical listing of GEMDOS functions	467
4.3	The blitter chip	469
4.3.1	The blitter registers	471
4.4	The Mega ST realtime clock	478
4.5	Blitter chip demonstration programs	479
	Index	491

List of Figures

1.1-1	68000 Registers	5
1.2-1	GLUE	14
1.2-2	MMU	16
1.2-3	SHIFTER	17
1.2-4	DMA	19
1.3-1	FDC 1772	21
1.4-1	MFP 68901	29
1.5-1	ACIA 6850	42
1.6-1	Sound Chip YM-2149	49
1.6-2	Envelopes of the PSG	53
1.7-1	I/O Assignments	62
1.7-2	Memory Map	63
1.7-3	Block Diagram of the Atari ST	64
2.1-1	6850 Interface to 68000	68
2.1-2	Block Diagram of Keyboard Circuit	70
2.1.1-1	The Mouse	72
2.1.1-2	Mouse control port	74
2.1.2-1	Atari ST Key Assignments	84
2.2-1	Diagram of Video Interface	86
2.2-2	Monitor Connector	87
2.3-1	Printer Port Pins	88
2.3-2	Centronics Connection	89
2.4-1	RS-232 Connection	92
2.5-1	MIDI System Connection	95
2.6-1	The Cartridge Slot	96
2.7-1	Disk Connection	100
2.8-1	DMA Port	102
2.8-2	DMA Connections	102
3.4-1	Lo-Res-Mode	208
3.4-2	Medium-Res-Mode	209
3.4-3	Hi-Res-Mode	210
4.3-1	BLITTER	469
4.3.1-1	BLITTER BLOCK DIAGRAM	471

Chapter One

The Integrated Circuits

1.1   The 68000 Processor
1.1.1   The 68000 Registers
1.1.2   Exceptions on the 68000
1.1.3   The 68000 Connections
1.2   The Custom Chips
1.3   The WD 1772 Floppy Disk Controller
1.3.1   1772 Pins
1.3.2   1772 Registers
1.3.3   Programming the FDC
1.4   The MFP 68901
1.4.1   68901 Connections
1.4.2   The MFP Registers
1.5   The 6850 ACIAs
1.5.1   The Pins of the 6850
1.5.2   The Registers of the 6850
1.6   The YM-2149 Sound Generator
1.6.1   Sound Chip Pins
1.6.2   The 2149 Registers and their Functions
1.7   I/O Register Layout of the ST

The Integrated Circuits

1.1 The 68000 Processor

The 68000 microprocessor is the heart of the entire Atari ST system. This 16-bit chip is in a class by itself; programmers and hardware designers alike find the chip very easy to handle. From its initial development by Motorola in 1977 to its appearance on the market in 1979, the chip was to be a competitor to the INTEL 8086/8088 (the processor used in the IBM-PC and its many clones). Before the Atari ST's arrival on the marketplace, there were no affordable 68000 machines available to the home user. Now, though, with 16-bit computers becoming more affordable to the *common* man, the 8-bit machines won't be around much longer.

What does the 68000 have that's so special? Here's a very incomplete list of features:

>16 data bits
>24 address bits (16-megabyte address range!!)
>all signals directly accessible without multiplexer
>hassle-free operation of "old" 8-bit peripherals
>powerful machine language commands
>easy-to-learn assembler syntax
>14 different types of addressing
>17 registers each having 32-bit widths

These specifications (and many yet to be mentioned here) make the 68000 an incredibly good microprocessor for home and personal computers. In fact, as the price of memory drops, you'll soon be seeing 68000-based 64K machines for the same price as present-day 8-bit computers with the same amount of memory.

1.1.1 The 68000 Registers

Let's take a look at 68000 design. Figure 1.1-1 shows the 17 onboard 32-bit registers, the program counter and the status register.

The eight data registers can store and perform calculations, as well as the normal addressing tasks. Eight-bit systems use the accumulators for this, which limits the programmer to a total of 8 accumulators. Our 68000 data registers are quite flexible; data can be handled in 1-, 8-, 16- and 32- bit sizes. Even four-bit operations are possible (within the limits of Binary Coded Decimal counting). When working with 32-bit data, all 32 bits can be handled with a single operation. With 8- and 16-bit data, only the 8th or 16th bit of the data register can be accessed.

The address registers aren't as flexible for data access as are the data registers. These registers are for addressing, not calculation. Processing data is possible only with word (16-bit) and longword (32-bit) operations. The address registers must be looked at as two distinct groups, the most versatile being the registers A0-A6. Registers A7 and A7' fulfill a special need. These registers are used as the stack pointer by the processor. Two stack pointers are needed to allow the 68000 to run in USER MODE and SUPERVISOR MODE. Register A7 declares whether the system is in USER or SUPERVISOR mode. Note that the two registers work "under" A7, but the register contents are only available to the respective operating mode. We'll discuss these operating modes later.

The program counter is also considered a 32-bit register. It is theoretically possible to handle an address range of over 4 gigabytes. But the address bits A24-A31 aren't used, which "limits" us to 16 megabytes.

The 68000 status register comprises 16 bits, of which only 10 bits are used. This status register is divided into two halves: The lower eight bits (bits 0 to 4 proper) is the "user byte". These bits, which act as flags most of the time, show the results of arithmetical and comparative operations, and can be used for program branches hinging on those results. We'll look at the user byte in more detail later; for now, here is a brief list:

```
BIT 0 = Carry flag      BIT 1 = Overflow flag
BIT 2 = Zero flag       BIT 3 = Negative flag
BIT 4 = eXtend flag
```

Figure 1.1-1   68000 Registers

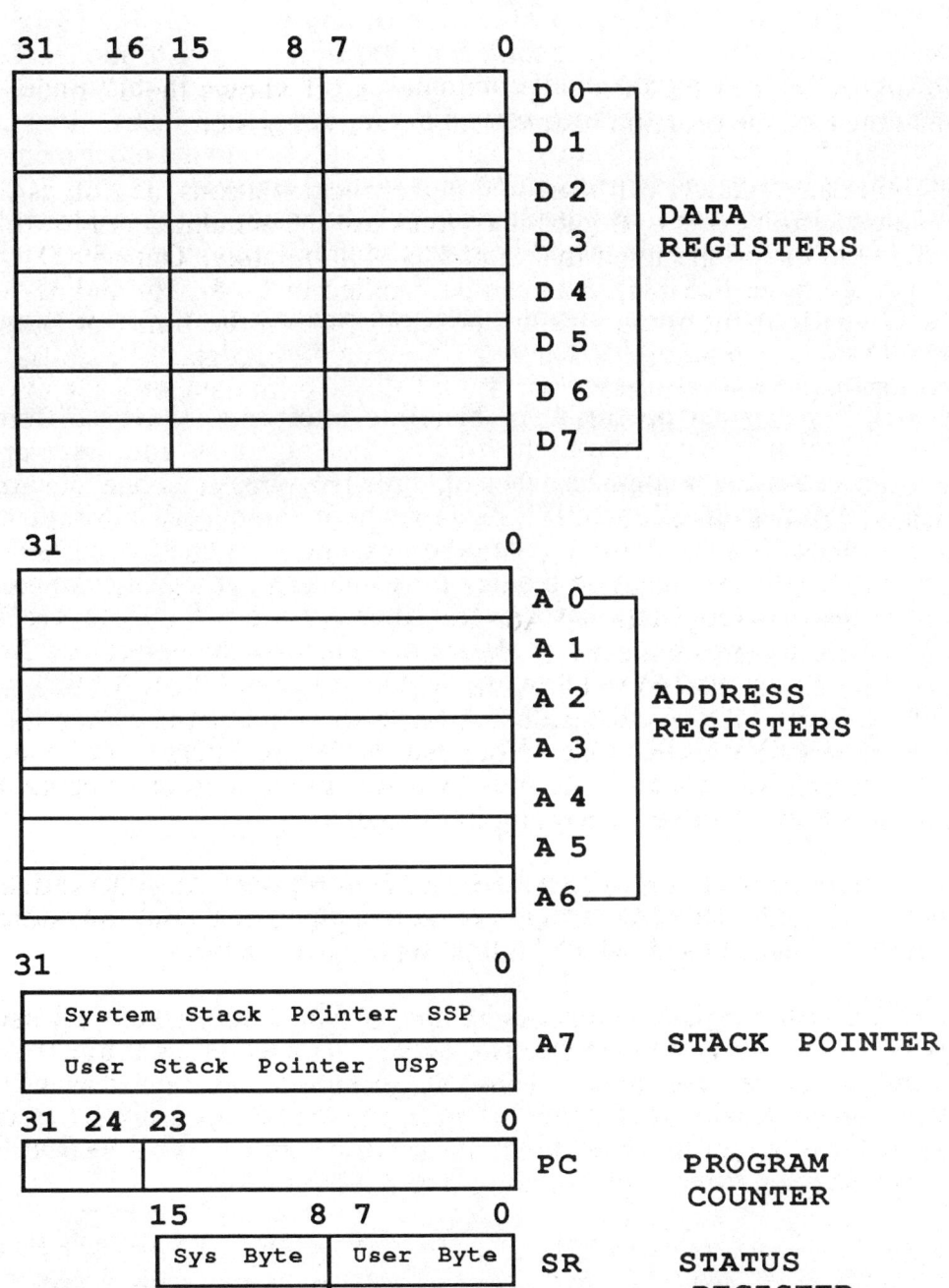

Bits 8-10, 13 and 15 make up the status register's system byte. The remaining bits are unused. Bit 15 works as a trace bit, which lets you do a software controlled single-step execution of any program. Bit 13 is the supervisor bit. When this bit is set, the 68000 is in supervisor mode. This is the normal operating mode; all commands are executed in this mode. In user mode, in which programs normally run, privileged instructions are inoperative. A special hardware design allows access into the other memory range while in user mode (e.g., important system variables, I/O registers). The system byte of the status register can only be manipulated in supervisor mode; but there's a simple method of switching between modes.

Bits 8 and 10 show the interrupt mask, and run in connection with pins IPL0-IPL2.

The 68000 has great potential for handling interrupts. Seven different interrupt priorities exist, the highest being the "non-maskable interrupt"; NMI. This interrupt recognizes when all three IPL pins simultaneously read low (0). If, however, all three IPL pins read high, there is no interrupt, and the system operates normally. The other six priorities can be masked by appropriate setting of the system byte of the status register. For example, if bit I2 of the interrupt mask is set, while I0 and I1 are off, only levels 7, 6 and 5 (000, 001 and 010) are recognized. All other combinations from IPL0-IPL2 are ignored by the processor.

1.1.2 Exceptions on the 68000

We've spoken of interrupts as if the 68000 behaves like other microprocessors. Interrupts, according to Motorola nomenclature, are an external form of an **exception** (the machine can interrupt what it's doing, do something else, and return to the interrupted task if needed). The 68000 distinguishes between normal operation and exception handling, rather than between user and supervisor mode. One such set of exceptions are the interrupts. Other things which cause exceptions are undefined opcodes, and word or longword access to a prohibited address.

To make exception handling quicker and easier, the 68000 reserves the first 1K of memory (1024 bytes, $000000-$0003FF). The exception table is located here. Exceptions are all coded as one of four bytes of a longword. Encountering an exception triggers the 68000, and the address of the corresponding table entry is output.

A special exception occurs on reset, which requires 8 bytes (two longwords); the first longword contains the standard initial value of the supervisor stack pointer, while the second longword contains the address of the reset routine itself. See Chapter 3.3 for the design and layout of the exception table.

1.1.3 The 68000 Connections

The connections on the 68000 are divided into eight groups (see Figure 1.1-3 on page 11).

The first group combines data and address busses. The data bus consists of pins D0-D15, and the address bus A1-A23. Address bit A0 is not available to the 68000. Memory can be communicated with words rather than bytes (1 word=2 bytes=16 bits, as opposed to 1 byte=8 bits). Also, the 68000 can access data located on odd addresses as well as even addresses. The signals will be dealt with later.

It's important to remember in connection with this, that by word access to memory, the byte of the odd address is treated as the low byte, and the even address is the high byte. Word access shouldn't stray from even addresses. That means that opcodes (whether all words or a single word) must always be located at even addresses.

When the data and address bus are in "tri-state" condition, a third condition (in addition to high and low) exists, in which the pins offer high resistance, and thus are inactive on the bus. This is important in connection with Direct Memory Access (DMA).

The second group of connections comprise the signals for asynchronous bus control. This group has five signals, which we'll now look at individually:

1) R/W (READ/WRITE)
The R/W signal is a familiar one to all microprocessors. This indicates to memory and peripherals whether the processor is writing to or reading data from the address on the bus.

2) AS (ADDRESS STROBE)
Every processor has a signal which it sends along the data lines signaling whether the address is ready to be used. On the 68000, this is known as the ADDRESS STROBE (low active).

3) UDS (UPPER DATA STROBE)
4) LDS (LOWER DATA STROBE)

If the 68000 could only process an entire memory word (two bytes) simultaneously, this signal wouldn't be necessary. However, for individual access to the low-byte and high-byte of a word, the processor must be able to distinguish between the two bytes. This is the task performed by UDS and LDS. When a word is accessed, both strobes are activated simultaneously (active=low). Accessing the data at an odd address activates the Lower Data Strobe only, while accessing data at an even address activates the Upper Data Strobe.

Bit A0 from the address bus is used in this case. After every access when the system must distinguish between three conditions (word, even byte, odd byte), A0 determines how to complete the access.

LDS and UDS are tri-state outputs.

5) DTACK

The above signals (with the exception of UDS and LDS) are needed by an 8-bit processor. DTACK takes a different path; DTACK must be low for any write or read access to take place. If the signal is not low within a bus cycle, the address and data lines "freeze up" until DTACK turns low. This can also occur in a WAIT loop. This way, the processor can slow down memory and peripheral chips while performing other tasks. If no wait cycles are used on the ST, the processor moves "at full tilt".

The third group of connections, the signals VMA, VPA and E are for synchronous bus control. A computer is more than memory and a microprocessor; interfaces to keyboard, screen, printer, etc. must be available for communication. In most cases, interfacing is handled by special ICs, but the 68000 has a huge selection of interface chips onboard. For hardware designers we'll take a little time explaining these synchronous bus signals.

The signal E (also known as $\Phi 2$ or phi 2) represents the reference count for peripherals. Users of 6800 and 6502 machines know this signal as the system counter. Whereas most peripheral chips have a maximum frequency of only 1 or 2 mHz, the 68000 has a working speed of 8 mHz, which can increased to 10 by the E signal. The frequency of E in the ST is 800 kHz. The E output is always active; it is not capable of a TRI-STATE condition.

The signal **VPA** (Valid Peripheral Address) sends data over the synchronous bus, and delegates this transfer to specific sections of the chip. Without this signal, data transfer is performed by the asynchronous bus. VPA also plays a role in generating interrupts, as we'll soon see.

VMA (Valid Memory Address) works in conjunction with the VPA to produce the CHIP-select signal for the synchronous bus.

The fourth group of 68000 signals allows simple DMA operation in the 68000 system. DMA (Direct Memory Access) directly accesses the DMA controllers, which control computer memory, and which is the fastest method of data transfer within a computer system.

To execute the DMA, the processor must be in an inactive state. But for the processor to be signaled, it must be in a "sleep" state; the low BR signal

(Bus Request) accomplishes this. On recognizing the BR signal, the 68000's read/write cycle ends, and the BG signal (Bus Grant) is activated. Now the DMA-requested chip waits until the signals AS, DTACK and (when possible) BGACK are rendered inactive. As soon as this occurs, the BGACK (Bus Grant Acknowledge) is activated by the requested chip, and takes over the bus. All essential signals on the processor are made high; in particular, the data, address and control busses are no longer influenced by the processor. The DMA controller can then place the desired address on the bus, and read or write data. When the DMA chip is finished with its task, the BGACK signal returns to its inactive state, and the processor again takes over the bus.

The fifth group of signals on the 68000 control interrupt generation. The 68000's "user's choice" interrupt concept is one of its most extraordinary performing qualities; you have 199 (!) interrupt vectors from which to choose. These interrupt vectors are divided into 7 non-auto-vectors and 192 auto-vectors, plus 7 different priority lines.

Interrupts are triggered by signals from the three lines IPL0 to IPL2; these three lines give you eight possible combinations. The combination determines the priority of the interrupt. That is, if IPL0, IPL1 and IPL2 are all set high, then the lowest priority is set ("no interrupt"). However, if all three lines are low, then highest priority takes over, to execute a non-maskable interrupt. All the combinations in between affect special bits in the 68000's status register; these, in turn, affect program control, regardless of whether or not a chosen interrupt is allowable.

Wait -- what are auto-vectors and non-auto-vectors? What do these terms mean?

If requesting an interrupt on IPL0-IPL2 while VPA is active (low), the desired code is directly converted from the IPL pins into a vector number. All seven interrupt codes on the IPL pins have their own vectors, though. The auto-vector concept automatically gives the vector number of the IPL interrupt code needed.

When DTACK, instead of VPA, is active on an interrupt request, the interrupt is handled as a non-auto-vector. In this case, the vector number from the triggered chip is produced by DTACK on the 8 lowest bits of the data bus. Usually (though not important here), the vector number is placed into the user-vector range ($40--$FF).

The sixth set of connections are the three "function code" outputs FC0 to FC2. These lines handle the status display of the processor. With the help of these lines, the 68000 can expand to four times 16 megabytes (64 megabytes). This extension requires the MMU (Memory Management Unit). This MMU does more than handle memory expansion on the ST; it also recognizes whether access is made to memory in user or supervisor mode. This information is conveyed to a memory range only accessible in supervisor mode. Also, the interrupt verification uses this information on the FC line. The figure below shows the possible combinations of functions.

Figure 1.1-3

FC2	FC1	FC0	Status
0	0	0	unused
0	0	1	User-mode data access
0	1	0	User-mode program
0	1	1	unused
1	0	0	unused
1	0	1	Supervisor data access
1	1	0	Supervisor program
1	1	1	Interrupt verification

The seventh group contains system control signals. This group applies to the input CLK and BERR, as well as the bidirectional lines RESET and HALT.

The input CLK will generate the working frequency of the processor. The 68000 can operate at different speeds; but the operating frequency must be specified (4, 6, 8, 10, or even 12.5 mHz). The ST has 8 mHz built in, while the minimum operating frequency is 2 mHz. The ST's 8 mHz was chosen as a "middle of the road" frequency to avoid losing data at higher frequencies.

The RESET line is necessary to check for system power-up. The 68000's data page distinguishes between two different reset conditions. On power-up, RESET and HALT are switched low for at least 100 milliseconds, to set up a proper initialization. Every other initialization requires a low impulse of at least 4 "beats" on the 68K.

Here is what RESET does in detail. The system byte of the status register is loaded with the value $27. Once the processor is brought into supervisor status, the Trace flag in the status register is cleared, and the interrupt level is set to 7 (lowest priority, all lines allowable). Additionally, the supervisor stack pointer and program counter are loaded with the contents of the first 8 bytes of memory, whereby the value of the program counter is set to the beginning of the reset routine.

However, since the RESET line is bi-directional, the processor can also have RESET under program control during the time the line is low. The RESET instruction serves this purpose, when the connection is low for 124 "beats". It's possible to re-initialize the peripheral ICs at any time, without resetting the computer itself. RESET time puts the 68000 into a NOP state -- a reset is unstoppable once it occurs.

The HALT pin is important to the RESET line's existence (as we mentioned above), in order to initialize things properly. This pin has still more functions: when the pin is low while RESET is high, the processor goes into a halt state. This state causes the DMA pin to set the processor into the tri-state condition. The HALT condition ends when HALT is high again. This signal can be used in the design of single-step control.

HALT is also bi-directional. When the processor signals this line to become low, it means that a major error has occurred (e.g., doubled bus and address errors).

A low state on the BERR pin will call up exception handling, which runs basically like an external interrupt. In an orderly system, every access to the asynchronous bus quits with the DTACK signal. When DTACK is outputting, however, the hardware can produce a BERR, which informs the processor of any errors found. A further use for BERR is in connection with the MMU, to test for proper memory access of a specific range; this access is signaled by the FC pins. If protected memory is tried for in user mode, a BERR will turn up.

When both BERR and HALT are low, the processor will "re-execute" the instruction at which it stopped. If it doesn't run properly on the second "go-round", then it's called a *doubled* bus error, and the processor halts.

The eighth group of connections are for voltage and ground.

1.2 The Custom Chips

The Atari ST has four specially developed ICs. These chips (GLUE, MMU, DMA and SHIFTER) play a major role in the low price of the ST, since each chip performs several hundred overlapping functions. The first prototype of the ST was 5 X 50 X 30 cm. in size, mostly to handle all those TTL ICs. Once multiple functions could be crammed into four ICs, the ST became a saleable item. Then again, the present ST hasn't quite reached the ultimate goal -- it still has eight TTLs.

Naturally, since these chips were specifically designed by Atari for the ST, they haven't been publishing any spec sheets. Even without any data specs, we can give you quite a bit of information on the workings of the ICs.

An interesting fact about these ICs is that they're designed to work in concert with one another. For example, the DMA chip can't operate alone. It hasn't an address counter, and is incapable of addressing memory on its own (functions which are taken care of by the MMU). It's the same with SHIFTER -- it controls video screen and color, but it can't address video RAM. Again, MMU handles the addressing.

The system programmer can easily figure out which IC has which register. It is only essential to be able to recognize the address of the register, and how to control it. We're going to spend some time in this chapter exploring the pins of the individual ICs.

The most important IC of the "foursome" is GLUE. Its title speaks for the function -- a glue or paste. This IC, with its 68 pins, literally holds the entire system together, including decoding the address range and working the peripheral ICs.

Furthermore, the DMA handshake signals BR, BG and BGACK are produced/output by GLUE. The time point for DMA request is dictated by GLUE by the signal from the DMA controller. GLUE also has a BG (Bus Grant) input, as well as a BGO (Bus Grant Out).

The interrupt signal is produced by GLUE; in the ST, only IPL1 and IPL2 are used for this. Without other hardware, you can't use NMI (interrupt level 7). The pins MFPINT and IACK are used for interrupt control.

Figure 1.2-1 GLUE

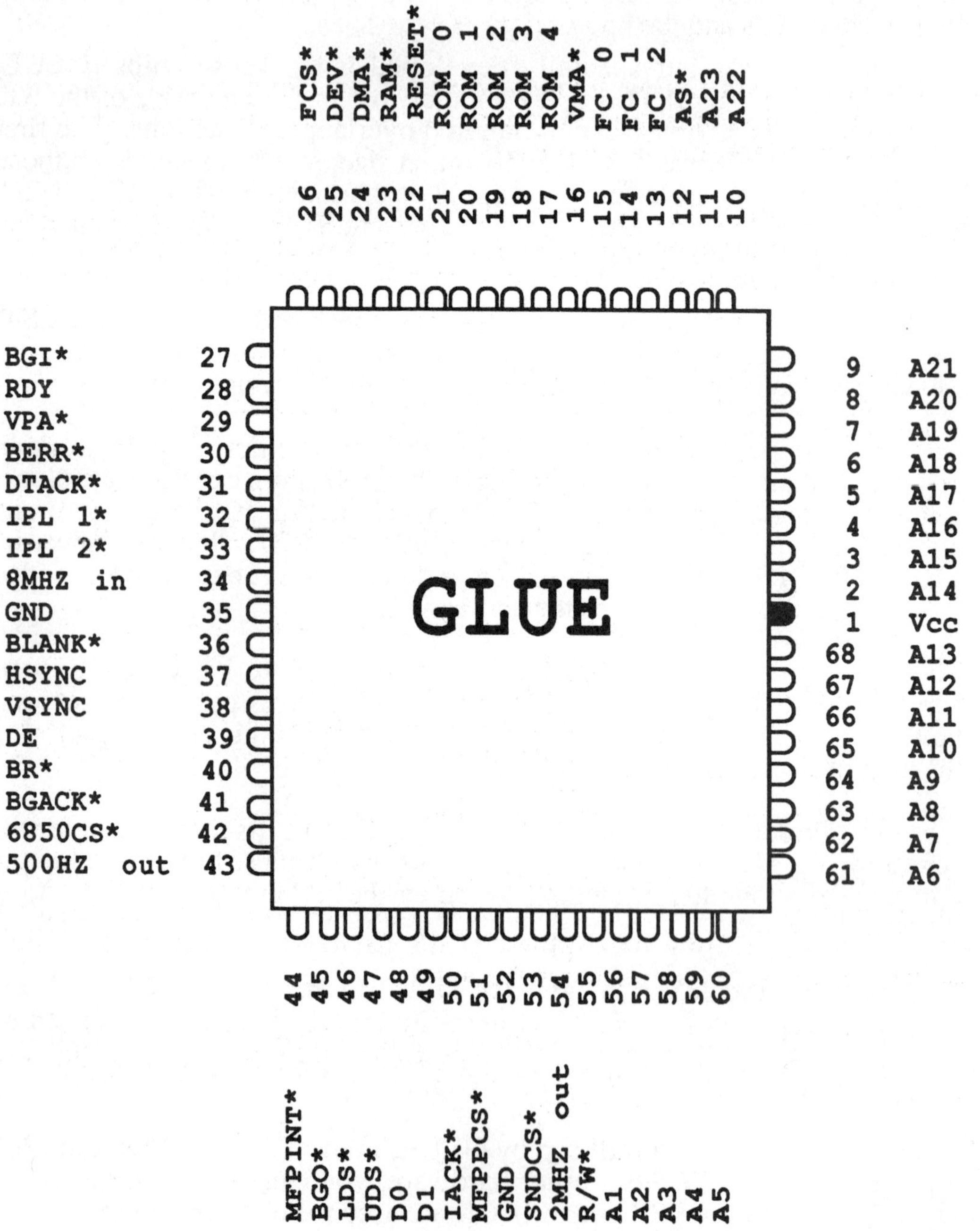

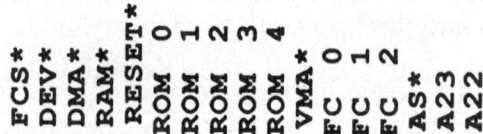

Pin	Signal		Pin	Signal
27	BGI*		9	A21
28	RDY		8	A20
29	VPA*		7	A19
30	BERR*		6	A18
31	DTACK*		5	A17
32	IPL 1*		4	A16
33	IPL 2*		3	A15
34	8MHZ in		2	A14
35	GND		1	Vcc
36	BLANK*		68	A13
37	HSYNC		67	A12
38	VSYNC		66	A11
39	DE		65	A10
40	BR*		64	A9
41	BGACK*		63	A8
42	6850CS*		62	A7
43	500HZ out		61	A6

Top pins (26–10): FCS*, DEV*, DMA*, RAM*, RESET*, ROM 0, ROM 1, ROM 2, ROM 3, ROM 4, VMA*, FC 0, FC 1, FC 2, AS*, A23, A22

Bottom pins (44–60): MFPINT*, BGO*, LDS*, UDS*, D0, D1, IACK*, MFPPCS*, GND, SNDCS*, 2MHZ out, R/W*, A1, A2, A3, A4, A5

The function code pins are guided by GLUE, where memory access tasks are performed (range testing and access authorization). Needless to say, the BERR signal is also handled by this chip. VPA is particularly important to the peripheral ICs and the appropriate select signals.

GLUE generates a timing frequency of 8 mHz. Frequencies between 2 mHz (sound chip's operating frequency) and 500 kHz (timing for keyboard and MIDI interface) can be produced.

HSYNC, VSYNC, BLANK and DE (Display Enable) are generated by GLUE for monitor operation. The synchronous timing can be switched on and off, and external sync-signals sent to the monitor. This will allow you to synchronize the ST's screen with a video camera.

The MMU also has a total of 68 pins. This IC performs three vital tasks. The most important task is coupling the multiplexed address bus of dynamic RAM with the processor's bus (handled by address lines A1 to A21). This gives us an address range totaling 4 megabytes. Dynamic RAM is controlled by RAS0, RAS1, CAS0L, CAS0H, CAS1L and CAS1H, as well as the multiplexed address bus on the MMU. DTACK, R/W, AS, LDS and UDS are also controlled by MMU.

We've already mentioned another important function of the MMU: it works with the SHIFTER to produce the video signal (the screen information is addressed in RAM, and SHIFTER conveys the information). Counters are incorporated in the MMU for this; a starting value is loaded, and within 500 nanoseconds, a word is addressed in memory and the information is sent over DCYC. The starting value of the video counter (and the screen memory position) can be shifted in 256-byte increments.

Another integrated counter in MMU, as mentioned earlier, is for addressing memory using the DMA. This counter begins with every DMA access (disk or hard disk), loading the address of the data being transferred. Every transfer automatically increments the counter.

The SHIFTER converts the information in video RAM into impulses readable on a monitor. Whether the ST is in 640 X 200 or 320 X 200 resolution, SHIFTER is involved.

Figure 1.2-2 MMU

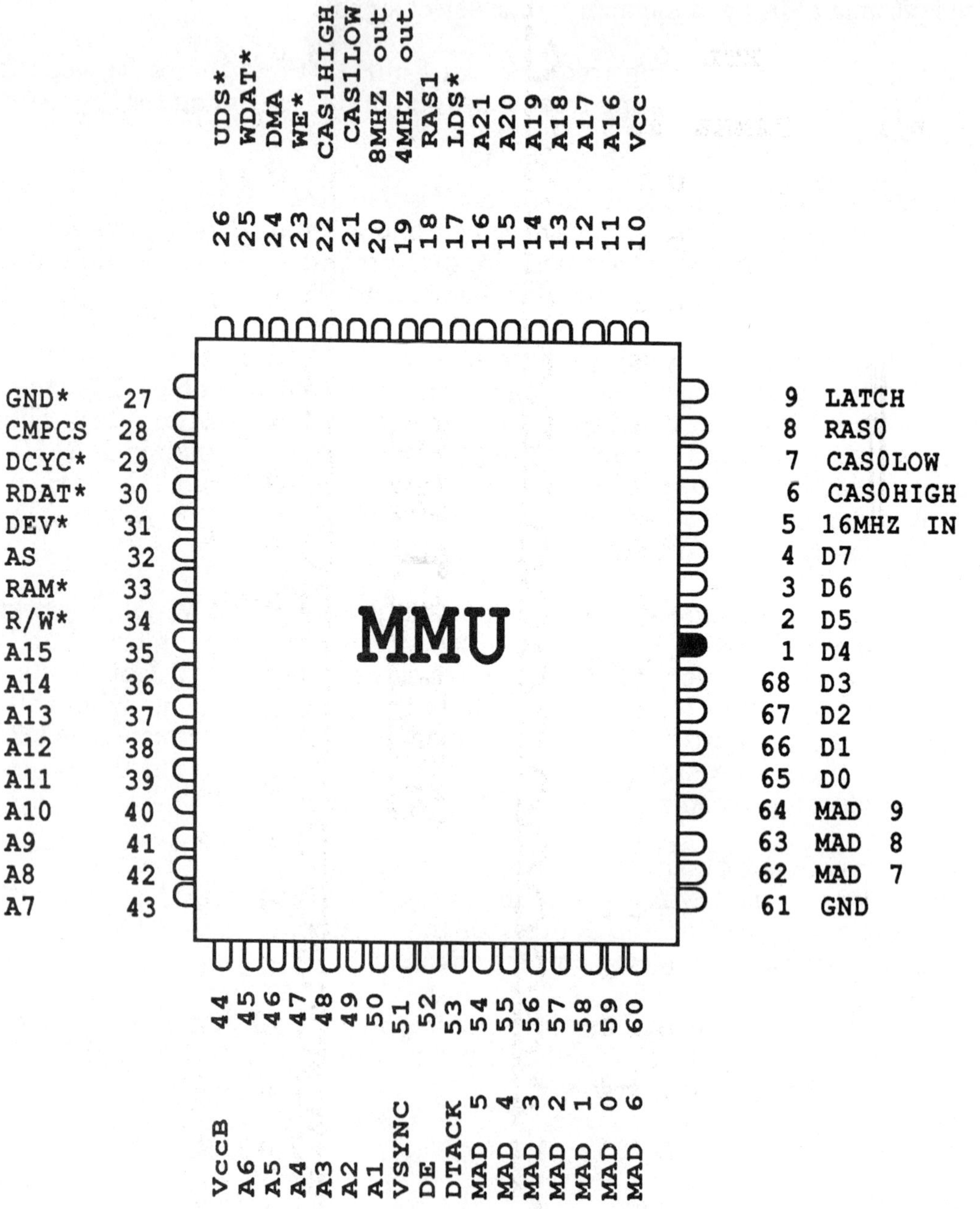

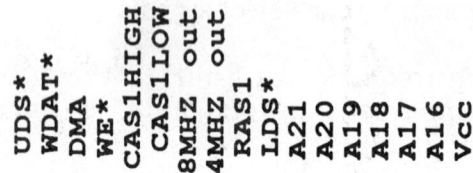

Figure 1.2-3 SHIFTER

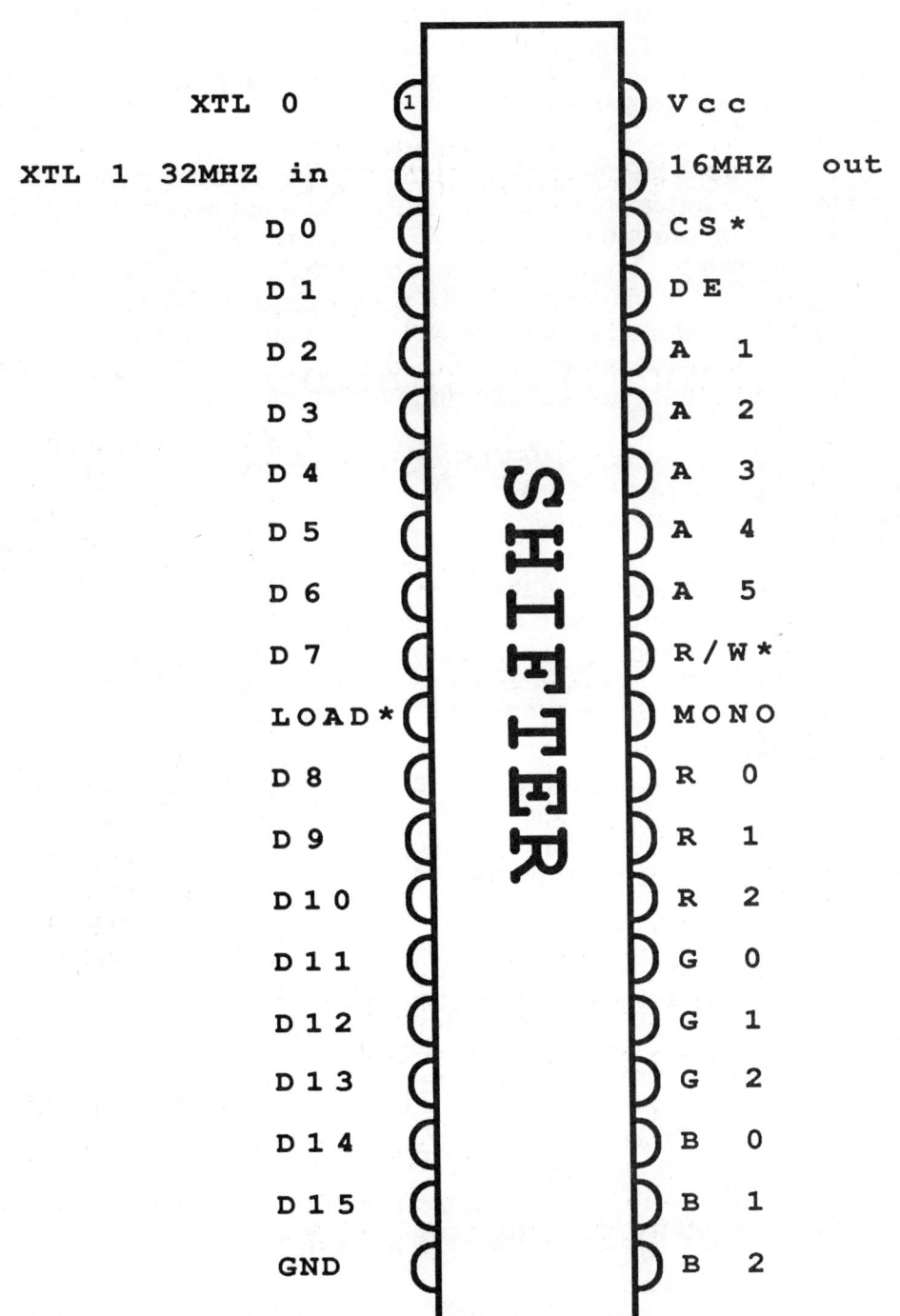

The information from RAM is transferred to SHIFTER on the signal LOAD. A resolution of 640 X 400 points sends the video signal over the MONO connector. Since color is impossible in that mode, the RGB connection is rendered inactive. The other two resolutions set MONO output to inactive, since all screen information is being sent out the RGB connection in those cases.

The third color connection works together with external equipment as a digital/analog converter. Individual colors are sent out over different pins, to give us color on our monitor. Pins R1- R5 on the address bus make up the "palette registers". These registers contain the color values, which are placed in individual bit patterns. The 16 palette registers hold a total of 16 colors for 320 X 200 mode. Note, however, that since these are based on the "primary" colors red, green and blue, these colors can be adjusted in 8 steps of brightness, bringing the color total to 512.

The DMA controller is like SHIFTER, only in a 40-pin housing; it is used to oversee the floppy disk controller, the hard disk, and any other peripherals that are likely to appear.

The speed of data transfer using the floppy disk drive offers no problems to the processor. It's different with hard disks; data moves at such high speed that the 68000 has to send a "pause" over the 8 mHz frequency. This pace is made possible by the DMA.

The DMA is joined to the processor's data bus to help transfer data. Two registers within the machine act as a bi-directional buffer for data through the DMA port; we'll discuss these registers later. One interesting point: The processor's 16-bit data bus is reduced to 8 bits for floppy/hard disk work. Data transfer automatically transfers two bytes per word.

The signals CA1, CA2, CR/W, FDCS and FDRQ manage the floppy disk controller. CA1 and CA2 are signals which the floppy disk controller (FDC) uses to select registers. CR/W determine the direction of data transfer from/to the FDC, and other peripherals connected to the DMA port.

The RDY signal communicated with GLUE (DMA-request) and MMU (address counter). This signal tells the DMA to transfer a word.

As you can see, these ICs work in close harmony with one another, and each would be almost useless on its own.

Figure 1.2-4 DMA

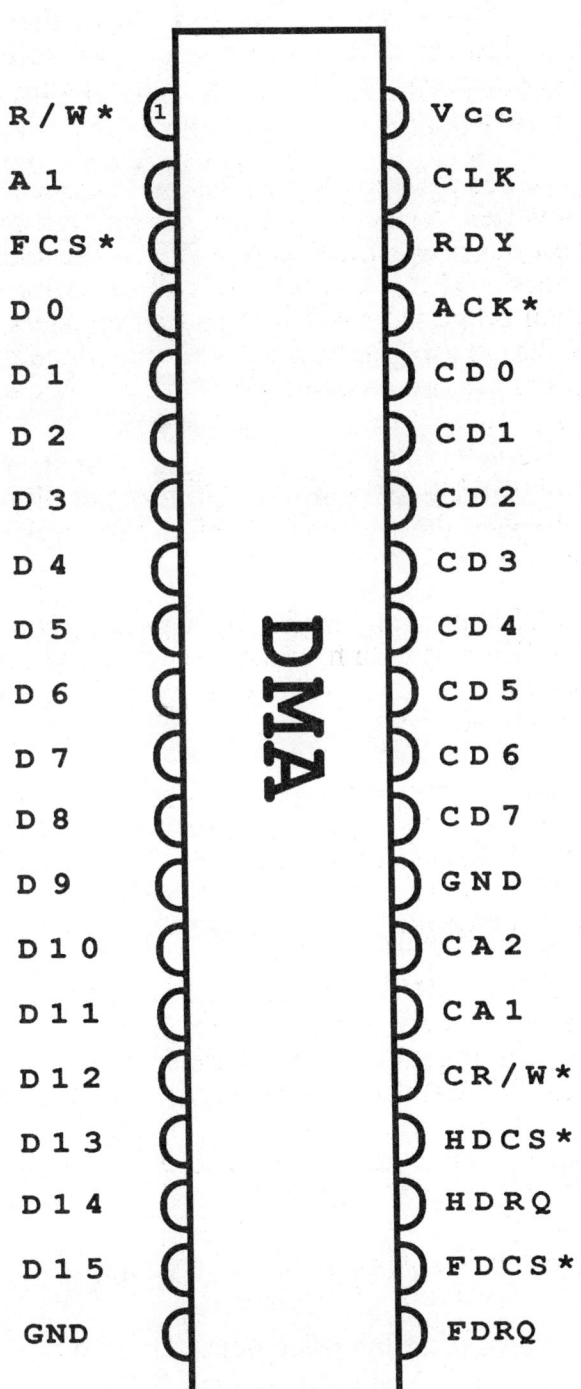

1.3 The WD 1772 Floppy Disk Controller

Although the 1772 from Western Digital has only 28 pins, this chip contains a complete floppy disk controller (FDC) with capabilities matching 40-pin controllers. This IC is software-compatible with the 1790/2790 series. Here are some of the 1772's features:

- Simple 5-volt current
- Built-in data separator
- Built-in copy compensation logic
- Single and double density
- Built-in motor controls

Although the user has his/her choice of disk format, e.g. sector length, number of sectors per track and number of tracks per diskette, the "normal" format is the optimum one for data transfer. So, Apple or Commodore diskettes can't be used.

Before going on to details of the FDC, let's take a moment to look at the 28 pins of this IC.

1.3.1 1772 Pins

These pins can be placed in three categories. The first group consists of the power connections.

Vcc:
    +5 volts current.

GND:
    Ground connection.

MR:
    Master reset. FDC reinitializes when this is low.

The second set are processor interface pins. These pins carry data between the processor and the FDC.

Figure 1.3-1 FDC 1772

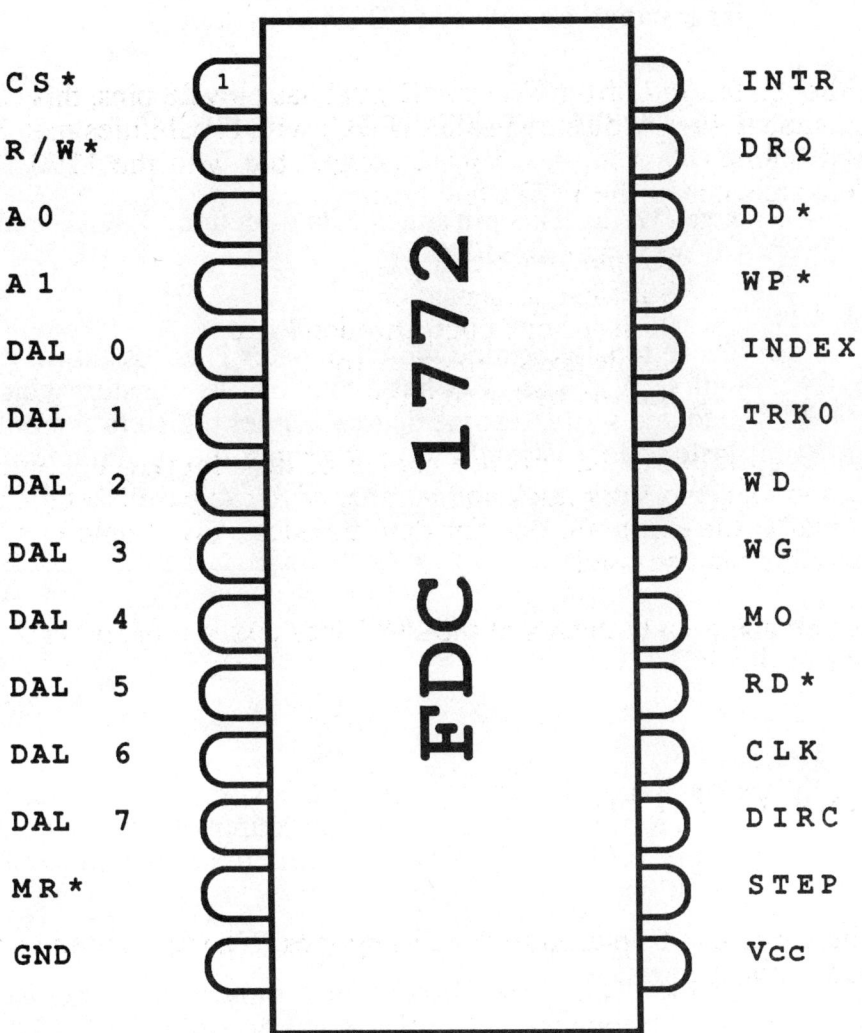

D0-D7:
>Eight-bit bi-directional bus; data, commands and status information go between FDC and system.

CS:
>FDC can only access registers when this line is low.

R/W:
>Read/Write. This pin states data direction. HIGH= read by FDC, LOW=write from FDC.

A0,A1:
>These bits determine which register is accessed (in conjunction with R/W). The 1772 has a total of five registers which can both read and write to some degree. Other registers can only read OR write. Here is a table to show how the manufacturer designed them:

A1	A0	R/W=1	R/W=0
0	0	Status Reg.	Command Reg.
0	1	Track Reg.	Track Reg.
1	0	Sector Reg.	Sector Reg.
1	1	Data Reg.	Data Reg.

DRQ:
>Data Request. When this output is high, either the data register is full (from reading), and must be "dumped", or the data register is empty (writing), and can be refilled. This connection aids the DMA operation of the FDC.

CLK:
>Clock. The clock signal counts only to the processor bus. An input frequency of 8 mHz must be on, for the FDC's internal timing to work.

The third group of signals make up the floppy interface.

STEP:
>Sends an impulse for every step of the head motor.

DIRC:
>Direction. This connection decides the direction of the head; high moves the head towards center of the diskette.

RD:
    Read Data. Reads data from the diskette. This information contains both timing and data impulses -- it is sent to the internal data separator for division.

MO:
    Motor On. Controls the disk drive motor, which is automatically started during read/write/whatever operations.

WG:
    Write Gate. WG will be low before writing to diskette. Write logic would be impossible without this line.

WD:
    Write Data. Sends serial data flow as data and timing impulses.

TR00:
    Track 00. This moves read/write head to track 00. TR00 would be low in this case.

IP:
    Index Pulse. The index pulses mark the physical beginnings of every track on a diskette. When formatting a disk, the FDC marks the start of each track before formatting the disk.

WPRT:
    Write Protect. If the diskette is write-protected, this input will react.

DDEN:
    Double Density Enable. This signal is confined to floppy disk control; it allows you to switch between single-density and double-density formats.

1.3.2 1772 Registers

CR (Command Register):
Commands are written in this 8-bit register. Commands should only be written in CR when no other command is under execution. Although the FDC only understands 11 commands, we actually have a large number of possibilities for these commands (we'll talk about those later).

STR (Status Register):
Gives different conditions of the FDC, coded into individual bits. Command writing depends on the meaning of each bit. The status register can only be read.

TR (Track Register):
Contains the current position of the read/write head. Every movement of the head raises or lowers the value of TR appropriately. Some commands will read the contents of TR, along with information read from the disk. The result affects the Status Register. TR can be read/written.

SR (Sector Register):
SR contains the number of sectors desired from read/write operations. Like TR, it can be used for either operation.

DR (Data Register):
DR is used for writing data to/ reading data from diskette.

1.3.3 Programming the FDC

Programming this chip is no big deal for a system programmer. Direct (and in most cases, unnecessary) programming is made somewhat harder AND drastically simpler by the DMA chip. The 11 FDC commands are divided into four types.

Type	Function
1	Restore, look for track 00
1	Seek, look for a track
1	Step, a track in previous direction
1	Step In, move head one track in (toward disk hub)
1	Step Out, move head one track out (toward edge of disk)
2	Read Sector
2	Write Sector
3	Read Address, read ID
3	Read Track, read entire track
3	Write Track, write entire track (format)
4	Force Interrupt

Type 1 Commands

These commands position the read/write head. The bit patterns of these five commands look like this:

	BIT							
	7	6	5	4	3	2	1	0
Restore	0	0	0	0	H	V	R1	R0
Seek	0	0	0	1	H	V	R1	R0
Step	0	0	1	U	H	V	R1	R0
Step In	0	1	0	U	H	V	R1	R0
Step Out	0	1	1	U	H	V	R1	R0

All five commands have several variable bits; bits R0 and R1 give the time between two step impulses. The possible combinations are:

```
R1  R0  STEP RATE
0   0   2 milliseconds
0   1   3 milliseconds
1   0   5 milliseconds
1   1   6 milliseconds
```

These bits must be set by the command bytes to the disk drive. The V-bit is the so-called "verify flag". When set, the drive performs an automatic verify after every head movement. The H-bit contains the spin-up sequence. The system delays disk access until the disk motor has reached 300 rpm. If the H-bit is cleared, the FDC checks for activation of the motor-on pins. When the motor is off, this pin will be set high (motor on), and the FDC waits for 6 index impulses before executing the command. If the motor is already running, then there will be no waiting time.

The three different step commands have bit 4 designated a U- bit. Every step and change of the head appears here.

Type 2 Commands

These commands deal with reading and writing sectors. They also have individual bits with special meanings.

```
BIT            7  6  5  4  3  2  1  0
Read Sector    1  0  0  M  H  E  0  0
Write Sector   1  0  1  M  H  E  P  A0
```

The H-bit is the previously described start-up bit. When the E-bit is set, the FDC waits 30 milliseconds before starting the command. This delay is important for some disk drives, since it takes time for the head to change tracks. When the E-bit reads null, the command will run immediately.

The M-bit determines whether one or several sectors are read one after another. On a null reading, only one sector will be read from/written to. Multi-sector reading sets the bit, and the FDC increments the counter at each new sector read.

Bits 0 and 1 must be cleared for sector reading. Writing has its own special meaning: the A0 bit conveys to bit 0 whether a cleared or normal data address mark is to be written. Most operating systems don't use this option (a normal data address mark is written).

The P-bit (bit 1) dictates whether pre-compensation for writing data is turned on or off. Pre-compensation is normally set on; it supplies a higher degree of protection to the inner tracks of a diskette.

Type 3 Commands

Read Address gives program information about the next ID field on the diskette. This ID field describes track, sector, disk side and sector length. Read Track gives all bytes written to a formatted diskette, and the data "between sectors". Write Track formats a track for data storage. Here are the bit patterns for these commands:

```
BIT           7 6 5 4 3 2 1 0
Read Address  1 1 0 0 H E 0 0
Read Track    1 1 1 0 H E 0 0
Write Track   1 1 1 1 H E P 0
```

The H- and E-bits also belong to the Type 2 command set (spin-up and head-settle time). The P-bit has the same function as in writing sectors.

Type 4 Commands

There's only one command in this set: Force Interrupt. This command can work with individual bits during another FDC command. When this command comes into play, whatever command was currently running is ended.

```
BIT              7 6 5 4 3  2  1  0
Force Interrupt  1 1 0 1 I3 I2 I1 I0
```

Bits I0-I3 present the conditions under which the interrupt is pressed. I0 and I1 have no meaning to the 1772, and remain low. If I2 is set, an interrupt will be produced with every index impulse. This allows for software controlled disk rotation. If I3 is set, an interrupt is forced immediately, and the currently-running command ends. When all bits are null, the command ends without interruption.

1.4 The MFP 68901

MFP is the abbreviation for Multi-Function Peripheral. This name is no exaggeration; wait until you see what it can do! Here's a brief list of the most noteworthy features:

> 8-bit parallel port
> Data direction of every port bit is individually programmable
> Port bits usable as interrupt input
> 16 possible interrupt sources
> Four universal timers
> Built-in serial interface

1.4.1 The 68901 Connections

The 48 pins of the MFP are set apart in function groups. The first function group is the power connection set:

GND, Vcc, CLK:
Vcc and GND carry voltage to and from the MFP. CLK is the clock input; this clock signal must not interfere with the system timer of the processor. The ST's MFP operates at a frequency of 4 mHz.

Communication with the data bus of the processor is maintained with D0-D7, DTACK, RS1-RS5 and RESET.

D0-D7:
These bi-directional pins normally work with the 8 lowest data bits of the 68000. It is also possible to connect with D8 through D15, but it's impossible to produce non-auto interrupts. Thus, interrupt vectors travel along the low order 8 data bits.

Figure 1.4-1 MFP 68901

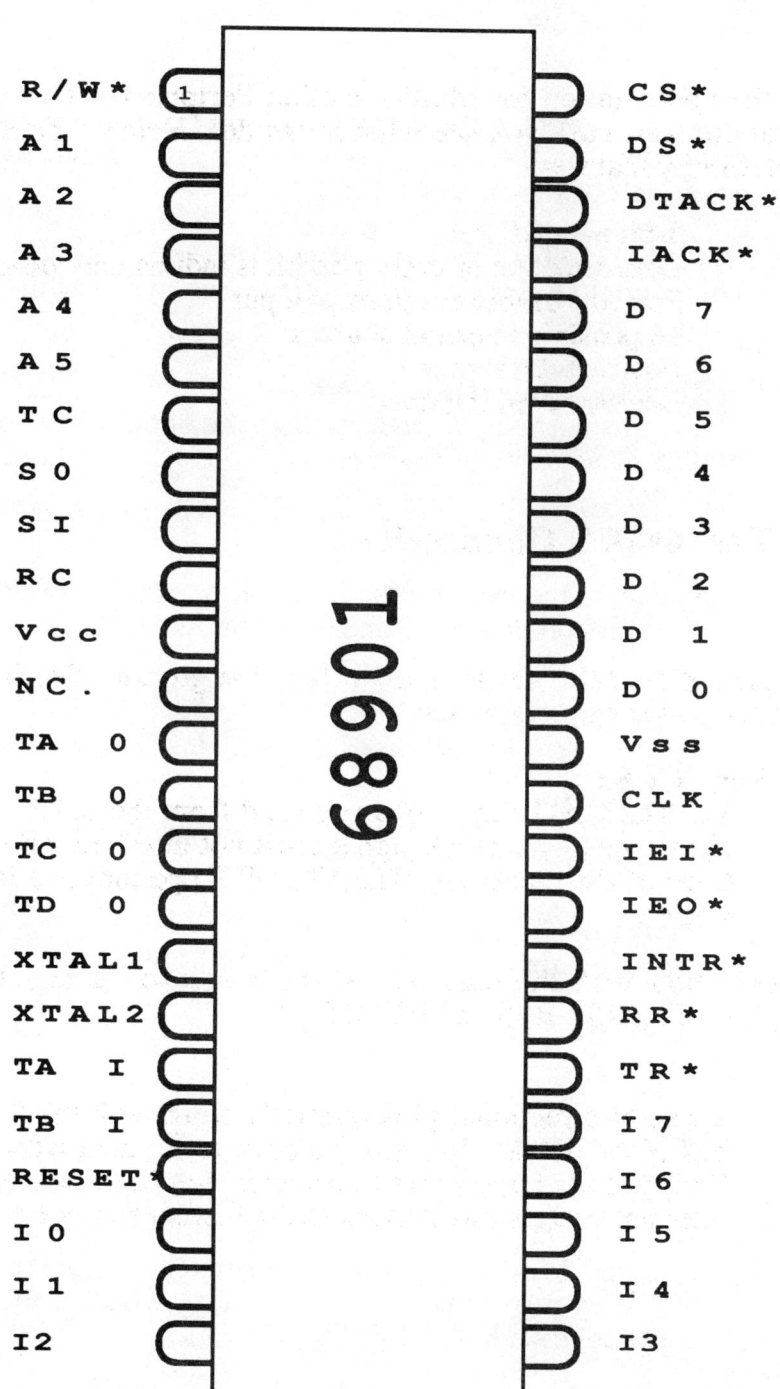

CS (Chip Select):
> This line is necessary to communication with the MFP. CS is active when low.

DS (Data Strobe):
> This pin works with either LDS or UDS on the processor. Depending on the signal, MFP will operate either the lower or upper half of the data bus.

DTACK (Data Transfer ACKnoledge):
> This signal shows the status of the bus cycle of the processor (read or write).

RS1-RS5 (Register Select):
> These pins normally connect with to the bottom five address lines of the processor, and serve to choose from the 24 internal registers.

RESET:
> If this pin is low for at least 2 microseconds, the MFP initializes. This occurs on power-up and a system reset.

The next group of signals cover interrupt connections (IRQ, IACK, IEI and IEO).

IRQ (Interrupt ReQuest):
> IRQ will be low when an interrupt is triggered in the MFP. This informs the processor of interrupts.

IACK (Interrupt ACKnowledge):
> On an interrupt (IRQ and IEI), the MFP sends a low signal over IACK and DS on the data lines. Since 16 different interrupt sources are available, this makes handling interrupts much simpler.

IEI, IEO (Interrupt Enable In/ Out):
> These two lines permit daisy-chaining of several MFPs, and determine MFP priority by their positioning in this chain. IEI would work through the MFP with the highest priority. IEO of the second MFP would remain unswitched. On an interrupt, a signal is sent over IACK, and the first MFP in the chain will acknowledge with a high IEO.

Next, we'll look at the eight I/O lines.

IO0-7 (Input/Output):
These pins use one or all normal I/O lines. The data direction of each port bit is set up in a data direction register of its own. In addition, though, every port bit can be programmed to be an interrupt input.

The timer pins make up yet another group of connections:

XTAL1,2 (Timer Clock Crystal):
A quartz crystal can be connected to these lines to deliver a working frequency for the four timers.

TAI,TBI (Timer Input):
Timers A and B can not only be used as real counters differently from timers C and D with the frequency from XTAL1 and 2, but can also be set up for event counting and impulse width measurement. In both these cases, an external signal (Timer Input) must be used.

TAO,TBO,TCO,TDO (Timer Output):
Every timer can send out its status on each peg (from 01 to 00). Each impulse is equal to 01.

The second-to-last set of signals are the connections to the universal serial interface. The built-in full duplex of the MFP can be run synchronously or asynchronously, and in different sending and receiving baud rates.

SI (Serial Input):
An incoming bit current will go up the SI input.

SO (Serial Output):
Outgoing bit voltage (reverse of SI).

RC (Receiver Clock):
Transfer speed of incoming data is determined by the frequency of this input; the source of this signal can, for example, be one of the four timers.

TC (Transmitter Clock):
Similar to RC, but for adjusting the baud-rate of data being transmitted.

The final group of signals aren't used in the Atari ST. They are necessary when the serial interface is operated by the DMA.

RR (Receiver Ready):
> This pin gives the status of the receiving data registers. If a character is completely received, this pin sends current.

TR (Transmitter Ready):
> This line performs a similar function for the sender section of the serial interface. Low tells the DMA controller that a new character in the MFP must be sent.

1.4.2 The MFP Registers

As we've already mentioned, the 68901 has a total of 24 different registers. This large number, together with the logical arrangement, makes programming the MFP much easier.

Reg 1 GPIP, General Purpose I/O Interrupt Port
> This is the data register for the 8-bit ports, where data from the port bits is sent and read.

Reg 2 AER, Active Edge Register
> When port bits are used for input, this register dictates whether the interrupt will be a low-high- or high-low conversion. Zero is used in the high-low change, one for low-high.

Reg 3 DDR, Data Direction Register
> We've already said that the data direction of individual port bits can be fixed by the user. When a DDR bit equals 0, the corresponding pin becomes an input, and 1 makes it an output. Port bit positions are influenced by AER and DDR bits.

Reg 4,5 IERA,IERB, Interrupt Enable Register

Every interrupt source of the MFP can be separately switched on and off. With a total of 16 sources, two 8-bit registers are needed to control them. If a 1 has been written to IERA or IERB, the corresponding channel is enabled (turned on). Conversely, a zero disables the channel. If it comes upon a closed channel caused by an interrupt, the MFP will completely ignore it. The following table shows which bit is coordinated with which interrupt occurrence:

```
IERA
Bit 7: I/O port bit 7 (highest priority)
Bit 6: I/O port bit 6
Bit 5: Timer A
Bit 4: Receive buffer full
Bit 3: Receive error
Bit 2: Sender buffer empty
Bit 1: Sender error
Bit 0: Timer B

IERB
Bit 7: I/O port bit 5
Bit 6: I/O port bit 4
Bit 5: Timer C
Bit 4: Timer D
Bit 3: I/O port bit 3
Bit 2: I/O port bit 2
Bit 1: I/O port bit 1
Bit 0: I/O port bit 0, lowest priority
```

This arrangement applies to the IP-, IM- and IS-registers discussed below.

Reg 6,7 IPRA,IPRB, Interrupt Pending Register

When an interrupt occurs on an open channel, the appropriate bit in the Interrupt Pending Register is set to 1. When working with a system that allows vector creation, this bit will be cleared when the MFP puts the vector number on the data bus. If this isn't possible, the IPR must be cleared using software. To clear a bit, a byte in the MFP will show the location of the specific bit.

The bit arrangement of the IPR bit arrangement is shown in the table for registers 4 and 5 (see above).

Reg 8,9 ISRA,ISRB,Interrupt In-Service Register
The function of these registers is somewhat complicated, and depends upon bit 3 of register 12. This bit is an S-bit, which determines whether the 68901 is working in "Software End-of-Interrupt" mode (SEI) or in "Automatic End-of-Interrupt" mode (AEI). AEI mode clears the IPR (Interrupt Pending Bit), when the processor gets the vector number from the MFP during an IACK cycle. The appropriate In-Service bit is cleared at the same time. Now a new interrupt can occur, even when the previous interrupt hasn't finished its work.

SEI mode sets the corresponding ISR-bit when the vector number of the interrupt is requested by the processor. At the interrupt routine's end, the bit designated within the MFP must be cleared. As long as the Interrupt In-Service bit is set, all interrupts of lower priority are masked out by the MFP. Once the Pending-bit of the active channel is cleared, the same sort of interrupt can occur a second time, and interrupts of lesser priority can occur as well.

Reg 10,11 IMRA,IMRB Interrupt Mask Register
Individual interrupt sources switched on by IER can be masked with the help of this register. That means that the interrupt is recognized from within and is signaled in the IPR, even if the IRQ line remains high.

Reg 12 VR Vector Register
In the cases of interrupts, the 68901 can generate a vector number corresponding to the interrupt source requested by the processor during an Interrupt Acknowledge Cycle. All 16 interrupt channels have their own vectors, with their priorities coded into the bottom four bits of the vector number (the upper four bits of the vector are copied from the vector register). These bits must be set into VR, therefore.

Bit 3 of VR is the previously mentioned S-bit. If this bit is set (like in the ST), then the MFP operates in "Software End-of-Interrupt" mode; a cleared bit puts the system into "Automatic End-of-Interrupt" mode.

Reg 13,14 TACR,TBCR   Timer A/B Control Register

Before proceeding with these registers, we should talk for a moment about the timer. Timers A and B are both identical. Every timer consists of a data register, a programmable feature and an 8-bit count-down counter. Contents of the counters will decrease by one every impulse. When the counter stands at 01, the next impulse changes the corresponding timer to the output of its pins. At the same time, the value of the timer data register is loaded into the timer. If this channel is set by the IER bit, the interrupt will be requested. The source of the timer beats will usually be those quartz frequencies from XTAL1 and 2. This operating mode is called delay mode, and is available to timers C and D.

Timers A and B can also be fed external impulses using timer inputs TAI and TBI (in event count mode). The maximum frequency on timer inputs should not surpass 1/4 of the MFP's operating frequency (that is, 1 mHz).

Another peculiarity of this operating mode is the fact that the timer inputs for the interrupts are I/O pins 13 and 14. By programming the corresponding bits in the AER, a pin-jump can be used by the timer inputs to request an interrupt. TAI is joined with pin 13, TBI by pin 14. Pins 13 and 14 can also be used as I/O lines without interrupt capability.

Timers A and B have yet a third operating mode (pulse-length measurement). This is similar to Delay Mode, with the difference that the timer can be turned on and off with TAI and TBI. Also, when pins 13 and 14 are used, the AER-bits can determine whether the timer inputs are high or low. If, say, AER-bit 4 is set, the counter works when TAI is high. When TAI changes to low, an interrupt is created.

Now we come to TACR and TBCR. Both registers only use the fifth through eighth bits. Bits 0 to 3 determine the operating mode of each timer:

```
BIT  3 2 1 0    Function

     0 0 0 0    Timer stop, no function executed
     0 0 0 1    Delay mode, subdivider divides by 4
     0 0 1 0    Delay mode, subdivider divides by 10
     0 0 1 1    Delay mode, subdivider divides by 16
     0 0 1 1    Delay mode, subdivider divides by 16
     0 1 0 0    Delay mode, subdivider divides by 50
     0 1 0 1    Delay mode, subdivider divides by 64
     0 1 1 0    Delay mode, subdivider divides by 100
     0 1 1 1    Delay mode, subdivider divides by 200
     1 0 0 0    Event Count Mode
     1 0 0 1    Pulse extension mode, subdivider divides by 4
     1 0 1 0    Pulse extension mode, subdivider divides by 10
     1 0 1 1    Pulse extension mode, subdivider divides by 16
     1 1 0 0    Pulse extension mode, subdivider divides by 50
     1 1 0 1    Pulse extension mode, subdivider divides by 64
     1 1 1 0    Pulse extension mode, subdivider divides by 100
     1 1 1 1    Pulse extension mode, subdivider divides by 200
```

Bit 4 of the Timer Control Register has a particular function. This bit can produce a low reading for the timer being used with it at any time. However, it will immediately go high when the timer runs.

Reg 15 TCDCR Timers C and D Control Register

Timers C and D are available only in delay mode; thus, one byte controls both timers. The control information is programmed into the lower three bits of the nibbles (four- bit halves). Bits 0 and 2 arrange Timer D, Timer C is influenced by bits 4 and 6. Bits 3 and 7 in this register have no function.

```
Bit  2 1 0      Function - Timer D
Bit  6 5 4      Function - Timer C
     0 0 0      Timer Stop
     0 0 1      Delay Mode, division by 4
     0 1 0      Delay Mode, division by 10
     0 1 1      Delay Mode, division by 16
     1 0 0      Delay Mode, division by 50
     1 0 1      Delay Mode, division by 64
     1 1 0      Delay Mode, division by 100
     1 1 1      Delay Mode, division by 200
```

Reg 16-19 TADR,TBDR,TCDR,TDDR Timer Data Registers
The four Timer Data Registers are loaded with a value from the counter. When a condition of 01 is reached, an impulse occurs. A continuous countdown will stem from this value.

Reg 20 SCR Synchronous Character Register
A value will be written to this register by synchronous data transfer, so that the receiver of the data will be alerted. When synchronous mode is chosen, all characters received will be stored in the SCR, after first being put into the receive buffer.

Reg 21 UCR,USART Control Register
USART is short for Universal Synchronous/Asynchronous Receiver/Transmitter. The UCR allows you to set all the operating parameters for the interfaces. Parameters can also be coded in with the timers.

```
Bit 0      : unused
Bit 1      : 0=Odd parity
             1=Even parity

Bit 2      : 0=No parity (bit 1 is ignored)
             1=Parity according to bit 1

Bits 3,4   : These bis control the number of
             start- and stopbits and the
             format desired.
     Bit 4 3 Start Stop Format
         0 0   0    0   Synchronous
         0 1   1    1   Asynchronous
         1 0   1    1,5 Asynchronous
         1 1   1    2   Asynchronous

Bits 5,6   : These bits give the
             "wordlength" of the data bits
             to be transferred.
     Bits 6 5 Word length
          0 0 8 bits
          0 1 7 bits
          1 0 6 bits
          1 1 5 bits
```

Bit 7   :   0=Frequency from TC and RC
                    directly used as transfer
                    frequency (used only for
                    synchronous transfer)
                    1=Frequency in TC and RC
                    internally divided by 16.

Reg 22 RSR Receiver Status Register

The RSR gives information concerning the conditions of all receivers. Again, the different conditions are coded into individual bits.

Bit 0 Receiver Enable Bit

When this bit is cleared, receipt is immediately turned off. All flags in RSR are automatically cleared. A set bit means that the receiver is behaving normally.

Bit 1 Synchronous Strip Enable

This bit allows synchronous data transfer to determine whether or not a character in the SCR is identical to a character in the receive buffer.

Bit 2 Match/Character in Progress

When in synchronous transfer format, this bit signals that a character identical with the SCR byte would be received. In asynchronous mode, this bit is set as soon as the startbit is recognized. A stopbit automatically clears this bit.

Bit 3 Found - Search/Break Detected

This bit is set in synchronous transfer format, when a character received coincides with one stored in the SCR. This condition can be treated as an interrupt over the receiver's error channel. Asynchronous mode will cause the bit to set when a BREAK is received. The break condition is fulfilled when only zeroes are received following a startbit. To distinguish between a BREAK from a "real" null, this line should be low.

Bit 4 Frame Error

A frame error occurs when a byte received is not a null, but the stopbit of the byte IS a null.

Bit 5 Parity Error
The condition of this bit gives information as to whether parity on the last received character was correct. If the parity test is off, the PE bit is untouched.

Bit 6 Overrun Error
This bit will be set when a complete character is in the receiver floating range but not read into the receive buffer. This error can be operated as an interrupt.

Bit 7 Buffer Full
This bit is set when a character is transferred from the floating register to the receive buffer. As soon as the processor reads the byte, the bit is cleared.

Reg 23 TSR Transmitter Status Register
Whereas the RSR sends receiver information, the TSR handles transmission information.

Bit 0 Transmitter Enable
The sending section is completely shut off when this bit is cleared. At the same time the End-bit is cleared and the UE-bit is set (see below). The output to the receiver is set in the corresponding H- and L-bits.

Bits 1,2 High- and Low-bit
These bits let the programmer decide which mode of output the switched-off transmitter will take on. If both bits are cleared, the output is high. High-bit only will create high output; low-bit, low output. Both bits on will switch on loop-back-mode. This state loops the output from the transmitter with receiver input. The output itself is on the high-pin.

Bit 3 Break
The break-bit has no function in synchronous data transfer. In asynchronous mode, though, a break condition is sent when the bit is set.

Bit 4 End of Transmission
> If the sender is switched off during running transmission, the end-bit will be set as soon as the current character has been sent in its entirety. When no character is sent, the bit is immediately set.

Bit 5 Auto Turnaround
> When this bit is set, the receiver is automatically switched on when the transmitter is off, and a character will eventually be sent.

Bit 6 Underrun Error
> This bit is switched on when a character in the sender floating register will be sent, before a new character is written into the send buffer.

Bit 7 Buffer Empty
> This bit will be set when a character from the send buffer will be transferred to the floating register. The bit is cleared when new data is written to the send buffer.

Reg 24 UDR, USART Data Register
Send/receive data is sent over this register. Writing sends data in the send buffer, reading gives you the contents of the receive buffer.

1.5 The 6850 ACIAs

ACIA is short for "Asynchronous Communications Interface Adapter". This 24-pin IC has all the components necessary for operating a serial interface, as well as error-recognizing and data-formatting capabilities. Originally for 6800-based computers, this chip can be easily tailored for 6502 and 68000 systems. The ST has two of these chips. One of them communicates with the keyboard, mouse, joystick ports, and runs the clock. Keyboard data travels over a serial interface to the 68000 chip. The second ACIA is used for operating the MIDI interface.

Parameter changes in the keyboard ACIA are not recommended: The connection between keyboard and ST can be easily disrupted. The MIDI interface is another story, though -- we can create all sorts of practical applications. Incidentally, nowhere else has it been mentioned that the MIDI connections can be used for other purposes. One idea would be to use the MIDI interfaces of several STs to link them together (for schools or offices, for example).

1.5.1 The Pins of the 6850

For those of you readers who aren't very well-acquainted with the principles of serial data transfer, we've included some fairly detailed descriptions in the pin layout which follows.

Vss
    This connection is the "ground wire" of the IC.

RX DATA Receive Data
    This pin receives data; a start-bit must precede the least significant data-bit before receipt.

Figure 1.5-1 ACIA 6850

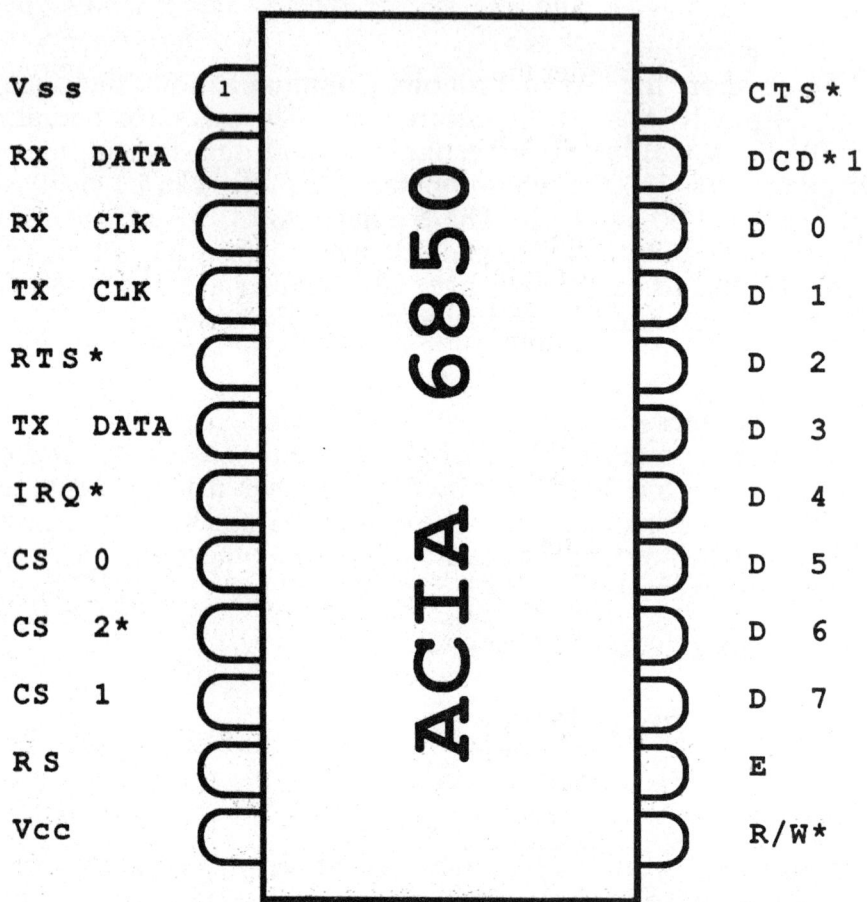

RX CLK Receive Clock
   This pin signal determines baud-rate (speed at which the data is received), and is synchronize to the incoming data. The frequency of RX CLK is patterned after the desired transfer speed and after the internally programmed division rate.

TX CLK Transmitter Clock
   Like RX CLK, only used for transmission speed.

RTS Request To Send
   This output signals the processor whether the 6850 is low or high; mostly used for controlling data transfer. A low output will, for example, signal a modem that the computer is ready to transmit.

TX DATA Transmitter Data
   This pin sends data bit-wise (serially) from the computer.

IRQ Interrupt Request
   Different circumstances set this pin low, signaling the 68000 processor. Possible conditions include completed transmission or receipt of a character.

CS 0,1,2 Chip Select
   These three lines are needed for ACIA selection. The relatively high number of CS signals help minimize the amount of hardware needed for address decoding, particularly in smaller computer systems.

RS Register Select
   This signal communicates with internal registers, and works closely with the R/W signal. We shall talk about these registers later.

Vcc Voltage
   This pin is required of all ICs -- this pin gets an operating voltage of 5V.

R/W Read/Write
   This tells the processor the "direction" of data traveling through the ACIA. A high signal tells the processor to read data, and low writes data in the 6850.

E Enable
> The E-signal determines the time of reading/writing. All read/write processes with this signal must be synchronous.

D0 - D7 Data
> These data lines are connected to those of the 68000. Until the ACIA is accessed, these bidirectional lines are all high.

DCD Data Carrier Detect
> A modem control signal, which detects incoming data. When DCD is high, serial data cannot be received.

CTS Clear To Send
> CTS answers the computer on the signal RTS. Data transmission is possible only when this pin is low.

1.5.2 The Registers of the 6850

The 6850 has four different registers. Two of these are read only. Two of them are write only. These registers are distinguished by R/W and RS, after the table below:

R/W	RS	Register	Access
0	0	Control Register	write
0	1	Sender Register	write
1	0	Status Register	read
1	1	Receive Register	read

The sender/receiver registers (also known as the RX- and TX- buffers) are for data transfer. When receiving is possible, the incoming bits are put in a shift register. Once the specified number of bits has arrived, the contents of the shift register are transferred to the TX buffer. The sender works in much the same way, only in the reverse direction (RX buffer to sender shift register).

The Control Register

The eight-bit control register determines internal operations. To solve the problem of controlling diverse functions with one byte, single bits are set up as below:

CR 0,1

These bits determine by which factor the transmitter and receiver clock will be divided. These bits also are joined with a master reset function. The 6850 has no separate reset line, so it must be accomplished through software.

```
CR1   CR0
 0     0     RXCLK/TXCLK without division
 0     1     RXCLK/TXCLK by 16 (for MIDI)
 1     0     RXCLK/TXCLK by 64 (for keyboard)
 1     1     Master RESET
```

CR 2,3,4

These so-called Word Select bits tell whether 7 or 8 data-bits are involved; whether 1 or 2 stop-bits are transferred; and the type of parity.

```
CR4   CR3   CR2
 0     0     0     7 databits, 2 stopbits, even parity
 0     0     1     7 databits, 2 stopbits, odd  parity
 0     1     0     7 databits, 1 stopbit,  even parity
 0     1     1     7 databits, 1 stopbit,  odd  parity
 1     0     0     8 databits, 2 stopbit,  no   parity
 1     0     1     8 databits, 1 stopbit,  no   parity
 1     1     0     8 databits, 1 stopbit,  even parity
 1     1     1     8 databits, 1 stopbit,  odd  parity
```

CR 6,5

These Transmitter Control bits set the RTS output pin, and allow or prevent an interrupt through the ACIA when the send register is emptied. Also, BREAK signals can be sent over the serial output by this line. A BREAK signal is nothing more than a long sequence of null bits.

CR6	CR5	
0	0	RTS low, transmitter IRQ disabled
0	1	RTS low, transmitter IRQ enabled
1	0	RTS high, transmitter IRQ disabled
1	1	RTS low, transmitter IRQ disabled, BREAK sent

CR 7

The Receiver Interrupt Enable bit determines whether the receiver interrupt will be on. An interrupt can be caused by the DCD line changing from low to high, or by the receiver data buffer filling. Besides that, an interrupt can occur from an OVERRUN (a received character isn't properly read from the processor).

CR7	
0	Interrupt disabled
1	Interrupt enabled

The Status Register

The Status Register gives information about the status of the chip. It also has its information coded into individual bytes.

SR0

When this bit is high, the RX data register is full. The byte must be read before a new character can be received (otherwise an OVERRUN happens).

SR1

This bit reflects the status of the TX data buffer. An empty register sets the bit.

SR2

A low-high change on pin DCD sets SR2. If the receiver interrupt is allowable, the IRQ will be cancelled. The bit is cleared when the status register and the receiver register are read. This also cancels the IRQ. SR2 register remains high if the signal on the DCD pin is still high; SR2 registers low if DCD becomes low.

SR3

    This line shows the status of CTS. This signal cannot be altered by a master reset, or by ACIA programming.

SR4

    Shows "Frame errors". Frame errors are when no stop-bit is recognized in receiver switching. It can be set with every new character.

SR5

    This bit displays the previously mentioned OVERRUN condition. SR5 is reset when the RX buffer is read.

SR6

    This bit recognizes whether the parity of a received character is correct. The bit is set on an error.

SR 7

    This signals the state of the IRQ pins; this bit makes it possible to switch several IRQ lines on one interrupt input. In cases where an interrupt is program-generated, SR7 can tell which IC cut off the interrupt.

The ACIAs in the ST

The ACIAs have lots of extras unnecessary to the ST. In fact, CTS, DCD and RTS are not connected.

The keyboard ACIA lies at the addresses $FFFC00 and $FFFC02. Built-in parameters are: 8-bit word, 1 stopbit, no parity, 7812.5 baud (500 kHz/64).

The parameters are the same for the MIDI chip, EXCEPT for the baud rate, which runs at 31250 baud (500 kHz/16).

1.6 The YM-2149 Sound Generator

The Yamaha YM-2149, a PSG (programmable sound generator) in the same family as the General Instruments AY-3-8190, is a first-class sound synthesis chip. It was developed to produce sound for arcade games. The PSG also has remarkable capabilities for generating/altering sounds. Additionally, the PSG can be easily controlled by joysticks, the computer keyboard, or external keyboard switching. The PSG has two bidirectional 8-bit parallel ports. Here's some general data on the YM-2149:

- three independently programmable tone generators
- a programmable noise generator
- complete software-controlled analog output
- programmable mixer for tone/noise
- 15 logarithmically raised volume levels
- programmable envelopes (ASDR)
- two bidirectional 8-bit data ports
- TTL-compatible
- simple 5-volt power

The YM-2149 has a total of 16 registers. All sound capabilities are controlled by these registers.

The PSG has several "functional blocks" each with its own job. The tone generator block produces a square-wave sound by means of a time signal. The noise generator block produces a frequency-modulated square-wave signal, whose pulse-width simulates a noise generator. The mixer couples the three tone generators' output with the noise signal. The channels may be coupled by programming.

The amplitude control block controls the output volume of the three channels with the volume registers; or creates envelopes (Attack, Decay, Sustain, Release, or ADSR), which controls the volume and alters the sound quality.

The D/A converter translates the volume and envelope information into digital form, for external use. Finally one function block controls the two I/O ports.

Figure 1.6-1 Sound chip YM-2149

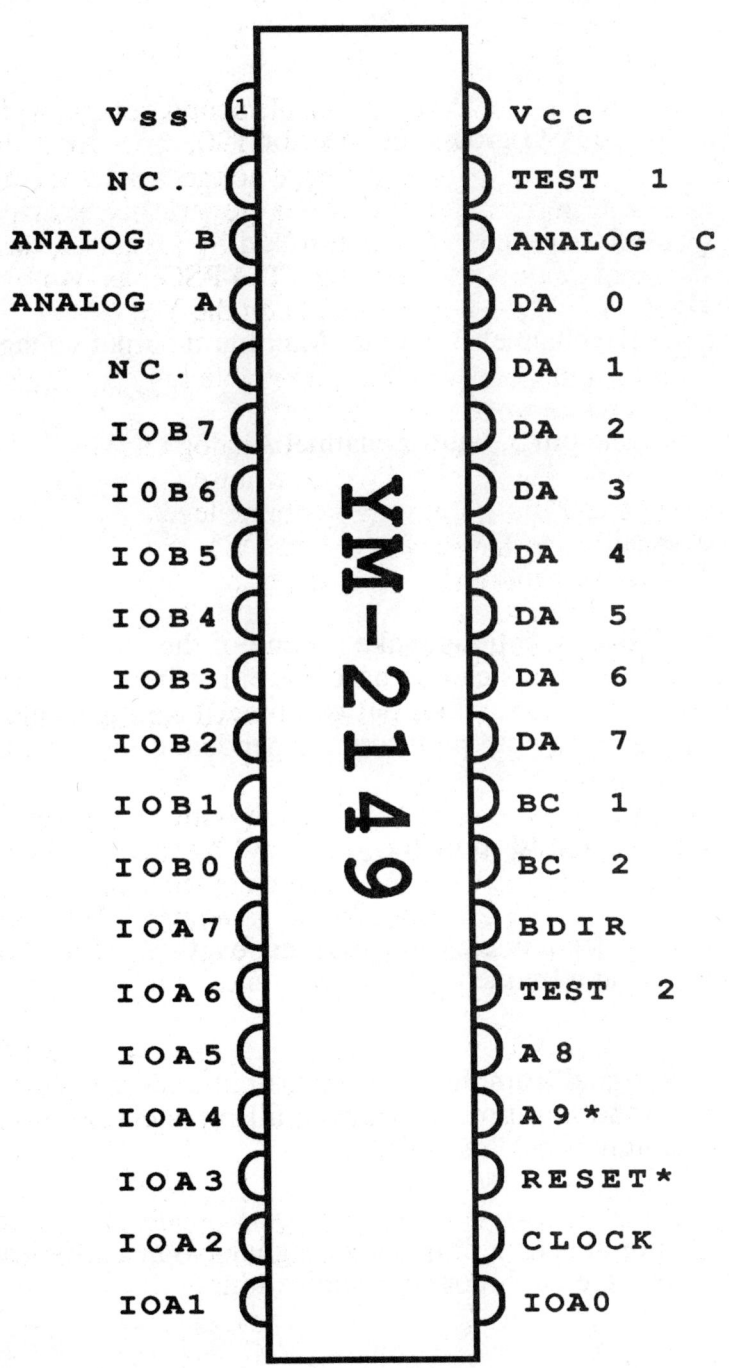

1.6.1 Sound Chip Pins

Vss:
>This is the PSG ground connection.

NC.:
>Not used.

ANALOG B:
>This is the channel B output. Maximum output voltage is 1 vss.

ANALOG A:
>Works like pin 3, but for channel A.

NC.:
>Not used.

IOB7 - 0:
>The IOB connections make up one of the two 8-bit ports on the chip. These pins can be used for either input or output. Mixed operation (input and output combined) is impossible within one port, however both ports are independent of one another.

IOA7 - 0:
>Like IOB, but for port A.

CLOCK:
>All tone frequencies are divided by this signal. This signal operates at a frequency between 1 and 2 mHz.

RESET:
>A low signal from this pin resets all internal registers. Without a reset, random numbers exist in all registers, the result being a rather unmusical "racket".

A9:
>This pin acts as a chip select-signal. When it is low, the PSG registers are ready for communication.

A8:
>Similar to A9, only it is active when high.

TEST2:
>Test2 is used for testing in the factory, and is unused in normal operation.

BDIR & BC1,2:
>The BDIR (Bus DIRection), BC1 and BC2 (Bus Control) pins control the PSG's register access.

```
BDIR BC2 BC1  PSG function
0    0   0    Inactive
0    0   1    Latch address
0    1   0    Inactive
0    1   1    Read from PSG
1    0   0    Latch address
1    0   1    Inactive
1    1   0    Write to PSG
1    1   1    Latch address
```

>Only four of these combinations are of any use to us; those with a 5+ voltage running over BC2. So, here's what we have left:

```
BDIR BC1 Function
0    0   Inactive, PSG data bus high
0    1   Read PSG registers
1    0   Write PSG registers
1    1   Latch, write register number(s)
```

DA0 - 7:
>These pins connect the sound chip to the processor, through the data bus. The identifier DA means that both data and (register) addresses can be sent over these lines.

ANALOG C:
>Works with channel C (see ANALOG B, above).

TEST1:
>See TEST2.

Vcc:
>+5 volt pin.

1.6.2 The 2149 Registers and their Functions

Now let's look at the functions of the individual registers. One point of interest: the contents of the address register remain unaltered until reprogrammed. You can use the same data over and over, without having to send that data again.

Reg 0,1:
These register determine the period length, and the pitch of ANALOG A. Not all 16 bits are used here; the eight bits of register 0 (set frequency) and the four lowest bits of register 1 (control step size). The lower the 12-bit value in the register, the higher the tone.

Reg 2,3:
Same as registers 0 and 1, only for channel B.

Reg 4,5:
Same as registers 0 and 1, only for channel C.

Reg 6:
The five lowest bits of this register control the noise generator. Again, the smaller the value, the higher the noise "pitch".

Reg 7:

```
Bit 0:Channel A tone  on/off     0=on  /1=off
Bit 1:Channel B tone  on/off     0=on  /1=off
Bit 2:Channel C tone  on/off     0=on  /1=off
Bit 3:Channel A noise on/off     0=on  /1=off
Bit 4:Channel B noise on/off     0=on  /1=off
Bit 5:Channel C noise on/off     0=on  /1=off
Bit 6:Port A in/output           0=in  /1=out
Bit 7:Port B in/output           0=in  /1=out
```

Figure 1.6-2 Envelopes of the PSG

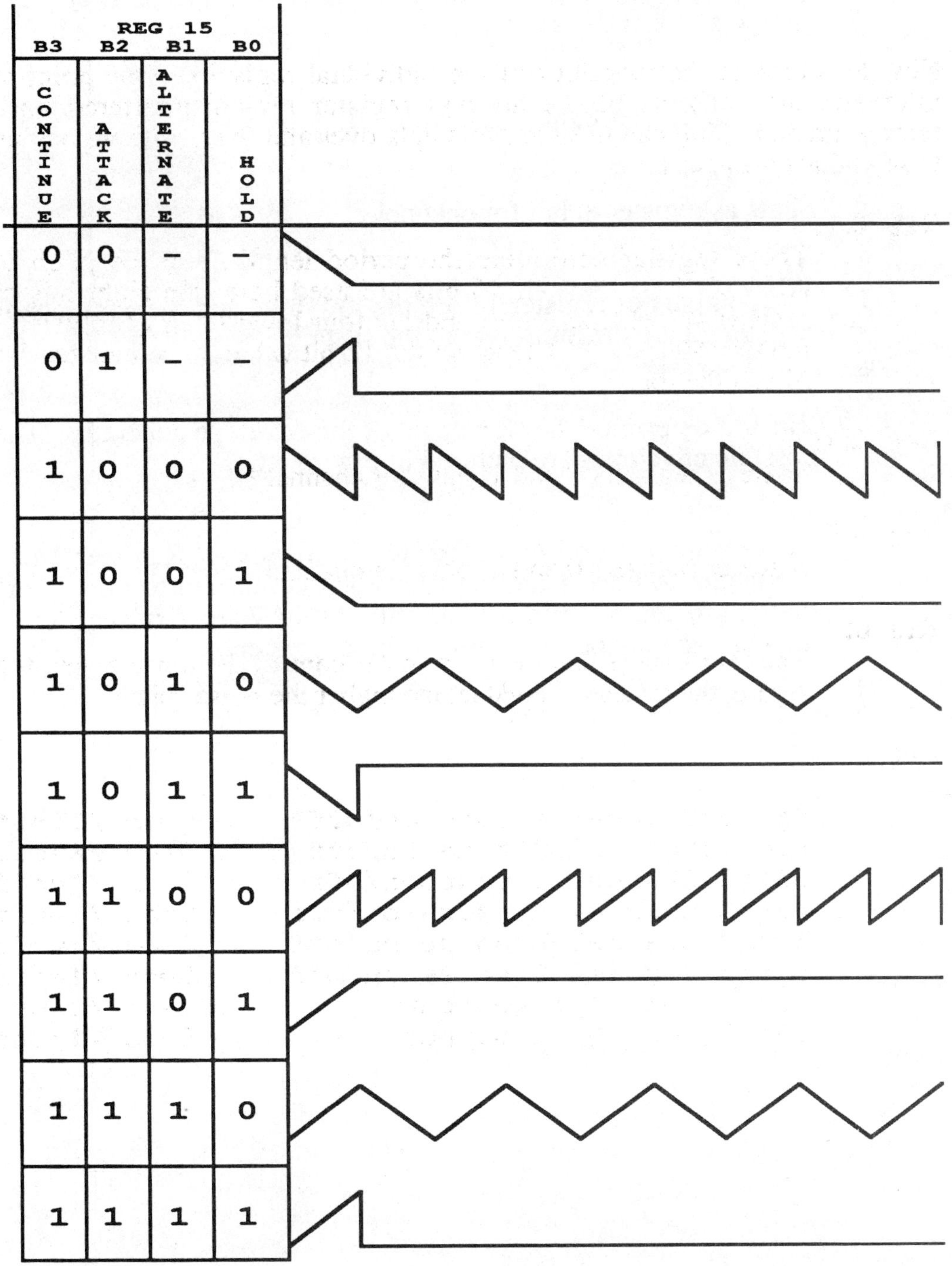

B3 CONTINUE	REG 15 B2 ATTACK	B1 ALTERNATE	B0 HOLD	Envelope
0	0	–	–	╲_____
0	1	–	–	╱‾‾‾‾‾‾‾
1	0	0	0	╲╲╲╲╲╲
1	0	0	1	╲_____
1	0	1	0	╲╱╲╱╲╱
1	0	1	1	╲‾‾‾‾‾‾‾
1	1	0	0	╱╱╱╱╱╱
1	1	0	1	╱‾‾‾‾‾‾‾
1	1	1	0	╱╲╱╲╱╲
1	1	1	1	╱_____

Reg 8:
    Bits 0-3 of this register control the signal volume of channel A. When bit 4 is set, the envelope register is being used and the contents of bits 0-3 are ignored.

Reg 9:
    Same as register 8, but for channel B.

Reg 10:
    Same as register 8, but for channel C.

Reg 11,12:
    The contents of register 11 are the low-byte and the contents of register 12 are the high-byte of the sustain.

Reg 13:
    Bits 0-3 determine the waveform of the envelope generator. The possible envelopes are pictured in Figure 1.6-2.

Reg 14,15:
    These registers comprise the two 8-bit ports. Register 14 is connected to Port A and register 15 is connected to Port B. If these ports are programmed as output (bits 7 and 8 of register 7) then values may be sent through these registers.

1.7 I/O Register Layout in the ST

The entire I/O range (all peripheral ICs and other registers) is controlled by a 32K address register -- $FF8000 - $FFFFFF. Below is a complete table of the different registers. CAUTION: The I/O section can be accessed only in supervisor mode. Any access in user mode results in a bus-error.

```
$FF8000      Memory configuration
$FF8200      Video display register
$FF8400      Reserved
$FF8600      DMA/disk controller
$FF8800      Sound chip
$FFFA00      MFP 68901
$FFFC00      ACIAs for MIDI and keyboard
```

The addresses given refer only to the start of each register, and supply no hint as to the size of each. More detailed information follows.

$FF8000   Memory Configuration

There is a single 8-bit register at $FF8001 in which the memory configuration is set up (four lowest bits). The MMU-IC is designed for maximum versatility within the ST. It lets you use three different types of memory expansion chips: 64K, 256K, and the 1M chips. Since all of these ICs are bit-oriented instead of byte-oriented, 16 memory chips of each type are required for memory expansion. The identifier for 16 such chips (regardless of memory capacity) is BANK. So, expansion is possible to 128 Kbyte, 512 Kbyte or even 2 Megabytes.

MMU can control two banks at once, using the RAS- and CAS- signals. The table on the next page shows the possible combinations:

$FF8001	Bit	Memory configuration	
	3-0	Bank 0	Bank 1
	0000	128K	128K
	0001	128K	512K
	0010	128K	2 M
	0011	reserved	
	0100	512K	128K
	0101	512K	512K
	0100	512K	2 M, normally reserved
	0100	reserved	
	1000	2M	128K
	1001	2M	512K
	1010	2M	2M
	1011	reserved	
	11XX	reserved	

The memory configuration can be read from or written to.

$FF8200   Video Display Register

This register is the storage area that determines the resolution and the color palette of the video display.

```
$FF8201    8-bit    Screen memory position (high-byte)
$FF8203    8-bit    Screen memory position (low-byte)
```

These two read/write registers are located at the beginning of the 32K video RAM.

In order to relocate video RAM, another register is used. This register is three bytes long and is located at $FF8205. Video RAM can be relocated in 256-byte increments. Normally the starting address of video RAM is $78000.

```
$FF8205    8-bit    Video address pointer (high-byte)
$FF8207    8-bit    Video address pointer (mid-byte)
$FF8209    8-bit    Video address pointer (low-byte)
```

These three registers are read only. Every three microseconds, the contents of these registers are incremented by 2.

```
$FF820A BIT        Synchronization mode
        1 0
        : :-- 0=internal,1=external synchronization
        :---- 0=60 Hz, 1=50Hz screen frequency
```

The bottom two bits of this register control synchronization mode; the remaining bits are unused. If bit 0 is set, the HSync and VSync impulses are shut off, which allows for screen synchronization from external sources (monitor jack). This offers new realm of possibilities in video, synchronization of your ST and a video camera, for example.

Bit 1 of the sync-mode register handles the screen frequency. This bit is useful only in the two "lowest" resolutions. High-res operation puts the ST at a 70 Hz screen frequency.

Sync mode can be read/written.

```
$FF8240     16-bit      Color palette register 0
$FF8242     16-bit      Color palette register 1
   :          :
   :          :         Color palette registers 2-13
   :          :
$FF825C     16-bit      Color palette register 14
$FF825E     16-bit      Color palette register 15
```

Although the ST has a total of 512 colors, only 16 different colors can be displayed on the screen at one time. The reason for this is that the user has 16 color pens on screen, and each can be one of 512 colors. The color palette registers represent these pens. All 16 registers contain 9 bits which affect the color:

```
FEDCBA9876543210
.....XXX.XXX.XXX
```

The bits marked X control the registers. Bits 0-2 adjust the shade of blue desired; 4-6, green hue; and 8-A, red. The higher the value in these three bits, the more intense the resulting color.

Middle resolution (640 X 200 points) offers four different colors; colors 4 through 15 are ignored by the palette registers.

When you want the maximum of 16 colors, it's best to zero-out the contents of the palette registers.

High-res (640 X 400 points) gives you a choice on only one "color"; bit 0 of palette register 0 is set to the background color. If the bit is cleared, then the text is black on a light background. A set bit reverses the screen (light characters, black background). The color register is a read/write register.

```
$FF8260    Bit   Resolution
           1 0
           0 0   320 X 200 points, four focal planes
           0 1   640 X 200 points, two focal planes
           1 0   640 X 400 points, one focal planes
```

This register sets up the appropriate hardware for the graphic resolution desired.

$FF8600   DMA/Disk Controller

```
$FF8600                    reserved
$FF8602                    reserved

$FF8604    16-bit          FDC access/sector count
```

The lowest 8 bits access the FDC registers. The upper 8 bits contain no information, and consistently read 1. Which register of the FDC is used depends upon the information in the DMA mode control register at $FF8606. The FDC can also be accessed indirectly.

The sector count-register under $FF8604 can be accessed when the appropriate bit in the DMA control register is set. The contents of these addresses are both read/write.

```
$FF8606    16-bit          DMA mode/status
```

When this register is read, the DMA status is found in the lower three bits of the register.

```
Bit 0   0=no error, 1=DMA error
Bit 1   0=sector count = null, 1=sector count<>null
Bit 2   Condition of FDC DATA REQUEST signal
```

Write access to this address controls the DMA mode register.

Bit 0		unused
Bit 1		0=pin A0 is low
		1=pin A0 is high
Bit 2		0=pin A1 is low
		1=pin A1 is high
Bit 3		0=FDC access
		1=HDC access
Bit 4		0=access to FDC register
		1=access to sector count register
Bit 5		0, reserved
Bit 6		0=DMA on
		1=no DMA
Bit 7		0=hard disk controller access (HDC)
		1=FDC access
Bit 8		0=read FDC/HDC registers
		1=write to FDC/HDC registers
$FF8609	8-bit	DMA basis and counter high-byte
$FF860B	8-bit	DMA basis and counter mid-byte
$FF860D	8-bit	DMA basis and counter low-byte

DMA transfer will tell the hardware at which address the data is to be moved. The initialization of the three registers must begin with the low-byte of the address, then mid-byte, then high-byte.

$FF8800 Sound Chip

The YM-2149 has 16 internal registers which can't be directly addressed. Instead, the number for the desired register is loaded into the select register. The chosen registers can be read/write, until a new register number is written to the PSG.

$FF8800	8-bit	Read data/Register select

Reading this address gives you the last register used (normally port A), by which disk drive is selected. This can be accomplished with write-protect signals, although these protected contents can be accessed by another register. Port A is used for multiple control functions, while port B is the printer data port.

PORT A
  Bit 0   Page-choice signal for double-sided
            floppy drive
  Bit 1   Drive select signal -- floppy drive 0
  Bit 2   Drive select signal -- floppy drive 1
  Bit 3   RS-232 RTS-output
  Bit 4   RS-232 DTR output
  Bit 5   Centronics strobe
  Bit 6   Freely usable output (monitor jack)
  Bit 7   reserved

When $FF8800 is written to, the select register of the PSG is alerted. The information in the bottom four bits are then considered as register numbers. The necessary four-bit number serves for writing to the PSG.

$FF8802   8-bit   Write data

Attempting to read this address after writing to it will give you $FF only, while BDIR and BC1 are nulls.

Writing register numbers and data can be performed with a single MOVE instruction.

$FFFA00   MFP 68901

The MFP's 24 registers are found at odd addresses from $FFFA01-$FFFA2F:

    $FFFA01   8-bit   Parallel port
    $FFFA03   8-bit   Active Edge register
    $FFFA05   8-bit   Data direction
    $FFFA07   8-bit   Interrupt enable A
    $FFFA09   8-bit   Interrupt enable B
    $FFFA0B   8-bit   Interrupt pending A
    $FFFA0D   8-bit   Interrupt pending B
    $FFFA0F   8-bit   Interrupt in-service A
    $FFFA11   8-bit   Interrupt in-service B
    $FFFA13   8-bit   Interrupt mask A
    $FFFA15   8-bit   Interrupt mask B
    $FFFA17   8-bit   Vector register
    $FFFA19   8-bit   Timer A control
    $FFFA1B   8-bit   Timer B control

```
$FFFA1D    8-bit    Timer C & D control
$FFFA1F    8-bit    Timer A data
$FFFA21    8-bit    Timer B data
$FFFA23    8-bit    Timer C data
$FFFA25    8-bit    Timer D data
$FFFA27    8-bit    Sync character
$FFFA29    8-bit    USART control
$FFFA2B    8-bit    Receiver status
$FFFA2D    8-bit    Transmitter status
$FFFA2F    8-bit    USART data
```

See the chapter on the MFP for details on the individual registers.

```
I/O Port
Bit 0    Centronics busy
Bit 1    RS-232 data carrier detect - input
Bit 2    RS-232 clear to send - input
Bit 3    reserved
Bit 4    keyboard and MIDI interrupt
Bit 5    FDC and HDC interrupt
Bit 6    RS-232 ring indicator
Bit 7    Monochrome monitor detect
```

Timers A and B each have an input which can be used by external timer control, or send a time impulse from an external source. Timer A is unused in the ST, which means that the input is always available, but it isn't connected to the user port, so the Centronics busy pin is connected instead. You can use it for your own purposes.

Timer B is used for counting screen lines in conjunction with DE (Display Enable).

The timer outputs in A-C are unused. Timer D, on the other hand, sends the timing signal for the MFP's built-in serial interface.

$FFFC00   Keyboard and MIDI ACIAs

The communications between the ST, the keyboard, and musical instruments are handled by two registers in the ACIAs.

```
$FFFC00    8-bit      Keyboard ACIA control
$FFFC02    8-bit      Keyboard ACIA data
$FFFC04    8-bit      MIDI ACIA control
$FFFC06    8-bit      MIDI ACIA data
```

Figure 1.7-1 I/O Assignments

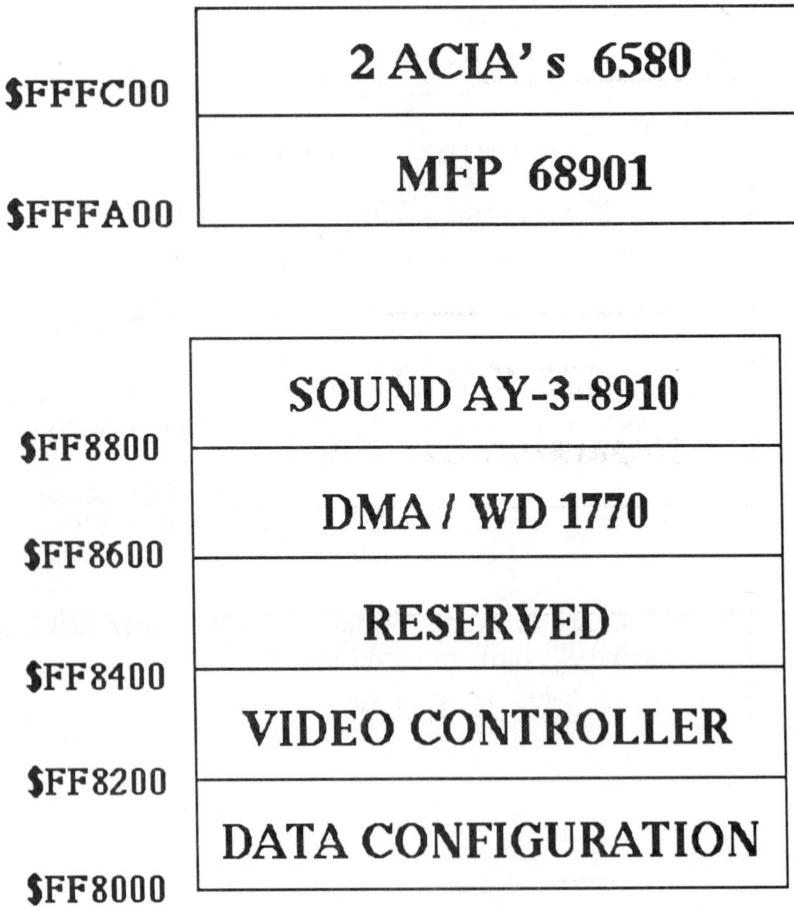

$FFFC00	2 ACIA's 6580
$FFFA00	MFP 68901

$FF8800	SOUND AY-3-8910
$FF8600	DMA / WD 1770
$FF8400	RESERVED
$FF8200	VIDEO CONTROLLER
$FF8000	DATA CONFIGURATION

Abacus Software   Atari ST Internals

Figure 1.7-2 Memory Map of the ATARI ST

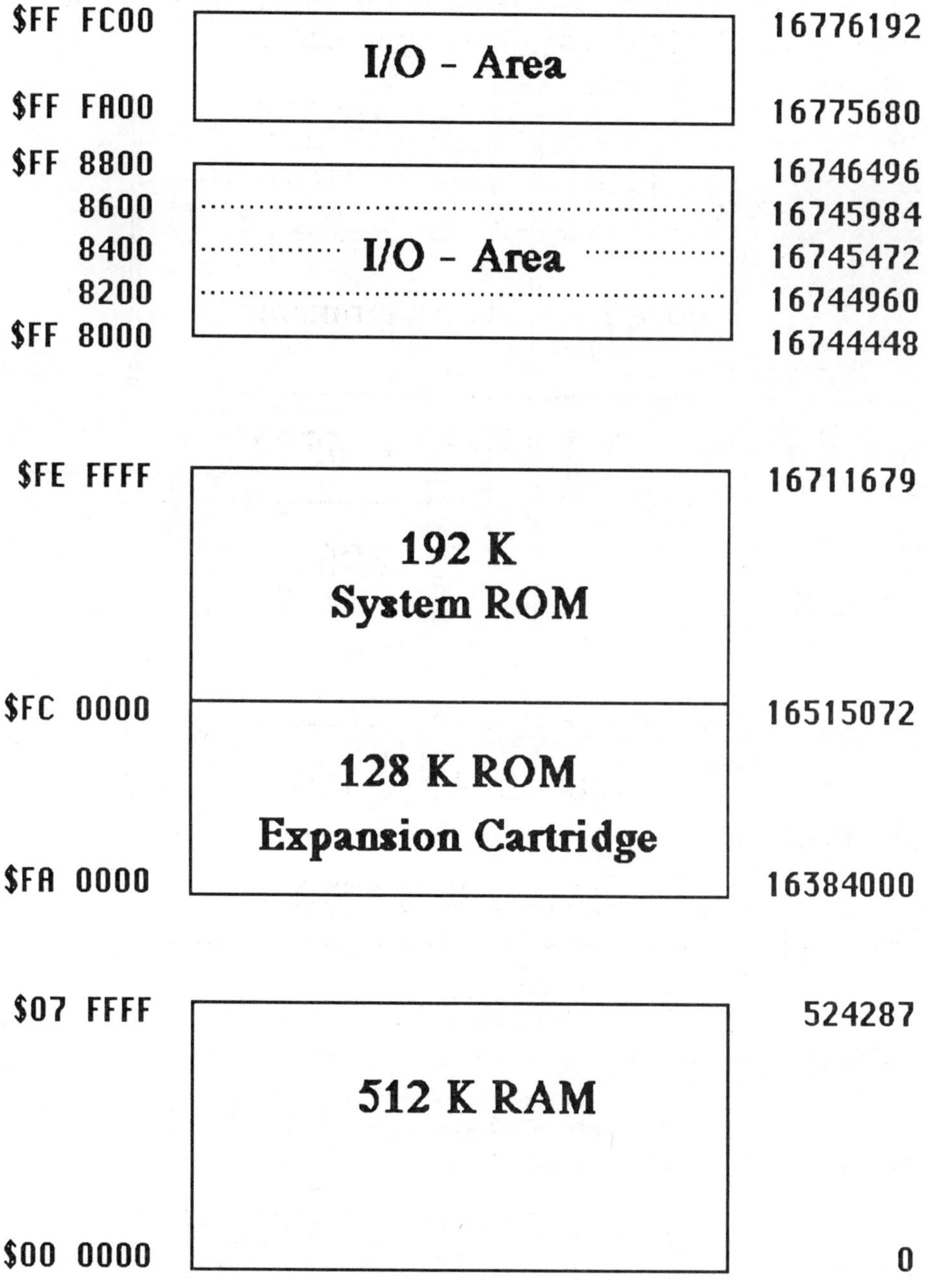

Address	Region	Decimal
$FF FC00	I/O - Area	16776192
$FF FA00		16775680
$FF 8800	I/O - Area	16746496
8600		16745984
8400		16745472
8200		16744960
$FF 8000		16744448
$FE FFFF	192 K System ROM	16711679
$FC 0000	128 K ROM Expansion Cartridge	16515072
$FA 0000		16384000
$07 FFFF	512 K RAM	524287
$00 0000		0

BLOCK DIAGRAM of the ATARI ST

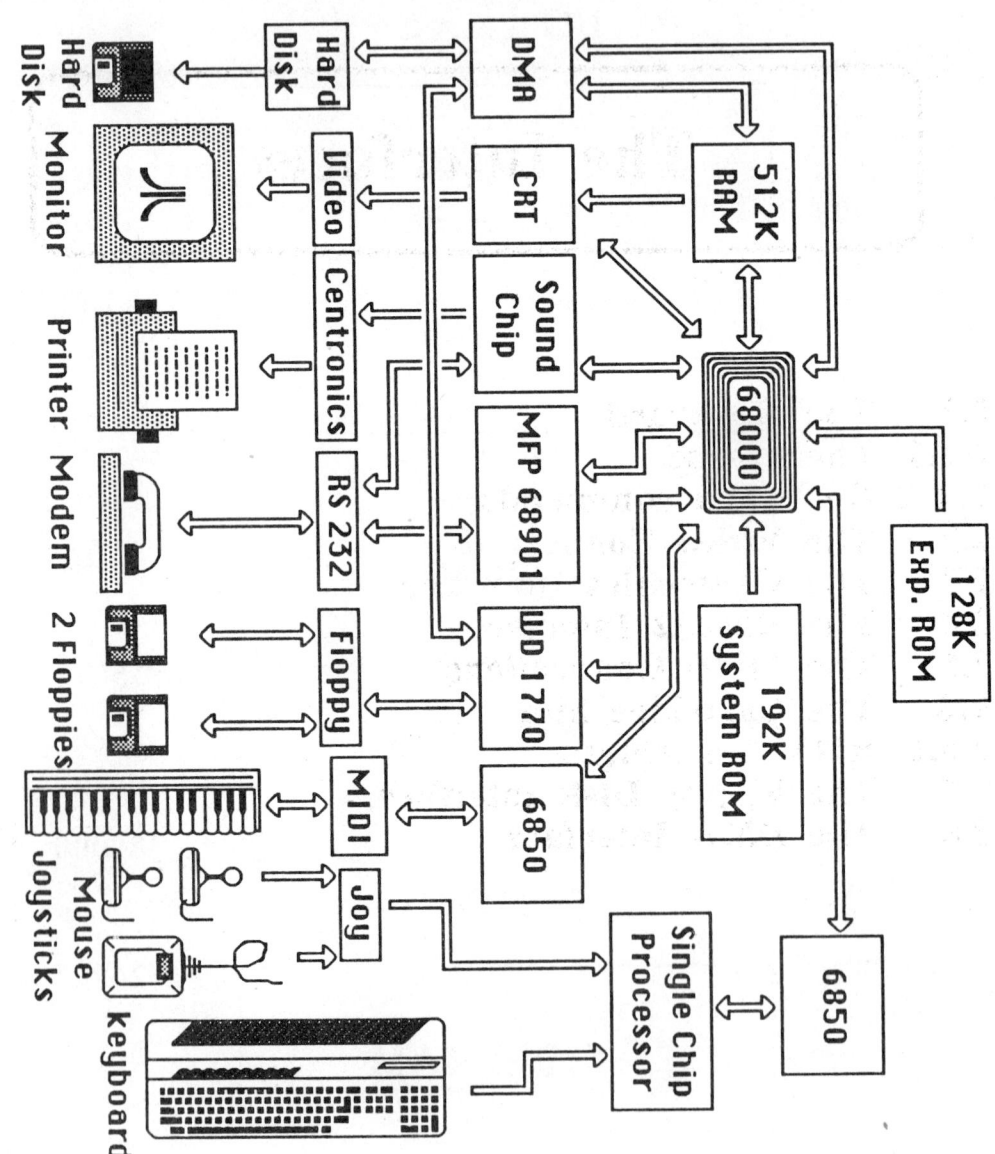

Chapter Two

The Interfaces

2.1 The Keyboard
2.1.1 The Mouse
2.1.2 Keyboard commands
2.2 The Video Connection
2.3 The Centronics Interface
2.4 The RS-232 Interface
2.5 The MIDI Connections
2.6 The Cartridge Slot
2.6.1 ROM Cartridges
2.7 The Floppy Disk Interface
2.8 The DMA Interface

The Interfaces

2.1 The Keyboard

Do you think it's really necessary to give a detailed report on something as trivial as the keyboard, since keyboards all function the same way? Actually the title should read "Keyboard Systems" or something similar. The keyboard is controlled by its own processor. You will soon see how this affects the assembly language programmer.

The keyboard processor is single-chip computer (controller) from the 6800 family, the 6301. Single chip means that everything needed for operation is found on a single IC. In actuality, there are some passive components in the keyboard circuit along with the 6301.

The 6301 has ROM, RAM, some I/O lines, and even a serial interface on the chip. The serial interface handles the traffic to and from the main board.

The advantage of this design is easy to see. The main computer is not burdened by having to continually poll the keyboard. Instead it can dedicate itself completely to processing your programs. The keyboard processor notifies the system if an event occurs that the operating system should be aware of.

The 6301 is not only responsible for the relatively boring task of reading the keyboard, however. It also takes care of the rather complicated tasks required in connection with the mouse. The main processor is then fed simply the new X and Y coordinates when the mouse is moved. Naturally, anything to do with the joysticks is also taken care of by the keyboard controller.

In addition, this controller contains a real-time clock which counts in one-second increments.

Figure 2.1-1 6850 Interface to 68000

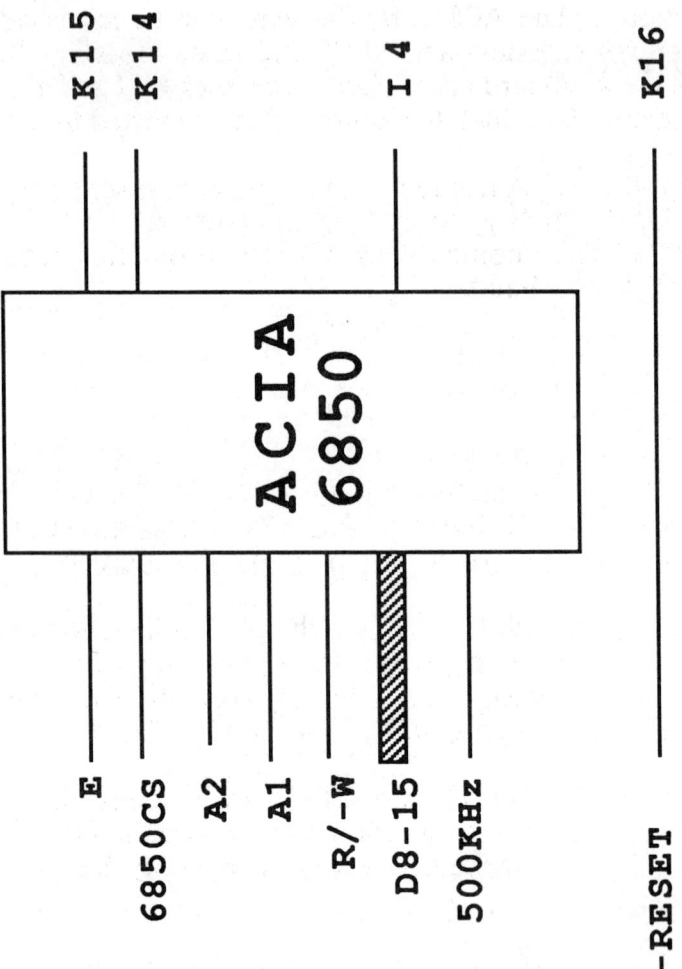

In Figure 2.1-1 is an overview of the interface to the 68000. As you see, the main processors is burdened as little as possible. The ACIA 6850 ensures that it is disturbed only when a byte has actually been completely received from the keyboard. The ACIA, by the way, can be accessed at addresses $FFFC00 (control register) and $FFFC02 (data register). The individual connection to the keyboard takes place over lines K14 and K15. K indicates the plug connection by which the keyboard is connected to the main board.

The signal that the ACIA has received a byte is first sent over line 14 to the MFP 68901 which then generates an interrupt to the 68000. The clock frequency of 500KHz comes from GLUE. From this results the "odd" transfer rate of 7812.5 baud.

In case you were surprised that data can also be sent *to* the keyboard processor, you will find the solution to the puzzle in Chapter 2.1.2.

The block diagram of the keyboard circuit is found in Figure 2.1-2. The function is as simple as the figure is easy to read. The processor has 4K of ROM available. The 128 bytes of RAM is comparatively small, but it is used only as a buffer and for storing pointers and counters.

The lines designated with K are again the plug connections assigned to the main board. With few exceptions, the connections for the joystick and mouse are also put through. K16 is the reset line from the 68000. K15 carries the send data from the 6850, K14 the send data from the 6301.

The I/O ports 1(0-7), 3(1-7), and 4(0-7) are responsible for reading the keyboard matrix. One line from ports 3 and 4 is pulled low in a cycle. The state of port 1 is the checked. If a key is pressed, the low signal comes through on port 1.

Each key can be identified from the combination of value placed on ports 3 and 4 and the value read from port 1.

If none of the lines of Port 3 and 4 are placed low and a bit of port 1 still equals zero, a joystick is active on the outer connector 1. The data from outer connector 0, to which a mouse or a joystick can be connected, does not come through by chance since it must first be switched through the NAND gate with port 2 (bit 0). The buttons on the mouse or the joystick then arrive at port 2 (1 and 2).

Figure 2.1-2 Block Diagram of Keyboard Circuit

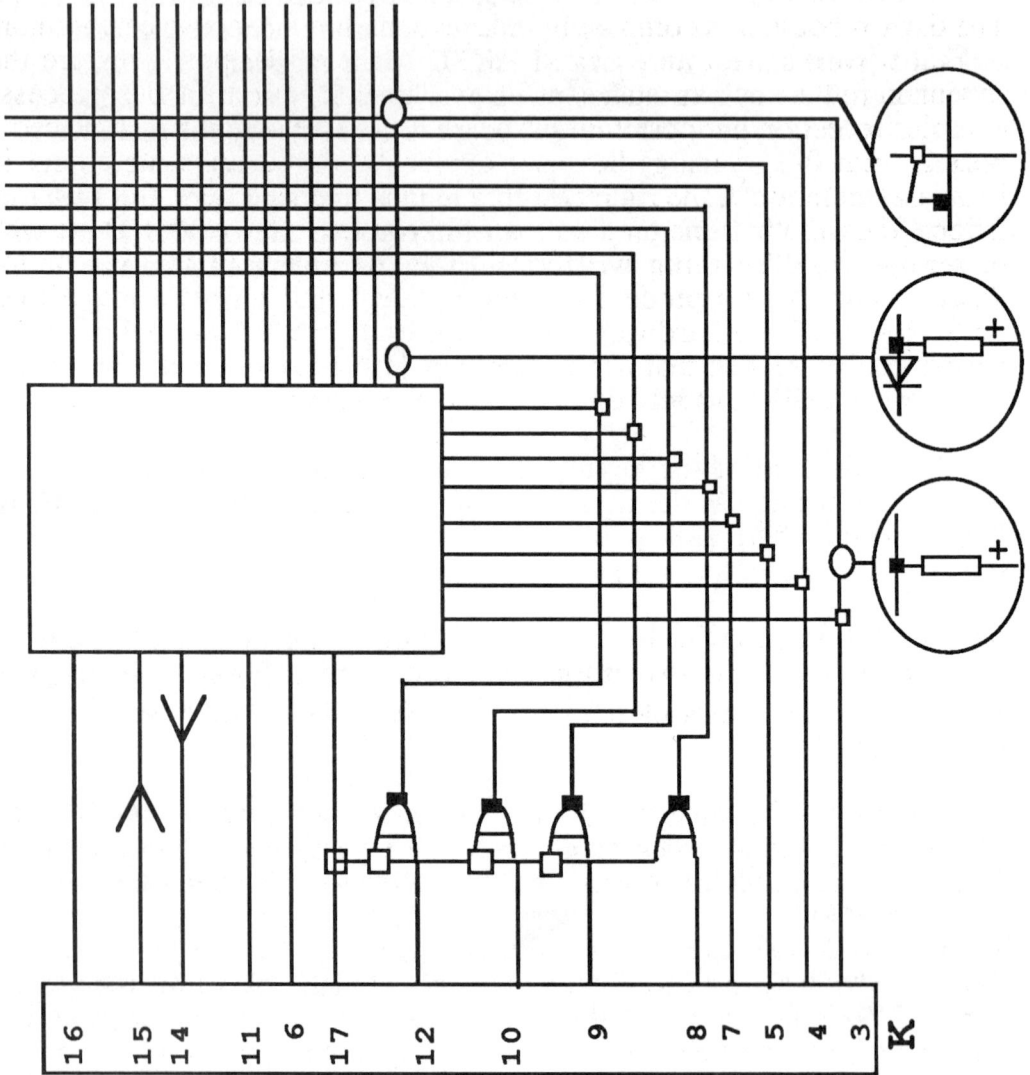

The assignments of the K lines to the signal names on the outer connector are found in the next section.

The 6301 processor is completely independent, but it can also be configured so that it works with an external ROM. Some of the port lines are then reconfigured to act as address lines. The configuration the processor assumes (one of eight possibilities) depends on the logical signal placed on port 2 (bits 0-2) during the reset cycle. All three lines high puts the processor in mode 7, the right one for the task intended here. But bits 1 and 2 depend on the buttons on the mouse. If you leave the mouse alone while powering-up, everything will be in order. If you hold the two buttons down, however, the processor enters mode 1 and makes a magnificent belly-flop, since the hardware for this operating mode is not provided. You notice this by the fact that the mouse cursor does not move on the screen if you move the mouse. Only the reset button will restore the processor.

2.1.1 The Mouse

The construction of this little device is quite simple, but effective. Essentially, it consists of four light barriers, two encoder wheels, and a drive mechanism.

The task of the mouse is to give the computer information about its movements. This information consists of the components: direction on the X-axis, direction on the Y-axis, and the path traveled on each axis.

In order to do this, the rubber-covered ball visible from the outside drives two encoder wheels whose drive axes are at angle of 90 degrees to each other. The one or the other axis rotates more or less, forwards or backwards, depending on the direction the mouse is moved.

It is no problem to determine the absolute movement on each axis. The encoder wheels alternately interrupt the light barriers. One need only count the pulses from each wheel to be informed about the path traveled on each axis.

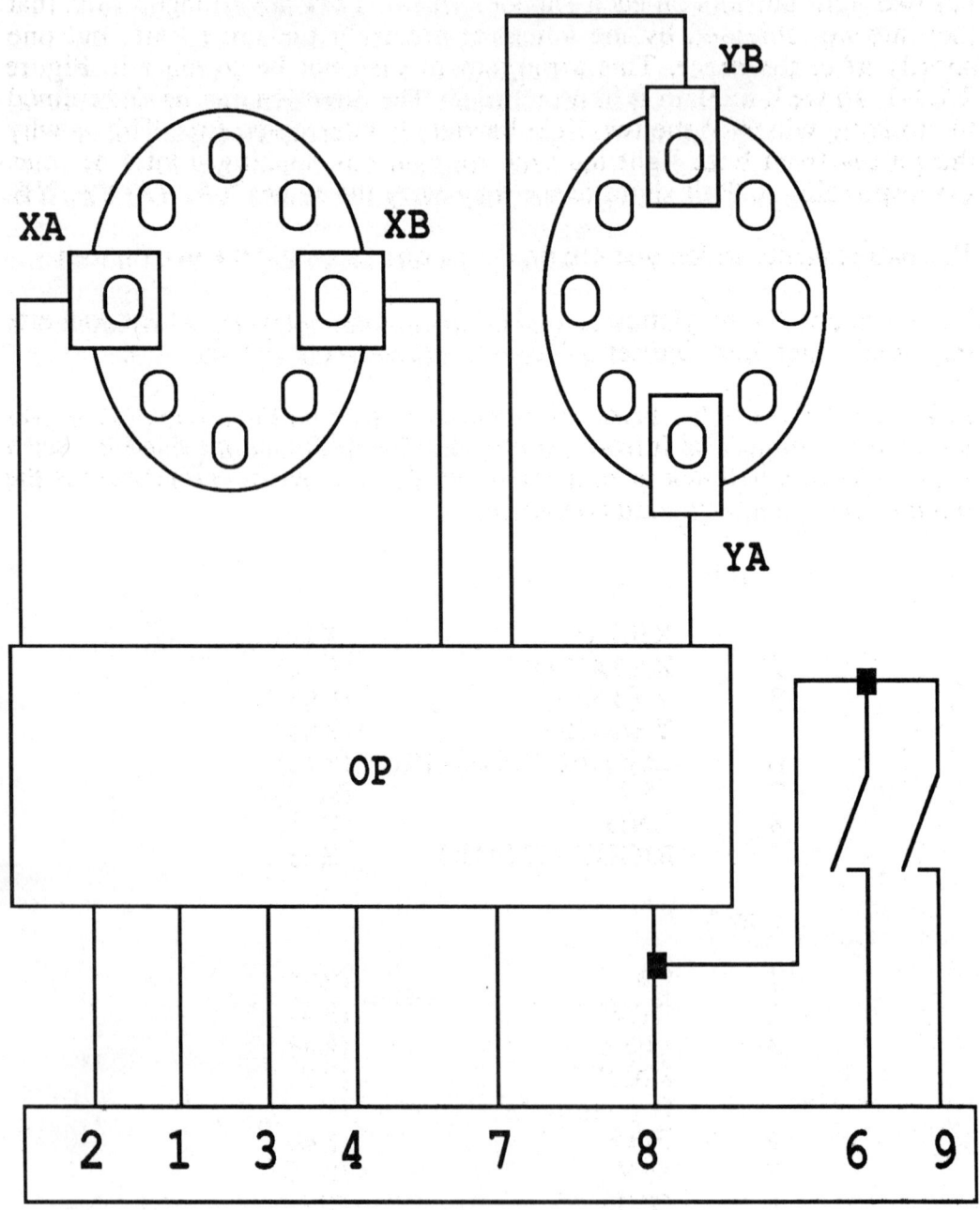

Figure 2.1.1-1 The Mouse

It is more difficult when the direction of movement is also required. The designers of the mouse used a convenient trick for this. There are not one, but two light barriers on each encoder wheel. They are arranged such that they are not shielded by the wheel at precisely the same time, but one shortly after the other. This arrangement may not be so clear in Figure 2.1.1-1, so we'll explain it in more detail The direction can be determined by noticing which of the two light barriers is interrupted first. This is why the pulses from both light barriers are sent out, making a total of four. Corresponding to their significance they carry the names XA, XB, YA, YB.

The two contacts which you see on the picture represent the two buttons.

The large box on the picture is a quad operational amplifier which converts the rather rough light-barrier pulses into square wave signals.

In Figure 2.1.1-2 is the layout of the control port on the computer, as you see it when you look at it from the outside. The designation behind the slash applies when a joystick is connected and the number in parentheses is the pin number of the keyboard connector.

Port 0

1	XB/UP	(K12)
2	XA/DOWN	(K10)
3	YA/LEFT	(K9)
4	YB/RIGHT	(K8)
6	LEFT BUTTON/FIRE	(K11)
7	+5V	(K13)
8	GND	(K1)
9	RIGHT BUTTON	(K6)

Port 1

1	UP	(K7)
2	DOWN	(K5)
3	LEFT	(K4)
4	RIGHT	(K3)
5	Port 0 enable	(K17)
6	FIRE	(K6)
7	+5V	(K13)
8	GND	(K1)

Figure 2.1.1-2 Mouse control port

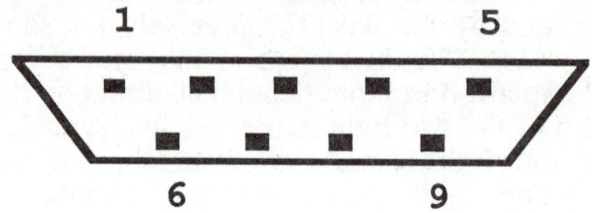

2.1.2 Keyboard commands

The keyboard processor "understands" some commands pertaining to such things as how the mouse is to be handled, etc. You can set the clock time, read the internal memory, and so on. You can find an application example in the assembly language listing on page 80 (after command $21).

The "normal" action of the processor consists of keeping an eye on the keyboard and announcing each keypress. This is done by outputting the number of the key when the key is pressed. When the key is released the number is set again, but with bit 7 set. The result of this is that no key numbers greater than 127 are possible. You can find the assignment of the key numbers to the keys at the end of this section in figure 2.1.2-1. In reality these numbers only go up to 117 because values from $F6 up are reserved for other purposes. There must be a way to pass more information than just key numbers to the main processor, information such as the clock time or the current position of the mouse. This cannot be handled in a single byte but only in something called a package, so the bytes at $F6 signal the start of a package. Which header comes before which package is explained along with the individual commands.

A command to the keyboard processor consists of the command code (a byte) and any parameters required. The following description is sorted according to command bytes.

$07
Returns the result of pressing one of the two mouse buttons. A parameter byte with the following format is required:

Bit 0 =1: The absolute position is returned when a mouse button is pressed. Bit 2 must =0.
Bit 1 =1: The absolute position is returned when a mouse button is released. Bit 2 must =0.
Bit 2 =1: The mouse buttons are treated like normal keys. The left button is key number $74, the right is $75.
Bits 3-7   must always be zero.

$08
Returns the relative mouse position from now on. This command tells the keyboard processor to automatically return the relative position (the distance from the previous position) whenever the mouse is moved. A movement is given when the number of encoder wheel pulses has reached a given threshold. See also $0B. A relative mouse package looks like this:

```
1 byte   Header in range $F8-$FB. The two lowest
         bits of the header indicate the condition
         of the two mouse buttons.
1 byte   Relative X-position (signed!)
1 byte   Relative Y-position (signed!)
```

If the relative position changes substantially between two packages so that the distance can no longer be expressed in one byte, another package is automatically created which makes up for the remainder.

$09
Returns the absolute mouse position from now on. This command also sets the coordinate maximums. The internal coordinate pointers are at the same time set to zero. The following parameters are required:

```
1 word   Maximum X-coordinate
1 word   Maximum Y-coordinate
```

Mouse movements under the zero point or over the maximums are not returned.

$0A
With this command it is possible to get the key numbers of the cursor keys instead of the coordinates. A mouse movement then appears to the operating system as if the corresponding cursor keys had been pressed. These parameters are necessary:

```
1 byte  Number of pulses (X) after which the key
        number for cursor left (or right) will be
        sent.
1 byte  Number of pulses (Y) after which the key
        number for cursor up (or down) will be sent.
```

$0B

This command sets the trigger threshold, above which movements will be announced. A certain number of encoder pulses elapse before a package is sent. This functions only in the relative operating mode. The following are the parameters:

```
1 byte     Threshold in X-direction
1 byte     Threshold in Y-direction
```

$0C

Scale mouse. Here is determined how many encoder pulses will go by before the coordinate counter is changed by 1. This command is valid only in the absolute. The following parameters are required:

```
1 byte     X scaling
1 byte     Y scaling
```

$0D

Read absolute mouse position. No parameters are required, but a package of the following form is sent:

```
1 byte     Header = $F7
1 byte     Button status
     Bit 0 = 1: Right button was pressed since the
                last read
     Bit 1 = 1: Right button was not pressed
     Bit 2 = 1: Left button was pressed since the
                last read
     Bit 3 = 1: Left button was not pressed
```

From this strange arrangement you can determine that the state of a button has changed since the last read if the two bits pertaining to it are zero.

```
1 word Absolute X-coordinate
1 word Absolute Y-coordinate
```

$0E
Set the internal coordinate counter. The following parameters are required:

```
1 byte     =0 as fill byte
1 word     X-coordinate
1 word     Y-coordinate
```

$0F
Set the origin for the Y-axis is down (next to the user).

$10
Set the origin for the Y-axis is up.

$11
The data transfer to the main processor is permitted again (see $13).
Any command other than $13 will also restart the transfer.

$12
Turn mouse off. Any mouse-mode command ($08, $09, $0A) turns the mouse back on. If the mouse is in mode $0A, this command has no effect.

$13
Stop data transfer to main processor.
NOTE: Mouse movements and key presses will be stored as long as the small buffer of the 6301 allows. Actions beyond the capacity of the buffer will be lost.

$14
Every joystick movement is automatically returned. The packages sent have the following format:

```
1 byte     Header = $FE or $FF for joystick 0/1
1 byte     Bits 0-3 for the position (a bit for each
           direction), bit 7 for the button
```

$15
End the automatic-return mode for the joystick. When needed, a package must be requested with $16.

$16
Read joystick. After this command the keyboard sends a package as described above.

$17
Joystick duration message. One parameter is required.

1 byte	Time between two messages in 1/100 sec.

From this point on, packages of the following form are sent continuously (as long as no other mode is selected):

1 byte	Bit 0 for the button on joystick 1, bit 1 for that of joystick 0
1 byte	Bits 0-3 for the position of joystick 1, bits 4-7 for the position of joystick 0

NOTE: The read interval should not be shorter than the transfer channel needs to send the two bytes of the package.

$18
Fire button duration message. The condition of the button in joystick 1 (!) is continually tested and the result packed into a byte. This means that a message byte contains 8 such tests, whereby bit 7 is the most recent. The keyboard controller determines the time between byte fetches by the main processor. This time is divided into eight equal intervals in which the button is polled. The polling then takes place as regularly as possible. This mode remains active until another command is received.

$19
Cursor key simulation mode for joystick 0 (!). The current position of the joystick is sent to the main processor as if the corresponding cursor keys had been pressed (as often as necessary). To avoid having to explain the same things for the following parameters, here are the most important: All times are assumed to be in tenths of seconds. R indicates the time, when reached, cursor clicks will be sent in intervals of T. After this the interval is V. If R=0, only V is responsible for the interval. Naturally, this mechanism comes into play only when the joystick is held in the same position for longer than T or R.

1 byte	RX
1 byte	RY
1 byte	TX
1 byte	TY
1 byte	VX
1 byte	VY

$1A
Turn off joysticks. Any other joystick command turns them on again.

$1B
Set clock time. This command sets the internal real-time clock in the keyboard processor. The values are passed in packed BCD, meaning a digit 0-9 for each half byte, yielding a two-digit decimal number per byte. The following parameters are necessary:

```
1 byte     Year, two digit (85, 86, etc.)
1 byte     Month, two digit (12, 01, etc.)
1 byte     Day, two digit (31,01,02, etc.)
1 byte     Hours, two digit
1 byte     Minutes, two digit
1 byte     Seconds, two digit
```

Any half byte which does not contain a valid BCD digit (such as F) is ignored. This makes it possible to change just part of the date or clock time.

$1C
Read clock time. After receiving this command the keyboard processor returns a package having the same format as the one described above. A header is added to the package, however, having the value $FC.

$20
Load memory. The internal memory of the keyboard processor (naturally only the RAM in the range $80 to $FF makes sense) can be written with this command. It is not clear to us of what use this is since according to our investigations (we have disassembled the operating system of the 6301), no RAM is available to be used as desired. Perhaps certain parameters can be changed in this manner which are not accessible through "legal" means. Here are the parameters:

```
1 word     Start address
1 byte     Number of bytes (max. 128)
Data bytes (corresponding to the number)
```

The interval at which the data bytes will be sent must be less than 20 msec.

$21

Read memory. This command is the opposite of $20. These parameters are required:

1 word   Address at which to read

A package having the following format is returned:

1 byte   Header 1 =$F6. This is the status header which precedes all packages containing any operating conditions of the keyboard processor. We will come to the general status messages shortly.
1 byte   Header 2 =$20 as indicator that this package carries the memory contents.
6 bytes   Memory contents starting with the address given in the command.

Here is a small program which we used to read the ROM in the 6301 and output it to a printer. Here you also see how the status packages arrive from the keyboard. These are normally thrown away by the 68000 operating system. Section 3.1 contains information about the GEMDOS and XBIOS calls used.

```
            prt     equ     0
            chout   equ     3
            gemdos  equ     1
            bios    equ     13
            xbios   equ     14
            stvec   equ     12
            rdm     equ     $21
            wrkbd   equ     25
            kbdvec  equ     34
            term    equ     0
start:
            move.w  #kbdvec,-(a7)
            trap    #xbios
            addq.l  #2,a7
            move.l  d0,a0
            lea     keyin,a1
            move.l  d0,savea
            move.l  stvec(a0),save
```

```
            move.l    a1,stvec(a0)
            move.w    #$f000,d4            Starting address
loop:
            move.w    d4,tbuf+1            Current address
            bsr       keyout
wait:
            cmpi.b    rbuf
            beq       wait
            moveq.w   #5,d6
            bsr       bufout
            addq.w    #6,d4                Ending address?
            bmi       loop
            bra       exit
bufout:
            lea       rbuf+2,a4
bytout:
            move.b    (a4)+,d0
            bsr       hexout
            dbra      d6,bytout
            rts
hexout:
            movea.w   d0,a1
            lsr.b     #4,d0
            andi.w    #15,d0
            lea       table,a3
            move.b    0(a3,d0),d2
            lsl.w     #8,d2
            move.w    a1,d0
            andi.w    #15,d0
            move.b    0(a3,d0),d2
            move.w    d2,d0
            move.w    d2,-(a7)
            lsr.w     #8,d0
            bsr       chrout
            move.w    (a7)+,d0
            bsr       chrout
            move.b    #" ",d0
chrout:
            move.w    d0,-(a7)
            move.w    #prt,-(a7)
            move.w    #chout,-(a7)
            trap      #bios
            addq.l    #6,a7
            rts
exit:
            movea     savea,a0
            move.l    save,stvec(a0)
```

```
            move.w    #term,-(a7)
            trap      #gemdos
keyout:
            move.b    rbuf
            pea       tbuf
            move.w    #2,-(a7)
            move.w    #wrkbd,-(a7)
            trap      #xbios
            addq.l    #8,a7
            rts
keyin:
            moveq     #7,d0
            lea       rbuf,a1
repin:
            move.b    (a0)+,(a1)+
            dbra      d0,repin
            rts
table:
            dc.b      "0123456789ABCDEF"

            rbuf:     ds.b    8
            save      ds.l    1
            savea     ds.l    1
            dummy     ds.b    1
            tbuf      dc.b    rdm
            ds.b      2
            .end
```

$22
Execute routine. With this command you can execute a subroutine in the 6301. Naturally, you must know exactly what it does and where it is located, so long as you have not transferred it yourself to RAM with $20 (assuming you found some free space). The only required parameters are:

```
1 word   Start address
```

Status messages
You can at any time read the operating parameters of the keyboard by simply adding $80 to the command byte with which you would to set the operating mode (whose parameters you want to know). You then get a status package back (header=$F6), whose format corresponds exactly to those which would be necessary for setting the operating mode.

An example makes it clearer: you want to know how the mouse is scaled. So you send as the command the value $8C (since $0C sets the scaling). You get the following back:

```
1 byte  Status header =$F6
1 byte  X-scaling
1 byte  Y-scaling
```

This is the same format which would be necessary for the command $0C. For commands which do not require parameters, you get the evoked command back as such. For example, say you want to know what operating mode the joystick is in ($14 or $15). You send the value $94 (or $95, it makes no difference). As status package you receive, in addition to the header, either $14 or $15 depending on the operating mode of the joystick handler.

Allowed status checks are: $87, $88, $89, $8A, $8B, $8C, $8F, $90, $92, $94, $99, and $9A.

In conclusion we have a tip for those for whom the functions of the keyboard are too meager and who want to give it more "intelligence". The processor 6301 is also available in "piggy-back" version, the 63P01 (Hitachi). This model does not have ROM built in, but has a socket on the top for an EPROM of type 2732 or 2764 (8K!). You can then realize your own ideas and, for example, use the two joystick connections as universal 4-bit I/O ports, for which you can also extend the command set in order to access the new functions from the XBIOS as well.

Figure 2.1.2-1 ATARI ST Key Assignments

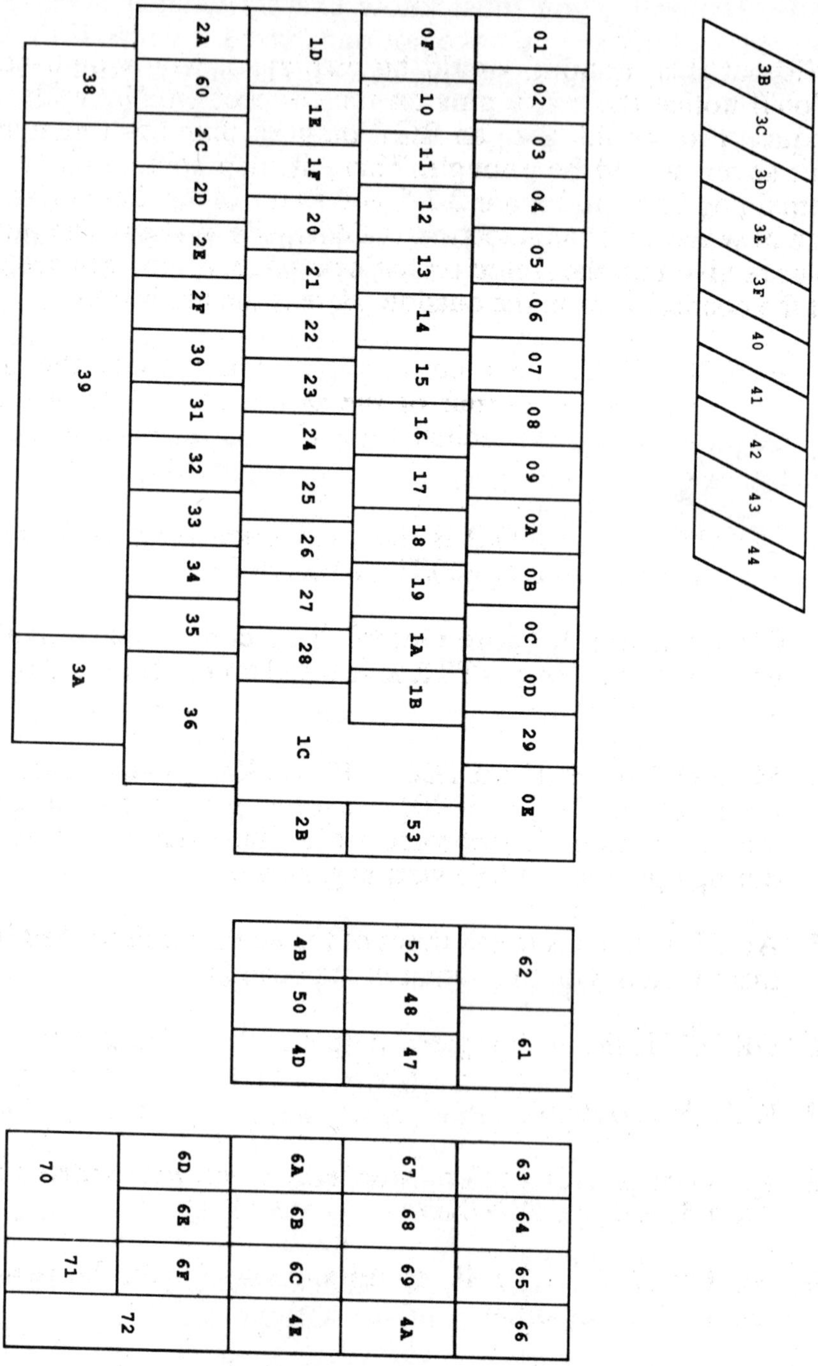

2.2 The Video Connection

Without this, nothing would be displayed. You would be typing blind. You'll notice the many pins on the connection. Naturally more lines are required for hooking up an RGB monitor than for a monochrome screen, but seven would be enough. There is also something special about the remaining lines. In Figure 2.2-1 you find a block diagram in which you can see how the video connection is tied to the system. The numbering of the pins is given on the figure on the next page, as you can see, when you look at the connector from the outside. Here is the pin layout:

1 AUDIO OUT. This connection comes from the amplifier connected to the output of the sound chip. A high-impedance earphone can be attached here if you do not use the original monitor.

2 COMPOSITE VIDEO is the connection from 9-12. This is not available on the early 520ST or 1040 ST.

3 GPO, General Purpose Output. This connection is available for your use. The line has TTL levels and comes from I/O port A bit 6 of the sound chip.

4 MONOCHROME DETECT. If this line, which leads to the I7 input of the MFP 68901, is low, the computer enters the high-resolution monochrome mode. If the state of the line changes during operation, a cold start is generated.

5 AUDIO IN leads to the input of the amplifier described in 1 and is there mixed with the output of the sound chip.

6 GREEN is the analog green output of the video shifter.

7 RED. Red output.

8 +12 control voltage for color televisions with video connectors. Atari 520ST = GROUND.

9 HORIZONTAL SYNC is responsible for the horizontal beam return of the monitor.

Figure 2.2-1 Diagram of Video Interface

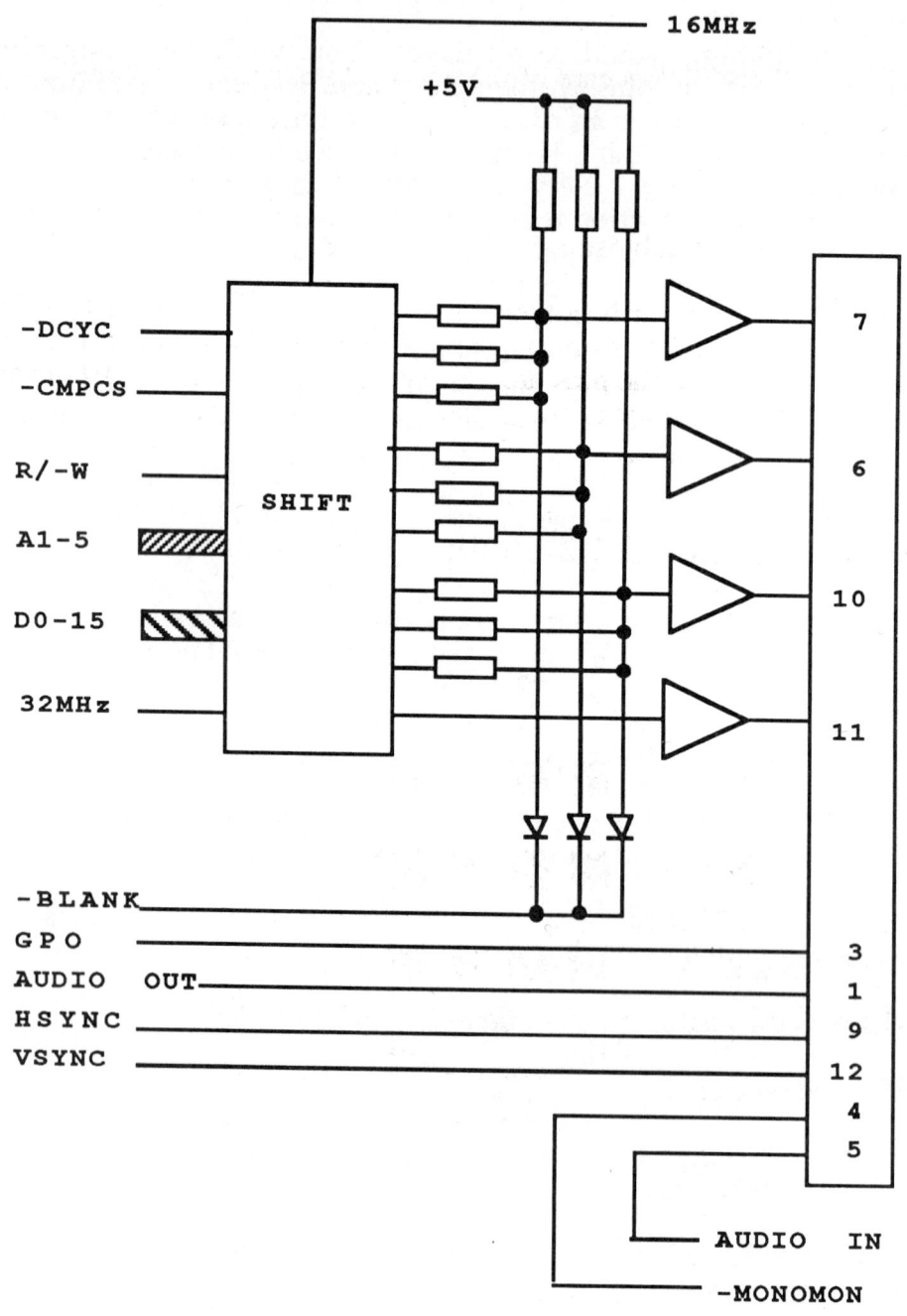

10 BLUE is the analog blue output of the video shifter.

11 MONOCHROME provides a monochrome monitor with the intensity signal.

12 VERTICAL SYNC takes care of the beam return at the end of the screen.

13 GROUND.

A tip for the hardware hobbyist:

A plug to fit this connector is not available. If you want to make a plug for connecting other monitors, simply use a piece of perf board in which you have soldered pins, since the pins are fortunately organized in a 1/10" array. Pin 13 is out of order, but it is not needed since pin 8 is also available for ground.

Figure 2.2-2 Monitor Connector

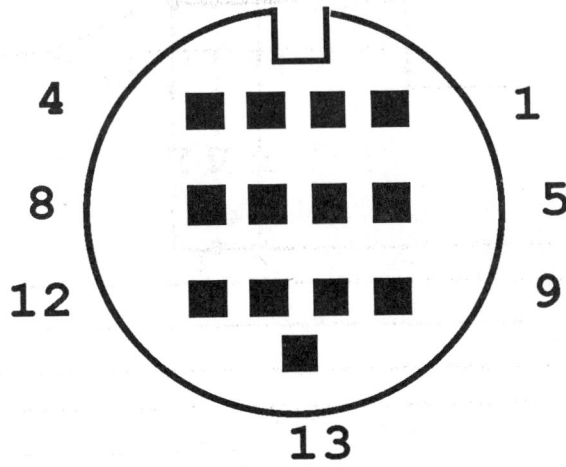

2.3 The Centronics Interface

A standard Centronics parallel printer can be connected to this interface, provided that you have the proper cable. As you can see in Figure 2.3-2, the connection to the system is somewhat unusual. The data lines and the strobe of the universal port of the sound chip are used. So you find these too on the picture, in which the other lines, which will not be described in the section, will not disturb you. They belong to the disk drive and RS-232 interface and are handled there.

Here is the pin description:

1   -STROBE indicates the validity of the byte on the data lines to the connected device by a low pulse.

2-9   DATA

11   BUSY is always placed high by the printer when it is not able to receive additional data. This can have various causes. Usually the buffer is full or the device is off line.

18-25   GROUND.

All other pins are unused.

A tip for making a cable. Get flat-cable solderless connectors. You need a type D25-subminiature, a Cinch 36-pin (3M,AMP) and the appropriate length of 25-conductor flat ribbon cable. You squeeze the connectors on the cable so that pins 1 match up on both sides (they are connected together). The other connections then match automatically. Note that there will naturally be some pins free on the printer side.

Figure 2.3-1 Printer Port Pins

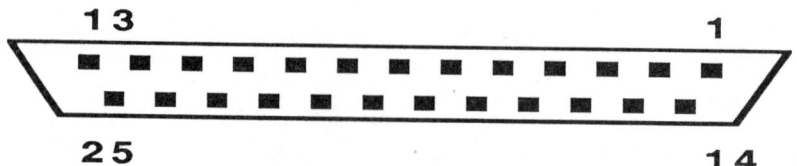

Figure 2.3-2 Centronics Connection

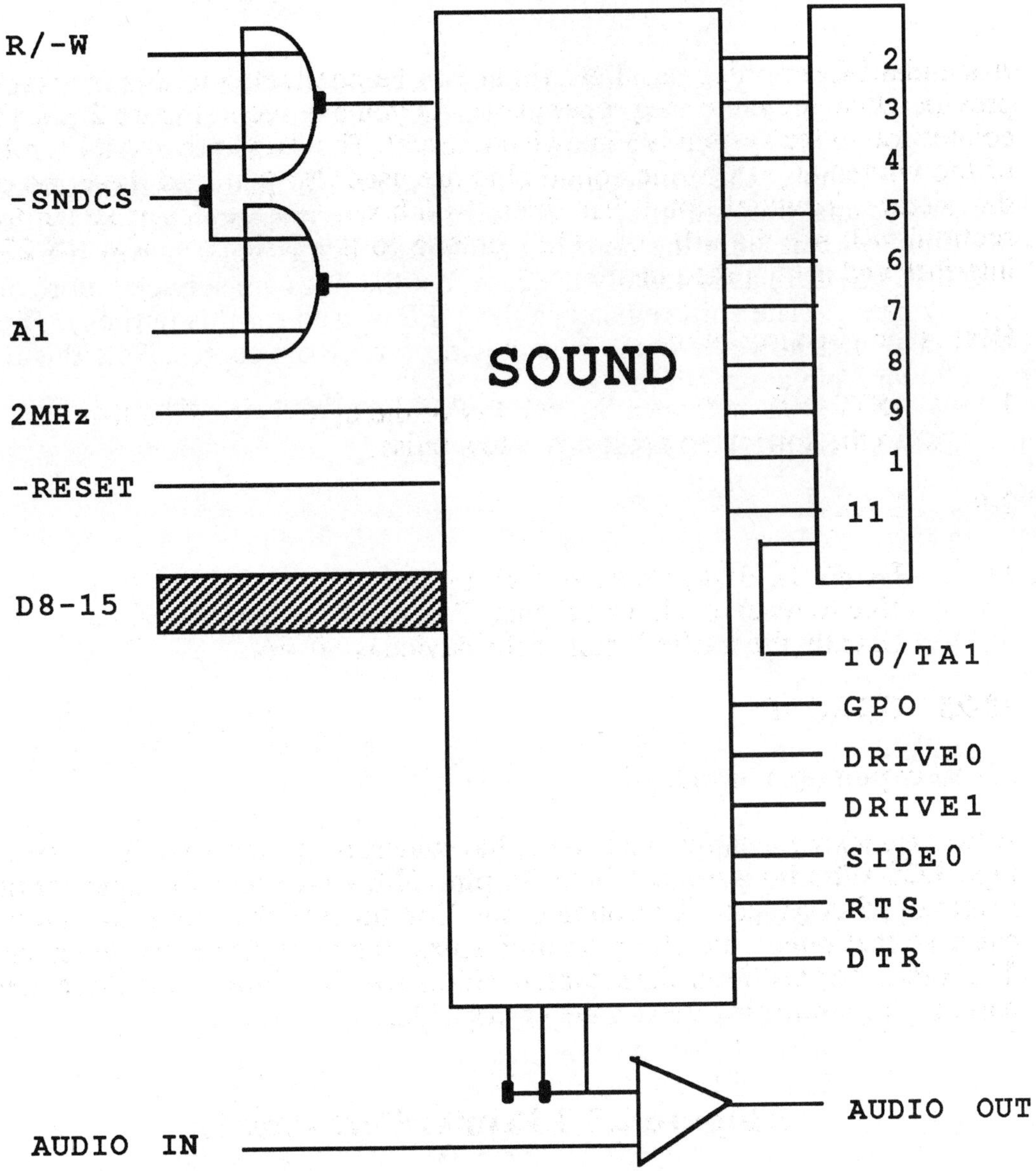

2.4 The RS-232 Interface

This interface usually serves for communication with other computers and modems. You can also connect a printer here. Note the description of pin 5!

Figure 2.4-1 shows the connection to the system. Normally you don't have to do any special programming to use this interface. It is taken care of by the operating system. Here the control of the interface is not controlled by a special IC (UART) as is usually the case, but the lines are serviced more or less "by hand." The shift register in the MFP is used for this purpose. The handshake lines however come from a wide variety of sources. Note this in the following pin description:

1   CHASSIS GROUND (shield)
     This is seldom used.

2   TxD
     Send data

3   RxD
     Receive data

4   RTS
     Ready to send comes from I/O port A bit 3 of the sound chip and is always high when the computer is ready to receive a byte. On the Atari, this signal is first placed low after receiving a byte and is kept low until the byte has been processed.

5   CTS
     Clear to send of a connected device is read at interrupt input I2 of the MFP. At the present time this signal is handled improperly by the operating system. Therefore it is possible to connect only devices which "rattle" the line after every received byte (like the 520ST with RTS). The signal goes to input I2 of the MFP, but unfortunately is tested only for the signal edge. You will not have any luck connecting a printer because they usually hold the CTS signal high as long as the buffer is not full. There is no signal edge after each byte, which means that only the first byte of a text is transmitted, and then nothing.

7   GND
    Signal ground.

8   DCD
    Carrier signal detected. This line, which goes to interrupt input I1 of the MFP, is normally serviced by a modem, which tells the computer that connection has been made with the other party.

20 DTR
    Device ready. This line signals to a device that the computer is turned on and the interface will be serviced as required. It comes from I/O port A bit 4 of the sound chip.

22 RI
    Ring indicator is a rather important interrupt on I6 of the MFP and is used by a modem to tell the computer that another party wishes connection, that is, someone called.

Figure 2.4-1 RS-232 Connection

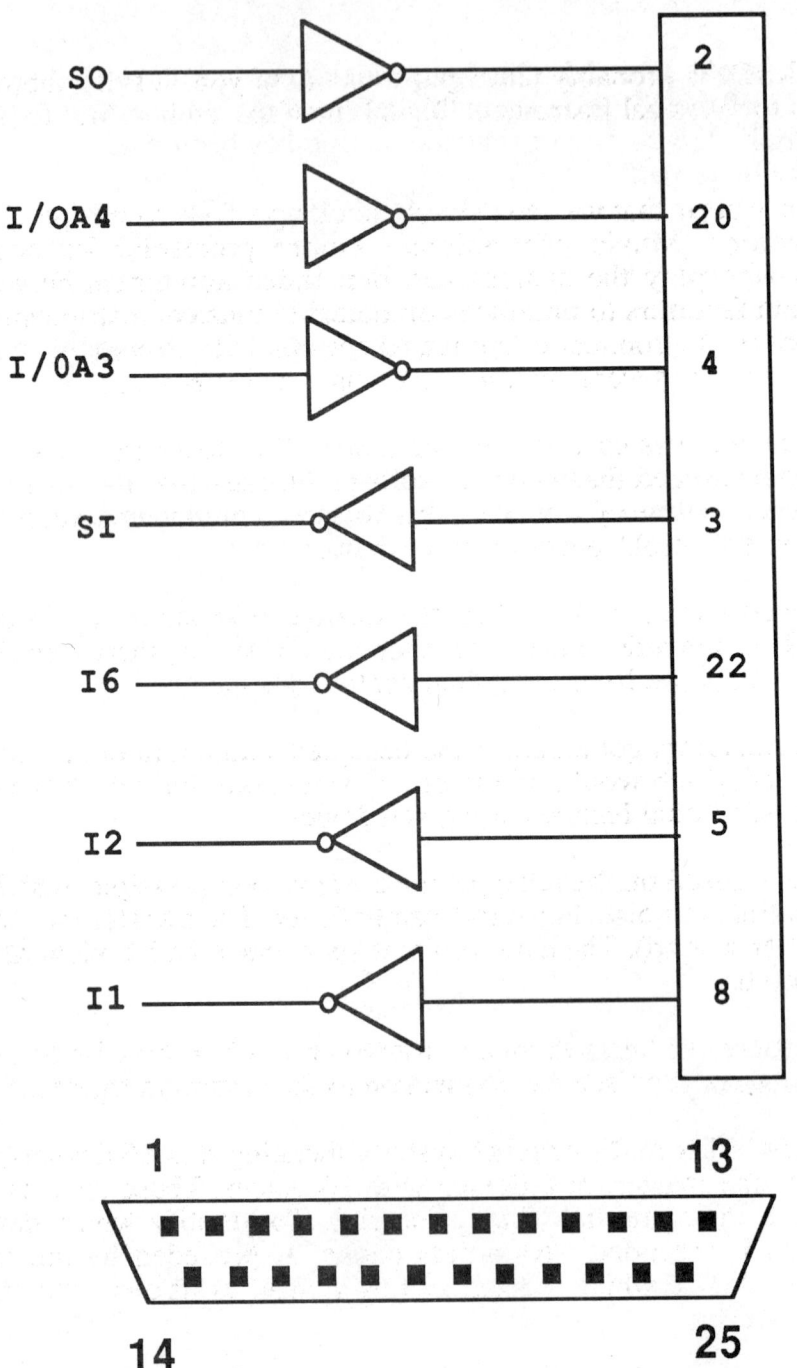

2.5 The MIDI Connections

The term MIDI is probably unknown to many of you. It is an abbreviation and stands for Musical Instrument Digital Interface, an interface for musical instruments.

It is certainly clear that we can't simply hook up a flute to this port. So first a little history. Music professionals (more precisely: keyboardists, musicians who play the synthesizer) demanded agreement between the various manufacturers to interface computers to musical instruments. They found it absurd to connect complicated set-ups with masses of wire. The idea was to service several synthesizers from one keyboard.

The tone created was basically analog (and still is, to a degree), so that the manufacturers agreed that a control voltage difference of 1V corresponded to a difference in tone of 1 octave. This way one could play several devices under "remote control," but not service them.

This changed substantially when the change was made to digital tone creation. Here one didn't have to turn a bunch of knobs, there were buttons to press, whereby the basis for digital control was created.

Some manufacturers got together and designed a digital interface, the basic commands of which would be the same throughout, but which would still support the additional features of a given device.

The device is based on the teletype, the current-loop principle, which is not very susceptible to noise, but significantly faster. The transfer rate is 31250 baud (bits per second). The data format is set at one start bit, eight data bits, and one stop bit.

An IC can therefore be used for control which would otherwise be used for RS-232 purposes. You see the connection to the system in figure 2.5-1.

Logically, MIDI is multi-channel system, meaning that 16 devices can be serviced by one master, or a device with 16 voices. These devices are all connected to the same line (bus principle). To identify which device or which voice is intended, each data packet is preceded by the channel number. The device which recognizes this number as its own then executes the desired action.

You may wonder what such an interface is doing in a computer. A computer can provide an entire arsenal of synthesizers with settings or complete melodies (sequencer) because of its high speed and memory capacity. It can also be used to record and store input from a synthesizer keyboard.

For this purpose the ST has the interfaces MIDI-IN and MIDI-OUT. The interfaces are even supported by the XBIOS so you don't have to worry about their actual operation.

The current loop travels on pins 4 and 5, out through pin 4 (+) of MIDI-OUT and in at 5, when a device is connected.

For MIDI-IN the situation is reversed because the current flows in through pin 4 and back out through pin 5. It goes though something called an optocoupler which electrically isolates the computer from the sender.

The received data are looped back to MIDI-OUT (pins 1 and 3), which implements the MIDI-THRU function, although not entirely according to the standard.

Figure 2.5-1 MIDI System Connection

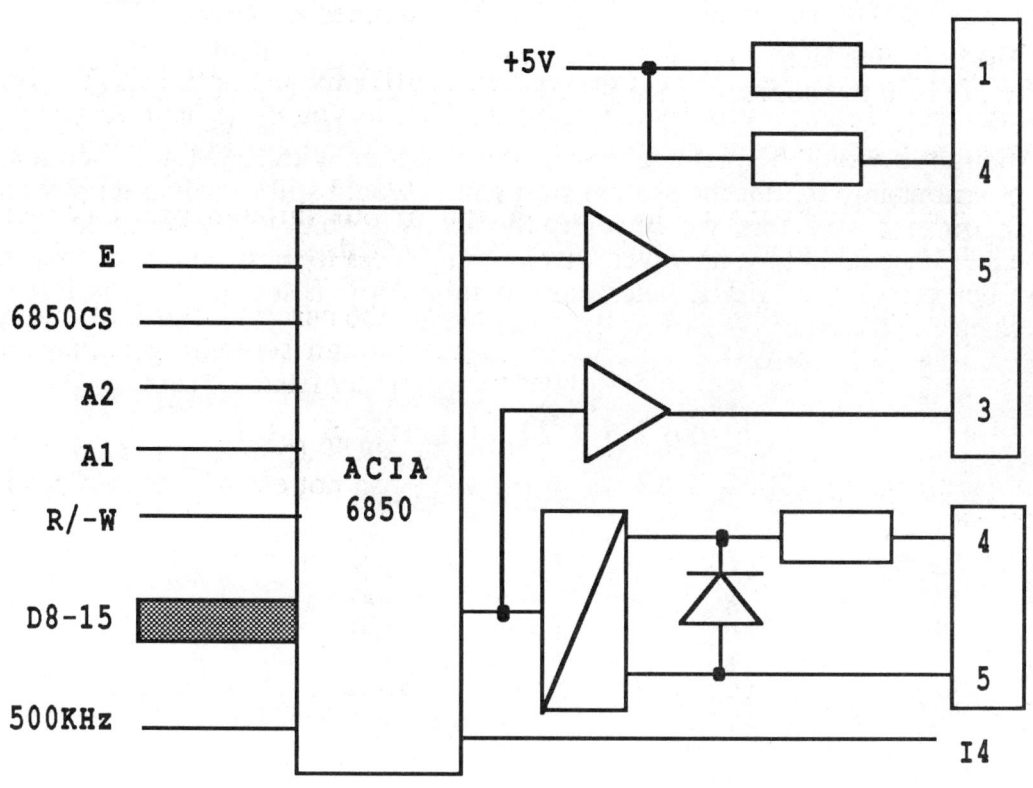

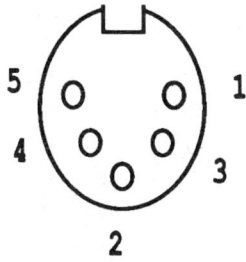

2.6 The Cartridge Slot

The cartridge slot can be used *exclusively* for inserting ROM cartridges. Up to 128K in the address space $FA0000 to $FBFFFF can be addressed. The reason we stressed the exclusivity of the read access is the following. We thought it would be practical to outfit a cartridge with RAM and then load programs into it after the system start which would still remain after a reset. In order to try this we brought the R/-W signal to the outside. The experience taught us, however, that a write access to these addresses creates a bus error. The GLUE takes care of this. As you see, nothing is left to chance in the Atari.

Figure 2.6-1 The Cartridge Slot

```
 1 = +5VDC              21 = Address  8
 2 = +5VDC              22 = Address  14
 3 = Data   14          23 = Address  7
 4 = Data   15          24 = Address  9
 5 = Data   12          25 = Address  6
 6 = Data   13          26 = Address  10
 7 = Data   10          27 = Address  5
 8 = Data   11          28 = Address  12
 9 =   Data  8          29 = Address  11
10 =   Data  9          30 = Address  4
11 =   Data  6          31 = ROM Select  3
12 =   Data  7          32 = Address  3
13 =   Data  4          33 = ROM Select  4
14 =   Data  5          34 = Address  2
15 =   Data  2          35 = Upper Data Strobe
16 =   Data  3          36 = Address  1
17 =   Data  0          37 = Lower Data Strobe
18 =   Data  1          38 = GND
19 = Address 13         39 = GND
20 = Address 15         40 = GND
```

Position:

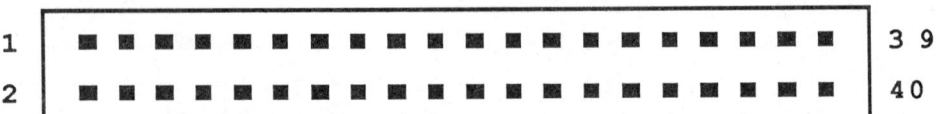

2.6.1 ROM Cartridges

We want to spend this section telling you how a program is put into ROM, as well as how the operating system recognizes and loads such a program.

These cartridges are technically feasible, since many manufacturers are now making ROM cartridge boards and programming devices for the ST computers.

The most important aspect is the first longword in ROM, which must contain an index number, or "magic number". This is read when the system start occurs—it checks to see whether there is a program cartridge or a diagnostic cartridge plugged into the cartridge port. The former must contain the index number $ABCDEF42, the latter the index number $FA52255F.

We wouldn't want to go any farther with the diagnostic cartridge. It should be enough that the operating system jumps to immediately test the address $FA0004 without initializing GEMDOS. You won't get any system processes anyway from this cartridge.

The program cartridges are what interest us. We can call up several programs from a ROM module of this type. Every program must have an introductory section, or application header, to be started by the operating system. The first must begin right after the magic number (from $FA0004), and must be made up of the following:

1 longword:
Address of the next header, when multiple programs reside in one cartridge. The header of the last (or only) program must contain $00000000.

1 longword:
Initialization code. This is where GEMDOS gets information, first about the handling of the program. In particular, this longword is made up of an address which points to the initialization routine (when needed). The most significant byte in this longword states at which point in time this routine should jump.

This is arranged as follows:

BIT
- 0   The routine will be executed before the interrupt vectors, video RAM, etc., is installed.
- 1   The routine will be executed before GEMDOS is initialized.
- 3   The routine will be executed before GEMDOS is loaded. NOTE: This function is not accessible to computers which have GEMDOS in ROM!
- 5   Character which indicates that the program should be handled as an accessory.
- 6   Character which identifies the program as a .TOS type, and not requiring the GEM system.
- 7   Character which identifies the program as a .TTP type, and requiring starting parameters.

1 longword:
Starting address of the program, i.e. where it would start if you double-clicked it.

1 word:
Time in DOS format; has no meaning during runtime.

1 word:
Date in DOS format, see the previous entry.

1 longword:
Program length in bytes; has no meaning during runtime.

String:
Program name in explanatory text. The program name is inserted according to normal conventions, i.e., up to 8 characters, a period (.), and three characters after the period. **NOTE**: The string absolutely must be concluded by $00.

So, that's it. As for the rest: We've neglected to give you any information on clicking. Some program cartridges have their own icons, similar to a disk drive icon. Click this icon. It will show the programs contained in the cartridge; you may then start the desired program.

2.7 The Floppy Disk Interface

The interface for floppy disk drives is conspicuous because of the unusual connector, a 14-pin DIN connector. All of the signals required for the operation of two disk drives are available on it.

You know most of the signals from the description of the disk controller 1772, since nine of the available connections are connected to the controller either directly or through a buffer. Only the drive select 1 and drive select 2 signals and the side 0 select are not derived from the disk controller. These signals come from port A of the sound chip.

Pinout of the disk connector:

```
1 READ DATA           8 MOTOR ON
2 SIDE 0 SELECT       9 DIRECTION IN
3 GND                10 STEP
4 INDEX              11 WRITE DATA
5 DRIVE 0 SELECT     12 WRITE GATE
6 DRIVE 1 SELECT     13 TRACK 00
7 GND                14 WRITE PROTECT
```

Figure 2.7-1 Disk Connection

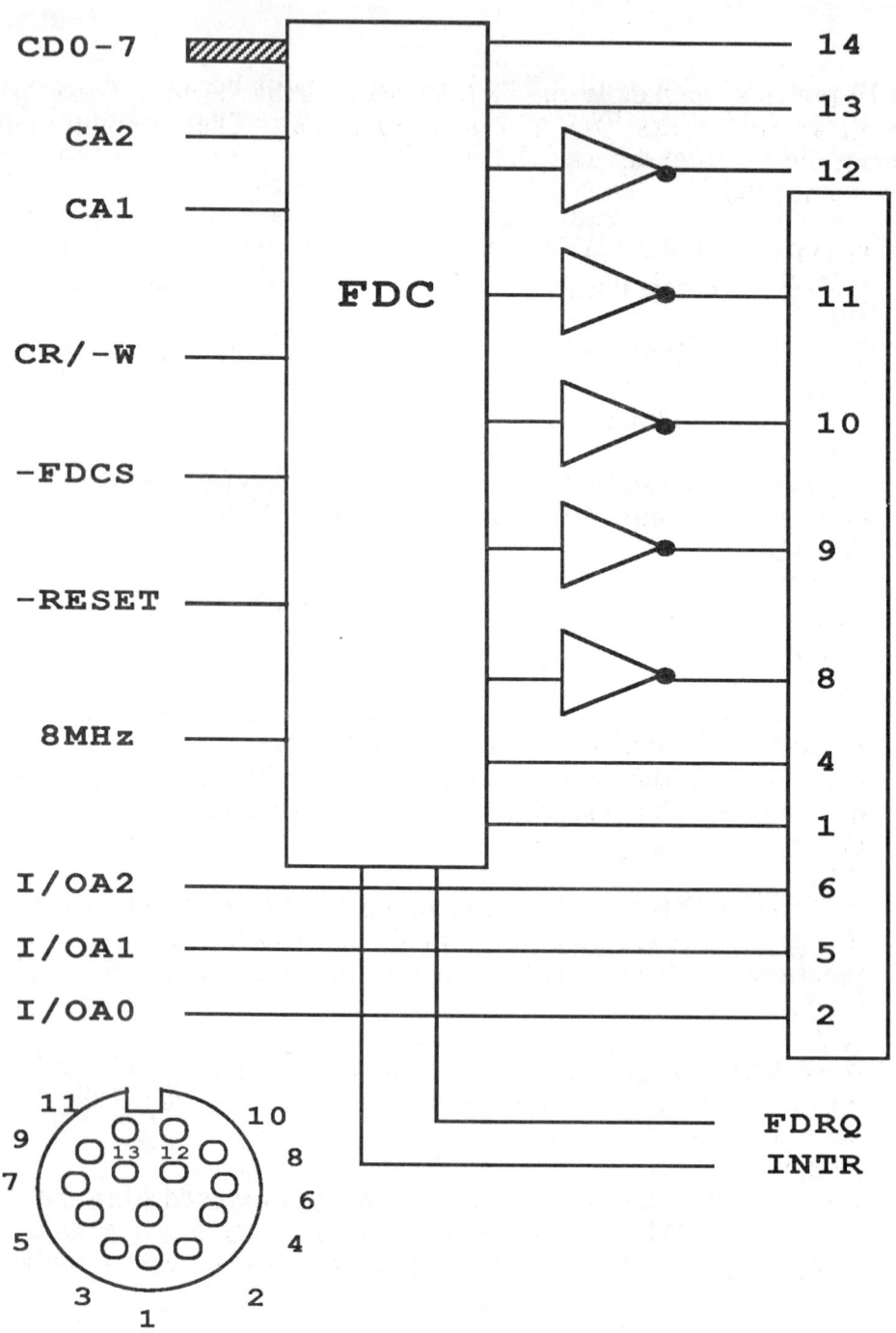

2.8 The DMA Interface

This 19-pin jack can handle up to 8 DMA-compatible devices. These include hard disks, networks, and even coprocessors. The communications between the external devices and the ST run at a speed of up to 1 million bytes per second.

1-8 D0-D7
   Bidirectional data lines
9 CS
   Chip Select, low-active. This line is activeated from the computer when either commands are sent to the device, or status bytes are read from there. If DMA transfer is in process, the signal is in a wait state.
10 IRQ
   Interrupt Request, low=active. This signal is produced by the device, and tells the computer that an action is done (e.g., DMA transfer).
11 GND
12 RST
   Reset, low=active.
13 GND
14 ACK
   Acknowledge, low-active. This signal only has meaning during DMA transfer. This indicates the device to the computer's DMA controller, depending on the data direction, whether a byte is received from the device or whether a legal data byte lies on the bus.
15 GND
16 A1
   Address 1. This signal tells the device's DMA controller whether the device address is set on bus with all commands (A1=low) or whether parameter bytes are handled (usually 5 parameter bytes; A1=high).
17 GND
18 R/W
   Read/Write. This line also controls the controller, and is valid only when initializing. Write(=low): Command bytes snet; Read (=high): Waiting for a status byte.
19 DRQ
   Data Request, low=active. This signal is produced from the device only during DMA transfer, depending upon data direction, when it can receive a byte from the controller; or otherwise, set a byte on the bus.

There are two different methods of transfer. One is a computer controlled data transfer using the A1, CS and R/W lines. The other transfer of data, controlled from the device itself (the DMA transfer), runs without the computer with the help of the DRQ and ACK lines.

A connection can be seen between the chip description of the DMA controller, and the reset routine in the operating system, which checks for all eight possible DMA devices.

Figure 2.8-1 DMA Port

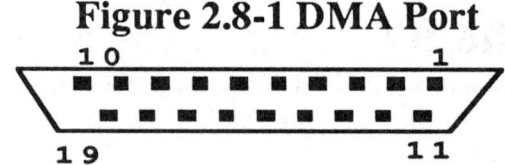

Figure 2.8-2 DMA Connections

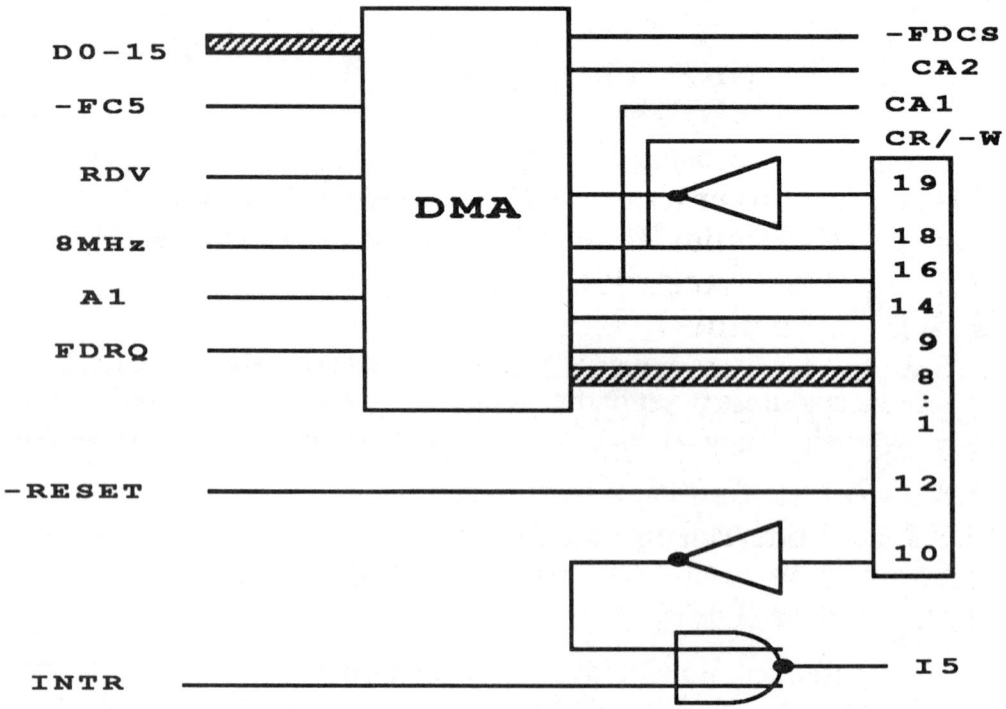

Chapter 3

The ST Operating System

3.1 The GEMDOS
3.1.1 Memory, files and processes
3.2 The BIOS Functions
3.3 The XBIOS
3.4 The Graphics
3.4.1 An overview of the line-A variables
3.4.2 Examples for using the line-A opcodes
3.5 The Exception Vectors
3.5.1 The line-F emulator
3.5.2 The interrupt structure of the ST
3.6 The ST VT52 Emulator
3.7 The ST System Variables
3.8 The 68000 Instruction Set
3.8.1 Addressing modes
3.8.2 The instructions
3.9 The BIOS listing

The ST Operating System

GEMDOS--what is it? Is it in the ST? The operating system is supposed to be TOS, though. Or is it CP/M 68K? Or what?

These questions can be answered with few words. The operating system in the ST is named TOS--Tramiel Operating System--after the head of Atari. This TOS, in contrast to earlier information has nothing to do with CP/M 68K from Digital Research. At the start of development of the ST, CP/M 68K was implemented on it, but this was later changed because CP/M 68K is not exactly a model of speed and efficiency. A 68000 running at 8MHz and provided with DMA would be slowed considerably by the operating system.

At the beginning of 1985, Digital Research began developing a new operating system for 68000 computers, which would include a user-level interface. This operating system was named GEMDOS. It is exactly this GEMDOS which makes up the hardware-independent part of TOS. Like CP/M, TOS consists of a hardware-dependent and a hardware-independent part. The hardware-dependent part is the BIOS and the XBIOS, while the hardware-independent part is called GEMDOS. A large number of functions are built into GEMDOS, through which the programmer can control the actual input/output functions of the computer. Functions for keyboard input, text output on the screen or printer, and the operation of the various other interfaces are all present. Another quite important group contains the functions for file handling and for logical file and disk management.

3.1 The GEMDOS

When you look at the functions available under GEMDOS, you will eventually come to the conclusion that the whole thing is not really new. All the functions in GEMDOS are very similar to the functions of the MS-DOS operating system. Even the functions numbers used correspond to those of MS-DOS. But not all MS-DOS functions are implemented in GEMDOS. Especially in the area of file management, only the UNIX compatible functions are implemented in GEMDOS. The "old" block-oriented functions which are included in MS-DOS to maintain compatibility with CP/M are missing from GEMDOS. Also, special functions relating to the hardware of MS-DOS computers (8088 processor) are missing.

Another essential difference between MS-DOS and GEMDOS is that for GEMDOS calls as well as for the BIOS and XBIOS, the function number, the number of the desired GEMDOS routine, and the required parameters are placed on the stack and are not passed in the registers. The 68000 is particularly suited to this type of parameters passing. GEMDOS is called with `trap #1` and the function is executed according to the contents of the parameter list. After the call, the programmer must put the stack back in order himself, by clearing the parameters from memory.

The basic call of GEMDOS functions differs from the BIOS and XBIOS calls only in the trap number.

In regard to all GEMDOS calls, it must be noted that registers D0 and A0 are changed in all cases. If a value is returned, it is returned in D0, or D0 may contain an error number, and after the call A0 (usually) points to the stack address of the function number. Any parameters required in D0 or A0 must be placed there before GEMDOS is called.

The remainder of this section describes the individual GEMDOS functions.

$00 TERM

`C: void Pterm0()`

Calling GEMDOS with function number 0 ends the running program and returns to the program from which it was started. For applications (programs started from the desktop), control is returned to the desktop. If the program was called from a different program, control is passed back to the calling program. This point is important for chaining program segments.

```
clr.w    -(sp)
trap     #1
```

$01 CONIN

`C: long Cconin()`

CONIN gets a single character from the keyboard. The routine waits until a character is available. The character read from the keyboard is returned in the D0 register. The ASCII code of the pressed key is returned in the low byte of the low word, while the low byte of the high word of the register contains the scan code from the keyboard. This is important for reading keys which have no ASCII code, such as the 10 function keys or the editing keys. These keys return the ASCII value zero when pressed.

The scan code can be used to determine if the keypad or the main keys were pressed. These keys have identical ASCII codes, but different scan codes.

In addition, Shift status can be determined from the upper eight bits (bits 24 to 31) by calling Cconin. In this case, bits 24-31 correspond to bits 0 to 7 in BIOS function 11 ("kbshift"). The information can only be sent on a Cconin call when bit 3 of the memory location "conterm" (address $484) is set. If this bit is unset, then the shift bits after Cconin are deleted.

Cconin does not recognize <Control><C>.

```
move.w  #1,-(sp)     Function number on the stack
trap    #1           Call GEMDOS
addq.l  #2,sp        Correct stack
```

$02 CONOUT

```
C: void Cconout(c)
   int c;
```

CONOUT, also known as Cconout, represents the simplest and most primitive character output of GEMDOS. With this function only one character is printed on the screen. The character to be displayed is placed on the stack as the first word. The ASCII value of the character to be printed must be in the low byte of the word and the high byte should be zero.

The character printed by CONOUT is sent to device number 2, the normal console output. Control characters and escape sequences are interpreted normally.

```
move.w  #65,-(sp)       Output an A
move.w  #2,-(sp)        CONOUT
trap    #1              Call GEMDOS
addq.l  #4,sp           Correct stack
```

$03 AUXILIARY INPUT

```
C: int Cauxin()
```

The RS-232 interface of the ST goes under the designation "auxiliary port". A character can be read from the interface with the Cauxin function. The function returns when a character has been completely received. The character is returned in the lower eight bits of register D0.

```
move.w  #3,-(sp)        Cauxin
trap    #1              Call GEMDOS, output character
addq.l  #2,sp           Correct stack
                        Character in D0
```

$04 AUXILIARY OUTPUT

```
C: void Cauxout(c)
   int c;
```

A character can be transmitted over the serial interface, similar to the input of characters. With this function the programmer should clear the upper eight bits of the word and pass the character to be sent in the lower eight bits.

```
move.w  #$41,-(sp)      An A should be output
move.w  #4,-(sp)        Cauxout
trap    #1              Call GEMDOS, output character
addq.l  #4,sp           Correct stack
```

$05 PRINTER OUTPUT

```
C: void Cprnout(c)
   int c;
```

PRINTER OUTPUT is the simplest method of operating a printer connected to the Centronics interface. One character is printed with each call.

An important part of PRINTER OUTPUT is the return value in D0. If the character was sent to the printer, the value -1 ($FFFFFFFF) is returned in D0. If, after 30 seconds, the printer was unable to accept the character (not turned on, OFF LINE, no paper, etc.), GEMDOS returns a time out to the program. D0 then contains a zero.

```
move.w  #65,-(sp)       Output an A
move.w  #5,-(sp)        Function number
trap    #1              Call GEMDOS, output character
addq.l  #4,sp           Correct stack
tst.w   D0              Affect flags
beq     printererror
```

$06 RAWCONIO

```
C: long Crawio(c)
   int c;
```

RAWCONIO is a somewhat unusual mixture of keyboard input and screen output; it also receives a parameter on the stack.

The keyboard is tested with a function value of $FF. If a character is present, the ASCII code and scan code are passed to D0 as described for CONIN. If no key value is present, the value zero is passed as both the ASCII code and the scan code in D0. The call to RAWCONIO with parameter $FF is comparable to the BASIC INKEY$ function.

If a value other than $FF is passed to the function, the value is interpreted as a character to be printed and it is output at the current cursor position. This output also interprets the control characters and escape sequences properly.

```
START:

        move.w  #$ff,-(sp)      Function value test keyboard
        move.w  #6,-(sp)        Function number
        trap    #1              Call GEMDOS, test keyboard
        addq.l  #4,sp           Correct stack
        tst.w   D0              Character arrived?
        beq     START           Not yet
        cmp.b   #3,D0           ^C selected as the end marker
        beq     END
        move    D0,-(sp)        Character for output on the stack
        move    #6,-(sp)        Function number
        trap    #1              Call GEMDOS, test keyboard
        addq.l  #4,sp           Correct stack
        bra     START           Get new character
```

$07 DIRECT CONIN WITHOUT ECHO

```
C: long Crawcin()
```

The function $07 differs from $01 only in that the character received from the keyboard is not displayed on the screen. It waits for a key just as does CONIN.

```
move.w  #8,-(sp)        Cauxin
trap    #1              Call GEMDOS, output character
addq.l  #2,sp           Adjust stack
.                       Character in D0
```

$08 CONIN WITHOUT ECHO

C: long Cnecin()

Both function $08 and function $07 have exactly the same effect. The reason for this seemingly nonsensical behavior lies in the abovementioned compatibility to MS-DOS. Under MS-DOS these two functions are different in that with $08, certain keys not present on the ATARI are evaluated correctly, while this evaluation does not take place with function $07.

```
move.w  #8,-(sp)        Cauxin
trap    #1              Call GEMDOS, output character
addq.l  #2,sp           Adjust stack
.                       Character in D0
```

$09 PRINT LINE

C: void Cconws(c)
   int c;

You are already familiar with functions that output individual characters on the screen (see CONOUT and RAWCONIO). PRINT LINE offers you an easy way to output text. An entire string can be printed at the current cursor position with this function. To do this, the address of the string is placed on the stack as a parameter. The string itself is concluded with a zero byte. Escape sequences and control characters can also be displayed with this function.

After the call, D0 contains the number of characters which were printed. The length of the string is not limited.

```
move.l   #text,-(sp)     Address of the string on the stack
move     #$09,-(sp)      Function number PRT LINE
trap     #1              Call GEMDOS
addq.l   #6,sp           Clear the stack
.
.
text     .dc.b 'This is the string to be printed',$0D,$0A,0
```

$0A READLINE

```
C; void Cconrs(buf)
   char *buf;
```

READLINE is a very easy-to-use function for reading characters from the keyboard. In contrast to the "simpler" character-oriented input functions, an entire input line can be taken from the keyboard with READLINE. The characters entered are displayed on the screen at the same time.

The address of an input buffer is passed to the function as the parameter. The value of the first byte of the input buffer determines the maximum length of the input line and must be initialized before the call. At the end of the routine, the second byte of the buffer contains the number of characters entered. The characters themselves start with the third byte.

The routine used by READLINE for keyboard input is quite different from the character-oriented console inputs. Escape sequences are not interpreted during the output. Only control characters like <Control><H> (backspace) and <Control><I> (TAB) are recognized and handled appropriately. The following control characters are possible:

```
^C   Ends input and program (!)
^H   Backspace one position
^I   TAB
^J   Linefeed, end input
^M   CR, end input
^R   Entered line is printed in new line
^U   Don't count line, start new line
^X   Clear line, cursor at start of line
```

A function like ^H (deleting a character entered) is useful, but for large programs you should write your own input routine because ^C is very "dangerous." Unlike CP/M, the program will be ended even if the cursor is not at the very start of the input line.

If more characters are entered than were indicated in the first byte of the buffer at the initialization, the input is automatically terminated. If the input is terminated by ENTER, ^J, or ^M, the terminating character will not be put in the buffer.

After the input, D0 contains the number of characters entered, excluding ENTER, which can be found at buffer+1.

```
pea     buffer          Address of the input buffer
move    #$0A,-(sp)      Function number
trap    #1
addq.l  #6,(sp)         Make room on stack
.
.
buffer dc.b 20          We want a maximum of 20 characters
       dc.b 0           Number of given characters
       ds.b 20          of the input buffer
```

$0B CONSTAT

`C: int CConis()`

All key presses are first stored in a buffer in the operating system. This buffer is 64 bytes in length. The key values stored there are taken from the buffer when a call to a GEMDOS output routine is made.

CONSTAT can be used to check if characters are stored in the keyboard buffer. After the call, D0 contains the value zero or $FFFF. A zero in D0 indicates that no characters are available.

```
testloop:
move    #$0B,-(sp)      Function number
trap    #1
addq.l  #2,(sp)         Make room on stack
tst.w   D0              Character available?
beq     testloop        NO, then look again
```

$0E SETDRV

```
C: long Dsetdrv(drv)
   int drv;
```

The current drive can be set with the function SETDRV. A 16-bit parameter containing the drive specification is passed to the routine. Drive A is addressed with the number 0 and drive B with the number 1.

After the call, D0 contains the number of the drive active before the call.

```
move    #$2,-(sp)       Drive C, e.g. RAMdisk
move    #$0E,-(sp)      Function number
trap    #1
addq.l  #4,(sp)         Make room on stack
.                       Previous current drive in D0
```

$10 CONOUT STAT

```
C: int Cconos()
```

CONOUT STAT returns the console status in D0. If the value $FFFF is returned, a character can be displayed on the screen. If the returned value is zero, no character output is possible on the screen at that time. Incidentally, all attempts failed at creating a not-ready status at the console. The only imaginable possibility for the not-ready status would be if the output of the individual bit pattern of a character was interrupted and the interrupt routine itself tried to output a character. This case could not, however, be created.

```
move    #$10,-(sp)      Function number
trap    #1
addq.l  #2,(sp)         Make room on stack
.                       Always $FFFF in D0
```

$11 PRTOUT STAT

C: int Cprnos()

This function returns the status, the condition of the Centronics interface. If no printer is connected (or turned off, or off line), D0 contains the value zero after the call to indicate "printer not available." If, however, the printer is ready to receive, D0 contains the value $FFFF.

```
move     #$11,-(sp)      How's the printer doing?
trap     #1
addq.l   #2,(sp)         Make room on the stack
tst      d0
beq      printererror    Go here if not ready
```

$12 AUXIN STAT

C: int Cauxis(c)

AUXIN STAT shows whether a character is available from the serial interface receiver ($FFFF) or not ($0000). The value is returned in D0.

```
waitloop:
move     #$12,-(sp)      We wait for a character
trap     #1              from the serial interface
addq.l   #2,(sp)         Make room on the stack
tst      d0              Is there a character there?
bne      waitloop        No, not yet
```

$13 AUXOUT STAT

C: int Cauxos()

AUXOUT STAT gives information about the state of the serial bus. A value of $FFFF indicates that the serial interface can send a character, while zero indicates that no characters can be sent at this time.

```
waitloop:
move    #$13,-(sp)      Wait for a character
trap    #1              from the serial interface
addq.l  #2,(sp)         Make room on the stack
tst     d0              Received one yet?
bne     waitloop        No, not yet
```

$19 CURRENT DISK

C: int Dgetdrv()

For many applications it is necessary to know which drive is currently active. The current drive can be determined by the function $19. After the call, D0 contains the number of the drive. The significance of the drive numbers is the same as for $0E, SET DRIVE (0=A, 1=B).

```
move    #$19,-(sp)      Which drive is active?
trap    #1              It will be sent over
                        the serial interface
addq.l  #2,(sp)         Make room on the stack
ADD     D0,'A'          There will now be a character in
                        D0 between 'A' and 'P'
```

$1A SET DISK TRANSFER ADDRESS

C: void Fsetdta(buf)
   char *buf;

The disk transfer address is the address of a 44-byte buffer required for various disk operations (especially directory operations). Along with the GEMDOS functions SEARCH FIRST and SEARCH NEXT are examples for using the DTA.

```
move.l  #DTADDRESS,-(sp)  Address of the 44-byte DTA buffer
move.w  #$1a,-(sp)        Function number SET DTA
trap    #1                Set DTA
addq.l  #6,sp             Clean up the stack
```

$20 SUPER

This function is especially interesting for programmers who want to access the peripherals or system variables available only in the supervisor mode while running a program in the user mode. After calling this function from user mode, the 68000 is placed in the supervisor mode. In contrast to the XBIOS routine for enabling the supervisor mode, additional GEMDOS, BIOS, and XBIOS calls can be made after a successful SUPER call.

Calling the SUPER function with a value of -1L ($FFFFFFFF) tells us the processor's current operating mode. If the result in D0 after the call is 0, the processor is in user mode. A value of $0001 signifies that the processor is in supervisor mode. Switching modes is not carried out yet.

A program in user mode can call the SUPER function with a zero on the stack. In this case, the supervisor mode will be turned on. The supervisor stack pointer points to the current value of the user stack, and the original value of the supervisor stack is in D0. This value must be stored in the program to later return to the user mode. If the change to user mode is not made before the end of the program, the odds of a system crash are good.

If a value other than zero is passed to the SUPER function the first time it is called, this value is interpreted as the desired value of the supervisor stack pointer. In this case as well, D0 contains the original value of the supervisor stack pointer, which the program should save.

As mentioned above, the user mode should be reenabled before the end of the program. This change of modes requires setting the address used by the supervisor stack pointer back to its original value.

The SUPER function differs from all other GEMDOS functions in one very important respect. Under certain circumstances, this call can also change the contents of A1 and D1. If you store important values in these registers, you must save the values somewhere before calling the SUPER function.

```
                        The 68000 is in the user mode
clr.l    -(sp)          User stack becomes supervisor stack
move.w   #$20,-(sp)     Call SUPER
trap     #1             Supervisor mode is active after TRAP
add.l    #6,sp          D0 = old supervisor stack
move.l   d0,_SAVE_SSP   Save value
.
.        Here processing can be done in the supervisor mode
```

```
move.l  _SAVE_SSP,-(sp)    Old supervisor stack pointer
move.w  #$20,-(sp)         Call SUPER
trap    #1                 Now we are back in the user mode
add.l   #6,sp
```

$2A GET DATE

C: int Tgetdate()

You have no doubt experimented with the status field at one time or another. Among other functions, the status field contains a clock with time and date. It can be useful for some applications to have that data available. The date can be easily determined by GET DATE. This call requires no parameters and puts the date in the low word of register D0. It is thoroughly encoded, though, so the result in D0 must be prepared to get the correct date.

The day in the range 1 to 31 is coded in the lower five bits. Bits 5 to 8 contain the month in the range 1 to 12, and the year is contained in bits 9 to 15. The range of these "year bits" goes from 0 to 119. The value of these bits must be added to the value 1980 to get the actual year. The date 12/12/1992, for example, would be %0001100.1100.01100 in binary, or $198C in D0. The lengths of the three fields are marked with periods.

```
move    #$2a,-(sp)         We want to get some data
trap    #1
addq.l  #2,(sp)
move    d0,d1              Store result in D1 for now
and     #%11111,D0         Mask the day bits and
move    d0,DAY             store them
LSR     #5,d1              Shift the 5 day bits
move    d1,d0
and     #%1111,d0          and mask the month bits
move    D0,MONTH           Store the month number
LSR     #4,d1              Shift the month bits
move    d1,YEAR            Year is in D1
.
DAY     ds.w    1
MONTH   ds.w    1
YEAR    ds.w    1
```

$2B SET DATE

```
C: int Tsetdate(date)
   int date;
```

The clock time and date can also be set from application programs. This is particularly interesting for programs which use the date and/or clock time. An example of this would be invoice processing in which the current date is inserted in the invoice. Such programs can then ask the user to enter the date. This avoids the problems that occur if the user forgets to set the date and clock time on the status field beforehand.

The date must be passed to the function SET DATE in the same format as it is received from GET DATE, bits 0-4 = day, bits 5-8 = month, bits 9-15 = year-1980.

```
move.w  #%101101011001,-(sp)    Set date to 10/25/1985
move.w  #$2b,-(sp)              Function number of SET DATE
trap    #1                      Set date
addq.l  #4,sp                   Repair stack
```

$2C GET TIME

```
C: int Tgettime()
```

The function GET TIME returns the current (read: set) time from the GEMDOS clock. Similar to the date, the clock time is coded in a special pattern in individual bits of the register D0 after the call. The seconds are represented in bits 0-4. But since only values from 0 to 31 can be represented in 5 bits, the internal clock runs in two second increments. In order to get the correct seconds-result the contents of these five bits must be multiplied by two. The number of minutes is contained in bits 5 to 10, while the remaining bits 11-15 give information about the hour in 24-hour format.

```
waitloop:

move     #$2c,-(sp)     Is it noon yet?
trap     #1             Get the time from GEMDOS
addq.l   #2,sp
move     d0,d1          Store result in D1
```

```
and      #$1111,D0       Store seconds in steps
move     D0,SEC          of two
LSR      #4,D1           Shift 4 second bits
bne      waitloop        No, not yet
```

$2D SET TIME

```
C:  int Tsettime(time)
    int time;
```

It is also possible to set the clock time under GEMDOS. The function SET TIME expects a 16-bit value (word) on the stack, in which the time is coded in the same form as that in which GET TIME returns the clock time.

When GEMDOS has the given time, D0 returns the value 0; otherwise the value returned is $FFFFFFFF. GEMDOS handles time much as it does the date. Time changes through GEMDOS cannot be conveyed through the XBIOS. Select either XBIOS or GEMDOS. If you cross the two, you will end up with some very unpleasant complications.

```
move.w   #%1000101010111101,-(sp)   Clock time 17:21:58
move.w   #$2D,-(sp)                 Function # of GET TIME
trap     #1                         Set date
addq.l   #4,sp                      Repair stack
```

$2F GET DTA

```
C:  long Fgetdta()
```

The function $2F is the counterpart of SET DTA ($1A). A call to GET DTA returns the current disk transfer buffer address in D0. A description of this buffer is found with the functions SEARCH FIRST and SEARCH NEXT.

```
move     #$2f,-(sp)          Function number Fgetdta
trap     #1                  Get DTA
addq.l   #2,sp
move.l   d0,DTAPOINTER       and mark for later
.
```

$30 GET VERSION NUMBER

```
C: int Sversion()
```

Calling this function returns in D0 the version number of GEMDOS. In the version of GEMDOS currently in release, this question is always answered with $0D00, corresponding to version 13.00. Official Atari documentation claims that a value of $0100 should be returned for this version, though perhaps the value should indicate that the present GEMDOS version is the $D = diskette version.

```
move     #30,-(sp)       Look to see which
trap     #1              version we have
addq.l   #2,sp
cmp      #$1300,d0       The recognized version?
bne      not_tos         It can't be given
.
```

$31 KEEP PROCESS

```
C: void Ptermres(keepcnt,retcode)
   long keepcnt;
   int retcode;
```

This function is comparable to the GEMDOS function TERM $00. The program is also ended after a call to this function. $31 does differ from $00 in several important points.

After processing TRAP #1, like TERM, control is passed back to the program which started the program just ended. In contrast to TERM, a termination condition can be communicated to the caller. While TERM returns the termination value zero (no error), zero or one may be selected as the termination value for $31. A value other than zero means that an error occurred during program processing.

Another essential point lies in the memory management of GEMDOS. When a program is started, the entire available memory space is made available to it. If the program is ended with TERM, the memory space is released and made available to GEMDOS. The entire area of memory released is also cleared, filled with zeros. The program actually physically disappears from the memory. With function $31, however, an area of memory can be protected at the start address of the program. This memory area is not released when the program is ended and it is also not cleared. The program could be restarted without having to load it in again.

Practical applications for Ptermres() are spoolers, RAM disks and other utilities which are installed once and remain in memory for storage or processing. At the same time, such programs must be ended correctly after installation to allow other programs to be loaded and started.

KEEP PROCESS is called with two parameters. The example program shows the parameter passing. It is also important that memory additionally reserved for programs be Malloc not be freed up. If files are opened by Ptermres() at that time, these will be closed by GEMDOS.

```
move.w  #0,-(sp)         Error code no error, else 1
move.l  #$1000,-(sp)     Protect $1000 bytes at program start
move.w  #$31,-(sp)       Function number, end program
trap    #1                   ....now.
.                        This time, don't clear the stack!
```

$36 GET DISK FREE SPACE

```
C:  void Dfree(buffer,drive)
    long *buffer
    int drive
```

It can be very important for disk-oriented programs to determine the amount of free space on the diskette, then warn the user to change disks. "Disk full" messages or even data loss can then be avoided.

Function $36, Dfree(), returns this information. The number of the desired disk drive and the address of a 16-byte buffer must be passed to the function. If the value 0 is passed as the drive number, the information is fetched from the active drive, a 1 takes the information from drive A, and a 2 from drive B.

The information passed in the buffer is divided into four longwords. The first longword contains the number of free allocation units. Each file, even if it is only eight bytes long, requires at least one such allocation unit.

The second longword gives information about the number of allocation units present on the disk, regardless of whether they are already used or are still free. For the "small" single-sided diskettes this value is $15C or 351, while the double-sided disks have $2C7 = 711 allocation units.

The third longword contains the size of a disk sector in bytes. For the Atari this is always 512 bytes ($200 bytes).

The last longword is the number of physical sectors belonging to an allocation unit. This is normally 2. Two sectors form one allocation unit.

The amount of free disk space can be easily calculated from this data.

```
move.w  #0,-(sp)        Information from the active drive
pea     BUFFER          Address of the 16-byte buffer
move    #$36,-(sp)      Function number
trap    #1
addq.l  #6,sp           Clean up stack
.
.
.
BUFFER:
freal:  .ds.l   1       Free allocation units
total:  .ds.l   1       Total allocation units
bps:    .ds.l   1       Bytes/physical sector
pspal:  .ds.l   1       Phys. sectors/alloc. unit
```

$39 MKDIR

```
C:  int Dcreate(path)
    char *path;
```

A subdirectory can be created from the desktop with the menu option "NEW FOLDER". Such a subdirectory can also be created from an application program with a call to $39.

In order to create a new folder, the function $39 is given the address of the folder name, also called the pathname. This name may consist of 8 characters and a three-character extension. The same limitations apply to pathnames as do to filenames. The pathname must be terminated with a zero byte when calling MKDIR.

After the call, D0 indicates whether the operation was performed successfully. If D0 contains a zero, the call was successful. Errors are indicated through a negative number in D0. At the end of this chapter you will find an overview of all of the error messages occurring in connection with GEMDOS functions.

```
move.l  pathname            Address of the pathname
move    #$39,-(sp)          Function number
trap    #1
addq.l  #6,sp               Repair stack
tst.w   d0                  Error occurred?
bne     error               Apparently
.
pathname:
        .dc.b   'private.dat',0
```

$3A RMDIR

```
C: int  Ddelete(path)
   char *path;
```

A subdirectory created with MKDIR can be removed with $3A. As before, the pathname, terminated with a zero, is passed to RMDIR. The error messages also correspond to those for MKDIR, with zero for success or a negative value for errors. An important error message should be mentioned at this point. It is the message -36 ($FFFFFFCA). This is the error message you get when the subdirectory you are trying to remove contains files.

Only empty subdirectories can be removed with RMDIR. If you get an error, erase directory files with UNLINK ($41), then call RMDIR again.

```
pea     pathname            Address of the pathname
move.w  #$3A,-(sp)          Function #
trap    #1
addq.l  #6,sp               Repair stack
tst.w   D0                  Is there an error?
bne     era_sub_dir         It appears that way
.
pathname:
    .dc.b   'tmpfiles.a_z',0
```

$3B CHDIR

```
C: int Dsetpath(path)
   char *path;
```

The system of subdirectories available under GEMDOS is exactly the same form available under UNIX. This system is now running on systems with diskette drives, but its advantages become noticeable first when a large mass storage device such as a hard disk with several megabytes of storage capacity is connected to the system. After a while, most of the time would probably be spent looking for files in the directory.

To better organize the data, subdirectories can be placed within subdirectories. It can therefore become necessary to specify several subdirectories until one has the directory in which the desired file is stored. An example might be:

       \hugos.dat\cfiles.s\csorts.s\cqsort.s

Translated this would mean: load the file `cqsort.s` from the subdirectory `csorts.s`. This subdirectory `csorts.s` is found in the subdirectory `cfiles.s`, which in turn is a subdirectory of `hugos.dat`. If the whole expression is given as a filename, the desired file will actually be loaded (assuming that the file and all of the subdirectories are present). If you want to access another file via the same path (do you understand the term pathname?), the entire path must be entered again. But you can also make the subdirectory specified in the path into the current directory, by calling CHDIR with the specification of the desired path. After this, all of the files in the selected subdirectory can be accessed just by the filenames. The path is set by the function.

```
move.l  path,-(sp)      Address of the path
move.w  #$3b,-(sp)      Function number
trap    #1
addq.l  #6,sp           Repair stack
tst.w   d0              Error occurred?
bne     error           Apparently
.
.
path:
        .dc.b   ' \hugos.dat\cfiles.s\csorts.s\cqsort.s',0
```

$3C CREATE

```
C:  int   Fcreate(fname,attr)
    char  *fname;
    int   attr;
```

In all operating systems, the files are accessed through the sequence of opening the file, accessing the data (reading or writing), and then closing the file. This "trinity" also exists under GEMDOS, although there is an exception. Under CP/M, for example, a non-existent file can also be opened. When a file which does not exist is opened, it is created. Under GEMDOS, the file must first be created. The call $3C, CREATE, is used for this purpose. Two parameters are passed to this GEMDOS function: the address of the desired filename, and an attribute word.

If a zero is passed as the attribute word, a normal file is created, a file which can be written to as well as read from. If the value 1 is passed as the attribute the file will only be able to be read after it is closed. This is a type of software write-protect (which naturally cannot prevent the file from disappearing if the disk is formatted).

Other possible attributes are $02, $04, and $08. Attribute $02 creates a "hidden" file and attribute $04 a "hidden" system file. Attribute $08 creates a file with a "volume label." The volume label is the (optional) name which a disk can be given when it is formatted. The disk name is then created from the maximum of 11 characters in the name and the extension. Files with one of the last three attributes are excluded from the normal directory search in the Desktop. On the ST, however, they appear in the directory, e.g. as COMMAND.PRG.

When the function CREATE is ended, a file descriptor, also called a file handle, is returned in D0. All additional accesses to the file take place over this file handle (a numerical value between 6 and 45). The handle must be given when reading, writing, or closing files. A total of $28 = 40 files can be opened at the same time.

If CREATE is called and a file with this name already exists, it is cut off at zero length. This is equivalent to the sequence delete the old file and create a new file with the same name, but it goes much faster.

If after calling CREATE you get a handle number back in D0, the file need not be opened again with $3D OPEN.

```
move.w  #$0,-(sp)       File should have R/W status
pea     filename        Address of the filename on stack
move.w  #$3c,-(sp)      Fcreate function number
trap    #1              Call GEMDOS
addq.l  #8,sp           Clean up stack
tst     d0              Error occurred?
bmi     error           It appears so
move    d0,handle       Save file handle for later access
.
filename:               Don't forget the zero byte
        .dc.b   'myfile.dat',0
.
handle:
        .ds.w   1
```

$3D OPEN

```
C:  int Fopen(fname,mode)
    char *fname;
    int mode;
```

You can only create new files with CREATE, or shorten existing files to zero length. But you must be able to process existing files further as well. To do this, such files must be opened with the OPEN function.

The first parameter of the OPEN function is the mode word. With a zero in the mode word, the opened file can only be read, with one it can only be written. With a value of 2, the file can be read as well as written. The filename, ended with a zero byte, is passed as the second parameter.

The OPEN function returns the handle number in D0 as the result if the file is present and the desired access mode is possible. Otherwise D0 contains an error number. See the end of the chapter for a list of the error numbers.

Up until now, when we've discussed file functions, we have referred only to files. This is only half the story; devices can be opened and closed as well as files. These devices are the console (keyboard) and monitor, the serial port and the printer connection. See Chapter 3.1.1 for more information on GEMDOS and the file/device concept. We want to show you for now how a device is opened, and what handle to give it. This information is important insofar as device handles are different from file handles.

To open a device, the device name is given as a filename. The device names are: "CON:" for the console, "AUX:" for the serial interface and "PRN:" for the printer interface. After opening with the appropriate name, you'll get a word-negative handle. $FFFF(-1) is returned for CON:, $FFFE(-2) is returned for AUX: and $FFFD(-3) is the handle for the printer port.

```
move.w  #$2,-(sp)       File read and write
pea     filename        Address of the filename on the stack
move.w  #$3d,-(sp)      Function number
trap    #1              Call GEMDOS
addq.l  #8,sp           Clean up the stack
tst.l   d0              Error occurred?
bmi     error           Apparently
move    d0,fhandle      Save file handle for later accesses
.
filename:               Don't forget zero byte!
        .dc.b    'myfile.dat',0
handle:
        .ds.w    1
```

$3E CLOSE

```
C:  int   Fclose(handle)
    int   handle;
```

Every opened file should be closed when it is no longer needed within a program, or when the program itself is ended. Especially when writing, files must absolutely be closed before the program ends or data may be lost.

Files are closed by the call CLOSE, to which the handle number is passed as a parameter. The return value will be zero if the file was closed correctly.

```
move.w  handle,-(sp)    Handle number
move.w  #$3e,-(sp)      Function number
trap    #1              Call GEMDOS
addq.l  #4,sp           Error occurred?
bmi     error           Apparently
.
handle:
        .ds.w    1
```

$3F READ

```
C: long Fread(handle, count, buff)
   int  handle;
   long count;
   char *buff;
```

Opening and closing files is naturally only half of the matter. Data must be stored and the retrieved later. Reading such files can be done in a very elegant manner with the function READ. READ expects three parameters: first the address of a buffer in which the data is to be read, then the number of bytes to be read from the file, and finally the handle number of the file. This number you have (hopefully) saved from the previous OPEN.

As return value, D0 contains either an error number (hopefully not) or the number of bytes read without error. No message regarding the end of the file is returned. This is not necessary, however, since the size of the file is contained in the directory entry (see SEARCH FIRST/SEARCH NEXT). If the file is read past the logical end, no message is given. The reading will be interrupted at the end of the last occupied allocation unit of the file. The number of bytes read in this case is always divisible by $400.

```
pea      buffer            Address of the data buffer
move.l   #$100,-(sp)       Read 256 bytes
move.w   handle,-(sp)      Space for the handle number
move.w   #$3f,-(sp)        Function number
trap     #1
add.l    #12,sp
tst.l    d0                Did an error occur
bmi      error             Apparently
cmp.l    #$100,d0          256 bytes read?
bne      end_of_file       Not enough data in file
.
.
handle:
         .ds.w  1          Space for the handle number
.
buffer:
         .ds.b  $100       Suffices in our example
```

$40 WRITE

```
C: long Fwrite(handle, count, buff)
   int   handle;
   long  count;
   char  *buff;
```

Writing to a file is just as simple as reading from it. The parameters required are also the same as those required for reading. The file descriptors from OPEN and CREATE calls can be used as the handle, but the device numbers listed for READ can also be used. The output of a program can be sent to the screen, the printer, or in a file just by changing the handle number.

```
pea     buffer              Address of the data buffer
move.l  #$100,-(sp)         Read 256 bytes
move.w  handle,-(sp)        Space for the handle number
move.w  #$40,-(sp)          WRITE request
trap    #1
add.l   #12,sp
tst.l   d0                  Did an error occur?
bmi     error               Apparently
 .
 .
handle:
        .ds.w   1           Space for the handle number
 .
buffer:
        .ds.b   $100        Suffices in our example
```

$41 UNLINK

```
C: int  Fdelete(fname)
   char *fname;
```

Files which are no longer needed can be deleted with UNLINK. To do this, the address of the filename or, if necessary, the complete pathname must be passed to the function. If the D0 register contains a zero after the call, the file has been deleted. Otherwise D0 will contain an error number.

```
pea      fname              Name of the file to be scratched
move.w   #$41,-(sp)         Function number Fdelete()
trap     #1
add.l    #6,sp
tst.l    d0                 Did an error occur?
bmi      error              Apparently
.
.
fname:
         .dc.b    'b:\hugos.dat\cfiles\csorts\cqsort.s',0
```

$42 LSEEK

```
C: long Fseek(offset, handle, seekmode)
   long offset;
   int  handle;
   int  seekmode;
```

Up to now we have become acquainted only with sequential data accesses. We can read through any file from the beginning until we come the desired information. An internal file pointer which points to the next byte to be read goes along with each read. We can only move this pointer continuously in the direction of the end of file by reading. A few bytes forward or backward, setting the pointer as desired, is not something we can do. This is required for many applications, however.

LSEEK offers an extraordinarily easy-to-use method of setting the file pointer to any desired byte within the file and to read or write at this point. This UNIX-compatible option of GEMDOS is much easier to use than the relative file management methods available under CP/M, for instance.

A total of three parameters are passed to the LSEEK function. The first parameter specifies the number of bytes by which the pointer should be moved. An additional parameter is the handle number of the file. The last parameter is a mode word which describes how the file is to be moved. A zero as the mode moves the pointer to the start of the file and from there the given number of bytes toward the end of the file. Only positive values may be used as the number. With a mode value of 1, the pointer is moved the desired positive or negative amount from the current position, and a 2 as the mode value means the distance specified is from the end of the file. Only negative values are allowed in this mode.

After the call, D0 contains the absolute position of the pointer from the start of the file, or an error message.

```
move.w  #1,-(sp)         Relative from the current file ptr
move.w  handle,-(sp)     File handle
move.l  #$-20,-(sp)      32 bytes back
move.w  #$42,-(sp)       Function number
trap    #1
add.l   #10,sp
tst.w   d0               Did an error occur?
bmi     error            Apparently
.
.
handle:
        .ds.w   1        Space for the handle number
```

$43 CHANGE MODE (CHMOD)

```
C:  int   Fattrib(fname, flag, attrib)
    char  *fname;
    int   flag;
    int   attrib;
```

With the CREATE function a file can be assigned a specific attribute. This attribute can be determined and subsequently changed only with the function CHANGE MODE. The name of the file must be known because the address of the name or the complete pathname must be passed to CHMOD. Another parameter word specifies whether the file attribute is to be read or set. Moreover, a word must be passed which contains the new attribute. When reading the attribute of a file this word is not necessary, but should be passed to the routine as a dummy value. We indicated the possible file attributes in our discussion of the function CREATE, but here they are again in a table:

```
$00 = normal file status, read/write possible
$01 = File is READ ONLY
$02 = "hidden" file
$04 = system file
$08 = file is a volume label, contains disk name
$10 = file is a subdirectory
$20 = file is written and closed correctly
```

Attributes $10 and $20 cannot be specified when the file is created. Attribute $20 is given by the operating system, while the GEMDOS function MKDIR is used to create a subdirectory. The MKDIR function not only creates the directory entry with the appropriate attribute, it also physically arranges the subdirectory on the disk.

After the call, D0 will contain the current attribute value, which will be the new value after setting the attribute, or a negative error number.

First example:

```
move.w  #1,-(sp)        Give file READ ONLY attribute
move.w  #1,-(sp)        Set attribute identifier
pea     pathname        We also need the pathname
move.w  #$43,-(sp)      Function number
trap    #1
add.l   #10,sp
tst.w   d0              Did an error occur?
bmi     error           Apparently
.
pathname:               Don't forget zero byte at end!
        .dc.b   'killme.not',0
```

Second example:

```
move.w  #0,-(sp)        Dummy value, not actually required
move.w  #0,-(sp)        Read attribute
pea     pathname        and the pathname
move.w  #$43,-(sp)      Function number
trap    #1
add.l   #10,sp
tst.w   d0              Did an error occur?
bmi     error           Apparently
.
.
.
pathname:               Don't forget zero byte at the end!
        .dc.b   'what-am.i',0
```

$45 DUP

```
C: int  Fdup(handle)
   int  handle;
```

As mentioned in connection with the functions READ and WRITE, the devices console, line printer and RS-232 are available to the programmer. This permits input and output to be redirected to these devices. One of the devices can be assigned a file handle number with the DUP function. After the call the next free handle number is returned.

```
move.w  STDH,-(sp)    Parameter is standard handle number (0-5)
move.w  #$45,-(sp)    Execute DUP
trap    #1
addq.l  #4,sp
tst.l   d0            -35,-37 or 0 are possible
bmi     DUPERR
move    d0,NSTDH      Result is non standard handle
                      number (6-45)
```

$46 FORCE

```
C: int  Fforce(stdh,nonstdh)
   int  stdh;
   int  nonstdh;
```

The FORCE function allows further manipulation of handle numbers. If in a program the console input and output are used exclusively via the READ and WRITE functions with the handle numbers 0 and 1, input or output can be redirected with a call to this function. Screen outputs are written to a file, inputs are not taken from the keyboard, but from a previously-opened file.

```
move.w  NSTDH,-(sp)   Parameter is non-standard handle
move.w  STDH,-(sp)    Standard handle (0-5)
move.w  #$46,-(sp)    Execute FORCE
trap    #1
addq.l  #6,sp
tst.l   d0            -37 or 0 are possible
bne     FORCE_ERR
```

$47 GETDIR

```
C: void Dgetpath(buf, drive)
   char *buf;
   int  drive;
```

A given subdirectory can be made into the current directory with the function $37. All file accesses with a pathname then run only in the set subdirectory. Under certain presumptions it can be possible to determine the pathname to the current subdirectory. This is accomplished by the function call GETDIR, $47. This call requires the designation of the desired disk drive (0=current drive, 1=drive A, 2=drive B, etc.) and a pointer to a 64-byte buffer. The complete pathname to the current directory will be placed in this buffer. The pathname will be terminated by a zero byte. If the function is called when the main directory is active, no pathname will be returned. In this case, the first byte in the buffer will contain zero. After the call, D0 must contain the value zero. If the value is negative, an error occurred, for example if an incorrect drive number was passed.

```
move.w  #0,-(sp)        Get pathname of the current drive
pea     buffer          Address of the 64-byte buffer
move.w  #$47,-(sp)      Function number
trap    #1
addq.l  #8,sp
.
.
buffer:
        .ds.b    128    Better to play it safe
```

$48 MALLOC

```
C: long Malloc(number)
   long number;
```

The MALLOC function and the two that follow it, MFREE and SETBLOCK, are concerned with the memory organization of GEMDOS. As already mentioned in conjunction with function $31, KEEP PROCESS, a program is assigned all of the entire memory space available after it is loaded. This is uncritical in many cases, because only a single program is running.

There are applications under GEM in which at least a part of memory is free from the start of the program, to allow memory to be called for different GEM functions with MALLOC. One good example is the item selector box, which will not appear when no more memory is available.

Other applications are programs which work with overlays, for example. To load an overlay from the diskette, GEMDOS must have memory available. For this reason, every program must only have enough memory reserved for program and data code. The unused memory can then be returned to GEMDOS by the SETBLOCK command.

If the program needs some of the memory it released, it can request memory from GEMDOS via the function MALLOC (memory allocate). The number of bytes required is passed to MALLOC. After the call, D0 contains the starting address of the memory area reserved by the call or an error message if an attempt is made to reserve more memory than is actually available.

If -1L is passed as the number of bytes to be allocated, the number of bytes available is returned in D0.

Example 1:

```
move.l  #-1,-(sp)         Determine number of free bytes
move.w  #$48,-(sp)        Function number
trap    #1
addq.l  #6,sp             Number of free bytes in D0
.
```

Example 2:

```
move.l  #$1000,-(sp)      Get hex 1000 bytes for the program
move.w  #$48,-(sp)        Function number
trap    #1
addq.l  #6,sp
tst.l   d0                Error or address of memory?
bmi     error             Negative long word = error!
move.l  d0,mstart         Else start addr of the reserved area
.
mstart:
        .ds.l   1
```

$49 MFREE

```
C: long Mfree(addr)
   long addr;
```

An area of memory reserved with MALLOC can be released at any time with MFREE. To do this, GEMDOS is passed the address of the memory to be released. The value will usually be the address returned by MALLOC.

If a value of zero is returned in D0, the memory was released by GEMDOS without error. Negative values indicates errors.

```
move.l  mstart,-(sp)      Addr of a previously allocated area
move.w  #$49,-(sp)        Function number
trap    #1
addq.l  #6,sp             Number of free bytes in D0
tst.l   d0                Error?
bne     error             D0<>0 is error!
.
.
mstart:
        .ds.l  1
```

$4A SETBLOCK

```
C: int   Mshrink(dummy, block, newsize)
   word dummy = 0;
   long block;
   long newsize;
```

In contrast to the MALLOC function, a specific area of memory can be reserved with the function SETBLOCK. The memory beginning at the specified address is returned to GEMDOS, even if it was reserved before. This function can be used to reserve the actual memory requirements of a program and release the remaining memory.

The parameters the function requires are the starting address and the length of the area to be reserved. The area specified with these parameters is then reserved by GEMDOS and is not released again until the end of the program or after calling the MFREE function.

Usually programs will begin with the following command sequence or something similar. After the call, D0 must contain zero, otherwise an error occurs.

```
move.l  a7,a5           Save stack pointer in A5
move.l  #ustck,a7       Set up stack for the program
move.l  4(a5),a5        A5 now points to the base-page start
                        exactly $100 bytes below the prg start
move.l  $c(a5),d0       $C(A5) contains length of the prg area
add.l   $14(a5),d0      $14(A5) containing the length of the
                        initialized data area
add.l   $1C(a5),d0      $1C(A5) contains length of the
                        uninitialized data area
add.l   #$100,d0        Reserve $100 bytes base page
move.l  d0,-(sp)        D0 contains the length of the area
                        to be reserved
move.l  a5,-(sp)        A5 contains the start of the area
                        to be reserved
move.w  #0,-(sp)        Meaningless word, but still necessary!
move.w  #$4a,-(sp)      Function number
trap    #1
add.l   #12,sp          Clean up the stack as usual
tst.l   d0              Did an error occur?
bne     error           Stop
.                       Here the program continues...
```

$4B EXEC

```
C: long Pexec(mode, ptr1, ptr2, ptr3)
   int   mode;
   char  *ptr1;
   char  *ptr2;
   char  *ptr3;
```

The Pexec() function permits loading and chaining programs. If desired, the program loaded can be automatically started. In addition to the function number, the addresses of three strings and a mode word are expected on the stack.

Let's talk a bit about the mode word. This word has a value of 0, 3, 4 or 5.

Mode=0 represents the LOAD'N'GO option: In this case, the file is loaded from diskette and the filename and pathname are received in PTR1. PTR2 contains the option of the command tail, comparable to choosing .TTP in a dialog box. PTR2 stands for the environment string, which apparently has no function under GEMDOS. If the command tail and the environment string aren't used, then there is a null-byte at this point.

After loading the program, the system automatically starts the program. The called program, started by the Pexec() call, remains in memory. Eventually opened files will pass on the most recently started program. This new program will be classified as a "child process." Once the child process is done, control returns to the original program, or "parent process."

If the mode word is a three, the parameters PTR1 to PTR3 are handled in the same form as when mode = 0, except that the program will not be executed once it is loaded into memory. After calling Pexec() with mode = 3, the address of the basepage of the loaded program is found in D0.

At first glance this may not make sense, but this function is the minimum that any good debugger should have. When you want to search a program for errors with a debugger, you would want control to go to the debugger, instead of the program loading and immediately executing. If the program ran without the debugger, and it had errors, it would crash. The LOAD option of Pexec() offers help.

If the mode word = 4, the program found in memory will be started. PTR1 waits for the address of the necessary basepage. PTR2 and PTR3 are unused. This way you can start a program previously loaded with Pexec(), mode = 3.

The last option is a mode word of 5. This option sets up the basepage in memory, as well as allocating the largest free block of memory. Naturally, no more data can go into the basepage after this call, especially text, data and BSS ranges. These must be provided for by the programmer.

```
pea      env              Environment
pea      com              Command line
pea      fil              Filename
move.w   #0,-(sp)         Load and start, please
move.w   #$4b,-(sp)       Function number
trap     #1
add.l    #16,sp           Here we come to the end of the
.                         chained program or loaded module
```

```
fil:                    Load sort routine
        .dc.b   'qsort.prg',0
com:                    Sort the file in ascending order
        .dc.b   'up data.asc',0
env:                    No environment
        .dc.w   0
.
```

$4C TERM

```
C: void Pterm(retcode)
   int  retcode;
```

TERM $4C represents the third method, after Pterm0(), function number $00, and Ptermres(), function number $31, of ending a program. Pterm() automatically makes the memory used by the program available to GEMDOS again. Unlike TERM $00, however, a programmer-defined value other than zero can be returned to the caller. This allows a short message to be passed back to the calling program.

All files opened in this process will be automatically closed from PTERM.

```
move.w  #37,-(sp)       Any 2-byte value
move.w  #$4c,-(sp)      End program
trap    #1                      ...now
.                       We never get here
```

$ 4E SFIRST

```
C: int  Fsfirst(fnam,attr)
   char *fnam;
   int  attr;
```

The SFIRST function can be used to check to see if a file with the given name is present in the directory. If a file with the same name is found, the filename, the file attribute, data and time of creation, and the size of the file in bytes is returned. This information is placed in the DTA buffer, whose address is set with the SETDTA function, by GEMDOS.

One feature of this function is that the filename need not be specified in its entirety. Individual characters in the filename can be exchanged for a question mark "?", and entire groups of letters can also be replaced by a "*". In the extreme form a filename would be reduced to the string "*.*". In this case the first file in the directory would satisfy the conditions and the filename would appear in the DTA buffer along with the other information.

In addition to the filename, the SFIRST function must also be given a search attribute. The possible parameters of the search attribute correspond to the attributes which can be specified in CHMOD function:

```
$00 = Normal access, read/write possible
$01 = Normal access, write protected
$02 = Hidden entry (ignored by the ST desktop)
$04 = Hidden system file (ignored like $02)
$08 = Volume label, diskette name
$10 = Subdirectory
$20 = File will be written and closed
```

The following rules apply when searching for files:

- If the attribute word is zero, only normal files are recognized. System files or subdirectories are not recognized.
- System files, hidden files, and subdirectories are found when the corresponding attribute bits are set. Volume labels are not recognized, however.
- In order to get the volume label, this option must be expressly set in the attribute word. All other files are then ignored.
- After the call, D0 contains zero if the desired file has been found. The 44-byte DTA buffer is then constructed as follows:

Bytes	0-20	Reserved for GEMDOS
Byte	21	File attribute
Bytes	22-23	Clock time of file creation
Bytes	24-25	Date of file creation
Bytes	26-29	File size in bytes (long)
Bytes	30-43	Name and extension of the file

If, however, no file is found which corresponds to the specified search string, the error message -33, file not found, is returned.

```
pea     dta                 Set up DTA buffer
move.w  #1a,-(sp)           Function number SETDTA
```

```
trap    #1
addq.l  #6,SP
move.w  #attrib,-(sp)    Attribute value
move.l  #filnam,-(sp)    Name of file to search for
move.w  #$4e,-(sp)       Function number
trap    #1
addq.l  #8,sp
tst     d0               File found?
bne     notfound         Apparently not
.
.
.
attrib:
        .dc.b   0        Search for normal files only
filnam:
        .dc.b   '*.*',0  Search for the 1st possible file
.
.
.
dta:
        .ds.b   44       Space for the DTA buffer
```

$4F SNEXT

C: int   Fsnext()

The SNEXT function (Search next) can be used to see if there are other files on the disk which match the filename given. To do this, only the function number need be passed; SNEXT does not require any parameters. All of the parameters are set from the SFIRST call.

If the search string is very global, as in the previous example, all of the files on a diskette can be determined and displayed one after the other with SFIRST and SNEXT. This makes it rather easy to display a directory within a program. The SNEXT function is called repeatedly and the contents of D0 are check afterwards. If D0 contains a value other than zero, either an error occurred, or all of the directory entries have been searched.

```
move.w  #$4f,-(sp)   Search next
trap    #1           Is it still there?
addq.l  #2,sp
tst.l   d0           No more by negative values
```

$56 RENAME

```
C: int   Frename(dummy, oldname, newname)
   int   dummy = 0;
   char *oldname;
   char *newname;
```

Files are renamed under GEMDOS with the RENAME function, which requires two pointers to file or pathnames. The first pointer points to the new name, with the specification of the pathname if necessary; the second pointer points to the previous name. A 2-byte parameter is required in addition to the two pointers. We were unable to determine the function of the additional word parameter. Different values had no (recognizable) effect.

As a return value, D0 contains either zero, meaning that the name was changed correctly, or an error code.

```
        pea     newnam              New filename
        pea     oldname             File to rename
        move.w  #0,-(sp)            Dummy
        move.w  #$56,-(sp)          Function number
        trap    #1
        add.l   #12,sp
        tst.l   d0                  Test for error
.
oldnam:                             Don't forget zero byte at end!
        .dc.b   'oldfile.dat',0
newnam:
        .dc.b   'newname.dat',0
```

$57 GSDTOF

```
C: void Fdatime(timeptr, handle, flag)
   int   handle;
   char *timeptr;
   int   flag;
```

If the directory is displayed as text rather than icons on the desktop, the date and time of file creation as well as the size of the file in bytes is shown. The time and date can either be set or read with function $57. To do this it is necessary that the file be already opened by OPEN or CREATE. The handle number obtained at the opening must be passed to the function. Additional parameters are a word which acts as a flag as to whether the time and date are to be set (0) or read (1), and a pointer to a 4-byte buffer which either contains the result or will be provided with the required data before the call.

This date buffer contains the time in the first two byes and the date in the last two bytes. The data format is identical to that of the functions for setting/reading the time and date.

A word of warning about this section. Programmers who call this function in C and assembler must make allowances. In the include file OSBIND.H, the parameters 'timeprt' and 'handle' are exchanged. A C call must follow this scheme when using the abovementioned include file. In assembler programs, however, the normal sequence of parameters must be followed.

Example 1:

```
move.w  #1,-(sp)         Read time and date
pea     buff             4 byte buffer
move.w  #handle,-(sp)    File must first be opened
move.w  #$57,-(sp)       Function number
trap    #1
add.l   #10,sp
handle:
        .ds.b   2
buff:
        .ds.b   4
```

Example 2:

```
move.w  #0,-(sp)         Set time and date
pea     buff             4 byte buffer
move.w  #handle,-(sp)    File must first be opened
move.w  #$57,-(sp)       Function number
trap    #1
add.l   #10,sp
handle:
        .ds.b   2
buff:
        .ds.b   4
```

3.1.1 Memory, files and processes

Will it never end? You just mastered getting around the operating system of your C-64, Atari 800 or other 8-bit machine, then suddenly you're confronted with new things such as memory management, handles, and even parent/child processes. Other computers don't have these knickknacks. Is it really that important to have them? Doesn't the computer run fine without them? And then there are these types that don't stay at the memory address you want them to operate. It was so much simpler in the past. Those were the days when you knew where a program loaded and ran, and when you assembled things at the necessary addresses.

I/O conversion, Malloc, basepage, Pexec or Dup are such obscure terms. Yes, everything was a lot simpler in the good old days.

We're here to help you overcome the "culture shock" that hits most 8-bit owners when they get a 16-bit computer. In order to ease you into the most effective use of the Atari ST operating system, we want to show you what special functions like MALLOC, SETBLOCK, TERM and PEXEC are, as well as the use and design of the basepage. We'll close with DUP and FORCE, the input/output division.

The concept of memory processing

When the ST is first turned on, it goes through a normal boot sequence. This sequence happens regardless of the ROMs or operating system in your ST. The system boots, then displays the Desktop on the monitor.

Up to this time there have already been a number of procedures done within the ST. So other memory, peripheral chips and operating system routines are initialized, and the programs in the Auto folder executed.

The Desktop itself is an independent program, the same as an editor, BASIC interpreter or compiler. Whether it is in ROM or on the TOS.IMG disk, it starts like a program loaded from disk. One specific task of the Desktop is to load other programs and give computer control to these programs. As we said earlier, we'll take a closer look.

The function call Pexec is used by the Desktop in loading programs. When you choose a program with the mouse, a corresponding Pexec call with the filename and parameters given in the dialog box is executed. GEMDOS takes control from the call and looks for free memory. But what's "free memory"? Every program has its memory range; free memory is unoccupied memory, into which a program can be loaded. The start of free memory (TPA) will then have a basepage added to it. This basepage is 256 bytes ($100 bytes) in size, and contains special information about the program being loaded. The basepage's design looks like this:

Offset	Identifier	Function
0x00	p_lowtpa	Pointer to start of basepage
0x04	p_hitpa	Pointer to the end of free memory
0x08	p_tbase	Pointer to beginning of program (text segment)
0x0c	p_tlen	Program size (Text segment)
0x10	p_dbase	Pointer to start of data segment
0x14	p_dlen	Data segment size
0x18	p_bbase	Pointer to beginning of BSS segments
0x1c	p_len	BSS segment size
0x20	p_dta	Pointer to DTA buffer
0x24	p_parent	Pointer to parent's basepage
0x28	(reserved)	
0x2c	p_env	Pointer to environment string
0x80	cmdlin	Command line

The range between 0x30 and 0x7f is used by the operating system. You should not use this range.

Although the basepage is sent from the system, there aren't many other things that need to be done. First, after the program is loaded directly behind the basepage, the data is made available and put into the appropriate areas.

The program is relocated after loading (if needed). The programmer as a rule has no control over the memory where the program resides, since Pexec controls the free memory, and loads the program into that memory. The classic 8-bit computer must load a program into a specific range of memory, which easily allows combining multiple programs into one memory register. These combinations should be avoided at all costs under "proper" GEMDOS programming. Instead, assemble the program, putting relevant addresses into a loader that Pexec will load first, then act upon these addresses before loading the main program.

The program will start after this work. It is now a child of a program that it has called. The calling program will be identified as a parent. This parent has no gender; the general reference of parent and child solves any linguistic problems.

For the moment, let's concentrate on the child. This process has from the first set up the entire free memory needed. The first action should be to determine the amount of memory needed in any program, and hand the rest over to GEMDOS. And how do you allocate memory? Once you know it, it's simple to follow.

After the start of the program, you'll find the address of the basepage on the stack. All the program data and calculations for memory requirements is in the basepage. These data are p_tlen, p_dlen and p_blen. Add these values together, and there you have your range needed by the program. In addition, you have to reserve memory for the stack, which lies in protected memory.

When you analyze the beginning of a program with a disassembler, you'll frequently find the following or a similar sequence:

```
move.l  a7,a5           store stack to determine basepage
move.l  4(a5),a5        base page is now in a5
move.l  $c(a5),d0       text segment length stands in d0
add.l   $14(a5),d0      add to that the length of the data- and
add.l   $1c(a5),d0      the bss segments
add.l   #$500,d0        and to that add the amount needed for the stack

move.l  d0,d1
add.l   a5,d1           length + address of basepage
and.l   #-2,d1          be sure that the stack starts at an even address
move.l  d1,a7           now put the stack where you want it
move.l  d0,-(sp)        size of reserved area
move.l  a5,-(sp)        from where you want it reserved (base page)
clr.w   -(sp)           dummy
move.w  #$4a,-(sp)      setblock-function number
trap    #1              call gemdos
add.l   #12,sp          and clear off the stack
```

This program section takes up all tasks which were demanded from GEMDOS. After GEMDOS has reduced the amount of available memory accordingly, the program can then continue.

What is released memory? This is done by GEMDOS for further Pexec calls. The child process has no access authority. You should ideally be able to use memory without further measurements. When you keep putting data into this range, the data could occasionally become "overstuffed". Different functions of GEMDOS, the VDI and AES are reserved by Malloc, and putting data into the received range. When you haven't protected your data, the chances are good that you'll lose your data.

When you have not set up available memory, then you can call Malloc from the operating system. After the call, you get the starting address of the reserved range. This range is "safe"—you can't put any other process into this range. When the memory is no longer free, the best thing to do is call Mfree. Then you can choose from another process.

When you hold to these conventions, then one can't get past. The memory is again protected, and you can load in any other programs. Every new loading makes up another child of the parent program. So overlaying programs is only allowed when the available memory is protected.

If a program ends with Pterm0 or Pterm, then the designated memory is released from the program. Additional memory reserved by Malloc will be released. Also, any open files will be closed. Then control returns to the parent, whereas it was previously held by the child.

Handles, files, devices

The basic file handling functions in GEMDOS are quite simple. Fopen or Fcreate open a file; this file is read from with Fread, and written to with Fwrite. Fclose closes the file. All file accesses run under a number, initially stated in Fopen or Fcreate. This number between 6 and 45 is called a "non standard handle." Non standard handles are used only in conjunction with files.

It is logical to assume that there are also "standard handles." And so there are; these are the handles between 0 and 5. These handles can be organized as either a file or as a "character device." Character devices in the ST consist of the keyboard, the monitor, the printer interface and the serial interface. Here is the normal assignment for these standard handles:

```
Handle     Device
  0        Console input (Stdin)
  1        Console output (Stout)
  2        Serial interface (AUX)
  3        Printer interface (PRN)
```

The standard handles 4 and 5 aren't used in ST GEMDOS as a rule. The "correct" GEMDOS layout sees handle 2 as a standard error device (Stderr). These will shift AUX and PRN over one place. Handle 5 is originally used as a null-device. This null-device can store output in an empty space. This setup is unfortunately not implemented in the ST.

That's not all. There are also character handles which are assigned in connection with the character devices. These character handles are received only after an Fopen or Fcreate, and give the names of the desired character devices. The names of the character devices are "CON:", "AUX:" and "PRN:".

Standard handles serve two distinct purposes. The first is that you can use them for Fopen or Fcreate without actually having Fopen or Fcreate. These handles will perform any process arranged by the parent process. The second purpose is the allowance for altering standard handles.

For example: You work on a program which waits for a quantity of data from the keyboard; this data is processed, saved to disk, and the results sent to a printer. Now, you could do every test run by hand, and end up with a pile of paper, until the program runs free of error. However, you could just as easily pass along the keyboard input and the printer output by writing all the keyboard input into a file, and having the file data do the typing. You could also have the printer output sent to a file instead of the printer, so you could save yourself a waste of paper, and still see the result later.

These conversions use both standard and non standard handles, controlled by the Force function. Here is a program fragment which contains the necessary calls for using a file to send "keyboard" input from a file:

```
move.w  #0,-(sp)         "read only" mode
pea     fil_nam          name of the input file
move.w  #$3d,-(sp)       fopen()
trap    #1               gemdos call
addq.l  #8,sp
tst.l   d0               did fopen work?
bmi     opn_err          negative long is an error!
move.w  d0,f_handle      the handle we need is our
move.w  d0,-(sp)         our non std handle
move.w  #0,-(sp)         std handle console
move.w  #$46,-(sp)       force()
trap    #1               call gemdos
addq.l  #6,sp
tst.l   d0               read error
bmi     frc_err
.
.                        input starts from
.                        file here
```

After this call (and this is extremely important), every GEMDOS call for a character from the keyboard will get it from the file. The keyboard must not be read with Fread(). Cconin(), Crawio(), Cconrs() and the other functions dealing with keyboard data also look to the file data instead of the keyboard. The use of character functions (Conin, etc.) in connection with this are problematical. These functions have no options in working with the called program when the file ends. This information can be had only by using the Fread() function.

An exception is when you mark the input file with a special end-of-file (EOF) indicator. One character frequently used for this purpose is <Control><Z>, with an ASCII value of 26 or 0x1a. When you reserve this character for an EOF character, then you can read this character in addition to the standard arrangement of 0. For particularly elegant programming, you can follow it with the Fdup function. Here's a short example:

```
        move.w   #0,-(sp)         our std handle
        move.w   #$45,-(sp)       dup()
        trap     #1               call gemdos
        addq.l   #4,sp
        tst.l    d0               was there still a non std handle free?
        bmi      no_more          evidently not
        move.w   d0,dup_han       make a note of it!
        .
        .
*    here the key/file transfer program can follow
        .
        .
*    Here is the program itself. Now you can only start with keyboard
*    input
        .
        .
        move.w   dup_han,-(sp)    our non std handle from dup()
        move.w   #0,-(sp)         there should be a std handle
        move.w   #$46,-(sp)       force()
        trap     #1               call gemdos
        addq.l   #6,sp
        tst.l    d0               read error
        bmi      frc_err
        .
        .                         from this point on, the input is again
        .                         handed over to the keyboard
```

First, the handle from Stdin, the 0, is duplicated by the Dup function. The keyboard is accessed by the standard handle as well as the non standard handle. (only with Fread, naturally). The input routine then switches over to the file, giving the effect described above. All characters that you would normally send over the keyboard are read from the file. When the input is ended, then the duplicated handle is returned to keyboard input with a Force call. The still open file should be closed by an Fclose call.

From reading the above, it should be clear to you the way that the printer output works. Again, open a file with Fcreate(). The handle used can be Forced from the printer. Then all data that would normally go to the printer will be sent to a file.

A further application would be when you move output from the screen to the printer. This can also be easily realized.

GEMDOS error codes and their meaning

The GEMDOS functions return a value giving information about whether or not an error occurred during the execution of the function. A value of zero means no error; negative values have the following meanings:

```
-32   Invalid function number
-33   File not found
-34   Pathname not found
-35   Too many files open (no more handles left)
-36   Access not possible
-37   Invalid handle number
-39   Not enough memory
-40   Invalid memory block address
-46   Invalid drive specification
-49   No more files
```

In addition to these error messages, the BIOS error messages may occur. These error messages have numbers -1 to -31 and are described in section 3.3

3.2 The BIOS Functions

The software interface between GEMDOS and the hardware of the computer is the BIOS (Basic Input Output System). The BIOS, as the name suggests, is concerned with the fundamental input/output functions. This includes screen output, keyboard input, printer output, RS-232 functions and, of course, disk input and output.

The BIOS functions are also available to user programs. The `TRAP` instruction of the 68000 processor is used to call them. Any data required is passed through the stack and the result of the function is returned in the D0 register. The machine language programmer should be aware that the contents of D0-D2 and A0-A2 are changed when calling BIOS functions; the remaining registers remain unchanged.

BIOS function calls are even simpler if you program in C. Here you can use simple function calls with the corresponding parameter lists. The function calls are stored as macros in an include file. In the examples, the definition of the function and its parameters in C will be shown. For assembly language programmers, the use is described in an example.

`TRAP #13` is reserved for the BIOS functions.

0 Getmpb *get memory parameter block*

C: void Getmpb(pointer)
   long pointer;

Assembler:

```
move.l   pointer,-(SP)
move.w   #0,-(SP)
trap     #13
addq.l   #6,sp
```

This function fills a 12-byte block whose address is contained in `pointer` with the memory parameter block. This block contains three pointers:

```
long    md_mfl          Memory free list
long    md_mal          Memory allocated list
long    md_rover        Roving pointer
```

The structures to which each pointer points are constructed as follows:

```
long    md_link         Pointer to next block
long    md_start        Start address of the block
long    md_length       Length of the block in bytes
long    md_own          Process descriptor
```

Example:

```
move.l #buffer,-(sp)    Buffer for MPB
move.w #0,-(sp)         getmpb
trap   #13              Call BIOS
addq.l #6,sp            Stack correction
```

We get the values $48E, 0, and $48E. The following data are at address $48E (for 1MB RAM):

```
m_link    0             No additional block
m_start   $3B900        Start address of the free memory
m_length  $3C700        Length of the free memory
m_own     0             No process descriptor
```

1 Bconstat   *return input device status*

```
C:  int Bconstat(dev)
    int dev;
```

Assembler:

```
    move.w dev,-(sp)
    move.w #1,-(sp)
    trap   #13
    addq.l #4,sp
```

This function returns the status of an input device, defined as follows:

```
    Status 0         No characters ready
    Status -1        (at least) one character ready
```

The parameter `dev` specifies the input device:

```
    dev     Input device
     0      PRT:, Centronics interface
     1      AUX:, RS-232 interface
     2      CON:, Keyboard and screen
     3      MIDI, MIDI interface
     4      IKBD, Keyboard port
```

The following table lists the allowed accesses to these devices:

Operation	PRT:	AUX:	CON:	MIDI	IKBD
Input status	no	yes	yes	yes	no
Input	yes	yes	yes	yes	no
Output status	yes	yes	yes	yes	yes
Output	yes	yes	yes	yes	yes

This example waits until a character from the RS-232 interface is ready.

```
wait move.w #1,-(sp)         RS-232
     move.w #1,-(sp)         bconstat
     trap   #13
     addq.l #4,sp
     tst    d0                character available?
     beq    wait              no, wait
```

2 Bconin — *read character from device*

C: `long Bconin(dev)`
     `int dev;`

Assembler:

```
move.w  dev,-(sp)
move.w  #2,-(sp)
trap    #13
addq.l  #4,sp
```

This function fetches a character from an input device. The parameter `dev` has the same meaning as in the previous function. The function returns when a character is ready.

The character received is in the lowest byte of the result. If the input device was the keyboard (con, 2), the key scan code is also returned in the lower byte of the upper word (see the description of the keyboard processor).

Example:

```
move.w  #2,-(sp)     con
move.w  #2,-(sp)     bconin
trap    #13
addq.l  #4,sp
```

3 Bconout — *write character to device*

C: `void Bconout(dev, c)`
     `int dev, c;`

Assembler:

```
move.w  c,-(sp)
move.w  dev,-(sp)
move.w  #3,-(sp)
trap    #13
addq.l  #6,sp
```

This function serves to output a character "c" to the output device `dev` (meaning is the same as for the previous function). The function returns when the character has been outputted.

Example:

```
move.w  #'A',-(sp)
move.w  #0,-(sp)      PRT:
move.w  #3,-(sp)      Bconout
trap    #13
addq.l  #6,sp
```

The example outputs the letter "A" to the printer.

4 Rwabs   *read and write disk sector*

```
C: long Rwabs(rwflag, buffer, number, recno,dev)
   long buffer;
   int rwflag, number, recno, dev;
```

Assembler:

```
move.w  dev,-(sp)
move.w  recno,-(sp)
move.w  number,-(sp)
move.l  buffer,-(sp)
move.w  rwflag,-(sp)
move.w  #4,-(sp)
trap    #13
add.l   #14,sp
```

This function serves to read and write sectors on the disk. The parameters have the following meanings:

rwflag	Meaning
0	Read sector
1	Write sector
2	Read sector, ignore disk change
3	Write sector, ignore disk change

The parameter `buffer` is the address of a buffer into which the data will be read from the disk or from which the data will be written to the disk. The buffer should begin at an even address, or the transfer will run very slowly.

The parameter `number` specifies how many sectors should be read or written during the call. The parameter `recno` specifies which logical sector the process will start with.

The parameter `dev` determines which disk drive will be used:

dev	Drive
0	Drive A
1	Drive B
2+	Hard disk, RAM disk, network

The function returns an error code as the result. If this value is zero, the operation was performed without error. The returned value will be negative if an error occurred (please see the **Floprd** entry of the XBIOS listing for error codes and their meanings).

Example:

```
        move.w  #0,-(sp)          Drive A
        move.w  #10,-(sp)         Start at logical sector 10
        move.w  #2,-(sp)          Read 2 sectors
        move.l  #buffer,-(sp)     Buffer address
        move.w  #0,-(sp)          Read sectors
        move.w  #4,-(sp)          rwabs
        trap    #13
        add.l   #14,sp
        ...
buffer  ds.b    2*512
```

5 Setexec   *set exception vectors*

```
C: long Setexec(number, vector)
   int   number;
   long  vector;
```

Assembler:

```
    move.l vector,-(sp)
    move.w number,-(sp)
    move.w #5,-(sp)
    trap   #13
    addq.l #8,sp
```

The function `setexec` allows one of the exception vectors of the 68000 processor to be changed. The number of the vector must be passed in `number` and the address of the routine pertaining to it in `vector`. The function returns the old vector as the result. If you just want to read the vector, pass the value -1 as the new address. The 256 processor vectors as well as 8 vectors for GEM, which numbers $100 to $107 (address $400 to $41C) can be changed with this function.

Example:

```
    move.l #buserror,-(sp)
    move.w #2,-(sp)
    move.w #5,-(sp)
    trap   #13
    addq.l #8,sp
    ...
buserror ...
```

6 Tickcal   *return millisecond per tick*

C: `long Tickcal()`

Assembler:

```
move.w  #6,-(sp)
trap    #13
addq.l  #2,sp
```

This function returns the number of milliseconds between two system timer calls.

Example:

```
move.w  #6,-(sp)
trap    #13
addq.l  #2,sp
```

Result: 20 ms

---

7 Getbpb   *get BIOS parameter block*

C: `long Getbpb(dev)`
    `int dev;`

Assembler:

```
move.w  dev,-(sp)
move.w  #7,-(sp)
trap    #13
addq.l  #4,sp
```

This function returns a pointer to the BIOS Parameter Block of the drive `dev` (0=drive A, 1=drive B).

The BPB (BIOS Parameter Block) is constructed as follows:

```
int   recsiz    Sector size in bytes
int   clsiz     Cluster size in sectors
int   clsizb    Cluster size in bytes
```

```
int   rdlen    Directory length in sectors
int   fsiz     FAT size in sectors
int   fatrec   Sector number of the second FAT
int   datrec   Sector number of the first data cluster
int   numcl    Number of data clusters on the disk
int   bflags   Misc. flags
```

The function returns the address $3E3E for drive A and the address $3E5E for drive B. An address of zero indicates an error.

Example:

```
move.w  #0,-(sp)      Drive A
move.w  #7,-(sp)      getbpb
trap    #13
addq.l  #4,sp
```

Here are the BPB data for 80 track single and double-sided disk drives:

Parameter	80 track SS	80 track DS
recsiz	512	512
clsiz	2	2
clsizb	1024	1024
rdlen	7	7
fsiz	5	5
fatrec	6	6
datrec	18	18
numcl	351	711

8 Bcostat *return output device status*

```
C:  long Bcostat(dev)
    int  dev;
```

Assembler:

```
    move.w  dev,-(sp)
    move.w  #8,-(sp)
    trap    #13
    addq.l  #4,sp
```

This function tests to see if the output device specified by dev is ready to output the next character. dev can accept the values which are described in function one. The result of this function is either -1 if the output device is ready, or zero if it must wait.

Example:

```
    move.w  #0,-(sp)     Printer ready?
    move.w  #8,-(sp)     bcostat
    trap    #13
    addq.l  #4,sp
```

9 Mediach *inquire media change*

```
C:  long Mediach(dev)
    int dev;
```

Assembler:

```
    move.w  dev,-(sp)
    move.w  #9,-(sp)
    trap    #13
    addq.l  #4,sp
```

This function determines if the disk has been changed. The parameter dev, the drive number (0=drive A, 1=drive B), must be passed to the routine.

One of three values can occur as the result:

```
0    Diskette was definitely not changed
1    Diskette may have been changed
2    Diskette was definitely changed
```

Example:

```
move.w  #1,-(sp)        Drive B
move.w  #9,-(sp)        mediach
trap    #13
addq.l  #4,sp
```

10 Drvmap   *inquire drive status*

`C: long Drvmap()`

Assembler:

```
move.w  #10,-(sp)
trap    #13
addq.l  #2,sp
```

This function returns a bit vector which contains the connected drives. The bit number n is set if drive n is available (0 means A, etc.). Even if only one drive is connected, %11 is still returned, since two logical drives are assumed.

Example:

```
move.w  #10,-(sp)       drvmap
trap    #13
addq.l  #2,sp
```

11 Kbshift   *inquire/change keyboard status*

C: `long Kbshift(mode)`
    `int mode;`

Assembler:

```
move.w  mode,-(sp)
mode.w  #11,-(sp)
trap    #13
addq.l  #4,sp
```

With this function you can change or determine the status of the special keys on the keyboard. If mode is -1, you get the status, a positive value will be accepted as the status. The status is a bit vector constructed as follows:

Bit	Meaning
0	Right shift key
1	Left shift key
2	Control key
3	ALT key
4	Caps Lock on
5	Right mouse button (CLR/HOME)
6	Left mouse button (INSERT)
7	Unused

Example:

```
move.w  #-1,-(sp)       Read shift status
move.w  #11,-(sp)       kbshift
trap    #13
addq.l  #4,sp
```

3.3 The XBIOS

To support the special hardware features of the Atari ST, there are extended BIOS (XBIOS) functions, which are called by a `TRAP #14` instruction. These functions, like the normal BIOS functions, can be called from assembly language as well as from C. When calling from C, a small TRAP handler in machine language is again necessary, which is contained in OSBIND and can look like this:

```
trap14:
        move.l  (sp)+,retsave   Save return address
        trap    #14             Call XBIOS
        move.l  retsave,-(sp)   Restore return address
        rts

        .bss
retsave ds.l    1               Space for the return address
```

Macro functions can be used in C which allow the extended BIOS functions (eXtended BIOS, XBIOS) to be called by name. The appropriate function number and TRAP call will be created when the macro is expanded.

When working in assembly language, the function number of the XBIOS routine need simply be passed on the stack. The XBIOS has 40 different functions whose significance and use are described on the following pages.

0 Initmous *initialize mouse*

```
C: void Initmous(type, parameter, vector)
   int type;
   long parameter, vector;
```

Assembler:

```
    move.l  vector,-(sp)
    move.l  parameter,-(sp)
    move.w  type,-(sp)
    move.w  #0,(-sp)
    trap    #14
    add.l   #12,sp
```

This **XBIOS** function initializes the routines for mouse processing. The parameter `vector` is the address of a routine which will be executed following a mouse-report from the keyboard processor. The parameter `type` selects from among the following alternatives:

```
type
  0     Disable mouse
  1     Enable mouse, relative mode
  2     Enable mouse, absolute mode
  3     unused
  4     Enable mouse, keyboard mode
```

This allows you to select if mouse movements are to be reported and in what manner this will occur.

The parameter `parameter` points to a parameter block, which is constructed as follows:

```
    char topmode
    char buttons
    char xparam
    char yparam
```

The parameter `topmode` determines the layout of the coordinate system. A 0 means that Y=0 lies in the lower corner, 1 means that Y=0 lies in the upper corner.

The parameter `buttons` is a parameter for the command "set mouse buttons" of the keyboard processor (see description of the IKBD, intelligent keyboard).

The parameters `xparam` and `yparam` are scaling factors for the mouse movement. If you have selected 2 as the `type`, the absolute mode, the parameter block determines four more parameters:

```
int   xmax
int   ymax
int   xstart
int   ystart
```

These are the X- and Y-coordinates of the maximum value which the mouse position can assume, as well as the start value to which the mouse will be set.

Example:

```
    move.l  #vector,-(sp)      Address of the mouse position
    move.l  #parameter,-(sp)   Address of the parameter block
    move.w  #1,-(sp)           Enable relative mouse mode
    move.w  #0,-(sp)           Init mouse
    trap    #14
    add.l   #12,sp
    ...
parameter dc.b ......
    ...
vector    ...                  Mouse interrupt routine
```

1 Ssbrk   *save memory space*

C: `long Ssbrk(number)`
   `int number;`

Assembler:

```
move.w  number,-(sp)
move.w  #1,-(sp)
trap    #14
addq.l  #4,sp
```

This function reserves memory space. The number of bytes must be passed in `number`. Space is prepared at the upper end of memory. The function returns the address of the reserved memory area as the result. This function must be called before initializing the operating system, meaning that it must be called from the boot ROM, before the operating system is loaded.

Example:

```
move.w  #$400,-(sp)     Reserve 1K
move.w  #1,-(sp)        ssbrk
trap    #14
addq.l  #4,sp
```

2 Physbase   *return screen RAM base address*

C: `long Physbase()`

Assembler:

```
move    #2,-(sp)
trap    #14
addq.l  #2,sp
```

This function returns the base of the physical screen RAM. The physical screen RAM is the area of memory displayed by the video shifter. The result is a long word.

Example:

```
$F8000, base address of the screen for 1 MB RAM
$78000, base address of the screen for 512 KB RAM
```

3 Logbase   *get logical screen base*

C: `long Logbase()`

Assembler:

```
move    #3,-(sp)
trap    #14
addq.l  #2,sp
```

The logical screen base is the address which is used for all output functions as the screen base. If the physical and logical screen bases are different, one screen will be displayed while another picture is being constructed in a different area of RAM, which will be displayed later. The result of this function call is again a longword.

Example:

```
$F8000, base address of the screen for 1 MB RAM
$78000, base address of the screen for 512 KB RAM
```

4 Getrez   *return screen resolution*

C: `int Getrez()`

Assembler:

```
move.w #4,-(sp)
trap   #14
addq.l #2,sp
```

This function call returns the screen resolution:

```
0 :=  Low resolution, 320*200 pixels, 16 colors
1 :=  Medium resolution, 640*200 pixels, 4 colors
2 :=  High resolution, 640*400, pixels, monochrome
```

Example:

```
2, monochrome
```

---

5 Setscreen   *set screen parameters*

C: `void Setscreen(logadr, physadr, res)`
   `long logadr, physadr;`
   `int res;`

Assembler:

```
move.w res,-(sp)
move.l physadr,-(sp)
move.l logadr,-(sp)
move.w #5,-(sp)
trap   #14
add.l  #12,sp
```

This function changes the screen parameters which can be read with the previous three functions. If a parameter should not be set, a negative value must be passed. The parameters are set in the next VBL routine so that no disturbances appear on the screen.

Example:

```
move.w  #-1,-(sp)        Retain resolution
move.l  #$70000,-(sp)    Physical base
move.l  #$70000,-(sp)    Logical base
move.w  #5,-(sp)         setscreen
trap    #14
add.l   #12,sp
```

Set the physical and the logical screen address to $70000, retain the resolution.

6 Setpalette   *set color palette*

C: `void Setpalette(paletteptr)`
   `long paletteptr;`

Assembler:

```
move.l  paletteptr,-(sp)
move.w  #6,-(sp)
trap    #14
addq.l  #6,sp
```

A new color palette can be loaded with this function. The parameter `paletteptr` must be a pointer to a table with 16 colors (each a word). The address of the table must be even. The colors will be loaded at the start of the next VBL.

Example:

```
         move.l  #palette,-(sp)   Address of the new color palette
         move.w  #6,-(sp)         set palette
         trap    #14
         addq.l  #6,sp
         ....
palette  dc.w    $777,$700,$070,$007,$111,$222,$333,$444
         dc.w    $555,$000,$001,$010,$100,$200,$020,$002
```

7 Setcolor   *set color*

C: `int Setcolor(colornum, color)`
   `int colornum, color`

Assembler:

```
move.w  color,-(sp)
move.w  colornum,-(sp)
move.w  #7,-(sp)
trap    #14
addq.l  #6,sp
```

This function allows just one color to be changed. The color number (0-15) and the color belonging to it (0-$777) must be specified. If -1 is given as the color, the color is not set but the previous color is returned.

Example:

```
move.w  #$777,-(sp)      Color white
move.w  #1,-(sp)         As color number 1
move.w  #7,-(sp)
trap    #14
addq.l  #6,sp
```

8 Floprd   *read diskette sector*

```
C: int Floprd(buffer, filler, dev, sector, track, side,
count)
    long buffer, filler;
    int  dev, sector, track, side, count;
```

Assembler:

```
move.w count,-(sp)
move.w side,-(sp)
move.w track,-(sp)
move.w sector,-(sp)
move.w dev,-(sp)
clr.l  -(sp)
move.l buffer,-(sp)
move.w #8,-(sp)
trap   #14
add.l  #20,sp
```

This function reads one or more sectors in from the diskette. The parameters have the following meaning:

- `count:` Specifies how many sectors are to be read. Values between one and nine (number of sectors per track) are possible.

- `side:` Selects the diskette side, zero for single-sided drives and zero or one for double-sided drives.

- `track:` Determines the track number (0-79 for 80-track drives or 0-39 for 40-track drives).

- `sector:` The sector number of the first sector to be read (1-9).

- `dev:` Determine drive number, 0 for drive A and 1 for drive B.

- `filler:` Unused long word.

- `buffer:` Buffer in which the diskette data should be written. The buffer must begin on a word boundary and be large enough for the data to be read (512 bytes times the number of sectors).

The function returns an error code which has the following meaning:

```
  0 OK, no error
 -1 General error
 -2 Drive not ready
 -3 Unknown command
 -4 CRC error
 -5 Bad request, invalid command
 -6 Seek error, track not found
 -7 Unknown media (invalid boot sector)
 -8 Sector not found
 -9 (No paper)
-10 Write error
-11 Read error
-12 General error
-13 Diskette write protected
-14 Diskette was changed
-15 Unknown device
-16 Bad sector (during verify)
-17 Insert diskette (for connected drive)
```

Example:

```
    move.w  #1,-(sp)            Read a sector
    move.w  #0,-(sp)            Page zero
    move.w  #0,-(sp)            Track zero
    move.w  #1,-(sp)            Sector one
    move.w  #1,-(sp)            Drive B
    clr.l   -(sp)
    move.l  #buffer,-(sp)
    move.w  #8,-(sp)            floprd
    trap    #14
    add.l   #20,sp
    tst     d0                  Did error occur?
    bmi     error               yes
    ...
buffer  ds.b 512                Buffer for a sector
```

9 Flopwr *write diskette sector*

```
C: int Floprd(buffer, filler, dev, sector, track, side,
              count)
   long buffer, filler;
   int  dev,sector,track,side,count;
```

Assembler:

```
    move.w count,-(sp)
    move.w side,-(sp)
    move.w track,-(sp)
    move.w sector,-(sp)
    move.w dev,-(sp)
    clr.l  -(sp)
    move.l buffer,-(sp)
    move.w #9,-(sp)
    trap   #14
    add.l  #20,sp
```

One or more sectors can be written to disk with this XBIOS function. The parameters have the same meaning as for the **Floprd** function. The function returns an error code which has the same meaning as for reading sectors.

Example:

```
    move.w #3,-(sp)         Write three sectors
    move.w #0,-(sp)         Side zero
    move.w #7,-(sp)         Track seven
    move.w #1,-(sp)         Sector one
    move.w #0,-(sp)         Drive A
    clr.l  -(sp)
    move.l #buffer,-(sp)    Address of the buffer
    move.w #9,-(sp)         flopwr
    trap   #14
    add.l  #20,sp
    tst    d0               Did an error occur?
    bmi    error            yes
    ...
buffer  ds.b 3*512          Buffer for three sectors
```

10 Flopfmt   *format diskette*

```
C: int Flopfmt(buffer, filler, dev, spt, track, side,
              interleave, magic, virgin)
   long buffer, filler, magic;
   int  dev, spt, track, side, interleave, virgin;
```

Assembler:

```
move.w  virgin,-(sp)
move.l  magic,-(sp)
move.w  interleave,-(sp)
move.w  side,-(sp)
move.w  track,-(sp)
move.w  spt,-(sp)
move.w  dev,-(sp)
clr.l   -(sp)
move.l  buffer,-(sp)
move.w  #10,-(sp)
trap    #14
add.l   #26,sp
```

This routine serves to format a track on the diskette. The parameters have the following meanings:

- `virgin:` The sectors are formatted with this value. The standard value is $E5E5. The high nibble of each byte may not contain the value $F.

- `magic:` The constant $87654321 must be used as `magic` or formatting will be stopped.

- `interleave:` Determines in which order the sectors on the disk will be written, usually one.

- `side:` Selects the disk side (0 or 1).

- `track:` The number of the track to be formatted (0-79).

- `spt:` Sectors per track, normally 9.

- `dev:` The drive, 0 for A and 1 for B.

filler: Unused long word.

buffer: Buffer for the track data; for 9 sectors per track the buffer mst be at least 8K large.

The function returns an error code as its result. The value -16, bad sectors, means that data in some sectors could not be read back correctly. In this case the buffer contains a list of bad sectors (word data, terminated by zero). You can format these again or mark the sectors as bad.

Example:

```
        move.w  #$E5E5,-(sp)            Initial data
        move.l  #$87654321,-(sp)        magic
        move.w  #1,-(sp)                interleave
        move.w  #0,-(sp)                side 0
        move.w  #79,-(sp)               track 79
        move.w  #9,-(sp)                9 sector per track
        move.w  #0,-(sp)                drive A
        clr.l   -(sp)
        move.w  #buffer,-(sp)
        move.w  #10,-(sp)               flopfmt
        trap    #14
        add.l   #26,sp
        tst     d0
        bmi     error

buffer  ds.b    $2000                   8K buffer
```

11 Unused

12 Midiws   *write string to MIDI interface*

```
C: void Midiws(count, ptr)
   int   count;
   long  ptr;
```

Assembler:

```
move.l ptr,-(sp)
move.w count,-(sp)
move.w #12,-(sp)
trap   #14
addq.l #8,sp
```

With this function it is possible to output a string to the MIDI interface (MIDI OUT). The parameter `ptr` must point to a string, count must contain the number of characters to be sent minus 1.

Example:

```
move.l #string,-(sp)              Address of the string
move.w #stringend-string-1,-(sp)  Length
move.w #12,-(sp)                  midiws
trap   #14
addq.l #8,sp

    ....

string    dc.b 'MIDI data"
stringend equ  *
```

13 Mfpint
initialize MFP format

C: `void Mfpint(number, vector)`
    `int   number;`
    `long  vector;`

Assembler:

```
move.l vector,-(sp)
move.w number,-(sp)
move.w #13,-(sp)
trap   #14
addq.l #8,sp
```

This function initializes an interrupt routine in the MFP. The number of the MFP interrupt is in `number` while `vector` contains the address of the corresponding interrupt routine. The old interrupt vector is overwritten.

Example:

```
move.l #busy,-(sp)      Busy interrupt routine
move.w #0,-(sp)         Vector number 0
move.w #13,-(sp)        mfpint
trap   #14
addq.l #8,sp
....
busy:
```

14 Iorec *return record buffer*

C: `long Iorec(dev)`
   `int dev;`

Assembler:

```
move.w  dev,-(sp)
move.w  #14,-(sp)
trap    #14
addq.l  #4,sp
```

This function fetches a pointer to a buffer data record for an input device. The following input devices can be specified:

```
dev     Input device
0       RS-232
1       Keyboard
2       MIDI
```

The buffer record for an input device has the following layout:

```
long  ibuf      Pointer to an input buffer
int   ibufsize  Size of the input buffer
int   ibufhd    Head index
int   ibuftl    Tail index
int   ibuflow   Low water mark
int   ibufhi    High water mark
```

The input buffer is a circular buffer; the `head index` specifies the next write position (the buffer is filled by an interrupt routine) and the `tail index` specifies from where the buffer can be read. If the head and tail indices are the same, the buffer is empty. The low and high marks are used in connection with the communications status for the RS-232 (XON/XOFF or RTS/CTS). If the input buffer is filled up to the `high water mark`, the sender is informed via XON or CTS that the computer cannot receive any more data. When data received by the computer can be processed again, so that the buffer contents sink below the `low water mark`, the transfer is resumed.

There is an identically-constructed buffer record for the RS-232 output which is located directly behind the input record.

The following table contains the data for all devices:

	RS-232 input	RS-232 output	Keyboard	MIDI
Address	$9D0	($9DE)	$942	$A00
Buffer address	$6D0	$7D0	$8D0	$950
Buffer length	$100	$100	$80	$80
Head index	0	0	0	0
Tail index	0	0	0	0
Low water mark	$40	$40	$20	$20
High water mark	$C0	$C0	$20	$20

Head and tail indices are naturally dependent on the current operating mode. High and low water marks are set at 3/4 and 1/4 of the buffer size. They have significance only for XON/XOFF or RTS/CTS in connection with RS-232.

Example:

```
    move.w  #1,-(sp)        Buffer record for keyboard
    move.w  #14,-(sp)       iorec
    trap    #14
    addq.l  #4,sp
    ...
```

Result: $9F2

15 Rsconf   *set RS-232 configuration*

C: `void Rsconf(baud, ctrl, ucr, rsr, tsr, scr)`
   `int baud, ctrl, ucr, rsr, tsr, scr;`

Assembler:

```
move.w scr,-(sp)
move.w tsr,-(sp)
move.w rsr,-(sp)
move.w ucr,-(sp)
move.w ctrl,-(sp)
move.w baud,-(sp)
move.w #15,-(sp)
trap   #14
add.l  #14,sp
```

This XBIOS function serves to configure the RS-232 interface. The parameters have the following significance:

```
scr:  Synchronous Character Register in the MFP
tsr:  Transmitter Status Register in the MFP
rsr:  Receiver Status Register in the MFP
ucr:  USART Control Register in the MFP
ctrl: Communications parameters
baud: Baud rate
```

See the section on the MFP 68901 for information on the MFP registers. If one of the parameters is -1, the previous value is retained. The handshake mode can be selected with the `ctrl` parameter:

```
ctrl  Meaning
  0   No handshake, default after power-up
  1   XON/XOFF
  2   RTS/CTS
  3   XON/XOFF and RTS/CTS (not useful)
```

The `baud` parameter contains an indicator for the baud rate:

```
baud  baud rate
  0     19200
  1      9600
  2      4800
```

baud	baud rate
3	3600
4	2400
5	2000
6	1800
7	1200
8	600
9	300
10	200
11	150
12	134
13	110
14	75
15	50

Example:

```
move.w  #-1,-(sp)
move.w  #-1,-(sp)      Don't change MFP registers
move.w  #-1,-(sp)
move.w  #-1,-(sp)
move.w  #1,-(sp)       XON/XOFF
move.w  #9,-(sp)       300 baud
move.w  #15,-(sp)      rsconf
trap    #14
add.l   #14,sp
```

16 Keytbl   *set keyboard table*

```
C: long Keytbl(unshift, shift, capslock)
   long unshift, shift, capslock;
```

Assembler:

```
    move.l  capslock,-(sp)
    move.l  shift,-(sp)
    move.l  unshift,-(sp)
    move.w  #16,-(sp)
    trap    #14
    add.l   #14,sp
```

With this function it is possible to create a new keyboard layout. To do this you must pass the address of the new tables which contain the key codes for normal keys (without shift), shifted keys, and keys with caps lock. The function returns the address of the vector table in which the three keyboard table pointers are located. If a table should remain unchanged, -1 must be passed as the address. A keyboard table must be 128 bytes long. It is addressed via the key scan code and returns the ASCII code of the given key.

Example:

```
    move.l  #-1,-(sp)         Don't change caps lock
    move.l  #shift,-(sp)      Shift table
    move.l  #unshift,-(sp)    Table without shift
    move.w  #16,-(sp)
    trap    #14
    addq.l  #14,sp

      ....
shift:    ...
unshift:  ...
```

17 Random *return random number*

C: `long Random()`

Assembler:

```
move.w  #17,-(sp)
trap    #14
addq.l  #2,sp
```

This function returns a 24-bit random number. Bits 24-31 are zero. With each call you receive a different result. After turning on the computer a different seed is created.

Example:

```
move.w  #17,-(sp)      random
trap    #14
addq.l  #2,sp
```

---

18 Protobt *produce boot sector*

C: `void Protobt(buffer, serialno,disktype, execflag)`
   `long buffer, serialno;`
   `int  disktype, execflag;`

Assembler:

```
move.w  execflag,-(sp)
move.w  disktype,-(sp)
move.l  serialno,-(sp)
move.l  buffer,-(sp)
move.w  #18,-(sp)
trap    #14
add.l   #14,sp
```

This function serves to create a boot sector. A boot sector is located on track 0, sector 1 on side 0 of a diskette and gives the DOS information about the disk type. If the boot sector is executable, it can be used to load the operating system. With this function you can create a new boot sector, for a different disk format or to change an existing boot sector.

The parameters:

`execflag`: determines if the boot sector is executable.

```
 0 not executable
 1 executable
-1 boot sector remains as it was
```

The disk type can assume the following values:

```
 0 40 track, single sided (180 K)
 1 40 track, double sided (360 K)
 2 80 track, single sided (360 K)
 3 80 track, double sided (720 K)
-1 Disk type remains unchanged
```

The parameter `serialno` is a 24-bit serial number which is written in the boot sector. If the serial number is greater than 24 bits ($01000000), a random serial number is created (with the above function). A value of -1 means that the serial number will not be changed.

The parameter `buffer` is the address of a 512-byte buffer which contains the boot sector or in which the boot sector will be created.

A boot sector has the following construction:

Address		40 track SS	40 track DS	80 track SS	80 track DS
0- 1	Branch instruction to boot program if executable				
2- 7	'Loader'				
8-10	24-bit serial number				
11-12	BPS	512	512	512	512
13	SPC	1	2	2	2
14-15	RES	1	1	1	1
16	FAT	2	2	2	2
17-18	DIR	64	112	112	112
19-20	SEC	360	720	720	1440
21	MEDIA	252	253	248	249
22-23	SPF	2	2	5	5
24-25	SPT	9	9	9	9
26-27	SIDE	1	2	1	2
28-29	HID	0	0	0	0
510-511	CHECKSUM				

BPS: Bytes per sector. The sector size is 512 bytes for all formats

SPC: Sectors per cluster. The number of sectors which are combined into one block by the DOS, 2 sectors equals 1K

RES: Number of reserved disk sectors, including the boot sector.

FAT: The number of file allocation tables on the disk.

DIR: The maximum number of directory entries.

SEC: The total number of sectors on the disk.

MEDIA: Media descriptor byte, not used by the ST-BIOS.

SPF: Number of sectors in each FAT.

SPT: Number of sectors per track.

SIDE: Number of sides of the diskette.

HID: Number of hidden sectors on the disk.

The boot sector is compatible with MS-DOS 2.x. This is why all 16-bit words are stored in 8086 format (first low byte, then high byte). If the checksum of the whole boot sector is $1234, the sector is executable. In this case the boot program is located at address 30.

This program adapts an existing boot sector for 80 tracks, double sided.

Example:

```
    move.w  #-1,-(sp)       Don't change executability
    move.w  #3,-(sp)        80 tracks DS
    move.l  #-1,-(sp)       Don't change serial number
    move.l  #buffer,-(sp)
    move.w  #18,-(sp)       protobt
    trap    #14
    add.l   #14,sp

buffer ds.b 512
```

19 Flopver *verify diskette sector*

```
C:  int Flopver(buffer,filler,dev,sector,track,side,count)
    long buffer, filler;
    int  dev, sector, track, side, count;
```

Assembler:

```
move.w count,-(sp)
move.w side,-(sp)
move.w track,-(sp)
move.w sector,-(sp)
move.w dev,-(sp)
clr.l  -(sp)
move.l buffer,-(sp)
move.w #19,-(sp)
trap   #14
add.l  #16,sp
```

This function verifies one or more sectors on the disk. The sectors are read from the disk and compared with the buffer contents in memory. The parameters are the same as for reading and writing sectors. If the sector and buffer contents agree, the result will be zero. If an error occurs, an error number will be returned in D0 (see **Read sector** for error codes). On an error, the buffer will contain a list of bad sectors (16-bit values) terminated by a zero word. If **Rwabs** was used to write the sectors and if *fverify* ($444) is set, the sectors will automatically be verified after they are written.

Example:

```
move.w #1,-(sp)          A sector
move.w #0,-(sp)          Side zero
move.w #39,-(sp)         Track 39
move.w #1,-(sp)          Sector 1
move.w #0,-(sp)          Drive A
clr.l  -(sp)
move.l #buffer,-(sp)     Buffer address
move.w #19,-(sp)         flopver
trap   #14
add.l  #16,sp
tst    d0                Error?
bmi    error
```

20 Scrdmp   *output screen dump*

C: void Scrdmp()

Assembler:

```
move.w  #20,-(sp)
trap    #14
addq.l  #2,sp
```

This function sends a hardcopy of the screen to a connected printer. The previously-set printer parameters ("desktop Printer setup") are used. You can also perform this function by simultaneously pressing the ALT and HELP keys or from the desktop through "Print Screen" from the "Options" menu.

Example:

```
move.w  #20,-(sp)       Hardcopy
trap    #14             Call XBIOS
addq.l  #2,sp
```

---

21 Cursconf   *set cursor configuration*

C: int Cursconf(function, rate)
   int function, rate;

Assembler:

```
move.w  rate,-(sp)
move.w  function,-(sp)
move.w  #21,-(sp)
trap    #14
addq.l  #6,sp
```

This XBIOS function serves to set the cursor function. The parameter `function` can have a value from 0-5, which have the following meanings:

```
function   meaning
    0      Disable cursor
    1      Enable cursor
```

```
function   meaning
   2       Flashing cursor
   3       Steady cursor
   4       Set cursor flash rate
   5       Get cursor flash rate
```

You can use this function to set whether the cursor is visible, and whether it is flashing or steady. The XBIOS function returns a result only if you fetch the old baud rate. The unit of the flash frequency is dependent on the screen frequency: It is 70 Hz for a monochrome monitor or 50 Hz for a color monitor. You can set a new flash rate with function number 5. You need only use the parameter rate if you want to pass a new flash rate.

Example:

```
move.w  #20,-(sp)        20/70 seconds
move.w  #4,-(sp)         Set flash rate
move.w  #21,-(sp)        cursconf
trap    #14
addq.l  #6,sp
```

22 Settime   *set clock time and date*

C: void Settime(time)
   long time;

Assembler:

```
move.l  time,-(sp)
move.w  #22,-(sp)
trap    #14
add.l   #6,sp
```

This function is used to set the clock time and date. The time is passed in the lower word of time and the date in the upper word. The time and date are coded as follows:

```
bits  0- 4   Seconds in two-second increments
bits  5-10   Minutes
bits 11-15   Hours
bits 16-20   Day 1-31
```

```
bits 21-24   Month 1-12
bits 25-31   Year 0-119(minus offset 1980)
```

Example:

```
move.l  #%10110011000001000000000000000,-(sp)
move.w  #22,-(sp)         settime
trap    #14
addq.l  #6,sp
```

This call sets the date to the 16th of September, 1985, and the clock time to 8 o'clock.

23 Gettime *return clock time and date*

C: `long Gettime()`

Assembler:

```
move.w  #23,-(sp)
trap    #14
addq.l  #2,sp
```

This function returns the current date and clock time in the following format:

```
bits  0- 4   Seconds in two-second increments
bits  5-10   Minutes
bits 11-15   Hours
bits 16-20   Day 1-31
bits 21-24   Month 1-12
bits 25-31   Year (minus offset 1980)
```

Example:

```
move.w  #23,-(sp)         gettime
trap    #14
addq.l  #2,sp
move.l  d0,time           Save time and date
```

24 Bioskeys   *restore keyboard table*

C: void Bioskeys()

Assembler:

```
move.w  #24,-(sp)
trap    #14
addq.l  #2,sp
```

If you have selected a new keyboard layout with the XBIOS function 16, *keytbl*, this function will restore the standard BIOS keyboard layout. You can call this function, for example, before exiting a program of your own which changed the keyboard layout.

Example:

```
move.w  #24,-(sp)        bioskeys
trap    #14
addq.l  #2,sp
```

25 Ikbdws   *intelligent keyboard send*

C: void Ikbdws(number, pointer)
    int   number;
    long pointer;

Assembler:

```
move.l  pointer,-(sp)
move.w  number,-(sp)
move.w  #25,-(sp)
trap    #14
addq.l  #8,sp
```

This XBIOS function serves to transmit commands to the keyboard processor (intelligent keyboard). The parameter `pointer` is the address of a string to be sent, `number` is the length of a string minus 1.

Example:

```
    move.l #string,-(sp)          Address of the string
    move.w #strend-string-1,-(sp) Length minus 1
    move.w #25,-(sp)              ikbdws
    trap   #14
    addq.l #8,sp
    ...
string     dc.b   $80,1
strend     equ    *
```

26 Jdisint *disable interrupts on MFP*

C: void Jdisint(number)
   int number;

Assembler:

```
    move.w number,-(sp)
    move.w #26,-(sp)
    trap   #14
    addq.l #4,sp
```

This function makes it possible to selectively disable interrupts on the MFP 68901. The parameter is the MFP interrupt number (0-15). The significance of the individual interrupts is described in the section on interrupts.

Example:

```
    move.w #10,-(sp)    Disable RS-232 transmitter interrupt
    move.w #26,-(sp)    Disable interrupt
    trap   #14
    addq.l #4,sp
```

27 Jenabint   *enable interrupts on MFP*

C: `void Jenabint(number)`
   `int number;`

Assembler:

```
move.w  number,-(sp)
move.w  #27,-(sp)
trap    #14
addq.l  #4,sp
```

This function can be used to re-enable an interrupt on the MFP. The parameter is again the number of the interrupt, 0-15.

Example:

```
move.w  #12,-(sp)       Enable RS-232 receiver interrupt
move.w  #27,-(sp)       Enable interrupt
trap    #14
addq.l  #4,sp
```

28 Giaccess   *access GI sound chip*

C: `char Giaccess(data, register)`
   `char data;`
   `int  register;`

Assembler:

```
move.w  #register,-(sp)
move.w  #data,-(sp)
move.w  #28,-(sp)
trap    #14
addq.l  #6,sp
```

This function allows access to the GI sound chip registers. `register` must contain the register number of the sound chip (0-15). The meaning of the individual registers is given in the hardware description of the sound chip.

Bit 7 of the register number determines whether the specified register will be written or read:

```
Bit 7  0: Read
       1: Write
```

When writing, an 8-bit value is passed in data; when reading, the function returns the contents of the corresponding register.

Example:

```
move.w  #$80+3,-(sp)      Write register 3
move.w  #$50,-(sp)        Value to write
move.w  #28,-(sp)
trap    #14
addq.l  #6,sp
```

29 Offgibit   *reset Port A GI sound chip*

C: void Offgibit(bitnumber)
    int bitnumber;

Assembler:

```
move.w  #bitnumber,-(sp)
move.w  #29,-(sp)
trap    #14
addq.l  #4,sp
```

A bit of port A of the sound chip can be selectively set with this function call. Port A is an 8-bit output port in which the individual bits have the following function:

```
Bit 0:  Select disk side 0/side 1
Bit 1:  Select drive A
Bit 2:  Select drive B
Bit 3:  RS-232 RTS (Request To Send)
Bit 4:  RS-232 DTR (Data Terminal Ready)
Bit 5:  Centronics strobe
Bit 6:  General Purpose Output
Bit 7:  unused
```

Example:

```
move.w  #4,-(sp)        DTR bit
move.w  #29,-(sp)       offgibit
trap    #14
addq.l  #4,sp
```

30 Ongibit *clear Port A of GI sound chip*

C: `void ongibit(bitnumber)`
   `int bitnumber;`

Assembler:

```
move.w  #bitnumber,-(sp)
move.w  #30,-(sp)
trap    #14
addq.l  #4,sp
```

This function is the counterpart of the previous function. With this it is possible to clear a bit of port A in the sound chip.

Example:

```
move.w  #4,-(sp)        DTR bit
move.w  #30,-(sp)       ongibit
trap    #14
addq.l  #4,sp
```

31 Xbtimer   *start MFP timer*

```
C:  void Xbtimer(timer, control, data, vector)
    int  timer, control, data;
    long vector;
```

Assembler:

```
move.l vector,-(sp)
move.w data,-(sp)
move.w control,-(sp)
move.w timer,-(sp)
move.w #31,-(sp)
trap   #14
add.l  #12,sp
```

This function allows you to start a timer in the MFP 68901 and assign an interrupt routine to it. `timer` is the number of the timer in the MFP:

    Timer A : 0 / Timer B : 1 / Timer C : 2 / Timer D : 3

The parameters `data` and `control` are the values placed in the control and data registers of the timer (see the hardware description of the MFP 68901).

The parameter `vector` is the address of the interrupt routine which will be executed when the timer runs out. The four timers in the MFP are already partly used by the operating system:

```
Timer A: Reserved for the end user
Timer B: Horizontal blank counter
Timer C: 200 Hz system timer
Timer D: RS-232 baud rate generator (interrupt vector free)
```

Example:

```
move.l #vector,-(sp)     Interrupt routine
move.w data,-(sp)        Data and
move.w control,-(sp)     Control registers
move.w #0,-(sp)          Timer A
move.w #31,-(sp)         xbtimer
trap   #14
add.l  #12,sp
```

32 Dosound   *set sound parameters*

C: `void Dosound(pointer)`
   `long pointer;`

Assembler:

```
move.l  pointer,-(sp)
move.w  #32,-(sp)
trap    #14
addq.l  #6,sp
```

This function allows for easy sound processing. The parameter `pointer` must point to a string of sound commands. The following commands can be used:

Commands $00-$0F
> These commands are interpreted as register numbers of the sound chip. A byte following this is loaded into the corresponding register.

Command $80
> An argument follows this command which will be loaded into a temporary register.

Command $81
> Three arguments must follow this command. The first argument is the number of the sound chip register in which the contents of the temporary register will be loaded. The second argument is a two's-complement value which will be added to the temporary register. The third argument contains an end criterion. The end is reached when the content of the temporary register is equal to the end criterion.

Commands $82-$FF
> One argument follows each of these commands. If this argument is zero, the sound processing is halted. Otherwise this argument specifies the number of timer ticks (20ms, 50Hz) until the next sound processing.

Example:

```
move.l  #pointer,-(sp)     Pointer to sound command
move.w  #32,-(sp)          dosound
```

```
trap    #14
addq.l  #6,sp
....
pointer dc.b 0,10,1,50,...
```

33 Setprt   *set printer configuration*

C: void Setprt(config)
   int config;

Assembler:

```
move.w config,-(sp)
move.w #33,-(sp)
trap   #14
addq.l #4,sp
```

This function allows the printer configuration to be read or changed. If `config` contains the value -1, the current value is returned, otherwise the value is accepted as the new printer configuration. The printer configuration is a bit vector with the following meaning:

Bit number	0	1
0	matrix printer	daisy-wheel
1	monochrome printer	color printer
2	Atari printer	Epson printer
3	Test mode	Quality mode
4	Centronics port	RS-232 port
5	Continuous paper	Single-sheet
6-14	reserved	
15	always 0	

Example:

```
move.w #%000100,-(sp)    Epson printer
move.w #33,-(sp)         setprt
trap   #14
addq.l #4,sp
```

34 Kbdvbase   *return keyboard vector table*

C: `long Kbdvbase()`

Assembler:

```
move.w  #34,-(sp)
trap    #14
addq.l  #2,sp
```

This XBIOS function returns a pointer to a vector table which contains the address of routines which process the data from the keyboard processor. The table is constructed as follows:

```
long    midivec     MIDI input
long    vkbderr     Keyboard error
long    vmiderr     MIDI error
long    statvec     IKBD status
long    mousevec    Mouse routines
long    clockvec    Clock time routine
long    joyvec      Joystick routines
long    midisys     MIDI system vector
long    ikbdsys     IKBD system vector
```

The parameter `midivec` points to a routine which writes data received from the MIDI input (byte in D0) to the MIDI buffer.

The parameters `vkbderr` and `vmiderr` are called when an overflow is signaled by the keyboard or MIDI ACIA.

The routines `statvec`, `mousevec`, `clockvec`, and `joyvec` process the data packages which come from the keyboard ACIA. A pointer to the packages received is passed to these routines in D0. The mouse vector is used by GEM. If you want to use your own routine, you must terminate it with RTS and processing time may take no longer than one millisecond.

The remaining routines `midisys` and `ikbdsys` are called when there is a character in the present ACIA. `midisys` holds the character and jumps to `midivec`; `ikbdsys` gets the data package from the ACIA, and branches to the abovementioned routines.

Example:

```
move.w  #34,-(sp)      kbdvbase
trap    #14
addq.l  #2,sp
```

We get $DCC as the result. The vector field contains the following values:

midivec	$FC2CE2/$8B70	
vkbderr	$FC288E/$871C	(RTS)
vmiderr	$FC288E/$871C	(RTS)
statvec	$FC230A/$8198	(RTS)
mousevec	$FD02C2/$16150	
clockvec	$FC1D12/$7BA0	
joyvec	$FC230A/$8198	(RTS)
midisys	$FC284A/$86D8	
ikbdsys	$FC285A/$86E8	

35 Kbrate   *set keyboard repeat rate*

```
C: int Kbrate(delay, repeat)
   int delay, repeat;
```

Assembler:

```
move.w  repeat,-(sp)
move.w  delay,-(sp)
move.w  #35,-(sp)
trap    #14
addq.l  #6,sp
```

The keyboard repeat can be controlled with this function. The parameter `delay` specifies the delay time after a key is pressed before the key will automatically be repeated. The parameter `repeat` determines the time span after which the key will be repeated again. These values can be changed from the desktop by means of the two slide controllers on the control panel. The times are based on the 50 Hz system clock. If -1 is specified for one of the parameters, the corresponding value is not set. The function returns the previous values as the result; bits 0-7 contain the `repeat` value and bits 8-15 the value of `delay`.

Example:

```
move.w  #-1,-(sp)      Read old values
move.w  #-1,-(sp)
move.w  #35,-(sp)      kbrate
trap    #14
addq.l  #6,sp
```

Result: D0 = $0B03

36 Prtblk   *output block to printer*

C: `void Prtblk(parameter)`
   `long parameter;`

Assembler:

```
move.l parameter,-(sp)
move.w #36,-(sp)
trap   #14
addq.l #6,sp
```

This function resembles and is used by the function **Scrdmp** (20). The function expects a parameter list, however, whose address is passed to it. This list is constructed as follows:

```
long    blkprt     Address of the screen RAM
int     offset
int     width      Screen width
int     height     Screen height
int     left
int     right
int     scrres     Screen resolution (0, 1, or 2)
int     dstres     Printer resolution (0 or 1)
long    colpal     Address of the color palette
int     type       Printer type (0-3)
int     port       Printer port (0=Centronics, 1=RS-232)
long    masks      Pointer to half-tone mask
```

Example:

```
    move.l #parameter,-(sp)    Address of the parameter block
    move.w #36,-(sp)           prtblk
    trap   #14
    addq.l #6,sp
    ...
parameter dc.l ...
```

37 Vsync   *wait for video*

`C: void Vsync()`

Assembler:

```
    move.w #37,-(sp)
    trap   #14
    addq.l #2,sp
```

This function waits for the next picture return. It can be used to synchronize graphic outputs with the beam return, for example.

Example:

```
    move.w #37,-(sp)    wait for vsync
    trap   #14
    addq.l #2,sp
```

38 Supexec   *set supervisor execution*

C: `void Supexec(address)`
   `long address;`

Assembler:

```
move.l address,-(sp)
move.w #38,-(sp)
trap   #14
addq.l #6,sp
```

A routine can be executed in supervisor mode with **Supexec**.

Example:

```
move.l #address,-(sp)
move.w #38,-(sp)
trap   #14
addq.l #6,sp
...
address    move.l $400,00
```

39 Puntaes   *disable AES*

C: `void Puntaes()`

Assembler:

```
move.w #39,-(sp)
trap   #14
addq.l #2,sp
```

The AES can be disabled with this function, provided it is not in ROM.

Example:

```
move.w #39,-(sp)
trap   #14
addq.l #2,sp
```

Abacus Software   **Atari ST Internals**

64 Blitmode   *read and alter blitter*

```
C:  int Blitmode(flag)
    int flag;
```

Assembler:

```
move.w   flag,-(sp)
move.w   #64,-(sp)
trap     #14
addq.l   #4,sp
```

This function lets you read and change an available blitter's configuration. **Blitmode** also lets you determine whether a blitter exists in the system (bit 1) and whether it is usable (bit 0). The ST reads the current configuration when `flag` has a value of -1 (0xffff). The result is a bitmask. Each bit represents the following:

Bit number	0	1
0	Blit-operation through software	Blit_operation through hardware
1	No blitter available	Blitter available
2-14	Undefined, reserved	
15	Always 0	

When a blitter is available, you can determine whether blit operations can be performed by software or by the blitter. This is established by clearing or setting bit 0.

Bit number	0	1
0	Blit-operation through software	Blit_operation through hardware
1-14	Undefined, reserved	
15	Always 0	

Example:

```
move     #-1,(sp)      set configuration
move     #64,-(sp)     blitmode
trap     #14
addq.l   #4,sp
btst     #1,d0         is blitter on hand?
beq      no_blit       no
```

```
bset    #0,d0
move    d0,-(sp)      blit operation through hardware
move    #64,-(sp)     blit-mode
trap    #14
addq.l  #4, sp
no_blit:
rts
```

The above sample program tests for an onboard blitter. If this is the case, the system bit 0 displays blit operations through hardware (the blitter). The test, once set to hardware, won't ignore onboard blitters in the system.

By setting the blit mode, this should call the configuration, and the bits 1-14 should be taken over. They are reserved for further graphic functions or graphic chips.

3.4 The Graphics

Next to the high processing speed and the large memory available, the graphics capability is certainly the most fascinating aspect of the ST. With the standard monochrome monitor and the resolution of 640x400 points, it creates a whole new price/performance class for itself. But also in the color resolution the ST can display 16 colors with 320x200 screen points.

In this chapter we want to explain how the graphics are organized and how you can create fast and effective graphics without using the GEM graphics package, which is rather complicated for beginners. The ST offers the assembler and C programmer very useful routines which don't exactly make graphics programming child's play, but which can take away a good deal of the programming work. Unfortunately, some of these functions are so comprehensive that a detailed description would exceed the scope of this book. We have therefore had to limit ourselves to the simpler, but no less interesting functions.

These graphics routines are called in a very elegant manner. The software developers have made use of the fact that there are two groups of opcodes in the 68000 which the 68000 does not "understand" and which generate a trap, or software interrupt, when they are encountered in a program. These are the two groups of opcodes which begin with $Axxx and $Fxxx. In the ST, the $Axxx opcode trap is used in order to access the graphics routines. The trap handler, the program called by the trap, checks the lowest byte of the "command" to see what value it has. Values between zero and $F are permissible here. This gives a total of 16 graphics routines, which should first be presented in an overview. Later we will talk about the actual commands in detail.

```
$A000   Determine address of required variable range
$A001   Set point on the screen
$A002   Determine color of a screen point
$A003   Draw a line on the screen
$A004   Draw a horizontal line (very fast!)
$A005   Fill rectangle with color
$A006   Fill polygon line by line
$A007   Bit block transfer
$A008   Text block transfer
$A009   Enable mouse cursor
$A00A   Disable mouse cursor
```

```
$A00B  Change mouse cursor form
$A00C  Clear sprite
$A00D  Enable sprite
$A00E  Copy raster form
$A00F  Contour fill (Flood fill)
```

These routines are the ground work for the hardware-dependent part of GEM. All GEM graphic and text output is performed by the routines of the $Axxx opcodes. The set of A-opcodes are very useful in games. In games windows are needed only in the rarest cases. Another important point is the speed of the line A-instructions. Using the graphic routines directly is clearly faster than if the output is handled by GEM. Before we describe the individual commands in detail, we will take a brief look at the construction of graphics in the various graphic modes of the ST.

Immediately after turning the ST on, an area of 32K bytes is initialized at the upper memory border as the video RAM. In normal operation this results in addresses $78000 to $7FFFF or $F8000 to $FFFFF acting as the screen RAM. This video RAM can be viewed as a window in the ST. The following description is a simplification of the features of the 260ST with "only" 512K.

We will start with the simplest mode, the 640x400 mode. In this case each set of 80 bytes, or better, each set of 40 words forms one screen line. The word with the lowest address is displayed on the left edge of the screen, the additional words are displayed in order from left to right. Within a word, the highest-order bit lies at the left and the lowest-order bit at the right.

With this data, any point on the screen can be easily controlled or read. For example, to set the first screen point, the value $8000 must be written into memory location $78000. There is one small limitation to this area. The position of ST screen RAM can be easily moved. For this reason, it is usually more advantageous to set the point with the "A" function $A001. Function $A001 assumes an X-Y coordinate system with origin in the upper left-hand corner, and determines the position of the video RAM itself in order to set the point at the proper screen location.

In this resolution mode, each screen point is represented by a bit. If the bit is set, the point appears dark, or bright if the inverse display mode is selected in color palette register 0. The screen consists of only one bit plane. Different colors cannot be represented with just one plane, however. This is why when the resolution increases in the color modes, the number of displayable colors decreases.

Figure 3.4-1 LO-RES-MODE (0)

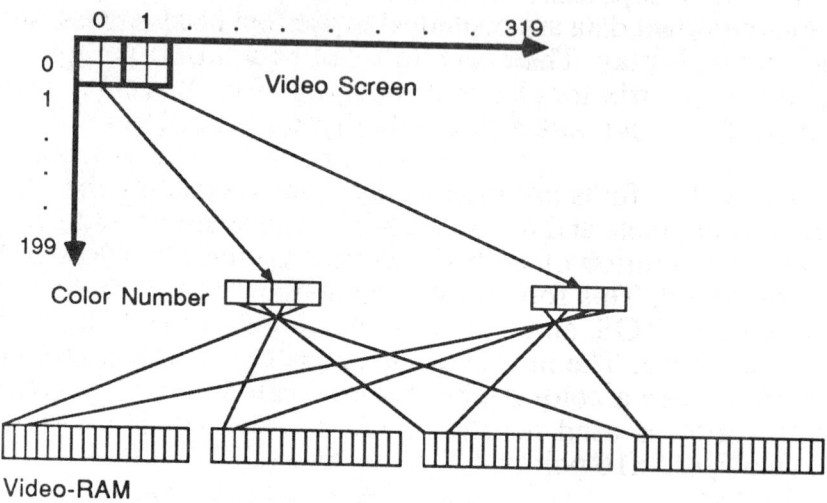

Four colors are possible in the 640x200 resolution mode. In this mode, two contiguous memory words form a single logical entity. The color of a point is determined by the value of the two corresponding bits in the two words. If both bits are zero, the background color results. Therefore two sequential words are used together for pixel representation. For the colors, however, all odd words belong to a plane. The second plane is made up of the even words. In this mode, there are two planes available.

Things become quite colorful in the mode with "only" 320x200 points. In this operating mode, 4 contiguous memory words form one entity which determines the color of the 16 pixels. To stick to the example we used before: in order to set the point in the upper left-hand corner, the topmost bits of words $78000, $78002, $78004, and $78006 must be manipulated. The desired color results from the bit pattern in the words.

It naturally requires some computer time to set a point in the desired color, independent of the mode. All of this work is handled by the $A001 routine, however. This routine sets all of the pertaining bits for the desired color in the current resolution. Naturally, all four planes are present in this mode. The first plane, keeping to our example, made up of the words at address $7F000, $7F008, $7F010, ..., and the other planes are composed of the other addresses correspondingly.

Another point to be clarified concerns the fonts or character sets. Since the ST does not have a text mode, only a graphics mode, the text output is created in high-resolution graphics. There are three different fonts built into the ST. You can load additional fonts from disk. Each font has a header which contains important information about the displayable characters. Since the important data are contained in the font header, there are unusually few limits for display. The characters can be arbitrarily high or wide. The age of the 8x8 matrix for character output is over. It is even possible to get cursive, bold, true proportional or other type on the screen.

The three built-in fonts are monospaced fonts, meaning they have a fixed defined size in pixels and a defined pitch. The smallest font has a matrix of 6x6. With a resolution of 640x400 points, 66 lines of 106 characters each can be displayed. This font is only accessible for output under GEM, not for output under TOS, and is used in the output of the directory in the icon form, for example. The next-largest type is composed of 8x8 points. This type is used when a color monitor is connected to the ST, while the third and largest font is used for the normal black-and-white mode. This font uses a matrix of 8x16 points.

Figure 3.4-2 MEDIUM-RES-MODE (1)

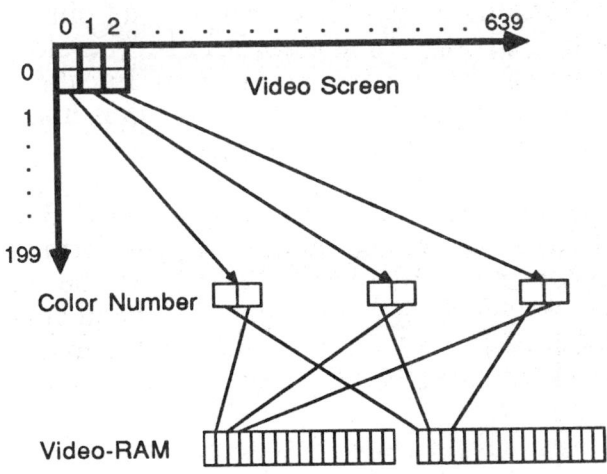

The exact layout of the font header is found under command $A008, which represents a very versatile text output which goes far beyond what is possible with the routine of the BIOS and GEMDOS.

Finally, we must clarify some of the terms which will come up often in the following descriptions, whose meanings may not be so clear. These are the terms Contrl array, Intin array, Intout array, Ptsin array and Ptsout array.

These arrays are mainly used by GEM to pass parameters to individual GEM functions or to store results from these functions. But line-A functions use parts of these arrays to pass parameters also. The arrays are defined in memory as data areas, whereby each element in the array consists of 2 bytes.

For GEM functions, the Contrl array always contains the number desired in the first element (Contrl(0)). This parameter is not used by the line-A commands, however. Contrl(1) contains the number of XY coordinates required for the function. These coordinates must be placed in the Ptsin array before the call. The element Contrl(2) is not supplied before the call. After the call it contains the number of XY coordinates in the Ptsout array. Contrl(3) specifies how many parameters will be passed to the function in the Intin array, while Contrl(4) contains the number of parameters in the Intout array after the call. The additional parameters of the Contrl array are not relevant for users of the line A.

Unfortunately, not all of the A opcode parameters can be in these arrays. For this reason there is another memory area which used as a variable area for (almost) all graphic outputs. The functions and uses of these over 50 variables are in a table at the end of this chapter. Important variables are also explained in conjunction with the functions requiring them.

By the way, you should be aware that registers D0 to D2 and A0 to A2 are changed by calling the functions. Important values contained in these registers should be saved before a call.

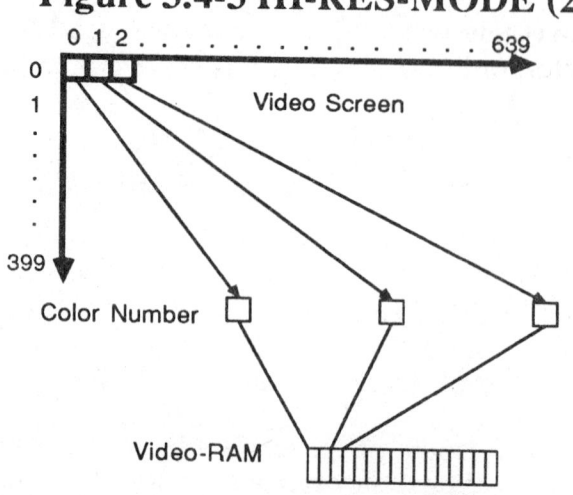

Figure 3.4-3 HI-RES-MODE (2)

$A000 Initialize

Initialize is really the wrong expression for this function. After the call, the addresses of the more important data areas are returned in registers D0 and A0 to A2. This function does not require input parameters.

The program is informed of the starting address of the line-A variables in D0 and A0. After the call, A1 points to a table with three addresses. These three addresses are the starting address of the three system font headers. Register A2 points to a table with the starting addresses of the 16 line-A routines.

This opcode destroys (at least) the contents of registers D0 to D2 and A0 to A2. Important values should be saved before the call.

$A001 PUT PIXEL

This opcode sets a point at the coordinates specified by the coordinates in `Ptsin(0)` and `Ptsin(1)`. The color is passed in `Intin(0)`. `Ptsin(0)` contains X-coordinate, `Ptsin(1)` the Y-coordinate.

The coordinate system used has its origin in the upper left corner. The possible range of the X and Y coordinates is naturally set according to the graphic mode enabled. Overflows in the X range are not handled as errors. Instead, the Y coordinate is simply incremented by the appropriate amount. No output is made if the Y range is exceeded.

The color in `Intin(0)` is dependent on the mode used. When driving the monochrome monitor, only bit zero of the value of `Intin(0)` is evaluated.

$A002 GET PIXEL

The color of a pixel can be determined with this opcode. As with $A001, the XY coordinates are passed in `Ptsin(0)` and `Ptsin(1)`; the color value is returned in the D0 register.

$A003 LINE

With the LINE opcode a line can be drawn between the points with coordinates x1,y1 and x2,y2. The parameters for this function are not passed via the parameter arrays, but must be transferred to the line-A variables before the call. The variables used are:

```
_X1       = x1 coordinate
_Y1       = y1 coordinate
_X2       = x2 coordinate
_Y2       = y1 coordinate
_FG_BP_1  = Plane 1 (all three modes)
_FG_BP_2  = Plane 2 (640x200, 320x200)
_FG_BP_3  = Plane 3 (only 320x200)
_FG_BP_4  = Plane 4 (only 320x200)
_LN_MASK  = Bit pattern of the line
            For example: $FFFF = filled
                         $CCCC = broken
_WRT_MOD  = Determines the write mode
_LSTLIN   = This variable should be set to -1 ($FFFF)
```

One point to be noted for some applications is the fact that when drawing a line, the highest bit of the line bit pattern is always set on the left screen edge. The line is always drawn from left to right and from top to bottom, not from x1,y1 to x2,y2.

Range overflows are handled as for PUT PIXEL. If an attempt is made to draw a line from 0,0 to 650,50, a line is actually drawn from, 0,0 to 639,48. The "remainder" results in an additional line from 0,49 to 10,50.

A total of four different write modes, with values 0 to 3, are available for drawing lines. With write mode zero, the original bit pattern "under" the line is erased and the bit pattern determined by _LN_MASK is put in its place (replace mode). In the transparent mode (_WRT_MOD=1), the background, the old bit pattern, is ORed with the new line pattern so only additional points are set. In the XOR mode (_WRT_MOD=2), the background and the line pattern are exclusive-ored. The last mode (_WRT_MOD=3) is the so-called "inverse transparent mode." As in the transparent mode, it involves an OR combination of the foreground and background data, in which the foreground data, the bit pattern determined by _LN_MASK, are inverted before the OR operation.

$A004 HORIZONTAL LINE

This function draws a line from x1,y1 to x2,y1. Drawing a horizontal line is significantly faster than when a line must be drawn diagonally. Diagonal lines are also created with this function, in which the line is divided into multiple horizontal lines segments. The parameters are entered directly into the required variables.

```
_X1       = x1 coordinate
_Y1       = y1 coordinate
_X2       = x2 coordinate
_FG_BP_1  = Plane 1 (all three modes)
_FG_BP_2  = Plane 2 (640x200, 320x200)
_FG_BP_3  = Plane 3 (only 320x200)
_FG_BP_4  = Plane 4 (only 320x200)
_WRT_MOD  = Determines the write mode
_patptr   = Pointer to the line pattern to use
_patmsk   = "Mask" for the line pattern
```

The valid values in _WRT_MOD also lie between 0 and 3 for this call. The contents of the variable _patptr is the address at which the desired line pattern or fill pattern is located. The H-line function is very well-suited to creating filled surfaces. The variable _patmsk plays an important role in this. The number of 16-bit values at the address in _patptr is dependent on the its value. If, for example, _patmsk contains the value 5, six 16-bit values should be located at the address in _patptr as the line pattern. If a horizontal line with the Y-coordinate value zero is to be drawn, the first bit pattern is taken as the line pattern. The second word is taken as the pattern for a line drawn at Y-coordinate 1, and so on. The pattern for a line with Y-coordinate 6 is again determined by the first value in the bit table. In this manner, very complex fill patterns can be created with relatively little effort.

$A005 FILLED RECTANGLE

The opcode $A005 represents an extension, or more exactly a special use, of opcode $A004. It is used to created filled rectangles. The essential parameters are the coordinates of the upper left and lower right corners of the of the rectangle.

```
_X1       = x1 coordinate, left upper
_Y1       = y1 coordinate
_X2       = x2 coordinate, right lower
```

```
_Y2       = y2 coordinate
_FG_BP_1  = Plane 1 (all three modes)
_FG_BP_2  = Plane 2 (640x200, 320x200)
_FG_BP_3  = Plane 3 (only 320x200)
_FG_BP_3  = Plane 4 (only 320x200)
_WRT_MOD  = Determines the write mode
_patptr   = Pointer to the fill pattern used
_patmsk   = "Mask" for the fill pattern
_CLIP     = Clipping flag
_XMN_CLIP = X minimum for clipping
_XMX_CLIP = X maximum for clipping
_YMN_CLIP = Y minimum for clipping
_YMX_CLIP = Y maximum for clipping
```

We have already explained all of the variables except the "clipping" variables. What is clipping? Clipping creates extracts or clippings of the total picture. If the clipping flag is set to one (or any value not equal to zero), the rectangle, drawn by $A005, is displayed only in the area defined by the clipping-area variables. An example may explain this behavior better: The values 100,100 and 200,200 are specified as the coordinates. The clip flag is 1 and the clip variables contain the values 150,150 for XMN_CLIP and YMN_CLIP as well as 300,300 for XMX_CLIP and YMX_CLIP. The value $FFFF will be chosen as the fill value for all of the lines. With these values, the rectangle will have the coordinate 150,150 as the upper left corner and 200,200 as the lower right. The "missing" area is not drawn because of the clip specifications. Clearing the clip flag draws the rectangle in the originally desired size.

$A006 FILLED POLYGON

$A006 is also an extension of $A004. Areas can be filled with a pattern with this function. The entire surface is not filled with the call: just one raster line is filled, a horizontal line with a width of one point. The result is that there are significantly more options for influencing the fill pattern.

The necessary variables are:

```
Ptsin     = Array with the XY coordinates
Contrl(1) = Number of coordinate pairs
_Y1       = y1 coordinate
_FG_BP_1  = Plane 1 (all three modes)
_FG_BP_2  = Plane 2 (640x200, 320x200)
```

```
_FG_BP_3   = Plane 3 (only 320x200)
_FG_BP_3   = Plane 4 (only 320x200)
_WRT_MOD   = Determines the write mode
_patptr    = Pointer to the fill pattern used
_patmsk    = "Mask" for the fill pattern
_CLIP      = Clipping flag
_XMN_CLIP  = X minimum for clipping
_XMX_CLIP  = X maximum for clipping
_YMN_CLIP  = Y minimum for clipping
_YMX_CLIP  = Y maximum for clipping
```

Basically, all of the parameters here are to be set exactly as they might be for a call to $A005. Only the first three coordinates are different. The XY coordinates are stored in the Ptsin array. It is important you specify the start coordinate again as the last coordinate as well. In order to fill a triangle, you must, for example, enter the coordinates (320,100), (120,300), (520,300), and (320,100). The number of effective coordinate pairs, three in our example, must be placed in Contrl(1), the second element of the array. With a call to the $A006 function you must also specify the Y-coordinate of the line to be drawn. Naturally you can fill all Y-coordinates from 0 to 399 (0 to 199 in the color modes) in order. But it is faster to find the largest and smallest of the XY values and call the function with only these as the range.

$A007 BITBLT

The BITBLock Transfer function copies a square source range into a target area. The source range can combine with a raster. Source and target range can be combined with 16 different logical operations. You can have these at any address. Normally it is at least the target area of video RAM; but it can also be copied within the screen or from an unused part of memory to another. If a blitter is onboard the ST, BITBLT uses hardware.

BITBLT is used by the line-A functions TEXTBLT and COPY RASTER FORM, as well as the VDI functions Copy Raster Opaque (vro_cpyfm) and Copy Raster Transparent (vrt_cpyfm). BITBLT's versatility involves the parameters used with the function call. These parameters are source, destination and pattern; information about the number of bitplanes (color or b/w) used; and logical operations combining source and destination. The data stands in a 76-byte parameter block, whose function address must be given through register A6. The parameter block looks like this:

```
Offset Length Name
  0      W    s_width  Pixel width of range being edited
  2      W    2_height Pixel height of range being edited
  4      W    planes   Number of bit planes
  6      W    fg-col   Foreground color
  8      W    bg_col   Background color
 10      L    op_tab   Logical operation
 14      W    s_xmin   Source upper left X-coordinate
 16      W    s_ymin   Source upper left Y-coordinate
 18      L    s_form   Source starting address
 22      W    s_nxwd   Byte offset of next source line
 24      W    s_nxln   Byte offset of next source line
 26      W    s_nxpl   Byte offset of next source color plane
 28      W    d_xmin   Destination upper left X-coordinate
 30      W    d_ymin   Destination upper left Y-coordinate
 32      L    d_form   Start address through destination
 36      W    d_nxwd   Byte offset of next destination word
 38      W    d_nxln   Byte offset of next destination line
 40      W    d_nxpl   Next destination color plane
 42      L    p_addr   Start address of pattern
 46      W    p_nxln   Byte offset of next raster line
 48      W    p_nxpl   Byte offset of next color plane
 50      W    p_mask   Raster height (raster index mask)
 52     12W   filler   Used internally by BITBLT
```

When destination and/or source ranges appear on the screen, the following values are used:

```
Resolution          320*200         640*200             640*400
Bitplanes           4               2                   1
d_form/s_form                       screen address
d_nxwd/s_nxwd       8               4                   2
d_nxln/s_nxln       160             160                 80
d_nxpl/s_nxpl       2               2                   2
```

Here are the 16 logical operations used in combining source and desination:

```
Operation  Function
   0       D' = 0        Set destination to background color
   1       D' = S &D
   2       D'= S & ~D
   3       D' = S        Replace Mode
```

```
 4         D' = ~S & D      Erase Mode
 5         D' = D
 6         D' = S ^ D       XOR Mode
 7         D' = S | D
 8         D' = ~ (S | D)
 9         D' = ~ (S ^ D)
10         D' = ~D
11         D' = S | ~D
12         D' = ~S
13         D' = ~S | D
14         D' = ~(S & D)
15         D' = 1           Set destination to foreground color
```

S=Source; D=Destination range before operation; D'=Destination range after the operation; &=logical AND; |=logical OR; ^=XOR (exclusive OR); ~=inversion.

Four such logical operations are given for BITBLT, addressed in the equation op = 2 * fg + bg. op is the used logical operation (0-3, relative to op_tab). fg is the foreground color and bg is the background color.

$A008 TEXTBLT

A character from any desired text font can be printed at any graphic position with the TEXT BLock Transfer function. In addition, the form of the character can be changed. The character can be displayed in italics, boldface, outlines, enlarged, or rotated. These things cannot be achieved with the "normal" character outputs via the BIOS or GEMDOS. TXTBLT often stands as the basic structure of all text output under VDI (v_gtext,etc.).

For the correct use of this function, a large number of parameters must be set and controlled. A rather complicated program must be written in order to output text with this function. If the additional options are not absolutely necessary, it is advisable not to use this function. But decide for yourself.

Before we produce a character on the screen, we must first concern ourselves with the organization of the fonts. We must take an especially close look at the font header because the font is described in detail by the information contained in it.

A font basically consists of four sets of data: font header, font data, character offset table and horizontal offset table. The font header contains general data about the font, such as its name and size, the number of characters it contains, and various other aspects. This information takes up a total of 88 bytes. The font data contains the bit pattern of the existing displayable characters. These data are organized to save as much space as possible.

In order to be able to better describe the organization, we will imagine a font with only two characters, such as "A" and "B". These characters are to be displayed in a 9x9 matrix. The font data are now in memory so that the bit pattern of the top scan line of the "A" is stored starting at a word boundary.

Since our font is 9 pixels = 9 bits wide, one byte is completely used, but only the top bit of the following byte. 7 bits must be wasted if the top scan line of the "B" is also to begin on a word boundary. This is not so, however, and the first scan line of the "B" starts with bit 6 of the second byte of the font data. Only the data of the second and further scan lines always start on a word boundary. In this manner, almost no bits are wasted in the font. Only the start of the scan lines of the first character actually begin on a word boundary; all other scan lines can begin at any bit position.

Because of this space-saving storage, the position of each character within the font must be calculated. The calculation of the scan-line positions is possible through the character offset table. This table contains one entry for each displayable character. For our example, such a table would contain the entries $0000, $0009, $0012. Through the direction of this table, it is possible to create true proportional type on the screen since the width of each character can be calculated. One subtracts the entry of the character to be displayed from the entry of the next character. The last entry is present so that the width of the last character can also be determined, although it is not assigned to a character.

In addition to the character offset table there is the horizontal offset table. This table is not used by most of the fonts, however. The fonts present in the ST do not use all the possibilities of this table either. If this table were present, it would contain a positive or negative offset value for each character, in order to shift the character to the right or left during output.

At the end of the description of the font construction are the meanings of the variables in the font header.

Bytes 0- 1 : Font identifier. A number which describes the font.   1=system font
Bytes 2- 3 : Font size in points (point is a measure used in typesetting).
Bytes 4-35 : The name of the font as an ASCII string.
Bytes 36-37 : Lowest ASCII value of displayable characters.
Bytes 38-39 : Highest ASCII value of displayable characters.
Bytes 40-49 : Relative distances of top, ascent, half, descent, and bottom line from the base line.
Bytes 50-51 : Width of the broadest character in the font.
Bytes 52-53 : Width of the broadest character cell. The cell is always at least one pixel wider than the actual character so that two characters next to each other are separated from each other.
Bytes 54-55 : Linker offset.
Bytes 56-57 : Right offset. The two offset values are used for displaying the font in italics (skewing).
Bytes 58-59 : Thickening. If a character is to be displayed in boldface, this variable is used.
Bytes 60-61 : Underline. Contains line height in pixels.
Bytes 62-63 : Lightening mask. "Light" characters are found on the desktop when an option on a pull-down menu is unavailable. This light grey character consists of masking the bits with the lightening mask. Usually the value is $5555.
Bytes 64-65 : Skewing mask. As before, only for displaying characters in italics.
Bytes 66-67 : Flag. Bit 0 is set if a system font is used.
Bit 1 must be set if the horizontal offset table is present.
Bit 2 is the so-called byte-swap flag. If it is set, the bytes in memory are in 68000 format (low byte-high byte). A cleared swap flag signals that the data is in INTEL format, reversed in memory. With this bit the fonts from the IBM version of GEM can be used on the ST and vice versa.
Bit 3 is set if the width of all characters in the font is equal.
Bytes 68-71 : Pointer to the horizontal offset table or zero.
Bytes 72-75 : Pointer to the character offset table.

Bytes 76-79 : Pointer to the font data.
Bytes 80-81 : Form width. This variable contains the sum of widths of all the characters. The value represents the length of the scan lines of all of the characters and thereby the start of the next line.
Bytes 82-83 : Form height. This variable contains the number of scan lines for this font.
Bytes 84-87 : Contain a pointer to the next font.

After so much talk, we should now list the parameters which must be noted or prepared for the $A008 opcode.

```
_WRT_MODE     = Write mode
_TEXT_FG      = Text foreground color
_TEXT_BG      = Text background color
_FBASE        = Pointer to the start of the font data
_FWIDTH       = Width of the font
_SOURCEX      = X-coordinate of the char in the font
_SOURCEY      = Y-coordinate of the char in the font
_DESTX        = X-coordinate of the char on the screen
_DESTY        = Y-coordinate of the char on the screen
_DELX         = Width of the character in pixels
_DELY         = Height of the character in pixels
_STYLE        = Bit-wise coded flag for special effects
_LITEMASK     = Bit pattern used for "lightening"
_SKEWMASK     = Bit pattern used for skewing
_WEIGHT       = Factor for character enlargement
_R_OFF        = Right offset of the char for skewing
_L_OFF        = Left offset of the char for skewing
_SCALE        = Flag for scaling
_XACC_DDA     = Accumulator for scaling
_DDA_INC      = Scaling factor
_T_SCLSTS     = Scaling direction flag
_CHUP         = Character rotation vector
_MONO_STATUS  = Flag for monospaced type
_scrtchp      = Pointer to buffer for effects
_scrpt2       = Offset scaling buffer in _scrtchp
```

As you can see, an enormous number of variables are evaluated for the output of graphic text. Here we can go into only the essential (and those we explored) variables.

The write mode allows the output of characters in the four known modes, replace, OR, XOR, and inverse OR. The variable _TEXT_FG is in connection with first four write modes. They form the foreground color used for display. The background color _TEXT_BG plays a role only with the 16 additional modes. It is clear that the additional modes are relevant only in connection with a color screen.

The variables _FBASE and _FWIDTH are set according to the desired font. You can find the start of the font data from the header of the desired font (bytes 76-79 in the header). _FWIDTH must be loaded with the contents of the bytes 80 and 81 of the header.

The parameter _SOURCEX determines which character you output. It should contain the ASCII value of the desired character. The parameter _SOURCEY is usually zero because the character is to be generated from the top to the bottom scan line.

The parameter _DELX can be calculated as the width of the character in which the entry in the character offset table of the desired character is subtracted from the next entry. The result is the width of the character in pixels. _DELY must be loaded with the value of byte 82-83 of the header.

The _STYLE is something special. Here you can specify if characters should be displayed normally or changed. The possible changes are boldface (thicken, bit 0), shading (lighten, bit 1), italic (bit 2), and outline (bit 4). The given change is enabled by setting the corresponding bit. Another change is scaling. The size of a character can be changed through scaling. Unfortunately, characters can only be enlarged on the ST.

If the scaling flag is cleared (zero), the character is displayed in its original size. The _T_SCLSTS flag determines if the font is to be reduced or enlarged. A value other than zero must be placed here for enlarging. _DDA_INC should contain the value of the enlargement or reduction. An enlargement could be produced only with a value of $FFFF.

Another interesting variable is _CHUP. With the help of this variable, characters can be rotated on the screen. The angle must be given in the range 0 to 360 degrees in tenths of a degree. A restriction must also be made for this function. Usable results are obtainable only with rotations by 90 degrees. The values are $0000 for normal, $0384 for 90-degree rotation, $0708 (upside-down type), and $0A8C for 270 degrees.

To work with the effects, _scrchp must contain a pointer to a buffer in which TEXTBLT can store temporary values. The exact size of this buffer is not known, but we always found a buffer of 1K to be sufficient. Another buffer must be specified for enlargement (_scrpt2). An offset is passed as a parameter which refers to the start of the _scrtchp buffer. A value of $40 proved to be sufficient here.

$A009 SHOW MOUSE

Calling this opcode enables the display of the mouse cursor. The cursor follows the mouse when it is moved. If the mouse cursor is disabled, the mouse can be used in programs which abandon the user interface GEM. This option is particularly useful for games.

The parameters required are passed in the Intin and Contrl arrays. Contrl(1) should be cleared before the call and Contrl(3) set to one. Intin(0) has a special significance. The routine for managing the mouse cursor counts the number of calls to remove and enable the cursor. If the cursor is disabled twice, two calls must be made to re-enable it before it will actually appear on the screen. This behavior can be changed by clearing Intin(0). With this parameter the cursor is immediately set independent of the number of previous HIDE CURSOR calls. If the value in Intin(0) is not equal to zero the actually required number of $A009 calls must be made in order to make the cursor visible.

$A00A HIDE CURSOR

This functions hides the cursor. If this function is called repeatedly, the number is recorded by the operating system and determines the number of calls of SHOW CURSOR before the cursor actually appears.

$A00B TRANSFORM MOUSE

Is the arrow unsuited as a mouse cursor for games? Simply make your own cursor. How would it be if a little car moved across the screen instead of an arrow? The opcode $A00B gives your fantasy free reign, at least as far as it concerns the mouse cursor.

The parameters must be passed in the Intin array. A total of 34 words are necessary. The following table lists the uses and possible values:

```
Intin(3)  Mask color index, normally 0
Intin(4)  Data color index, normally 1
Intin(5) to Intin(20) contain 16 words of the cursor mask
Intin(21) to Intin (36) contain 16 words of cursor data
```

The form of the cursor is determined by the cursor data. Each 1 in the data creates a point on the screen. If a cursor is placed over a letter or pattern on the screen, the border between the cursor and the background cannot be determined. The mask enters at this point. Each set bit in the mask clears the background at the given location. This draws a light border around the cursor. Look at the normal cursor in order to see the operation of the mask.

$A00C UNDRAW SPRITE

This opcode is related to $A00D, DRAW SPRITE. The ST actually has no hardware sprites like the Commodore 64. ST sprites are organized purely in software. Each sprite is 16x16 pixels large. One example of an ST sprite is the mouse cursor. It is created with this function.

To clear a previously-drawn sprite, the address of a buffer in which the background was saved when the sprite was drawn is passed in register A2. The opcode simply transfers the contents of the background buffer to the right spot on the screen. The buffer itself must be 64 bytes large for each plane. Another 10 bytes are used, independent of the number of planes. For monochrome display, the buffer is a total of 74 bytes long, while in the 320x200 pixel resolution (for planes), it is 4x64+10=266 bytes large.

$A00D DRAW SPRITE

This function draws the desired sprite on the screen. Parameters must be passed in the D0, D1, A0, and A2 registers.

D0 and D1 contain the X and Y-coordinates of the position of the sprite on the screen, called the hot spot. A0 is a pointer to the so-called sprite definition block and A2 contains the address of the sprite buffer in which the background will be saved for erasing the sprite later.

The sprite definition block must have the following construction:

```
Word 1 : X offset to hot spot
Word 2 : Y offset to hot spot
```

```
Word 3 : Format flag 0=VDI format, -1=XOR format
Word 4 : Background color (bg)
Word 5 : Foreground color (fg)
```

Following this are 32 words which contain the sprite pattern. The pattern must be in memory in the following order:

```
Word 6 : Background pattern of the top line
Word 7 : Foreground pattern of the top line
Word 8 : Background pattern of the second line
Word 9 : Foreground pattern of the second line
etc.
```

The information in the format flag has the following significance:

```
          VDI Format
fg  bg    Result
 0   0    The background appears
 0   1    The color in word 4 appears
 1   0    The color in word 5 appears
 1   1    The color in word 5 appears

          XOR Format
fg  bg    Result
 0   0    The background appears
 0   1    The color in word 4 appears
 1   0    Th fb bit XORs the pixel on the screen
 1   1    The color in word 5 appears
```

$A00E COPY RASTER FORM

Arbitrary areas of the screen can be copied with the $A00E opcode. Not only areas within the screen, but also from the screen into free RAM, and even more important, from the RAM to the screen. Even complete screen pages can be copied very quickly with the COPY RASTER opcode. The name RASTER FORM does express one limitation of the function, however. Each raster form to be copied must begin on a word boundary and must be a set of words.

The parameters are quite numerous and are passed in the Contrl, Ptsin, and Intin arrays. In addition, two "memory form definition" blocks must be in memory for COPY RASTER. We will start with the MFD blocks.

Since a copy operation must always have a source and a destination, one block describes the source memory range and the second describes the destination. Each block consists of 10 words. The address of the memory described by the block is contained in the first two words. The third word specifies the height of the form in pixels. Word 4 determines the width of the form in words. Word 6 should be set to 1 and word 7 specifies the number of planes of which the form is composed. The remaining words should be set to zero because they are reserved for future extensions.

Necessary parameters for COPY RASTER:

```
INTIN[0]        Bit   0-3
                Opaque:Logical operation; Transparent:
                Writing mode (see $A007, BITBLT)
                Bit 4 = 0: no pattern used;
                      = 1: pattern used
INTIN[1]        Transparent only: 1 bit color index
INTIN[2]        Transparent only: 0 bit color index
PTSIN[0]        Upper left source X-coordinate
PTSIN[1]        Upper left source Y-coordinate
PTSIN[2]        Lower right source X-coordinate
PTSIN[3]        Lower right source Y-coordinate
PTSIN[4]        Upper left destination X-coordinate
PTSIN[5]        Upper left destination Y-coordinate
PTSIN[6]        Lower right destination X-coordinate
PTSIN[7]        Lower right destination Y-coordinate
CONTRL[7+8]     Address source MFDB
CONTRL[9+10]    Address destination MFDB
_patptr         Pattern pointer (when used)
_multifill      0 = pattern has one plane
                1 = pattern has several planes
_COPYTRAN       0 = opaque
                N-plane source and n-plane destination
                1 = transparent
                Source with a plane copied through all
                destination planes (transparent).
```

Memory Form Definition Block (MFDB) design:

```
Offset  Size  Meaning
  0     long  Pointer to raster image
  4     word  Raster width in pixels
  6     word  Raster height in pixels
```

```
    8       word  Raster width in words
   10       word  Format flag
                  0 = device-specific
                  1 = number of bit planes
   12       word  Number of bit planes
   14       word  Reserved
```

When the COPY RASTER function is used, the raster image in device-specific format must be laid out first. (Standard format arranges the bitplanes one after the other, instead of nesting them by words).

A few remarks about the words "opaque" and "transparent:" Opaque copying simply combines the corresponding color planes of source and destination, as well as the resulting raster, though a logical operation with a value from 0 to 15 (see also $A007, BITBLT). Here the number of color planes in source and destination must match, or else the function stops. Opaque copying doesn't require the values in INTIN[1] and INTIN[2]. Transparent copying copies a source range containing a single color plane to a multicolor destination range. The source range consists of only two different colors, represented by bits 0 and 1. You can determine which color appears in the source range pixels. Give the corresponding color numbers in INTIN[1] and INTIN[2].

In INTIN[0] writing mode is used instead of the logical operations:

```
INTIN[0]    Writing mode
   1        Replace mode
   2        Transparent mode
   3        XOR mode
   4        Reverse transparent mode
```

These procedures serve when a source range is only two colors, and when a monochrome as well as a color screen are used. Monochrome copying naturally displays in black and white; color screens can use the two colors from the available palette. The diskette icons from the Desktop are copied using these procedures.

Copy Raster Opaque is identical in the other respects to the VDI function 109, vro_cpyfm, while Copy Raster Transparent corresponds to the VDI function 121, vrt_cpyfm.

$A00F CONTOUR FILL (FLOOD FILL)

The line-A opcode $A00F is not documented by Atari at present. However, when you look at the program with the help of a disassembler, you can see a $A00x opcode execute. It's much more difficult to determine WHICH function the $A00F opcode performs. Now, this is our mystery to be unraveled. $A00F calls a fill routine. This fill is identical to the VDI function 103 Contour Fill.

Contour Fill requires an XY coordinate and a mode word for parameters. The coordinates are stored in PTSIN(0) and PTSIN(1), the mode word in INTIN(0). The mode word means the following: If we have a positive value, this value is established as the color value. An area is then filled with either the border color or the given color. If the value is negative, the fill is limited to the color of the starting point.

Some of the variables important to this command are clipping, write mode, pattern pointer and pattern mask without multifill.

3.4.1 An overview of the "line-A" variables

After the initialization $A000, D0 and A0 contain the address of a variable area which contains more than 50 line-A variables. The essential variables have been described along with the various calls, but not the location of the variables within the variable block. We will present this list shortly. When naming the variables we have remained with the names used in the official Atari documentation.

Offset is the value which must be given to access the value register relative. Variables supplied with a question mark could not be definitively explained.

Offset	Name	Size	Function
0	v_planes	word	Number of planes
2	v_lin_wr	word	Bytes per scan line
4	Contrl	long	Pointer to the Contrl array
8	Intin	long	Pointer to the Intin array
12	Ptsin	long	Pointer to the Ptsin array
16	Intout	long	Pointer to the Intout array
20	Ptsout	long	Pointer to the Ptsout array
24	_FG_BP_1	word	Plane 0 color value
26	_FG_BP_2	word	Plane 1 color value
28	_FG_BP_3	word	Plane 2 color value
30	_FG_BP_4	word	Plane 3 color value
32	_LSTLIN	word	Should be -1 ($FFFF) (?)
34	_LN_MASK	word	Line pattern for $A003
36	_WRT_MODE	word	Write mode (0=write mode 1=transparent 2=XOR mode 3=Inverse trans.)
38	_X1	word	X1-coordinate
40	_Y1	word	Y1-coordinate
42	_X2	word	X2-coordinate
44	_Y2	word	Y2-coordinate
46	_patptr	long	Fill pattern pointer (see $A004)
50	_patmsk	word	Fill pattern "mask" (see $A004)
52	_multifill	word	0=fill pattern for one plane 1=fill pattern for multiplane
54	_CLIP	word	0=no clipping (see $A005) unequal to 0=clipping
56	_XMN_CLIP	word	define upper left corner of
58	_YMN_CLIP	word	the visible clipping area and
60	_XMX_CLIP	word	define lower right corner of
62	_YMX_CLIP	word	the visible area for clipping
64	_XACC_DDA	word	Should be set to $8000 before each call to TXTBLT (?)
66	_DDA_INC	word	Enlargement/reduction factor $FFFF for enlargement, reduction doesn't work (?)
68	_T_SCLSTS	word	0=reduction (?) 1=enlargement

70	_MONO_STATUS	word	1=no proportional font 0=proportional type or width of character changed by bold or italics
72	_SOURCEX	word	X-coordinate of char in font
74	_SOURCEY	word	Y-coord of char in font (0)

Note: SOURCEX is the value of the character from the horizontal offset table (HOT) and can be calculated with the formula SOURCEX = HOT-element (ASCII value minus FIRST ADE). The variable FIRST ADE is contained in bytes 36,37 of the font header (see example)

76	_DESTX	word	X-position of char on screen
78	_DESTY	word	Y-position of char on screen
80	_DELX	word	Character width
82	_DELY	word	Character height

Note: DELX can be calculated with the formula DELX = SOURCEX+1 minus SOURCEX (see $A008). DELY is the value FORM height from bytes 82,83 of the font header.

84	_FBASE	long	Pointer to start of font data
88	_FWIDTH	long	Width of font form
90	_STYLE	word	Special effects flag (see $A008)
92	_LITEMASK	word	Mask for shading
94	_SKEWMASK	word	Mask for italic type
96	_WEIGHT	word	Number of bits by which the character will be expanded
98	_R_OFF	word	Offset for italic type
100	_L_OFF	word	Offset for italic type

Note: The above five variables should be loaded with the corresponding values from the font header.

102	_SCALE	word	0=no scaling 1=scaling (enlarge/reduce)
104	_CHUP	word	Angle for character rotation 0=normal char representation $384=rotated 90 degrees $708=rotated 180 degrees $A8C=rotated 270 degrees

106	_TEXT_FG	word	Text display foreground color
108	_scrtchp	long	Buffer address required for creating special text effects
112	_scrpt2	word	Offset of the enlargement buffer in the scrtchp buffer
114	_TEXT_BG	word	Background color for text rep
116	_COPYTRAN	word	(?)

3.4.2 Examples for using the line-A opcodes

To make your first experiments with the line-A opcodes easier, here are a few examples to serve you as a starting point. In the first example, $A001 sets a point is set on the screen with $A001, $A002 sets the point's color.

```
*************************************************************
*              Demo of $A000,$A001 and $A002 functions
*************************************************************

Intin      equ       8
Ptsin      equ       12

init       equ       $a000
setpix     equ       $a001
getpix     equ       $a002

start:
           .dc.w     init                      call $A000
           move.l    Intin(a0),a3              address of Intin-arrays
           move.l    Ptsin(a0),a4              address of Ptsin-arrays

           move      #300,(a4)                 X coordinate
           move      #100,2(a4)                Y coordinate

           move      #1,(a3)                   color set, pixel set
                                               0 erases pixel

           .dc.w     setpix                    set pixel

           move      #300,(a4)                 X coordinate
           move      #100,2(a4)                y coordinate
           .dc.w     getpix                    get color value

           d0 now contains color value
```

A monochrome monitor requires only the color values zero and one. Other values can be entered when working in one of the color modes, however.

The next example shows how a triangle can be drawn on the screen with the function FILLED POLYGON.

```
****************************************************
*             a006 - filled polygon
****************************************************

contrl       equ       4
ptsin        equ       12

fg_bp1       equ       24
fg_bp2       equ       26
fg_bp3       equ       28
fg_bp4       equ       30
wrt_mod      equ       36

y1           equ       40

patptr       equ       46
patmsk       equ       50
multifill    equ       52
clip         equ       54
xmn_clip     equ       56
ymn_clip     equ       58
xmx_clip     equ       60
ymx_clip     equ       62

init         equ       $a000
polygon      equ       $a006

             .dc.w     init              get variable block address
                                         from A0

             move.w    #1,fg_bp1(a0)     set colors for
             clr.w     fg_bp2(a0)        monochrome only
             clr.w     fg_bp3(a0)
             clr.w     fg_bp4(a0)
             move.w    #2,wrt_mod(a0)    replace mode

             move.l    #fill,patptr(a0)  pointer to the fill pattern
             move.w    #4,patmsk(a0)     four fill patterns
             clr.w     multifill(a0)     only one plane (monochrome)
             clr.w     clip(a0)          no clipping
             move.l    contrl(a0),a6     Contrl array address from A6
```

```
                addq.l      #2,a6               A6 > Contrl(1)
                move.w      #3,(a6)             the XY pair in Ptsin

                move.l      ptsin(a0),a6        Ptsin array address from A6
                move.l      #tab,a5             Coordinate table
                move.w      #8,d3               receive 8 coordinates
loop            move.w      (a5)+,(a6)+
                dbra        d3,loop

                move.w      #100,d3             first scanline
loop1           move.w      d3,y1(a0)           from Y1
                move.l      a0,-(sp)            store address variable block

                dc.w        polygon             fill scanline, destroy A0

                move.l      (sp)+,a0            restore A0
                addq.w       #1,d3              calculate next scanline
                cmp.w       #301,d3             last scanline?
                bne         loop1               no, next scanline
                rts                             subroutine all done

fill:
                dc.w        %1100110011001100
                dc.w        %0110110110110110
                dc.w        %0011001100110011
                dc.w        %1001100110011001

tab:
                dc.w        320,100
                dc.w        120,300
                dc.w        520,300
                dc.w        320,100
```

The next example shows how to enable the mouse and manipulate the cursor form. The example waits for a key press before returning.

```
*************************************************
*               show mouse - transform mouse
*************************************************
intin           equ     8

init_a          equ     $a000
show_mouse      equ     $a009
transmouse      equ     $a00b

start:
                .dc.w   init_a          address Intin from A5
                move.l  Intin(a0),a5
                move    #0,6(a5)        Intin (3) = mask color value
                move    #1,8(a5)        Intin (4) = data color value

                add.l   #10,a5          a5 > Intin (5)

                lea     maus,a4         data for new cursor
                move    #15,d0          32 words = 16 longs
loop:
                move.l  (a4)+,(a5)+     transfer Intin array
                dbra    d0,loop

                .dc.w   transmouse      and set form

                .dc.w   init_a

                move.l  Intin(a0),a0
                clr.w   (a0)            Number Hide Cursor -ignore call

                .dc.w   show_mouse      now the new cursor

                rts                     subroutine all done

maus:
maske:
                .dc.w   %0000000110000000
                .dc.w   %0000011111100000
                .dc.w   %0001111111111000
                .dc.w   %0111111111111110
                .dc.w   %1111111111111111
                .dc.w   %1111001111001111
                .dc.w   %1111001111001111
```

```
            .dc.w    %1111001111001111
            .dc.w    %0000001111000000
            .dc.w    %0000001111000000
            .dc.w    %0000001111000000
            .dc.w    %0000001111000000
            .dc.w    %0000001111000000
            .dc.w    %0000001111000000
            .dc.w    %0000000000000000
daten:
            .dc.w    %0000000000000000
            .dc.w    %0000000000000000
            .dc.w    %0000000110000000
            .dc.w    %0000011001100000
            .dc.w    %0110000110000110
            .dc.w    %0110000110000110
            .dc.w    %0000000110000000
            .dc.w    %0000000110000000
            .dc.w    %0000000110000000
            .dc.w    %0000000110000000
            .dc.w    %0000000110000000
            .dc.w    %0000000110000000
            .dc.w    %0000000110000000
            .dc.w    %0000000000000000
            .dc.w    %0000000000000000
```

3.5 The Exception Vectors

The first 1024 bytes of the 68000 processor are reserved for the exception vectors. Routines which use exception handling store the addresses they require in this range of memory.

A condition which leads to an exception can come either from the processor itself or from the peripheral components and controls units connected to it. The interrupts, described in the next section, belong to the class of external events. In addition, a so-called bus error can be created externally.

A bus error can be created by many circumstances. For one, certain memory areas can be protected from unauthorized access by it. As you may already know, the 68000 can run in one of two operating modes. The operating system is driven at the first level, the *supervisor mode*. The *user mode* is intended for user programs. In order that a user program not be able to access important system variables as well as the system components in an uncontrolled fashion, such an access in the user mode leads to a bus error. If such an error occurs, the processor stops execution of the instruction, saves the program counter and status register on the stack, and branches to a routine, the address of which it fetches from the lowest 1024 bytes of memory. In the case of the bus error, the address is at memory location 8 (one long word). What happens in this routine?

First the vector number of the interrupt is determined and placed in address $3C4. Then the registers will get up to 16 words from the system stack and store them. Therein is the address by which the interruption occurred, as well as the current system status. In the case of a bus or address error, these words contain the address at which the error occurred, as well as the type of access (see any 68000 user's manual). As many cherry bombs appear on the screen as the interrupt vector number. In the case of a bus error, for example, this number is 2. Execution then returns to the GEM Desktop.

The range in which the above information will be stored retains this information until the ST is reset. It therefore conveys the complete status of the processor until a crash occurs. The data lie at the following addresses:

```
$380   contains  $12345678 when the following data is valid
$384 - $3A3      D0 - D7
$3A4 - $3BF      A0 - A6
```

$3C0	SSP	
$3C4	Exception number	
$3C8	USP	
$3CC - $3EB	16 words from SSP	

The following table contains all of the exception vectors.

Vector number	Address	Exception vector meaning
0	$000	Stack pointer after reset
1	$004	Program counter after reset
2	$008	Bus error
3	$00C	Address error
4	$010	Illegal instruction
5	$014	Division by zero
6	$018	CHK instruction
7	$01C	TRAPV instruction
8	$020	Privilege violation
9	$024	Trace
10	$028	Line-A emulator
11	$02C	Line-F emulator
12-14	$030-$038	reserved
15	$03C	Uninitialized interrupt
16-23	$040-$05C	reserved
24	$060	Spurious interrupt
25	$064	Level 1 interrupt
26	$068	Level 2 interrupt
27	$06C	Level 3 interrupt
28	$070	Level 4 interrupt
29	$074	Level 5 interrupt
30	$078	Level 6 interrupt
31	$07C	Level 7 interrupt
32	$080	TRAP #0 instruction
33	$084	TRAP #1 instruction
34	$088	TRAP #2 instruction
35	$08C	TRAP #3 instruction
36	$090	TRAP #4 instruction
37	$094	TRAP #5 instruction
38	$098	TRAP #6 instruction
39	$09C	TRAP #7 instruction
40	$0A0	TRAP #8 instruction
41	$0A4	TRAP #9 instruction
42	$0A8	TRAP #10 instruction
43	$0AC	TRAP #11 instruction

44	$0B0	TRAP #12 instruction
45	$0B4	TRAP #13 instruction
46	$0B8	TRAP #14 instruction
47	$0BC	TRAP #15 instruction
48-63	$0C0-$0FC	reserved
64-255	$100-$3FC	User interrupt vectors

The following vectors are used on the ST:

Line-A emulator	$FC9CA2 / $FB30
Line-F emulator	$A30E / $3A6AE
Level 2 interrupt	$FC061E / $64AC
Level 4 interrupt	$FC0634 / $64C2
TRAP #1 GEMDOS	$FC4D48 / $ABD6
TRAP #2 GEM	$FE340E / $29B76
TRAP #13 BIOS	$FC074E / $65DC
TRAP #14 XBIOS	$FC0748 / $65D6

The first address refers to the ROM version; the second address is read when the operating system is found in RAM. The vector for division by zero points to `rte` and returns directly to the interrupted program. Vectors 64-79 are reserved for the MFP 68901 interrupts. All other vectors point to $FC0A1A/$68A8 which outputs the vector number and ends the program as described for the bus error.

All of the unused vectors can be used for your own purposes, such as the line-F emulator or the 12 unused traps.

3.5.1 The line-F emulator

The ST operating system uses the line-F emulator to replace frequently used command sequences with just one command. Since the better part of the operating system is written in C, especially the AES, you'll often find a sequence at the end of a C subroutine, generated by the compiler:

```
tst.l    (A7)+
movem.l  (A7)+,Dx-Dy/Ax-Ay
unlk     A6
rts
```

This sequence requires 5 words. A 16-bit mask in the `movem` command decides which register will be taken from the stack. Bits 0 - 7 stand for data registers D0 - D7, and bits 8 - 15 are for the address registers (A0 - A7). This mask is ORed by the opcode $F000 to shift the second bit to the right, and set bit 0. Thus it is possible to get the register contents of D3 - D7 and A0 - A5, which are used by the C compiler, from the stack. Four words will be stored during this procedure.

If bit 0 is not set in the line-F command, the opcode will be interpreted as a pointer in a table, from which the address of a routine will be taken. This routine will then branch to the return address previously placed on the stack. The opcode must be divisible by 4; e.g., $F000, $F004, etc., up to $F9CC. The jump table resides at $FEE8BC-$FEF28B or $34B60-$3552F.

Since the line-F routine contains self-modifying code, it is copied into RAM.

```
************************* LINE-F emulator
00A30E  341F            move.w   (A7)+,D2          Get status from stack
00A310  205F            move.l   (A7)+,A0          Return address
00A312  3218            move.w   (A0)+,D1          Get opcode
00A314  08010000        btst     #0,D1             Bit 0 set?
00A318  6614            bne      $A32E             Yes
00A31A  46C2            move.w   D2,SR             Set status
00A31C  2F08            move.l   A0,-(A7)          Return addr. from stack
00A31E  02410FFF        and.w    #$0FFF,D1         Delete bits 12-15
00A322  207C00FEE8BC    move.l   #$FEE8BC,A0       Base address of table
00A328  20701000        move.l   0(A0,D1.W),A0     Get address
00A32C  4ED0            jmp      (A0)              Execute routine
00A32E  02410FFE        and.w    #$0FFE,D1         Delete bits 12-15 and bit 0
00A332  6712            beq      $A346             $F001, then unlk/rts
00A334  E549            lsl.w    #2,D1             Shift mask
00A336  007C07000       or.w     #$700,SR          Save IPL 7, interrupts
00A33A  41FA0008        lea      $A344(PC),A0      Register mask address
00A33E  3081            move.w   D1,(A0)           Copy mask in program
00A340  588F            addq.l   #4,A7             Correct stack
00A342  4CDF2000        movem.l  (A7)+,A5          Get register again
00A346  46C2            move.w   D2,SR             Set status
00A348  4E5E            unlk     A6                release local variables
00A34A  4E75            rts                        Return from call

         Bit no.   : FEDCBA9876543210
         Opcode    : 1111XXXXXXXXXXX1
         Register  :       AAAAAADDDDD
                           54321076543
```

3.5.2 The interrupt structure of the ST

The interrupt capabilities offered by the 68000 microprocessor are put to good use in the ST. As you may have already gathered from the hardware description of the processor, the processor has seven interrupt levels with different priorities. The interrupt mask in the system byte of the status register determines which levels can generate an interrupt. An interrupt can only be generated by a level higher than the current contents of the mask in the status register. A interrupt of a certain priority is communicated to the processor by the three interrupt priority level inputs. The following assignment results:

Level	IPL 2	1	0
7 (NMI)	0	0	0
6	0	0	1
5	0	1	0
4	0	1	1
3	1	0	0
2	1	0	1
1	1	1	0
0	1	1	1

If all three lines are 1 (interrupt level 0), no interrupt is present. Interrupt level 7 is the NMI (non-maskable interrupt), which is executed even if the interrupt mask in the status register contains seven. Which interrupt is assigned which vector (that is, the address of the routine which will process the interrupt) depends on the peripheral component which generates the interrupt. For auto-vectors, the processor itself derives the interrupt number from the interrupt level. The following table is used in this process:

Level	Vector number	Vector address
IPL 1	25	$64
IPL 2	26	$68
IPL 3	27	$6C
IPL 4	28	$70
IPL 5	29	$74
IPL 6	30	$78
IPL 7	31	$7C

Only lines IPL 1 and IPL 2 are used on the Atari ST; Line IPL is permanently set to a 1 level so that only levels 2, 4 and 6 are available. The results in the following assignment:

```
IPL 2          HBL, horizontal blank, line return
IPL 4          VBL, vertical blank, picture return
IPL 6          MFP 68901
```

The HPL interrupt is generated on each line return from the video section. It is generated every 50 to 64 µs depending on the monitor connected (monochrome or color). It occurs very often and is normally not permitted by an interrupt mask of three. The standard HBL routine therefore only has the task of setting the interrupt mask to three if it is zero and allows the HBL interrupt so that no more HBL interrupts will occur. One use of the HBL interrupt could be for special screen effects. With the help of this routine, you know exactly which line of the screen has just been displayed. Of much greater importance, however, is the VBL interrupt, which is generated on each picture return. This occurs 50, 60, or 70 times per second depending on the monitor.

The vertical blank interrupt (VBL) routine accomplishes a whole set of a tasks which must be periodically executed or which concern the screen display. When entering the routine, the frame counter _frclock ($466) is first incremented. Next, a test is made to see if the VBL interrupt is software-disabled. This is the case if vblsem ($452) (vertical blank semaphore) is zero or negative. In this case the routine is exited immediately and execution returns to the interrupted program. Otherwise, all of the registers are saved on the stack and the counter _vbclock ($462), which counts the executed VBL routines, is incremented. Next, a check is made to see if a different monitor has been connected in the meantime. If a change was made from a monochrome to color monitor, the video shifter is reprogrammed accordingly. This is necessary because the high screen frequency of 70 Hz of the monochrome monitor could damage a color monitor. The routine to flash the cursor is called next. If you load a new color palette via the appropriate BIOS functions or want to change the screen address, this happens here in the VBL routine. Since nothing is displayed at this time, a change can be made here without disturbing anything else. If colorptr ($45A) is not equal to zero, it is interpreted as a pointer to a new color palette, and this is loaded into the video shifter. The pointer is then cleared again. If screenptr is set, this value is used as the new base address of the screen. This takes care of the screen specific portions.

Now the floppy VBL routine is called which, with the help of the write protect status, determines if a diskette was changed. An additional task of this routine is to deselect the drives after the disk controller has turned the drive motor off.

Now comes the most interesting part for the programmer, the processing of the VBL queue. There is a way to tell the operating system to execute your own routines within the VBL interrupt. The maximum number of routines possible is in nvbls ($454). This value is normally initialized to 8, but it can be increased if required. Address _vblqueue ($456) contains a pointer to a vector array which contains the (8) addresses of the VBL routines. Each address is tested within the VBL routine and the corresponding routine executed if the address is not zero.

If you want to install your own VBL routine, check the 8 entries until you find one which contains a zero. At this address you can write a pointer to your routine which from now on will be executed in every VBL interrupt. In all 8 entries are already occupied, you can copy the entries into a free area of memory, append the address of your routine, and redirect _vblqueue to point to the new vector array. Naturally, you must not forget to increment vbls, the number of routines, correspondingly. Your routine may change all registers with the exception of the USP.

As soon as the VBL routine is done, the _dmpflg ($4EE) is checked. If this memory location is zero, a hardcopy of the screen is outputted. The flag is set in the keyboard interrupt routine if the keys ALT and HELP are pressed at the same time. Finally, the register contents are restored, vblsem is released and execution returns to the interrupted routine.

The MFP 68901 occupies interrupt level six in our previous table. This component is in the position to create interrupt vectors on its own. These are referred to non-auto vectors in contrast to the auto vectors used above, because the processor does not generate the vector itself. In the Atari ST, the MFP 68901 works as the interrupt controller. It manages the interrupt requests of all peripheral components including its own.

The MFP can manage sixteen interrupts which are prioritized in reference to each other, similar to the seven levels of the processor. All MFP interrupts appear on level 6 to the 68000, therefore prioritized higher than HBL and VBL interrupts. The table on the next page contains the assignments within the MFP.

```
Level    Assignment
  15     Monochrome monitor detect
  14     RS-232 ring indicator
  13     System clock timer A
  12     RS-232 receive buffer full
  11     RS-232 receive error
```

Level	Assignment
10	RS-232 transmit buffer empty
9	RS-232 transmit error
8	Line return counter, timer B
7	Floppy controller and DMA
6	Keyboard and MIDI ACIAs
5	Timer C
4	RS-232 baud rate generator, timer D
3	unused
2	RS-232 CTS
1	RS-232 DCD
0	Centronics busy

Not all of these possible interrupt sources are enabled, however. Some signals are processed through polling. The following is a description of the interrupts which are used by the operating system.

Level 2, RS-232 CTS, address $FC26B2 / $8540

This interrupt is generated every time the RS-232 interface is informed via the CTS line that a connected receiver is ready to receive additional data. The routine then sends the next character from the RS-232 transmit buffer.

Level 5, Timer C, address $FC2F78 / $8E06

This timer runs at 200 Hz. The 200 Hz counter at $4BA is first incremented in the interrupt routine. The next actions are performed only every fourth call to the interrupt routine, that is, only every 20ms (50 Hz). First a routine is called which handles the sound processing. Another task of this interrupt is the keyboard repeat when a key is pressed and initial repeat. Finally, the `evt_timer` routine of GEM is called, which is accessed via vector $400.

Level 6, Keyboard and Midi, address $FC281C / $86AA

Two peripheral components are connected to this interrupt level of the MFP, the two ACIAs which receive data from the keyboard and the MIDI interface. In order to decide which of the two components has requested an interrupt, the interrupt request bits in the status registers of the ACIAs are tested and the received byte is fetched if required. If it comes from the keyboard, the scan code is converted to the ASCII code by means of the keyboard table and written into the receive buffer, which happens immediately for MIDI data. Mouse and joystick data also come from the keyboard ACIA and are also prepared accordingly.

Level 9, RS-232 transmit error, address $FC2718 / $85A6

If an error occurs while sending RS-232 data, this interrupt routine is activated. Here the transmitter status register is read and the status is saved in the RS-232 parameter block.

Level 10, RS-232 transmit buffer empty, address $FC2666 / $84F4

Each time the MFP has completely outputted a data byte via the RS-232 interface, it generates this interrupt. It is then ready to send the next byte. If data is still in the transmit buffer, the next byte is written into the transmit register, which can now be shifted out according to the selected baud rate.

Level 11, RS-232 receive error, address $FC26FA / $8588

If an error occurs when receiving RS-232 data, this interrupt routine is activated. This may involve a parity error or an overflow. The routine only clears the receiver status register and then returns.

Level 12, RS-232 receive buffer full, address $FC2596 / $8424

If the MFP has received a complete byte, this interrupt occurs. Here the character can be fetched and written into the receive buffer (if there is still room). This routine takes into account the active handshake mode (sending XON/XOFF or RTS/CTS).

The other interrupt possibilities of the MFP are not used, but they can be used for your own routines. For example, interrupt level 0, Centronics strobe, can be used for buffered printer output.

3.6 The Atari ST VT52 Emulator

There are two options for text output on the ST. You can work with the GEMDOS functions by means of `TRAP#1` or a direct BIOS call with `TRAP#13`. The other possibility consists of using the VDI functions.

You have special options for screen control with both variants. We will first take a look at output using the normal DOS or BIOS calls. Here a terminal of type VT52, which offers a wide variety of control functions, is emulated for screen output. These control characters are prefixed with a special character, the escape code. Escape, or ESC for short, has an ASCII code of 27. Following the escape code is a letter which determines the function, as well as additional parameters if required. The following list contains all of the control codes and their significance.

ESC A Cursor up
 This function moves the cursor up one line. If the cursor was already on the top line, nothing happens.

ESC B Cursor down
 This ESC sequence positions the cursor one line down. If the cursor is already on the bottom line, nothing happens.

ESC C Cursor right
 This sequence moves the cursor one column to the right.

ESC D Cursor left
 Moves the cursor one position to the left. This function is identical to the control code backspace (BS, ASCII code 8). If the cursor is already in the first column, nothing happens.

ESC E Clear Home
 This control sequence clears the entire screen and positions the cursor in the upper left corner of the screen (home position).

ESC H Cursor home
With this function you can place the cursor in the upper left corner of the screen without erasing the contents of the screen.

ESC I Cursor up
This sequence moves the cursor one line towards the top. In contrast to ESC A, however, if the cursor is already in the top line, a blank line is inserted and the remainder of the screen is scrolled down a line correspondingly. The column position of the cursor remains unchanged.

ESC J Clear below cursor
By means of this function, the rest of the screen below the current cursor position is cleared. The cursor position itself is not changed.

ESC K Clear remainder of line
This ESC sequence clears the rest of the line in which the cursor is found. The cursor position itself is also cleared, but the position is not changed.

ESC L Insert line
This makes it possible to insert a blank line at the current cursor position. The remainder of the screen is shifted down; the lowest line is then lost. The cursor is placed at the start of the new line after the insertion.

ESC M Delete line
This function clears the line in which the cursor is found and moves the rest of the screen up one line. The lowest screen line then becomes free. After the deletion, the cursor is moved up to the first column of the line that takes the place of the deleted line.

ESC Y Position cursor
This is among the most important functions. It allows the cursor to be positioned at any place on the screen. The function needs the cursor line and column as parameters, which are expected in this order with an offset of 32. If you want to set the cursor to line 7, column 40, you must output the sequence ESC Y CHR$(32+7) CHR$(32+40). Lines and columns are counter starting at zero; for an 80x25 screen the lines are numbered from 0 to 24 and the columns from 0 to 79.

The remaining ESC sequences of the VT52 terminal start with a lower case letter.

ESC b Select character color
With this function you can select the character color for further output. With a monochrome monitor you have choice between just 0=white and 1=black. For color display you can select from 4 or 16 colors depending on the mode. Only the lowest four bits of the parameters are evaluated (mod 16). You can use the digit "1" for the color 1 as well as the letters "A" or "a" in addition to binary one.

ESC c Select background color
This function serves to select the background color in a similar manner. If you choose the same color for character and background, you will, of course, not be able to see text output any more.

ESC d Clear screen to cursor position
This sequence causes the screen to be erased starting at the top and going to the current position of the cursor, inclusive. The position of the cursor is not changed.

ESC e Enable cursor
Through this escape sequence the cursor becomes visible. The cursor can, for example, be enabled when waiting for input from the user.

ESC f Disable cursor
Turns the cursor off again.

ESC j Save cursor position
If you want to save the current position of the cursor, you can use this sequence to do so. Unfortunately, this function is also used by other ESC sequences, so the stored value is no longer available to you if you use some other sequences.

ESC k Set cursor to the saved position
This is the counterpart of the above function. It sets the cursor to the position which was previously saved with ESC j. If no cursor position was saved, the cursor will go to the home position.

ESC l Clear line
Clears the line in which the cursor is located. The remaining lines remain unaffected. After the line is cleared, the cursor is located in the first column of the line.

ESC o Clear from start
This clears the current cursor line from the start to the cursor position, inclusive. The position of the cursor remains unchanged.

ESC p Reverse on
The reverse (inverted) output is enabled with this sequence. For all further output, the character and background colors are exchanged. A monochrome monitor will show white type on a black background.

ESC q Reverse off
This sequence serves to re-enable the normal character display mode.

ESC v Automatic overflow on
After executing this sequence, an attempted output beyond the end of line will automatically start a new line.

ESC w Automatic overflow off
This deactivates the above sequence. An attempt to write beyond the line will result in all following characters being written in the last column.

Similar functions are available to you under VDI. The VDI escape functions (opcode 5) serve this purpose. The appropriate screen function is selected by choosing the proper function number. Note, however, that under VDI the line and column numbering does not begin with zero but with one.

Under VDI there is also a function which outputs a string at specific screen coordinates. If necessary, you can use the ESC functions of the VT52 emulation in addition.

The output of "unprintable" control characters

The three system fonts of the ST have also been supplied with characters for the ASCII codes zero to 31, which are normally interpreted as control codes. On the ST, only codes 7 (BEL), 8 (BS backspace), 9 (TAB), as well as 10, 11, and 12 (LF linefeed, VT vertical tab, and FF form feed all generate a linefeed) plus 13 (CR carriage return) have effect, in addition to ESC. The remaining codes have no effect. How do we access the characters below 32?

To do this, an additional device number is provided in the BIOS function 3 "conout". Normally number 2 "con" serves for output to the screen. If one selects number 5, however, all the codes from, 0 to 255 are outputted as printable characters, control codes are no longer taken into account.

You will find the three ST system fonts pictured in the Appendix.

3.7 The ST System Variables

The ST uses a set of system variables whose significance and addresses will not change in future versions of the operating system. If you use other variables, such as those from the BIOS listing which are not listed here, you should always remember that these could have a different meaning in a new version of the operating system. The system variables are in the lower RAM area directly above the 68000 exception vectors, at address $400 to 1024. The address range from 0 to $7FF (2047) can be accessed only in the supervisor mode. An access in the user mode leads to a bus error.

In the following listing we will use the original names from Atari. In addition to the address of the given variable, typical contents and the significance will be described. Two values are sometimes given for one address: The first signifies the address in the ROM version of the operating system, while the second address refers to the operating system when in RAM, unless stated otherwise in the text.

```
Address length    name          sample contents
```

$400   L   etv_timer $FCA62A / $104B8

    This is the GEM event timer vector. It handles periodic GEM tasks.

$404   L   etv_critic $FC0744 / $65D2

    Critical error handler. Under GEM this pointer points to $FE3226/$294DE. There an attempt is made to correct disk errors, such as if a another disk is requested in a single-drive system.

$408   L   etv_term $FC05C0 / $644E

    This is the GEM vector for ending a program.

$40C   5L   etv_xtra

    Here is space for 5 additional GEM vectors, presently not yet used.

$420   L   memvalid $752019F3

    If the memory location contains the given value, the configuration of the memory controller is valid.

$424	W	memctrl	$05

This is a copy of the configuration value in the memory controller. The value given applies for a 1MB machine.

$426	L	resvalid	$31415926

A given value located here causes a jump to the reset vector ($42A).

$42A	L	resvector	$FC0008

See above.

$42E	L	phystop	$80000 / $100000

This is the physical end of the RAM memory; $80000 for a 512K machine and $100000 for a 1MB machine.

$432	L	_membot	$A100 / $39FF0

The user memory begins here (TPA, transient program area).

$436	L	_memtop	$F8000

This is the upper end of the user memory.

$43A	L	memval2	$237698AA

This value and "memvalid" declare the memory configuration.

$43E	W	flock	0

If this variable contains a value other than zero, a disk access is in progress and the VBL disk routine is disabled.

$440	W	seekrate	3

The seek rate (the time it takes to move the read/write head to the next track) is determined according to the following table:

Seek rate	Time
0	6 ms
1	12 ms
2	2 ms
3	3 ms

$442   W   _timer_ms $14, 20 ms

The time span between two timer calls, 20 ms corresponds to 50 Hz.

$444   W   _fverify $FF

If this memory location contains a value other than zero, a verify is performed after every disk write access.

$446   W   _bootdev   0

Contains the device number of the drive from which the operating system was loaded.

$448   W   palmode   0

If this variable contains a value other than zero, the system is in the PAL mode (50 Hz); if the value is zero, it means the NTSC mode.

$44A   W   defshiftmod   0

If the Atari is switched from monochrome to color, it gets the new resolution from here (0=low, 1 medium resolution).

$44C   W   sshiftmd $2

Here is a copy of the register contents for the screen resolution.

```
0   320x200, low resolution
1   640x200, medium resolution
2   640x400, high resolution
```

$44E   L   _v_bas_ad $F8000

This variable contains a pointer to video RAM (logical screen base). The screen address must always begin on a 256 byte boundary.

$452   W   vblsem   1

If this variable is zero, the vertical blank routine is not executed.

$454   W   nvbls   8

Number of vertical blank routines.

$456   L   _vblqueue $4CE

Pointer to a list of nvbls routines which will be executed during the VBL.

$45A   L   colorptr   0

If this value is not zero, it is interpreted as a pointer to a color palette which will be loaded at the next VBL.

$45E   L   screenpt   0

This is a pointer to the start of the video RAM, which will be set during the next VBL (zero if no new address is to be set).

$462   L   _vbclock $2D26A

Counter for the number of VBL interrupts.

$466   L   _frclock $2D267

Number of VBL routines executed (not disabled by vblsem).

$46A   L   hdv_init $FC0D60 / $6BEE

Vector for hard disk initialization.

$46E   L   swv_vec $FC0020 / $6120

Vector for monitor change. A branch is made through this vector when another monitor (color/monochrome) is connected (default is reset).

$472   L   hdv_bpb $FC0DE6 / $6C74

Vector to get the parameter block for a hard disk (BIOS function 7).

$476   L   hdv_rw $FC10D2 / $6F60

Read/write routine vector for a hard disk (BIOS function 4).

$47A   L   hdv_boot $FC137C / $720A

Vector for loading a boot sector.

$47E   L   hdv_mediach $FC0F96 / $6E24

Media change routine vector for hard disk (BIOS function 9).

$482   W   _cmdload   0

If the boot program sets this variable to a value other than zero, the ST attempts to load a program called "COMMAND.PRG" once the operating system loads (e.g. an application other than the Desktop).

$484   B   conterm   6

Attribute vector for console output:

```
Bit  Meaning
 0   Key click on/off
 1   Key repeat on/off
 2   Tone after CTRL G on/off
 3   "kbshift" is returned in bits 24-31 for the
     BIOS function "conin"
```

$48E   4L   themd   0

Memory descriptor, filled out by the BIOS function `getmpb`.

$49E   2W   ___md   0

Space for additional memory descriptors.

$4A2   L   savptr $90C

Pointer to a save area for the processor registers after a BIOS call.

$4A6   W   _nflops   2

Number of connected floppy disk drives (0 or 2).

$4A8   L   con_state $FC41BC / $A04A

Vector for screen output; set by ESC functions to the appropriate routine, for example.

$4AC   W   save_row   0

Temporary storage for positioning the cursor with ESC Y.

$4AE   L   sav_context   0

Pointer to a temporary areas for exception handling.

$4B2   2L   _bufl $60A4, $60CC

Pointer to two buffer list headers of GEMDOS. The first header is responsible for data sectors, the second for the FAT (file allocation table) and the directory. Each buffer control block (BCB) is constructed as follows:

```
long   BCB     $4F8A,  pointer to next BCB
int    drive   -1,     drive number or -1
int    type    2       buffer type
int    rec     $41C    record number in this buffer
int    dirty   0       dirty flag (buffer changed)
long   DMD     $2854   pointer to drive media descriptor
long   buffer  $4292   pointer to the buffer itself
```

$4BA   L   _hz_200 $71280

Counter for 200 Hz system clock

$4BE   4B   the_env   0

Default environment string, four zero bytes.

$4C2   L   _drvbits   3

32-bit vector for connected drives. Bit 0 stands for drive A, bit 1 for drive B, and so on.

$4C6   L   _dskbufp $167A

Pointer to a 1024-byte disk buffer. The buffer is used for GSX graphic operations and should not be used by interrupt routines.

$4CA   L   _autopath   0

Pointer to autoexecute path.

$4CE   8L   _vbl_list $FD03C4,0,0.. / $16252,0,0..

List of the eight standard VBL routines.

$4EE	W	_dumpflg	$FFFF

This flag is incremented by one when the ALT and HELP keys are pressed simultaneously. A value of one generates a hardcopy of the screen on the printer. A hardcopy can be interrupted by pressing ALT HELP again.

$4F2	L	_sysbase	$FC0000 / $6100

Pointer to start of the operating system.

$4F6	L	_shell_p	0

Global shell information.

$4FA	L	end_os	$A100 / $3A4A0

Pointer to the end of the operating system in RAM, start of the TPA.

$4FE	L	exec_os	$FD8E98 / $1F600

Pointer to the start of the AES. Normally branched to after the initialization of the BIOS.

$502	L	dump_vec	$FC0C2C / $6ABA

This vector is jumped to when a hardcopy is being printed (XBIOS function 20).

$506	L	prt_stat	$FC1F34 / $7D2E

Printer status vector for hardcopy.

$50A	L	prt_vec	$FC1EA0 / $7D2E

Printer output vector for hardcopy.

$50E	L	aux_stat	$FC1F6E / $7DFC

Vector for getting serial output status during hardcopy.

| $512 | L | aux_vec | $FC1F86 / $7E14 |

Vector for serial output of the hardcopy function.

| $51A | L | memval3 | $5555AAAA |

Contains the variable of the "magic number" memval. Keeps the memory configuration constant after a reset (together with memvalid and memvalid2).

| $51E | 8L | bconstat_vec | $FC0670, $FC2138, $FC2226, $FC2044, $FC0670, $FC0670, $FC0670, $FC0670 |

Eight pointer to routines for getting input status (BIOS function 1, bconstat). The first value applies to device number 0, the next for device 1, etc., up to device 7. The address $FC0670 points direct to an rts command.

| $53E | 8L | bconin_vec | $FC2104, $FC2150, $FC223C, $FC2060, $FC0670, $FC0670, $FC0670, $FC0670 |

The vector table has an equivalent function to the above. There, however, the addresses for BIOS function 2 (bconin) are kept.

| $55E | 8L | bcostat_vec | $FC2124, $FC219A, $FC226C, $FC21DC, $FC2004, $FC0670, $FC0670, $FC0670 |

These addresses contain the output status for device numbers 0 to 7. They are jumped to from BIOS function 8, bcostat.

| $57E | 8L | bconout_vec | $FC2090, $FC21B4, $FC434C, $FC2016, $FC21EE, $FC4340, $FC0670, $FC0670 |

These addresses are the ones for character output. These correspond to the BIOS function 3, bconout.

3.8 The 68000 Instruction Set

If you are already familiar with the machine language of some 8-bit processor, forget everything you know. If you do, it will make it easier to understand the following material!

The 68000 processor is fundamentally different in construction and architecture from previous processors (including the 8086!). The essential difference does not lie in the fact that the standard processing width is 16 and not 8 bits (which is sometimes a drawback and can lead to programming errors), but in the fact that, with certain exceptions, the internal registers are not assigned to a specific purpose, but can be viewed as general-purpose registers, with which almost anything is possible.

In earlier processors, the accumulator was always the destination for arithmetic operations, but it is completely absent in the 68000. There are eight data registers (D0-D7) with a width of 32 bits, and as a general rule, at least one of these is involved in an operation. There are also eight address registers (A0-A7), each with 32 bits, which are usually used for generating complex addresses. Register A7 has a set assignment--it serves as the stack pointer. It is also present twice, once as the user stack pointer (USP) and once as the supervisor stack pointer (SSP). The distinction is made because there are also two operating modes, namely the user mode and the supervisor mode.

These two are not only different in that they use different stack pointers, but in that certain instructions are not legal in the user mode. These are the so-called privileged instructions (see also instruction description), with whose help an unwary programmer can easily "crash" the system rather spectacularly. This is why these instructions create an exception in the user mode. An exception, by the way, is the only way to get from the user mode to the supervisor mode.

In addition there is the status register, the upper half of which is designated as the system byte because it contains such things as the interrupt mask, things which do not concern the "normal" user, making access to this byte also one of the privileged instructions. The lower byte, the user byte, contains the flags which are set or cleared based on the result of operations, such as the carry flag, zero flag, etc. As a general rule, the programmer works with these flags indirectly, such as when the execution of a branch is made conditional on the state of a flag.

Two things should be mentioned yet: Multi-byte values (addresses or operands) are not stored in memory as they are with 8-bit processors, in the order low byte/high byte, but the other way around. Four-byte expressions (long word) are stored in memory (and the registers of course) with the highest-order byte first.

The second is that unsupported opcodes do not lead to a crash, but cause a special exception, whose standard handling must naturally be performed by the operating system.

3.8.1 Addressing modes

This is probably the most interesting theme of the 68000 because the enormous capability first takes effect through the many various addressing modes.

The effective address (the address which, sometimes composed of several components, finally determines the operand) is fundamentally 32 bits wide, even if one or more the components specified in the instruction is shorter. These are always sign-extended to the full 32-bit width.

The charm of the addressing lies in the fact that almost all instructions (naturally with exceptions), both the source and destination operands, can be specified with one of the addressing modes. This means that even memory operations do not necessarily have to use one of the registers; memory-to-memory operations are possible.

In the assembler syntax, the source operand is given first, followed by the destination operand (behind the comma).

Register Direct

The operand is located in a register. There are two kinds of register direct addressing: data register direct and address register direct.

In the first case, the operand may be bit, byte, word, or long word-oriented; in the second case a word or long word is required, in case the address register is the destination of the operation.

Example: `ADD.B D0,D1 or ADDA.W D0,A2`

Absolute Data Addressing

The operand is located in the address space of memory. This can also be a peripheral component, naturally (see `MOVEP`). The address is specified in absolute form.

This can have a width of a long word, whereby the entire address space can be accessed, or it can be only one word wide. In this case is sign-extended (the sign being the highest-order bit) to 32 bits. For example, the word $7FFF becomes the long word $00007FFF, while $FFFF becomes $FFFFFFFF. Only the lower 32K and the upper 32K of the address space can be accessed with the short form. This addressing mode is often used in the operating system of the ST because important system variables are stored low in memory and all peripheral components are decoded at the top.

Example: `MOVE.L $7FFF,$01234567`

Instructions in which both operands are addressed with a long word are the longest instructions in the set, consisting of 10 bytes.

Program Counter Relative Addressing

This addressing mode allows even constants to be addressed in a completely relocatable program, since the base of the address calculation is the current state of the program counter.

The are two variations. In the first, a 16-bit signed offset is added to the program counter, and in the second, the contents of a register (sign-extended if only one word is specified) are also added in, though here the offset may be only 8 bits long.

Example: `MOVE.B $1234(PC),$12(PC,D0.W)`

Register Indirect Addressing

There are several variations of this, and they will be discussed individually.

Register Indirect

Here the operand address is located in an address register.

Example: `CLR.L (A0)`

Postincrement Register Indirect

The operand is addressed as above, but the contents of the address register are incremented by the operand length, by 1 for xxx.B or 4 for xxx.L.

Example: `MOVE.B #0,(A0+),(A1)+ or CMP.L #23,(A1)+`

Predecrement Register Indirect

Here the address register is decrement by the length of the operand before the addressing.

Example: `CMPI.W $0123,-(A3)`

Register Indirect with Offset

A 16 bit offset will be added to the contents of the address register.

Example: `EOR.L D0,$1234(A4)`

Indexed Register Indirect with Offset

As above, but the contents of another register (address or data) are also added in, taking the sign into account. The offset may have a width of 8 bits here, however.

Example: `MOVE.W $12(A5,A6.L),D1`

Immediate Addressing

Here the operand is contained as such in the instruction itself. Naturally, an operand specified in this manner can serve only as a source. The immediate operands can, as a general rule, be any of the allowed widths.

Example: `ADDI.W #$1234,D5`

In the variant QUICK, the constant may be only 3 bits long, therefore having a value from 0-7. An exception is the MOVE command, where the constant may have 8 bits, but in which only a data register is allowed as the destination.

Example: `ADDQ.L #1,A0 or MOVEQ #123,D1`

Implied Register

This addressing mode is mentioned only for the sake of completeness and in it, an operand address is already determined by the instruction itself. The operands are either in the program counter, in the status register, or the system stack pointer.

Example: `MOVE SR,D6`

Regarding the offsets, it should be noted that they are signed numbers in two's complement. Their highest-order bit forms the sign. With an 8-bit value, an offset of +127/-128 is possible, and about ±32K with 16 bits.

3.8.2 The instructions

In the following instruction description, the individual bit patterns are not listed since this would lead us too far in this connection. Additional information can be gathered from books like the *M68000 16/32-Bit Microprocessor Programmer's Reference Manual* (Motorola).

The instructions are also explained only in their base form and variations are mentioned only in name. We will briefly explain what the individual variations can look like here.

The variations are indicated by letter after the operand. This can be one of the following:

A   indicates that the destination of the operation is an address register. Word operations are sign-extended to 32 bits.

I   indicates an immediate operand as the source of the operation. I operands may assume all widths as a general width.

Q   means quick and represents a special form of immediate addressing. Such an operand is usually three bits wide, corresponding to a value range of 0 to 7. This limited range has the advantage that the operand will fit into the opcode. Since there is no special command for incrementing a register, something like ADDQ.L #1,A0 works well in its place. An exception is MOVEQ. Here the operand may have a value of 0-255.

X   indicates arithmetic operations which use the X flag. This flag has a special significance. It is set equal to the carry flag for all arithmetic operations. The carry flag, however, is also affected by transfer operations while the X flag is not so that it remains available for further calculations. This is especially useful for computations with higher precision than the standard 32 bits, where temporary results must first be saved, and where the carry flag can be changed as a result.

All instructions have a suffix after the opcode of the form .B, .W, or .L. This suffix indicates the processing width of the operation. Although a data register, for example, has a width of 32 bits = 4 bytes = 1 long word, the instruction CLR.B D0 clears only the lowest-order byte of the register. For registers, .W specifies the lower word. The higher-order word is not explicitly addressable. If the operand is in memory, it is important to know that .W and .L operands must begin on an even address. The same applies for the opcode as such, which also always comprises one word.

If the destination of an operation is an address register, only operands of type .W and .L are allowed, whereby the first is sign-extended to a long word.

Some listings contain instructions of the form MOVE.L #27,D0. The programmer then assumes that the assembler will produce #$0000001B from #27.

Now to the individual instructions:

ABCD Add Decimal with Extend
   There is one data format which we have not yet discussed: the BCD format. This means nothing more than "Binary-Coded Decimal" and it uses digits in the range 0-9. Since this information requires only 4 bits, a byte can store a two-digit decimal number. The instruction ABCD can then add two such numbers. The processing width is always 8 bits.

ADD Add Binary
   This instruction simply adds two operands.
   Variations are *ADDA, ADDQ, ADDI,* and *ADDX.*

AND Logical AND
   Two operand are logically combined with each other according the AND function.
   Variation: *ANDI*

ASL Arithmetic Shift Left
   The operand is shifted to the left byte by the number of positions given, whereby the highest-order bit is copied into the C and X flags. A 0 is shifted in at the right. If a data register is shifted, the processing width can be any. The number of places to be shifted is either specified as an I operand (3 bits) or is placed in an additional register. If a memory location is shifted, the processing width is always one word. A counter is then not given; it is always =1.

ASR Arithmetic Shift Right
   The operand is shifted to the right, whereby the lowest bit is copied to C and X. The sign bit is shifted over from the left. See ASL for information about processing width and counter.

Bcc Branch Conditionally

The branch destination is always a relative address which is either one byte or one word long (signed!). Correspondingly, the branch can jump over a range of +127/-128 bytes or +32K-1/-32K. The point of reference is the address of the following instruction.

Whether or not this instruction is actually executed depends on the required condition, which is verified by means of the flags. Here are the variations and their conditions. A minus sign before a flag indicates that it must be cleared to satisfy the condition. Logical operations are indicated with "*" for AND and "/" for OR.

BRA	Branch Always	no condition
BCC	Branch Carry Clear	-C
BCS	Branch Carry Set	C
BEQ	Branch Equal	Z
BGE	Branch Greater or Equal	N*V/-N*-V
BGT	Branch Greater Than	N*V*-Z/-N*-V*-Z
BHI	Branch Higher	-C*-Z
BLE	Branch Less or Equal	Z/N*-V/-N*V
BLS	Branch Lower or Same	C/Z
BLT	Branch Less Than	N*-V/-N*V
BMI	Branch Minus	N
BNE	Branch Not Equal	-Z
BPL	Branch Plus	-N
BVC	Branch Overflow Clear	-V
BVS	Branch Overflow Set	V

BCHG Bit Test and Change

The specified bit of the operand will be inverted. The original state can be determined from the Z flag. The operand is located either in memory (width=.B) or in a data register (width=.L). The bit number is given either as an I operand or is located in a data register.

BCLR Bit Test and Clear

The specified bit is cleared. Everything else is handled as per BCHG.

BSET Bit Test and Set

The specified bit is set. Boundary conditions are per BCHG.

BSR Branch to Subroutine

This is an unconditional branch to a subroutine. Branch distances as for Bcc.

BTST Bit Test
   The bit is only tested as to its condition. Everything else as per BCHG.

CHK Check Register Against Boundaries
   A data register is checked to see if its contents are less than zero or greater than the operand. Should this be the case, the processor executes an exception. The program is continued at the address in memory location $18 (vector 6). Otherwise no action is taken. The processing width is only word.

CLR Clear Operand
   The specified operand is cleared (set to zero).

CMP Compare
   The first operand is subtracted from the second without changing either of the two operands. Only the flags are set, according to the result.
   Variations: *CMPA* and *CMPI*
   Both operands are addresses with the addressing mode (Ax)+ with the variant *CMPM*.

DBcc Test Condition, Decrement and Branch
   A data register (word) is decremented and the flags are checked for the specified condition. A branch is performed if the condition is *not fulfilled and* the register is not -1. Branch conditions and ranges as per Bcc.

DIVS Divide Signed
   The second operand is divided by the first operand, taking the sign into account. Afterwards the second operand contains the integer quotient in the lower word and the remainder in the upper word, which has the same sign as the quotient. The data width of the first operand is set at .W and at .L for the second.

DIVU Divide Unsigned
   Operation as above, but the sign is ignored.

EOR Exclusive OR
   The two operands are logically combined according to the rules of EXOR.
   Variations: *EORI*

EXG Exchange Registers
   The two registers specified are exchanged with each other.

EXT Sign Extend
The operand is filled to the given processing width with its bit 7 (in the case of .B) or bit 15 (.W).

JMP Jump
Unconditional jump to the specified address. The difference between this and BRA is that here the address is not relative but absolute, that is, the actual jump destination.

JSR Jump to Subroutine
Jump to a subroutine. The difference from BSR is as above.

LEA Load Effective Address
This often-misunderstood instruction loads an address register not with the contents of the specified operand address as is normal for the other instructions, but *with the address as such*!

LINK Link Stack
This instruction first places the given address register on the stack. The contents of the stack pointer (A7) are then placed in this register and the offset specified is added to the stack pointer.

With this practical instruction, data areas can be reserved for a subroutine, without having to make room in the program itself, which would also be impossible in programs which run in ROM. The C-compiler makes extensive use of this capability for local variables.

LSL Logical Shift Left
Function and limitations as per ASL.

LSR Logical Shift Right
Function and limitations as per ASR, except here the sign is not shifted in on the left, but a 0.

MOVE
The first operand is transferred to the second.
Variations: *MOVEA, MOVEQ*

MOVEM Move Mulitple Registers
Here an operand can consist of a list of registers. This can be used to place all of the registers on the stack, for instance.
Example: MOVEM.L A0-A6/D0-D7,-(A7)

MOVEP Move Peripheral Data

This specialty is made expressly for the operation of peripheral components. As a general rule, these work only with an 8-bit data bus, and are then connected only to the upper or lower 8 bits of the 68000's data bus. If a word or long word is to be transferred, the bytes must be passed over either the upper or lower byte of the data bus, depending on whether the address is even or odd. The address is then always incremented by two so that the transfer always continues on the same half of the data bus on which it was begun. Corresponding to the purpose of this instruction, one operand is always a data register, and the other is always of type register indirect with offset.

MULS Multiply Signed

Signed multiplication of two operands.

MULU Multiply Unsigned

Multiplication of two operands, ignoring the sign.

NBCD Negate Decimal with Extend

A BCD operand is subjected to the operation 0-operand X.

NEG Negate Binary

The operand is subjected to the treatment 0-operand.
Variations: *NEGX*

NOP No Operation

As the name says, this instruction doesn't do anything.

NOT One's Complement

The operand is inverted.

OR Logical OR

The two operands are combined according to the rule for logical OR.

PEA Push Effective Address

The address itself, not its contents, is placed on the stack.

RESET Reset External Devices

The reset line on the 68000 is bidirectional. Not only can the processor be externally reset, but it can also use this instruction to reset all of the peripheral devices connected to the reset line.
This is a privileged instruction!

ROL Rotate Left
The operand is shifted to the left, whereby the bit shifted out on the left will be shifted back in on the right and the carry flag is affected. Processing widths and shift counter as per ASL.

ROR Rotate Right
As above, but shift from left to right.

ROXL Rotate Left with Extend
As ROL, but the shifted bit is first placed in the X flag, the previous value of which is shifted in on the right.

ROXR Rotate Right with Extend
As above, but reversed shift direction.

RTE Return from Exception
Return from an exception routine to the location at which the exception occurred.

RTS Return from Subroutine
Return from a subroutine to the location at which it was called.

RTR Return and Restore
As above, but the CC register (the one with the flags) is first fetched from the stack (on which it *must* have first been placed, because otherwise execution will not return to the proper address.

SBCD Subtract Decimal with Extend
The first operand is subtracted from the second. Refer to ABCD for information on the data format.

Scc Set Conditionally
The operand (only .B) is set to $FF if the condition is fulfilled. Otherwise it is cleared. Refer to Bcc for the possible condition codes.

STOP
The processor is stopped and can only be called back to life through an external interrupt.
This is a privileged instruction!

SUB Subtract Binary
The first operand is subtracted from the second.

SWAP Swap Register Halves
   The two halves of a data register are exchanged with each other.

TAS Test and Set Operand
   The operand (only .B) is checked for sign and 0 (affecting the C and N flags). Bit 7 is then set to 1.

TRAP
   The applications programmer uses this instruction when he wants to call functions of the operating systems. This instruction generates an exception, which consists of continuing the program at the address determined by the given vector number. See the chapter on the BIOS and XBIOS for the use of this instruction.

TRAPV Trap on Overflow
   If the V flag is set, an exception is generated by this instruction, resulting in program execution continuing at the address in vector 7 ($1C).

TST Test
   Action like TAS, but the operand is not changed.

UNLK Unlink
   This instruction is the counterpart of LINK. The stack pointer (A7) is loaded with the given address register and this is supplied with the last stack entry. In this manner the area reserved with LINK is released.

Addendum to the condition codes: The conditions listed under Bcc are not complete, because the additional conditions do not make sense at that point. But the instructions DBcc and Scc have the additional variations T (DBT, ST) and F (DBF, SF). T stands for true and means that the condition is always fulfilled. F stands for false and is the opposite: the condition is never fulfilled.

DBF can also use the syntax DBRA.

3.9 The BIOS Listing

The situation concerning ST software has changed radically since the Spring of 1985. Nowadays you can find a wealth of programs which are fully supported by GEM, and as a consequence are easy to operate. In addition, many dealers have gone over exclusively to the ST.

One thing is certain: If available software and hardware under development are any indicators, the Atari ST has caught on as an incredibly popular computer.

The following is the commented BIOS listing of the Atari ST. It is patterned after the ROM version of February 1986. The listing includes system initialization, the complete BIOS and XBIOS, as well as the VT52 screen driver. We don't expect any changes to this listing in the near future. Any alterations to the ST that affect this listing will be reflected in later editions of this book (we plan on keeping abreast of any changes, naturally).

The variables in the ROM version lie in the same range (up to $6100) as the diskette version of TOS from February 1986.

If you want to use system routines from TOS in your own programs you should only use the call through the corresponding TRAP. Otherwise, your program won't run with any altered versions of TOS. This applies at the same time to the use of variables which are not contained in the list of system variables.

Otherwise, you can call the BIOS routines as excellent illustrations in 68000 assembly language. If your own routines are to be complex and transparent, you can convert most of them to C compiled code. Then you can recognize most of these routines since they start with `link #n,A6`. A6 as a base register will communicate with given parameters if there is a positive offset; a negative offset will communicate with the local variables of this routine.

```
*************************
FC0000  601E                      bra      $FC0020              ATARI ST ROM-BIOS
FC0002  0100                      dc.b     1,0                  to start of program
FC0004  00FC0020                  dc.l     $FC0020              Version 1
FC0008  00FC0000                  dc.l     $FC0000              Reset address
FC000C  00006100                  dc.l     $6100                Start of the operating system
FC0010  00FC0020                  dc.l     $FC0020              Start of free RAM
FC0014  00FEFFF4                  dc.l     $FEFFF4              Default shell (reset)
FC0018  02061986                  dc.l     $02061986            Address for GEM magic
FC001C  0003                      dc.w     3                    Creation date 2/6/1986
FC001E  0C46                      dc.w     $0C46                Flag for PAL version
FC0020  46FC2700                  move.w   #$2700,SR            Date in DOS format
FC0024  4E70                      reset                         Supervisor mode, IPL 7
FC0026  0CB9FA52235F00FA0000      cmp.l    #$FA52235F,$FA0000   Reset peripherals
FC0030  660A                      bne      $FC003C              Diagnostic cartridge inserted ?
FC0032  4DFA0008                  lea      $FC003C(PC),A6       no
FC0036  4EF900FA0004              jmp      $FA0004              Load return address
                                                                Jump to cartridge

FC003C  4DFA0006                  lea      $FC0044(PC),A6       Load return address
FC0040  60000596                  bra      $FC05D8              Memory configuration valid?
FC0044  660A                      bne      $FC0050              no
FC0046  13F900000424FFFF8001      move.b   $424,$FFFF8001       Get memctrl
FC0050  9BCD                      sub.l    A5,A5                Clear A5
FC0052  0CAD31415926 0426         cmp.l    #$31415926,$426(A5)  resvalid, resvector valid ?
FC005A  6618                      bne      $FC0074              No
FC005C  202D042A                  move.l   $42A(A5),D0          Load resvector
FC0060  4A2D042A                  tst.b    $42A(A5)             Test bits 24-31
FC0064  660E                      bne      $FC0074              Set, vector invalid
FC0066  08000000                  btst     #0,D0                Address odd?
FC006A  6608                      bne      $FC0074              Yes, invalid
FC006C  2040                      move.l   D0,A0                Load address
FC006E  4DFAFFE0                  lea      $FC0050(PC),A6       Load return address
```

FC0072	4ED0	jmp	(A0)	Jump via vector
FC0074	41F9FFFF8800	lea	$FFFF8800,A0	Address of the PSG
FC007A	10BC0007	move.b	#7,(A0)	Port A and B
FC007E	117C00C00002	move.b	#$C0,2(A0)	To output
FC0084	10BC000E	move.b	#$E,(A0)	Select port A
FC0088	117C00070002	move.b	#7,2(A0)	Deselect floppies
FC008E	083A0000FF8B	btst	#0,$FC001B(PC)	Pal version ? (must be $FC001D)
FC0094	6710	beq	$FC00A6	No
FC0096	4DFA0006	lea	$FC009E(PC),A6	Load return address
FC009A	60000C48	bra	$FC0CE4	
FC009E	13FC0002FFFF820A	move.b	#2,$FFFF820A	Sync mode to 50 Hz Pal
FC00A6	43F9FFFF8240	lea	$FFFF8240,A1	Address of the color palette
FC00AC	303C000F	move.w	#$F,D0	16 colors
FC00B0	41FA054C	lea	$FC05FE(PC),A0	Address of the color table
FC00B4	32D8	move.w	(A0)+,(A1)+	Copy color in palette
FC00B6	51C8FFFC	dbra	D0,$FC00B4	Next color
FC00BA	13FC0001FFFF8201	move.b	#1,$FFFF8201	dbaseh
FC00C2	13FC0000FFFF8203	move.b	#0,$FFFF8203	dbasel, video address to $10000
FC00CA	9BCD	sub.l	A5,A5	Clear A5
FC00CC	1C2D0424	move.b	$424(A5),D6	memctrl
FC00D0	2A2D042E	move.l	$42E(A5),D5	phystop
FC00D4	4DFA0006	lea	$FC00DC(PC),A6	Load return address
FC00D8	600004FE	bra	$FC05D8	
FC00DC	670000E4	beq	$FC01C2	Memory configuration valid?
FC00E0	4246	clr.w	D6	Yes
FC00E2	13FC000AFFFF8001	move.b	#$A,$FFFF8001	Start value for memory controller
FC00EA	307C0008	move.w	#8,A0	Memory controller to 2 * 2 MB
FC00EE	43F900200008	lea	$200008,A1	Start address for memory test
FC00F4	4240	clr.w	D0	A1 points to second bank
FC00F6	30C0	move.w	D0,(A0)+	Clear bit pattern to be written
FC00F8	32C0	move.w	D0,(A1)+	Write pattern
FC00FA	D07CFA54	add.w	#$FA54,D0	Write to other address range
				Next bit pattern

273

```
FC00FE B1FC00000200    cmp.l     #$200,A0              End address reached?
FC0104 66F0            bne       $FC00F6               No
FC0106 223C00200000    move.l    #$200000,D1           D1 equals second bank
FC010C E44E            lsr.w     #2,D6
FC010E 307C0208        move.w    #$208,A0              Is bit pattern at $208 ?
FC0112 4BFA0006        lea       $FC011A(PC),A5        Load return address
FC0116 600004AA        bra       $FC05C2               Memory test
FC011A 6720            beq       $FC013C               OK, 128 K
FC011C 307C0408        move.w    #$408,A0              At $408 ?
FC0120 4BFA0006        lea       $FC0128(PC),A5        Load return address
FC0124 6000049C        bra       $FC05C2               Memory test
FC0128 6710            beq       $FC013A               OK, 512 K
FC012A 307C0008        move.w    #$8,A0                At $8
FC012E 4BFA0006        lea       $FC0136(PC),A5        Load return address
FC0132 6000048E        bra       $FC05C2               Memory test
FC0136 6604            bne       $FC013C               Nothing in this bank
FC0138 5846            addq.w    #4,D6
FC013A 5846            addq.w    #4,D6
FC013C 92BC00200000    sub.l     #$200000,D1           Configuration byte to 2 MB
FC0142 67C8            beq       $FC010C               Next bank
FC0144 13C6FFFF8001    move.b    D6,$FFFF8001          Test for first bank
FC014A 28790000008     move.l    $8,A4                 Program memory controller
FC0150 41FA0036        lea       $FC0188(PC),A0        Save Bus Error vector
FC0154 23C800000008    move.l    A0,$8                 Address of new Bus-Error routine
FC015A 363CFB55        move.w    #$FB55,D3             Set
FC015E 2E3C00020000    move.l    #$20000,D7            Start bit pattern
FC0164 2047            move.l    D7,A0                 Start address is 128 K
FC0166 2248            move.l    A0,A1                 Save current
FC0168 3400            move.w    D0,D2                 address
FC016A 722A            moveq.l   #42,D1                43 words
FC016C 3302            move.w    D2,-(A1)              Write bit pattern in RAM
FC016E D443            add.w     D3,D2                 Change pattern
```

FC0170	51C9FFFA	dbra	D1,$FC016C	Write next bit pattern
FC0174	2248	move.l	A0,A1	Repeat address
FC0176	722A	moveq.l	#42,D1	43 words
FC0178	B061	cmp.w	-(A1),D0	Is bit pattern in RAM?
FC017A	660C	bne	$FC0188	No, terminate test
FC017C	4251	clr.w	(A1)	Clear RAM
FC017E	D043	add.w	D3,D0	Change bit pattern
FC0180	51C9FFF6	dbra	D1,$FC0178	Test next word
FC0184	D1C7	add.l	D7,A0	Increment address by 128K
FC0186	60DE	bra	$FC0166	Continue testing
FC0188	91C7	sub.l	D7,A0	Address minus 128 K
FC018A	2A08	move.l	A0,D5	Save
FC018C	23CC00000008	move.l	A4,$8	Restore old Bus-Error vector
FC0192	2045	move.l	D5,A0	Highest address for clear
FC0194	283C00000400	move.l	#$400,D4	Lower bound for clear
FC019A	4CFA000F0450	movem.l	$FC05EC(PC),D0-D3	Clear registers D0-D3
FC01A0	48E0F000	movem.l	D0-D3,-(A0)	Clear 16 bytes
FC01A4	B1C4	cmp.l	D4,A0	Lower bound reached?
FC01A6	66F8	bne	$FC01A0	No, continue
FC01A8	9BCD	sub.l	A5,A5	Clear A5
FC01AA	1B460424	move.b	D6,$424(A5)	memctrl
FC01AE	2B45042E	move.l	D5,$42E(A5)	Highest RAM address as phystop
FC01B2	2B7C752019F30420	move.l	#$752019F3,$420(A5)	magic to memvalid
FC01BA	2B7C237698AA043A	move.l	#$237698AA,$43A(A5)	magic to memval2
FC01C2	9BCD	sub.l	A5,A5	Clear A5
FC01C4	307C093A	move.w	#$93A,A0	End of the system variables
FC01C8	227C00010000	move.l	#$10000,A1	to current video address
FC01CE	7000	moveq.l	#0,D0	
FC01D0	30C0	move.w	D0,(A0)+	Clear memory
FC01D2	B3C8	cmp.l	A0,A1	End address reached?
FC01D4	66FA	bne	$FC01D0	No

```
FC01D6 206D042E          move.l   $42E(A5),A0              phystop
FC01DA 91FC00008000      sub.l    #$8000,A0                minus 32 K
FC01E0 2B48044E          move.l   A0,$44E(A5)              equals _v_bs_ad
FC01E4 13ED044FFFFF8201  move.b   $44F(A5),$FFFF8201       dbaseh
FC01EC 13ED0450FFFF8203  move.b   $450(A5),$FFFF8203       dbasel
FC01F4 323C07FF          move.w   #$7FF,D1                 32 K
FC01F8 20C0              move.l   D0,(A0)+
FC01FA 20C0              move.l   D0,(A0)+                 Clear screen
FC01FC 20C0              move.l   D0,(A0)+
FC01FE 20C0              move.l   D0,(A0)+
FC0200 51C9FFF6          dbra     D1,$FC01F8               Next 16 bytes
FC0204 207AFE0E          move.l   $FC0014(PC),A0           Address os_magic
FC0208 0C9087654321      cmp.l    #$87654321,(A0)          magic present ?
FC020E 6704              beq      $FC0214                  Yes
FC0210 41FAFDF6          lea      $FC0008(PC),A0           Else use system addresses
FC0214 23E80004000004FA  move.l   4(A0),$4FA               end_os
FC021C 23E80008000004FE  move.l   8(A0),$4FE               exec_os
FC0224 2B7C00FC0D60046A  move.l   #$FC0D60,$46A(A5)        hdv_init
FC022C 2B7C00FC10D20476  move.l   #$FC10D2,$476(A5)        hdv_rw
FC0234 2B7C00FC0DE60472  move.l   #$FC0DE6,$472(A5)        hdv_bpb
FC023C 2B7C00FC0F96047E  move.l   #$FC0F96,$47E(A5)        hdv_mediach
FC0244 2B7C00FC137C047A  move.l   #$FC137C,$47A(A5)        hdv_boot
FC024C 2B7C00FC1F340506  move.l   #$FC1F34,$506(A5)        prt_stat
FC0254 2B7C00FC1EA0050A  move.l   #$FC1EA0,$50A(A5)        prt_vec
FC025C 2B7C00FC1F6E050E  move.l   #$FC1F6E,$50E(A5)        aux_stat
FC0264 2B7C00FC1F860512  move.l   #$FC1F86,$512(A5)        aux_vec
FC026C 2B7C00FC0C2C0502  move.l   #$FC0C2C,$502(A5)        dump_vec
FC0274 2B6D0044E0436     move.l   $44E(A5),$436(A5)        _v_bs_ad to _memtop
FC027A 2B6D04FA0432      move.l   $4FA(A5),$432(A5)        end_os to _membot
FC0280 4FF900004DB8      lea      $4DB8,A7                 Initialize system stack pointer
FC0286 3B7C00080454      move.w   #8,$454(A5)              nvbls
FC028C 50ED0444          st       $444(A5)                 _fverify
```

FC0290	3B7C00030440	move.w	#3,$440(A5)	seek rate to 3 ms
FC0296	2B7C0000167A04C6	move.l	#$167A,$4C6(A5)	_dskbufp
FC029E	3B7CFFFF04EE	move.w	#-1,$4EE(A5)	clear _dumpflg
FC02A4	2B7C00FC000004F2	move.l	#$FC0000,$4F2(A5)	_sysbase to ROM start
FC02AC	2B7C0000093A04A2	move.l	#$93A,$4A2(A5)	savptr for BIOS
FC02B4	2B7C00FC05C0046E	move.l	#$FC05C0,$46E(A5)	swv_vec for monitor change to rts
FC02BC	47FA0466	lea	$FC0724(PC),A3	Address rte
FC02C0	49FA02FE	lea	$FC05C0(PC),A4	Address rts
FC02C4	0CB9FA52235F00FA0000	cmp.l	#$FA52235F,$FA0000	Diagnostic cartridge inserted ?
FC02CE	6726	beq	$FC02F6	Yes
FC02D0	43FA0748	lea	$FC0A1A(PC),A1	Indicate address for exception
FC02D4	D3FC02000000	add.l	#$2000000,A1	Vector number in bits 24-31 to 2
FC02DA	41F900000008	lea	$8,A0	Start with Bus Error
FC02E0	303C003D	move.w	#$3D,D0	62 vectors
FC02E4	20C9	move.l	A1,(A0)+	Set vector
FC02E6	D3FC01000000	add.l	#$1000000,A1	Increment vector number
FC02EC	51C8FFF6	dbra	D0,$FC02E4	Initialize next exception vector
FC02F0	23CB00000014	move.l	A3,$14	'Division by Zero' to rte
FC02F6	2B7C00FC06340070	move.l	#$FC0634,112(A5)	VBL interrupt, IPL 4
FC02FE	2B7C00FC061E0068	move.l	#$FC061E,104(A5)	HBL interrupt, IPL 2
FC0306	2B4B0088	move.l	A3,136(A5)	TRAP #2 to rte
FC030A	2B7C00FC074E00B4	move.l	#$FC074E,180(A5)	TRAP #13 vector
FC0312	2B7C00FC074800B8	move.l	#$FC0748,184(A5)	TRAP #14 vector
FC031A	2B7C00FC9CA20028	move.l	#$FC9CA2,40(A5)	LINE A vector
FC0322	2B4C0400	move.l	A4,$400(A5)	etv_timer to rts
FC0326	2B7C00FC07440404	move.l	#$FC0744,$404(A5)	etv_critic vector
FC032E	2B4C0408	move.l	A4,$408(A5)	etv_term to rts
FC0332	41ED04CE	lea	$4CE(A5),A0	_vbl_list
FC0336	2B480456	move.l	A0,$456(A5)	as pointer to _vblqueue
FC033A	303C0007	move.w	#7,D0	8 entries
FC033E	4298	clr.l	(A0)+	clear
FC0340	51C8FFFC	dbra	D0,$FC033E	Next entry

277

```
FC0344  61001E6E              bsr      $FC21B4                        Initialize mfp
FC0348  7002                  moveq.l  #2,D0                          Bit 2
FC034A  6100024A              bsr      $FC0596                        cartscan
FC034E  1039FFFF8260          move.b   $FFFF8260,D0                   Video resolution
FC0354  C03C0003              and.b    #3,D0                          Isolate bits 0 and 1
FC0358  B03C0003              cmp.b    #3,D0                          Invalid value?
FC035C  6602                  bne      $FC0360                        No
FC035E  7002                  moveq.l  #2,D0                          Replace with 2 for high resolution
FC0360  13C00000004C          move.b   D0,$44C                        sshiftmod
FC0366  1039FFFFFA01          move.b   $FFFFFA01,D0                   mfp gpip, monomon
FC036C  6B18                  bmi      $FC0386                        No monochrome monitor?
FC036E  4DFA0006              lea      $FC0376(PC),A6                 No return address
FC0372  60000970              bra      $FC0CE4
FC0376  13FC0002FFFF8260      move.b   #2,$FFFF8260                   High resolution
FC037E  13FC00020000004C      move.b   #2,$44C                        sshiftmod
FC0386  4EB900FCA7C4          jsr      $FCA7C4                        Initialize screen output
FC038C  0C3900010000004C      cmp.b    #1,$44C                        sshiftmod
FC0394  660A                  bne      $FC03A0                        Not medium resolution ?
FC0396  33F9FFFF825EFFFF8246  move.w   $FFFF825E,$FFFF8246            Copy color 15 (black) to color 3
FC03A0  2B7C00FC0020046E      move.l   #$FC0020,$46E(A5)              swv_vec to teset
FC03A8  33FC00010000452       move.w   #1,$452                        vblsem
FC03B0  4240                  clr.w    D0                             Bit 0
FC03B2  610001E2              bsr      $FC0596                        cartscan
FC03B6  46FC2300              move.w   #$2300,SR                      IPL 3
FC03BA  7001                  moveq.l  #1,D0                          Bit 1
FC03BC  610001D8              bsr      $FC0596                        cartscan
FC03C0  61004798              bsr      $FC4B5A                        Initialize DOS
FC03C4  3F3900FC001E          move.w   $FC001E,-(A7)                  Creation date in DOS format
FC03CA  3F3C002B              move.w   #$2B,-(A7)                     Set date
FC03CE  4E41                  trap     #1                             GEMDOS
FC03D0  584F                  addq.w   #4,A7                          Correct stack pointer
FC03D2  610000B8              bsr      $FC048C                        Boot from floppy
```

Address	Hex	Instruction	Operand	Comment
FC03D6	610000D0	bsr	$FC04A8	Boot from DMA bus
FC03DA	61000944	bsr	$FC0D20	Execute reset-resident programs
FC03DE	4A7900000482	tst.w	$482	_cmdload ?
FC03E4	6718	beq	$FC03FE	No
FC03E6	61004194	bsr	$FC457C	Turn cursor on
FC03EA	61000728	bsr	$FC0B14	autoexec, execute programs in AUTO folder
FC03EE	487A0099	pea	$FC0489(PC)	Null name
FC03F2	487A0095	pea	$FC0489(PC)	Null name
FC03F6	487A007E	pea	$FC0476(PC)	'COMMAND.PRG'
FC03FA	4267	clr.w	-(A7)	Load and start program
FC03FC	605C	bra	$FC045A	Load to program
FC03FE	61000714	bsr	$FC0B14	autoexec, execute programs in AUTO folder
FC0402	41FA0066	lea	$FC046A(PC),A0	'PATH='
FC0406	327C0840	move.w	#$840,A1	Address for environment
FC040A	0C100023	cmp.b	#35,(A0)	'#', place holder for drive?
FC040E	6602	bne	$FC0412	No
FC0410	2449	move.l	A1,A2	Save address
FC0412	12D8	move.b	(A0)+,(A1)+	Copy filenames
FC0414	6AF4	bpl	$FC040A	Next byte
FC0416	10390000446	move.b	$446,D0	_bootdev
FC041C	D03C0041	add.b	#$41,D0	'A'
FC0420	1480	move.b	D0,(A2)	Insert drive number
FC0422	487900000840	pea	$840	environment
FC0428	487900FC0489	pea	$FC0489	Null name
FC042E	487A0059	pea	$FC0489(PC)	Null name
FC0432	3F3C0005	move.w	#5,-(A7)	Create base page
FC0436	3F3C004B	move.w	#$4B,-(A7)	exec
FC043A	4E41	trap	#1	GEMDOS
FC043C	DEFC000E	add.w	#$E,A7	Correct stack pointer
FC0440	2040	move.l	D0,A0	Address of the base page
FC0442	217900004FE0008	move.l	$4FE,8(A0)	exec_os, start address AES and Desktop
FC044A	487900000840	pea	$840	environment

```
FC0450  2F08                  move.l    A0,-(A7)              Address of the base page
FC0452  487A0035              pea       $FC0489(PC)           Null name
FC0456  3F3C0004              move.w    #4,-(A7)              Start program
FC045A  3F3C004B              move.w    #$4B,-(A7)            exec
FC045E  4E41                  trap      #1                    GEMDOS
FC0460  DEFC000E              add.w     #$E,A7                Correct stack pointer
FC0464  4EF900FC0020          jmp       $FC0020               it return to reset
FC046A  504154483D00          dc.b      'PATH=',0
FC0470  233A5C0000FF          dc.b      '#:\',0,0,$FF
FC0476  434F4D4D414E442E      dc.b      'COMMAND.PRG',0
FC047E  50524700
FC0482  47454D2E505247        dc.b      'GEM.PRG'
FC0489  000000                dc.b      0,0,0
*****************************************************
FC048C  7003                  moveq.l   #3,D0                 Boot from floppy
FC048E  61000106              bsr       $FC0596               Bit 3
FC0492  20790000047A          move.l    $47A,A0               cartscan
FC0498  4E90                  jsr       (A0)                  hdv_boot
FC049A  4A40                  tst.w     D0                    Load boot sector
FC049C  6608                  bne       $FC04A6               Executable ?
FC049E  41F90000167A          lea       $167A,A0              Address of the disk buffer
FC04A4  4E90                  jsr       (A0)                  Execute boot sector
FC04A6  4E75                  rts
*****************************************************
FC04A8  7E00                  moveq.l   #0,D7                 dmaboot, load boot sector from DMA bus
FC04AA  612A                  bsr       $FC04D6               Begin with device 0
FC04AC  6620                  bne       $FC04CE               dmaread, load boot sector
FC04AE  20790000004C6         move.l    $4C6,A0               Error, test next device
FC04B4  323C00FF              move.w    #$FF,D1               _dskbufp
FC04B8  7000                  moveq.l   #0,D0                 $100 words
FC04BA  D058                  add.w     (A0)+,D0              Clear sum
FC04BC  51C9FFFC              dbra      D1,$FC04BA            Generate checksum
                                                              Next word
```

```
FC04C0  B07C1234              cmp.w    #$1234,D0              Executable sector?
FC04C4  6608                  bne      $FC04CE                No
FC04C6  2079000004C6          move.l   $4C6,A0                _dskbufp
FC04CC  4E90                  jsr      (A0)                   Execute boot sector
FC04CE  DE3C0020              add.b    #$20,D7                Next device number
FC04D2  66D6                  bne      $FC04AA                All 8 devices?
FC04D4  4E75                  rts
*****************************************************
FC04D6  4DF9FFFF8606          lea      $FFFF8606,A6           dmaread, load boot sector from DMA bus
FC04DC  4BF9FFFF8604          lea      $FFFF8604,A5           DMA control register
FC04E2  50F90000043E          st       $43E                   DMA data register
FC04E8  2F39000004C6          move.l   $4C6,-(A7)             set flock
FC04EE  13EF0003FFFF860D      move.b   3(A7),$FFFF860D        _dskbufp
FC04F6  13EF0002FFFF860B      move.b   2(A7),$FFFF860B
FC04FE  13EF0001FFFF8609      move.b   1(A7),$FFFF8609        Set DMA address
FC0506  584F                  addq.w   #4,A7                  Correct stack pointer
FC0508  3CBC0098              move.w   #$98,(A6)              Toggle R/W,
FC050C  3CBC0198              move.w   #$198,(A6)             to allow READ
FC0510  3CBC0098              move.w   #$98,(A6)
FC0514  3ABC0001              move.w   #1,(A5)                sector-count register to 1
FC0518  3CBC0088              move.w   #$88,(A6)              Select DMA bus
FC051C  1007                  move.b   D7,D0                  Device number << 5
FC051E  803C0008              or.b     #8,D0                  OR with read command
FC0522  4840                  swap     D0
FC0524  303C0088              move.w   #$88,D0
FC0528  614C                  bsr      $FC0576                Output byte to DMA bus
FC052A  662A                  bne      $FC0556                timeout, terminate
FC052C  7C03                  moveq.l  #3,D6                  Counter to 4
FC052E  41FA0036              lea      $FC0566(PC),A0         Pointer to command word table
FC0532  2018                  move.l   (A0)+,D0               Get command
FC0534  6140                  bsr      $FC0576                Output on DMA bus
FC0536  661E                  bne      $FC0556                timeout, terminate
```

```
FC0538 51CEFFF8                dbra    D6,$FC0532      Next command
FC053C 2ABC0000000A            move.l  #$A,(A5)        Send byte 6 (last byte)
FC0542 323C0190                move.w  #$190,D1
FC0546 6132                    bsr     $FC057A         Write byte
FC0548 660C                    bne     $FC0556         timeout, terminate
FC054A 3CBC008A                move.w  #$8A,(A6)       Select status register
FC054E 3015                    move.w  (A5),D0         Read status
FC0550 C07C00FF                and.w   #$FF,D0         Isolate bits 0-7
FC0554 6702                    beq     $FC0558         ok
FC0556 70FF                    moveq.l #-1,D0          Return code for error
FC0558 3CBC0080                move.w  #$80,(A6)       DMA chip back to floppy operation
FC055C 4A00                    tst.b   D0              Set flags
FC055E 51F90000043E            sf      $43E            Clear flock
FC0564 4E75                    rts

***************************************************** Command words for DMA chip

FC0566 0000008A                dc.l    $0000008A
FC056A 0000008A                dc.l    $0000008A
FC056E 0000008A                dc.l    $0000008A
FC0572 0001008A                dc.l    $0001008A

*****************************************************

FC0576 2A80                    move.l  D0,(A5)         wcbyte, output byte to DMA bus
FC0578 720A                    moveq.l #10,D1          Output byte
FC057A D2B9000004BA            add.l   $4BA,D1         Wait 1/20 second
FC0580 08390005FFFFFA01        btst    #5,$FFFFFA01    _hz_200
FC0588 670A                    beq     $FC0594         mfp gpip, command processed?
FC058A B2B9000004BA            cmp.l   $4BA,D1         Yes
FC0590 66EE                    bne     $FC0580         _hz_200, time run out?
FC0592 72FF                    moveq.l #-1,D1          No, keep waiting
FC0594 4E75                    rts                     Return code for error
```

```
************************************************
FC0596  41F900FA0000   lea     $FA0000,A0          cartscan, test cartridge
FC059C  0C98ABCDEF42   cmp.l   #$ABCDEF42,(A0)+    Address of the cartridge
FC05A2  661A           bne     $FC05BE             User cartridge ?
FC05A4  01280004       btst    D0,4(A0)            Corresponding bit set?
FC05A8  670E           beq     $FC05B8             No
FC05AA  48E7FFFE       movem.l D0-D7/A0-A6,-(A7)   Save registers
FC05AE  20680004       move.l  4(A0),A0            Get address of the routine
FC05B2  4E90           jsr     (A0)                and execute
FC05B4  4CDF7FFF       movem.l (A7)+,D0-D7/A0-A6   Save registers
FC05B8  4A90           tst.l   (A0)                Further use?
FC05BA  2050           move.l  (A0),A0             Get address
FC05BC  66E6           bne     $FC05A4             Yes, keep testing
FC05BE  4E75           rts
************************************************
FC05C0  4E75           rts                         rts for dummy routines
************************************************
FC05C2  D1C1           add.l   D1,A0               Memory test
FC05C4  4240           clr.w   D0                  Start address
FC05C6  43E801F8       lea     $1F8(A0),A1         Clear bit pattern
FC05CA  B058           cmp.w   (A0)+,D0            End address
FC05CC  6608           bne     $FC05D6             Test for bit pattern
FC05CE  D07CFA54       add.w   #$FA54,D0           Not equal, error
FC05D2  B3C8           cmp.l   A0,A1               Next bit pattern
FC05D4  66F4           bne     $FC05CA             End address reached?
FC05D6  4ED5           jmp     (A5)                No
                                                   Back to call
************************************************
FC05D8  9BCD                   sub.l   A5,A5               Memory configuration valid?
FC05DA  0CAD752019F30420       cmp.l   #$752019F3,$420(A5) Clear A5
                                                            magic in memvalid ?
```

```
FC05E2  6608                bne     $FC05EC                         No
FC05E4  0CAD237698AA043A    cmp.l   #$237698AA,$43A(A5)             magic in memval2 ?
FC05EC  4ED6                jmp     (A6)                            Back to call
********************************************                        Zero-bytes to clear
FC05EE  00000000            dc.l    0
FC05F2  00000000            dc.l    0
FC05F6  00000000            dc.l    0
FC05FA  00000000            dc.l    0
********************************************                        Standard color palette
FC05FE  0777070000700770    dc.w    $777,$700,$070,$770             White, red, green, yellow
FC0606  0007070700770555    dc.w    $007,$707,$077,$555             blue, magenta, cyan, light gray
FC060E  0333073303730773    dc.w    $333,$733,$373,$773             gray, lt. red, lt. green, lt. yellow
FC0616  0337073703770000    dc.w    $337,$737,$377,$000             lt. blue, lt. magenta, lt. cyan, black
********************************************                        HBL interrupt
FC061E  3F00                move.w  D0,-(A7)                        Save D0
FC0620  302F0002            move.w  2(A7),D0                        Save status from stack
FC0624  C07C0700            and.w   #$700,D0                        Isolate IPL mask
FC0628  6606                bne     $FC0630                         Not IPL 0 ?
FC062A  006F03000002        or.w    #$300,2(A7)                     Else set IPL 3
FC0630  301F                move.w  (A7)+,D0                        D0 back again
FC0632  4E73                rte
********************************************                        VBL interrupt
FC0634  52B900000466        addq.l  #1,$466                         _frclock
FC063A  53790000452         subq.w  #1,$452                         vblsem
FC0640  6B0000DC            bmi     $FC071E                         VBL routine disabled?
FC0644  48E7FFFE            movem.l D0-D7/A0-A6,-(A7)                Save registers
FC0648  52B900000462        addq.l  #1,$462                         _vbclock
FC064E  9BCD                sub.l   A5,A5                           Clear A5
FC0650  1039FFFF8260        move.b  $FFFF8260,D0                    Get video resolution
```

284

FC0656 C03C0003	and.b	#3,D0	Isolate bits 0 and 1
FC065A B03C0002	cmp.b	#2,D0	High resolution ?
FC065E 6C18	bge	$FC0678	Yes
FC0660 08390007FFFFFA01	btst	#7,$FFFFFA01	Monochrome monitor connected ?
FC0668 6634	bne	$FC069E	No
FC066A 303C07D0	move.w	#$7D0,D0	Counter
FC066E 51C8FFFE	dbra	D0,$FC066E	Delay loop
FC0672 103C0002	move.b	#2,D0	High resolution
FC0676 6016	bra	$FC068E	
FC0678 08390007FFFFFA01	btst	#7,$FFFFFA01	Monochrome monitor connected ?
FC0680 671C	beq	$FC069E	Yes
FC0682 102D044A	move.b	$44A(A5),D0	defshiftmod
FC0686 B03C0002	cmp.b	#2,D0	High resolution ?
FC068A 6D02	blt	$FC068E	No
FC068C 4200	clr.b	D0	
FC068E 1B40044C	move.b	D0,$44C(A5)	sshiftmod
FC0692 13C0FFFF8260	move.b	D0,$FFFF8260	shiftmd, select resolution
FC0698 206D046E	move.l	$46E(A5),A0	swv_vec
FC069C 4E90	jsr	(A0)	Default is reset
FC069E 6100401A	bsr	$FC46BA	Flash cursor
FC06A2 9BCD	sub.l	A5,A5	Clear A5
FC06A4 4AAD045A	tst.l	$45A(A5)	colorptr
FC06A8 6718	beq	$FC06C2	Don't load color palette?
FC06AA 206D045A	move.l	$45A(A5),A0	colorptr
FC06AE 43F9FFFF8240	lea	$FFFF8240,A1	Address of the color register
FC06B4 303C000F	move.w	#$F,D0	16 colors
FC06B8 32D8	move.w	(A0)+,(A1)+	copy
FC06BA 51C8FFFC	dbra	D0,$FC06B8	next color
FC06BE 42AD045A	clr.l	$45A(A5)	colorptr
FC06C2 4AAD045E	tst.l	$45E(A5)	screenpt
FC06C6 671A	beq	$FC06E2	Don't change video address?

```
FC06C8  2B6D045E044E        move.l    $45E(A5),$44E(A5)      screenpt to _v_bs_ad
FC06CE  202D044E            move.l    $44E(A5),D0            _v_bs_ad
FC06D2  E088                lsr.l     #8,D0                  Bits 8-15
FC06D4  13C0FFFF8203        move.b    D0,$FFFF8203           as dbasel
FC06DA  E048                lsr.w     #8,D0                  Bits 16-23
FC06DC  13C0FFFF8201        move.b    D0,$FFFF8201           as dbaseh
FC06E2  610012CC            bsr       $FC19B0                flopvbl, floppy VBL routine
FC06E6  3E390000454         move.w    $454,D7                nvbls
FC06EC  6720                beq       $FC070E                VBL list empty?
FC06EE  5387                subq.l    #1,D7                  dbra counter
FC06F0  20790000456         move.l    $456,A0                _vblqueue
FC06F6  2258                move.l    (A0)+,A1               Get address of the routine
FC06F8  B3FC00000000        cmp.l     #0,A1                  Not used?
FC06FE  670A                beq       $FC070A                To next routine
FC0700  48E70180            movem.l   D7/A0,-(A7)            Save registers
FC0704  4E91                jsr       (A1)                   Execute routine
FC0706  4CDF0180            movem.l   (A7)+,D7/A0            Restore registers
FC070A  51CFFFEA            dbra      D7,$FC06F6             Next routine
FC070E  9BCD                sub.l     A5,A5                  Clear A5
FC0710  4A6D04EE            tst.w     $4EE(A5)               _dumpflg
FC0714  6604                bne       $FC071A                Not set
FC0716  61000502            bsr       $FC0C1A                Execute hardcopy
FC071A  4CDF7FFF            movem.l   (A7)+,D0-D7/A0-A6      Restore registers
FC071E  52790000452         addq.w    #1,$452                vblsem
FC0724  4E73                rte
************************************************************
FC0726  40E7                move.w    SR,-(A7)               wvbl, wait for VBL
FC0728  027CF8FF            and.w     #$F8FF,SR              Save status
FC072C  20390000466         move.l    $466,D0                IPL 0, enable interrupts
FC0732  B0B90000466         cmp.l     $466,D0                _frclock
FC0738  67F8                beq       $FC0732                _frclock not yet incremented?
                                                             No, wait
```

```
FC073A 46DF              move.w   (A7)+,SR                      Restore status
FC073C 4E75              rts

*********************************************************
FC073E 2F3900000404      move.l   $404,-(A7)                    Critical error handler
FC0744 70FF              moveq.l  #-1,D0                        etv_critic
FC0746 4E75              rts                                    Default to error
                                                                Execute routine

*********************************************************
FC0748 41FA0084          lea      $FC07CE(PC),A0                TRAP #14
FC074C 6004              bra      $FC0752                       Address of the TRAP #14 routines

*********************************************************
FC074E 41FA004C          lea      $FC079C(PC),A0                TRAP #13
FC0752 22790000004A2     move.l   $4A2,A1                       Address of the TRAP #13 routines
FC0758 301F              move.w   (A7)+,D0                      Load savptr
FC075A 3300              move.w   D0,-(A1)                      Status register to D0
FC075C 231F              move.l   (A7)+,-(A1)                   Save in save area
FC075E 48E11F1F          movem.l  D3-D7/A3-A7,-(A1)             Return address in save area
FC0762 23C9000004A2      move.l   A1,$4A2                       Register in save area
FC0768 0800000D          btst     #13,D0                        Update savptr
FC076C 6602              bne      $FC0770                       Call from supervisor mode?
FC076E 4E6F              move.l   USP,A7                        Yes
FC0770 301F              move.w   (A7)+,D0                      Else use USP
FC0772 B058              cmp.w    (A0)+,D0                      Get function number from stack
FC0774 6C10              bge      $FC0786                       Compare with maximum number
FC0776 E548              lsl.w    #2,D0                         Too big, ignore
FC0778 20300000          move.l   0(A0,D0.w),D0                 As long index
FC077C 2040              move.l   D0,A0                         Get address of the routine
FC077E 6A02              bpl      $FC0782                       To A0
FC0780 2050              move.l   (A0),A0                       Direct address
FC0782 9BCD              sub.l    A5,A5                         Else use indirect
                                                                Clear A5
```

```
FC0784  4E90              jsr     (A0)                    Execute routine
FC0786  2279000004A2      move.l  $4A2,A1                 Get savptr
FC078C  4CD9F8F8          movem.l (A1)+,D3-D7/A3-A7       Restore registers
FC0790  2F19              move.l  (A1)+,-(A7)             Return address on stack
FC0792  3F19              move.w  (A1)+,-(A7)             Status on stack
FC0794  23C900004A2       move.l  A1,$4A2                 Update savptr
FC079A  4E73              rte

*****************************************************

FC079C  000C              dc.w    12                      Addresses of the TRAP #13 routines
FC079E  00FC0910          dc.l    $FC0910                 Number of routines
FC07A2  00FC0876          dc.l    $FC0876                 0, getmpb
FC07A6  00FC087C          dc.l    $FC087C                 1, bconstat
FC07AA  00FC0888          dc.l    $FC0888                 2, bconin
FC07AE  80000476          dc.l    $476+$80000000          3, bconout
FC07B2  00FC093C          dc.l    $FC093C                 4, (indirect) rwabs
FC07B6  00FC0954          dc.l    $FC0954                 5, setexec
FC07BA  80000472          dc.l    $472+$80000000          6, tickcal
FC07BE  00FC0882          dc.l    $FC0882                 7, (indirect) getbpb
FC07C2  8000047E          dc.l    $47E+$80000000          8, bcostat
FC07C6  00FC08F8          dc.l    $FC08F8                 9, (indirekct) mediach
FC07C8  00FC08FE          dc.l    $FC08FE                 10, drvmap
                                                          11, shift

*****************************************************

FC07CE  0028              dc.w    40                      Addresses of the TRAP #14 routines
FC07D0  00FC2DDC          dc.l    $FC2DDC                 Number of routines
FC07D4  00FC05C0          dc.l    $FC05C0                 0, initmouse
FC07D8  00FC095C          dc.l    $FC095C                 1, rts
FC07DC  00FC0970          dc.l    $FC0970                 2, physbase
FC07E0  00FC0976          dc.l    $FC0976                 3, logbase
FC07E4  00FC0982          dc.l    $FC0982                 4, getrez
FC07E8  00FC09D0          dc.l    $FC09D0                 5, setscreen
                                                          6, setpalette
```

```
FC07EC  00FC09D8    dc.l    $FC09D8     7, setcolor
FC07F0  00FC159E    dc.l    $FC159E     8, floprd
FC07F4  00FC167C    dc.l    $FC167C     9, flopwr
FC07F8  00FC1734    dc.l    $FC1734    10, flopfmt
FC07FC  00FC0DDC    dc.l    $FC0DDC    11, getdsb
FC0800  00FC1E40    dc.l    $FC1E40    12, midiws
FC0804  00FC240E    dc.l    $FC240E    13, mfpint
FC0808  00FC2732    dc.l    $FC2732    14, iorec
FC080C  00FC275A    dc.l    $FC275A    15, rsconf
FC0810  00FC2EE2    dc.l    $FC2EE2    16, keytrans
FC0814  00FC132C    dc.l    $FC132C    17, rand
FC0818  00FC1414    dc.l    $FC1414    18, protobt
FC081C  00FC18CE    dc.l    $FC18CE    19, flopver
FC0820  00FC0C1A    dc.l    $FC0C1A    20, dumpit
FC0824  00FC46F2    dc.l    $FC46F2    21, cursconf
FC0828  00FC1D76    dc.l    $FC1D76    22, settime
FC082C  00FC1D5C    dc.l    $FC1D5C    23, gettime
FC0830  00FC2F0E    dc.l    $FC2F0E    24, bioskeys
FC0834  00FC1FBE    dc.l    $FC1FBE    25, ikbdws
FC0838  00FC2438    dc.l    $FC2438    26, jdisint
FC083C  00FC2472    dc.l    $FC2472    27, jenabint
FC0840  00FC2D4C    dc.l    $FC2D4C    28, giaccess
FC0844  00FC2DB6    dc.l    $FC2DB6    29, offgibit
FC0848  00FC2D90    dc.l    $FC2D90    30, ongibit
FC084C  00FC2EA6    dc.l    $FC2EA6    31, xbtimer
FC0850  00FC2F28    dc.l    $FC2F28    32, dosound
FC0854  00FC2F3C    dc.l    $FC2F3C    33, setprt
FC0858  00FC2F70    dc.l    $FC2F70    34, ikbdvecs
FC085C  00FC2F4E    dc.l    $FC2F4E    35, kbrate
FC0860  00FC30AE    dc.l    $FC30AE    36, prtblk
FC0864  00FC0726    dc.l    $FC0726    37, wvbl
FC0868  00FC0870    dc.l    $FC0870    38, supexec
```

```
FC086C  00FC09FE          dc.l    $FC09FE                 39, puntaes

************************************************************
FC0870  206F0004          move.l  4(A7),A0                Get address
FC0874  4ED0              jmp     (A0)                    Execute routine in the supervisor mode
************************************************************
FC0876  41FA0020          lea     $FC0898(PC),A0          bconstat, get input status
FC087A  6010              bra     $FC088C                 Status table
************************************************************
FC087C  41FA0032          lea     $FC08B0(PC),A0          bconin, input
FC0880  600A              bra     $FC088C                 Input table
************************************************************
FC0882  41FA0044          lea     $FC08C8(PC),A0          bcostat, get output status
FC0886  6004              bra     $FC088C                 Status table
************************************************************
FC0888  41FA0056          lea     $FC08E0(PC),A0          bconout, output
FC088C  302F0004          move.w  4(A7),D0                Output table
FC0890  E548              lsl.w   #2,D0                   Device number
                                                          times 4
FC0892  20700000          move.l  0(A0,D0.w),A0           Get address of the routine
FC0896  4ED0              jmp     (A0)                    Execute routine
************************************************************
FC0898  00FC05C0          dc.l    $FC05C0                 Input status
FC089C  00FC1F48          dc.l    $FC1F48                 rts
FC08A0  00FC1FD2          dc.l    $FC1FD2                 RS 232 status
FC08A4  00FC1E54          dc.l    $FC1E54                 Console status
FC08A8  00FC05C0          dc.l    $FC05C0                 MIDI status
FC08AC  00FC05C0          dc.l    $FC05C0                 rts
                                                          rts
```

```
*****************************************
FC08B0  00FC1F14            dc.l    $FC1F14             Input
FC08B4  00FC1F5E            dc.l    $FC1F5E             Parallel port
FC08B8  00FC1FE8            dc.l    $FC1FE8             RS 232 input
FC08BC  00FC1E70            dc.l    $FC1E70             Console input
FC08C0  00FC05C0            dc.l    $FC05C0             MIDI input
FC08C4  00FC05C0            dc.l    $FC05C0             rts
                                                        rts
*****************************************
FC08C8  00FC1F34            dc.l    $FC1F34             Output status
FC08CC  00FC1F6E            dc.l    $FC1F6E             Centronics status
FC08D0  00FC2018            dc.l    $FC2018             RS 232 status
FC08D4  00FC1F92            dc.l    $FC1F92             Console status
FC08D8  00FC1E14            dc.l    $FC1E14             MIDI status
FC08DC  00FC05C0            dc.l    $FC05C0             IKBD status
                                                        rts
*****************************************
FC08E0  00FC1EA0            dc.l    $FC1EA0             Output
FC08E4  00FC1F86            dc.l    $FC1F86             Centronics output
FC08E8  00FC41AC            dc.l    $FC41AC             RS 232 output
FC08EC  00FC1E26            dc.l    $FC1E26             Console output
FC08F0  00FC1FA4            dc.l    $FC1FA4             MIDI output
FC08F4  00FC41A0            dc.l    $FC41A0             IKBD output
                                                        ASCII output
*****************************************
FC08F8  202D04C2            move.l  $4C2(A5),D0         drvmap, active drives
FC08FC  4E75                rts                         _drvbits
*****************************************
                                                        Shift, keyboard status
FC08FE  7000                moveq.l #0,D0               Shift status
FC0900  102D0E1B            move.b  $E1B(A5),D0         new shift status
FC0904  322F0004            move.w  4(A7),D1
```

```
FC0908 6B04                bmi      $FC090E                   -1, not set
FC090A 1B410E1B            move.b   D1,$E1B(A5)               Use new status
FC090E 4E75                rts

;*********************************************
FC0910 206F0004            move.l   4(A7),A0                  getmpb, Memory Parameter Block
FC0914 43ED048E            lea      $48E(A5),A1               Address of the mpb
FC0918 2089                move.l   A1,(A0)                   themd, Memory Descriptor
FC091A 42A80004            clr.l    4(A0)                     mp_mfl = address of the MD
FC091E 21490008            move.l   A1,8(A0)                  mp_mal = zero
FC0922 4291                clr.l    (A1)                      mp_rover = address of the MD
FC0924 236D04320004        move.l   $432(A5),4(A1)            clear m_link
FC092A 202D0436            move.l   $436(A5),D0               _membot as m_start
FC092E 90AD0432            sub.l    $432(A5),D0               _memtop
FC0932 23400008            move.l   D0,8(A1)                  minus _membot
FC0936 42A9000C            clr.l    12(A1)                    length m_lenght
FC093A 4E75                rts      ;nliča3;                  m_own = zero

;*********************************************
FC093C 302F0004            move.w   4(A7),D0                  setexc, set exception vector
FC0940 E548                lsl.w    #2,D0                     Vector number
FC0942 91C8                sub.l    A0,A0                     times 4
FC0944 41F00000            lea      0(A0,D0.w),A0             Clear A0
FC0948 2010                move.l   (A0),D0                   Get address of the vector
FC094A 222F0006            move.l   6(A7),D1                  Old vector to D0
FC094E 6B02                bmi      $FC0952                   New vector
FC0950 2081                move.l   D1,(A0)                   Negative, don't set
FC0952 4E75                rts                                Set new vector

;*********************************************
FC0954 4280                clr.l    D0                        tickcal, timer value in milliseconds
FC0956 302D0442            move.w   $442(A5),D0               _timer_ms
FC095A 4E75                rts
```

```
************************************************ physbase, physical video address
FC095C 7000                   moveq.l  #0,D0
FC095E 1039FFFF8201           move.b   $FFFF8201,D0    dbaseh
FC0964 E148                   lsl.w    #8,D0
FC0966 1039FFFF8203           move.b   $FFFF8203,D0    dbasel
FC096C E188                   lsl.l    #8,D0           Result in D0
FC096E 4E75                   rts

************************************************ logbase, logical video address
FC0970 202D044E               move.l   $44E(A5),D0     _v_bs_ad
FC0974 4E75                   rts

************************************************ getrez, get video resolution
FC0976 7000                   moveq.l  #0,D0
FC0978 102D8260               move.b   $FFFF8260(A5),D0  sshiftmd
FC097C C03C0003               and.b    #3,D0           Isolate bits 0 and 1
FC0980 4E75                   rts

************************************************ setscreen, set screen address
FC0982 4AAF0004               tst.l    4(A7)           Logical address
FC0986 6B06                   bmi      $FC098E         Don't set?
FC0988 2B6F0004044E           move.l   4(A7),$44E(A5)  _v_bs_ad
FC098E 4AAF0008               tst.l    8(A7)           physical address
FC0992 6B10                   bmi      $FC09A4         Don't set?
FC0994 13EF0009FFFF8201       move.b   9(A7),$FFFF8201 dbaseh
FC099C 13EF000AFFFF8203       move.b   10(A7),$FFFF8203 dbasel
FC09A4 4A6F000C               tst.w    12(A7)          Video resolution
FC09A8 6B24                   bmi      $FC09CE         don't set
FC09AA 1B6F000D044C           move.b   13(A7),$44C(A5) sshiftmd
FC09B0 6100FD74               bsr      $FC0726         wvbl, wait for VBL
FC09B4 13ED044CFFFF8260       move.b   $44C(A5),$FFFF8260 sshiftmd to shiftmd
```

```
FC09BC  426D0452                clr.w    $452(A5)              vblsem, VBL disabled
FC09C0  4EB900FCA7C4            jsr      $FCA7C4               Initialize screen output
FC09C6  33FC000100000452        move.w   #1,$452               vblsem, enable VBL again
FC09CE  4E75                    rts
*****************************************************
FC09D0  2B6F0004045A            move.l   4(A7),$45A(A5)        setpalette, load new color palette
FC09D6  4E75                    rts                            colorptr, execution in VBL
*****************************************************
FC09D8  322F0004                move.w   4(A7),D1              setcolor, set single color
FC09DC  D241                    add.w    D1,D1                 Color number
FC09DE  C27C001F                and.w    #$1F,D1               times 2
FC09E2  41F9FFFF8240            lea      $FFFF8240,A0          Limit to valid numbers
FC09E8  30301000                move.w   0(A0,D1.w),D0         Address of color palette
FC09EC  C07C0777                and.w    #$777,D0              Get color
FC09F0  4A6F0006                tst.w    6(A7)                 Isolate RGB bits
FC09F4  6B06                    bmi      $FC09FC               New color
FC09F6  31AF00061000            move.w   6(A7),0(A0,D1.w)      negative ?
FC09FC  4E75                    rts                            Set color
*****************************************************
FC09FE  207AF614                move.l   $FC0014(PC),A0        puntaes, clear AES and restart
FC0A02  0C908765432l            cmp.l    #$87654321,(A0)       Address os_magic
FC0A08  660E                    bne      $FC0A18               magic ?
FC0A0A  B1F900000042E           cmp.l    $42E,A0               No, AES already disabled
FC0A10  6C06                    bge      $FC0A18               phystop, AES in ROM ?
FC0A12  4290                    clr.l    (A0)                  Yes, nothing to do
FC0A14  6000F60A                bra      $FC0020               clear magic
FC0A18  4E75                    rts                            to reset
```

```
*****************************************
FC0A1A 6102                      bsr      $FC0A1E                         term, end program after exception
FC0A1C 4E71                      nop                                      PC on stack
FC0A1E 23DF000003C4              move.l   (A7)+,$3C4                      Save PC including vector number
FC0A24 48F9FFFF00000384          movem.l  D0-D7/A0-A7,$384                Save registers
FC0A2C 4E68                      move.l   USP,A0                          USP
FC0A2E 23C8000003C8              move.l   A0,$3C8                         save
FC0A34 700F                      moveq.l  #15,D0                          16 words
FC0A36 41F9000003CC              lea      $3CC,A0                         Address save area
FC0A3C 224F                      move.l   A7,A1                           Get stack pointer
FC0A3E 30D9                      move.w   (A1)+,(A0)+                     Save 16 words from stack
FC0A40 51C8FFFC                  dbra     D0,$FC0A3E                      Next word
FC0A44 23FC12345678 00000380     move.l   #$12345678,$380                 magic for saved registers
FC0A4E 7200                      moveq.l  #0,D1
FC0A50 1239000003C4              move.b   $3C4,D1                         Vector number to D1
FC0A56 5341                      subq.w   #1,D1                           in dbra counter
FC0A58 6116                      bsr      $FC0A70                         Output appropriate number of "bombs"
FC0A5A 23FC0000093A 000004A2     move.l   #$93A,$4A2                      Reset savptr for BIOS
FC0A64 3F3C0001                  move.w   #1,-(A7)                        Return code for error
FC0A68 42A7                      clr.l    -(A7)                           term, end program
FC0A6A 4E41                      trap     #1                              GEMDOS
FC0A6C 6000F5B2                  bra      $FC0020                         if return, then reset
*****************************************
FC0A70 1E39FFFF8260              move.b   $FFFF8260,D7                    Write "bombs" to screen
FC0A76 CE7C0003                  and.w    #3,D7                           shiftmd, get resolution
FC0A7A DE47                      add.w    D7,D7                           Isolate significant bits
FC0A7C 4280                      clr.l    D0                              as word pointer
FC0A7E 1039FFFF8201              move.b   $FFFF8201,D0                    dbaseh
FC0A84 E148                      lsl.w    #8,D0
FC0A86 1039FFFF8203              move.b   $FFFF8203,D0                    dbasel
FC0A8C E188                      lsl.l    #8,D0
```

```
FC0A8E  2040              move.l   D0,A0                      yields video address
FC0A90  D0FB702C          add.w    $FC0ABE(PC,D7.w),A0        plus offset for screen center
FC0A94  43F900FC0CC4      lea      $FC0CC4,A1                 Address of the bit pattern for bombs
FC0A9A  3C3C000F          move.w   #$F,D6                     16 raster lines
FC0A9E  3401              move.w   D1,D2
FC0AA0  2448              move.l   A0,A2                      Save pointer to start of line
FC0AA2  3A3B7022          move.w   $FC0AC6(PC,D7.w),D5        Number of words (screen planes)
FC0AA6  30D1              move.w   (A1),(A0)+                 Write one raster line
FC0AA8  51CDFFFC          dbra     D5,$FC0AA6                 Next screen plane
FC0AAC  51CAFFF4          dbra     D2,$FC0AA2                 Next bomb, same raster line
FC0AB0  5449              addq.w   #2,A1                      Next word of the bit pattern
FC0AB2  D4FB701A          add.w    $FC0ACE(PC,D7.w),A2        Plus line length, next screen line
FC0AB6  204A              move.l   A2,A0                      Start of the line
FC0AB8  51CEFFE4          dbra     D6,$FC0A9E                 Next raster line
FC0ABC  4E75              rts
*****************************************************************
FC0ABE  3E80              dc.w     100*160                    Offset for screen center
FC0AC0  3E80              dc.w     100*160                    low resolution
FC0AC2  3E80              dc.w     200*80                     medium resolution
FC0AC4  3E80              dc.w     200*80                     high resolution
                                                              high resolution
*****************************************************************
FC0AC6  0003              dc.w     3                          Number of screen planes - 1
FC0AC8  0001              dc.w     1                          low resolution
FC0ACA  0000              dc.w     0                          medium resolution
FC0ACC  0000              dc.w     0                          high resolution
                                                              high resolution
*****************************************************************
FC0ACE  00A0              dc.w     160                        Line length in bytes
FC0AD0  00A0              dc.w     160                        low resolution
FC0AD2  0050              dc.w     80                         medium resolution
                                                              high resolution
```

```
FC0AD4  0050                    dc.w        80                              high resolution
        ****************************************************
FC0AD6  206F0004                move.l      4(A7),A0                        fastcopy, copy floppy sector
FC0ADA  226F0008                move.l      8(A7),A1                        Source address
FC0ADE  303C003F                moveq.l     #63,D0                          Destination address
                                                                            (63+1)*8 = 512 bytes
FC0AE2  12D8                    move.b      (A0)+,(A1)+
FC0AE4  12D8                    move.b      (A0)+,(A1)+
FC0AE6  12D8                    move.b      (A0)+,(A1)+
FC0AE8  12D8                    move.b      (A0)+,(A1)+                     Copy 8 bytes
FC0AEA  12D8                    move.b      (A0)+,(A1)+
FC0AEC  12D8                    move.b      (A0)+,(A1)+
FC0AEE  12D8                    move.b      (A0)+,(A1)+                     Next 8 bytes
FC0AF0  12D8                    move.b      (A0)+,(A1)+
FC0AF2  51C8FFEE                dbra        D0,$FC0AE2
FC0AF6  4E75                    rts
        ****************************************************
FC0AF8  2F390000046A            move.l      $46A,-(A7)                      hdv_init, initialize drive data
                                                                            hdv_init
FC0AFE  4E75                    rts                                         Execute routine
        ****************************************************
FC0B00  5C4155544F5C            dc.b        '\AUTO\'
FC0B06  2A2E50524700            dc.b        '*.PRG',0
FC0B0C  12345678                dc.l        $12345678
FC0B10  9ABCDEF0                dc.l        $9ABCDEF0
        ****************************************************
FC0B14  41FAFFEA                lea         $FC0B00(PC),A0                  autoexec, execute programs in auto folder
                                                                            Address of pathname '\AUTO\*.PRG'
FC0B18  43FAFFEC                lea         $FC0B06(PC),A1                  Address of filename '*.PRG'
FC0B1C  23DF0000093A            move.l      (A7)+,$93A                      Save return address
FC0B22  9BCD                    sub.l       A5,A5                           Clear A5
```

```
FC0B24 2B48093E            move.l   A0,$93E(A5)         pathname
FC0B28 2B490942            move.l   A1,$942(A5)         filename
FC0B2C 202D04C2            move.l   $4C2(A5),D0         _drvbits
FC0B30 32390000446         move.w   $446,D1             _bootdev
FC0B36 0300                btst     D1,D0               Drive active ?
FC0B38 6736                beq      $FC0B70             No, done
FC0B3A 41FAF94D            lea      $FC0489(PC),A0      Pointer to null name
FC0B3E 2F08                move.l   A0,-(A7)            Environment
FC0B40 2F08                move.l   A0,-(A7)            Command tail
FC0B42 2F08                move.l   A0,-(A7)            Filler
FC0B44 3F3C0005            move.w   #5,-(A7)            Create base page
FC0B48 3F3C004B            move.w   #$4B,-(A7)          exec
FC0B4C 4E41                trap     #1                  GEMDOS
FC0B4E DEFC0010            add.w    #$10,A7             Correct stack pointer
FC0B52 2040                move.l   D0,A0               Address of the base page
FC0B54 217C00FC0B780008    move.l   #$FC0B78,8(A0)      Start address
FC0B5C 2F0B                move.l   A3,-(A7)            Null string
FC0B5E 2F00                move.l   D0,-(A7)            Base page
FC0B60 2F0B                move.l   A3,-(A7)            Null string
FC0B62 3F3C0004            move.w   #4,-(A7)            Start program
FC0B66 3F3C004B            move.w   #$4B,-(A7)          exec
FC0B6A 4E41                trap     #1                  GEMDOS
FC0B6C DEFC0010            add.w    #$10,A7             Correct stack pointer
FC0B70 2F390000093A        move.l   $93A,-(A7)          Repeat return address
FC0B76 4E75                rts                          Back to call
****************************************************************************
FC0B78 42A7                clr.l    -(A7)               Call autoexec program
FC0B7A 3F3C0020            move.w   #$20,-(A7)          super
FC0B7E 4E41                trap     #1                  GEMDOS
FC0B80 5C4F                addq.w   #6,A7               Correct stack pointer
FC0B82 2840                move.l   D0,A4               Saved stack pointer
```

FC0B84	2A6F0004	move.l 4(A7),A5	Base page address
FC0B88	4FED0100	lea $100(A5),A7	Stack pointer to end of base page
FC0B8C	2F3C00000100	move.l #$100,-(A7)	$100 bytes for base page
FC0B92	2F0D	move.l A5,-(A7)	Address of the program
FC0B94	4267	clr.w -(A7)	
FC0B96	3F3C004A	move.w #$4A,-(A7)	setblock, release memory
FC0B9A	4E41	trap #1	GEMDOS
FC0B9C	5C4F	addq.w #6,A7	Correct stack pointer
FC0B9E	4A40	tst.w D0	ok ?
FC0BA0	666A	bne $FC0C0C	No, terminate
FC0BA2	3F3C0007	move.w #7,-(A7)	R/O, hidden and system files
FC0BA6	2F390000093E	move.l $93E,-(A7)	Filename
FC0BAC	3F3C004E	move.w #$4E,-(A7)	Search first
FC0BB0	7E08	moveq.l #8,D7	Bytes for stack correction
FC0BB2	48790000946	pea $946	DMA address for DOS
FC0BB8	3F3C001A	move.w #$1A,-(A7)	Setdta
FC0BBC	4E41	trap #1	GEMDOS
FC0BBE	5C4F	addq.w #6,A7	Correct stack pointer
FC0BC0	4E41	trap #1	GEMDOS
FC0BC2	DEC7	add.w D7,A7	Correct stack pointer
FC0BC4	4A40	tst.w D0	Matching file found?
FC0BC6	6644	bne $FC0C0C	No
FC0BC8	207900000093E	move.l $93E,A0	pathname
FC0BCE	247900000942	move.l $942,A2	filename
FC0BD4	43F900000972	lea $972,A1	autoname
FC0BDA	12D8	move.b (A0)+,(A1)+	copy path
FC0BDC	B5C8	cmp.l A0,A2	End of path segment?
FC0BDE	66FA	bne $FC0BDA	No, keep copying
FC0BE0	41F900000964	lea $964,A0	Name from DMA buffer
FC0BE6	12D8	move.b (A0)+,(A1)+	Append to pathname
FC0BE8	66FC	bne $FC0BE6	End of the name?
FC0BEA	487AF89D	pea $FC0489(PC)	Null name

```
FC0BEE 487AF899            pea       $FC0489(PC)              Null name
FC0BF2 48790000972         pea       $972                     Filename
FC0BF8 4267                clr.w     -(A7)                    Load and start program
FC0BFA 3F3C004B            move.w    #$4B,-(A7)               exec
FC0BFE 4E41                trap      #1                       GEMDOS
FC0C00 DEFC0010            add.w     #$10,A7                  Correct stack
FC0C04 7E02                moveq.l   #2,D7                    Bytes for stack correction
FC0C06 3F3C004F            move.w    #$4F,-(A7)               Search next
FC0C0A 60A6                bra       $FC0BB2                  Next program
FC0C0C 4FF900004DB8        lea       $4DB8,A7                 Stack pointer to start value
FC0C12 2F390000093A        move.l    $93A,-(A7)               Return address
FC0C18 4E75                rts

*******************************************
FC0C1A 20790000502         move.l    $502,A0                  scrdmp, screen hardcopy
FC0C20 4E90                jsr       (A0)                     dump_vec
FC0C22 33FCFFFF000004EE    move.w    #-1,$4EE                 Execute routine
FC0C2A 4E75                rts                                clear _dumpflg

*******************************************
FC0C2C 9BCD                sub.l     A5,A5                    scrdmp
FC0C2E 2B6D044E0992        move.l    $44E(A5),$992(A5)        Clear A5
FC0C34 426D0996            clr.w     $996(A5)                 _v_bs_ad
FC0C38 4240                clr.w     D0                       Offset to zero
FC0C3A 102D044C            move.b    $44C(A5),D0
FC0C3E 3B4009A0            move.w    D0,$9A0(A5)              sshiftmod
FC0C42 D040                add.w     D0,D0                    save
FC0C44 41FA006A            lea       $FC0CB0(PC),A0           times 2
FC0C48 3B7000000998        move.w    0(A0,D0.w),$998(A5)      Table for screen resolution
FC0C4E 3B70000006099A      move.w    6(A0,D0.w),$99A(A5)      Get screen width
FC0C54 426D099C            clr.w     $99C(A5)                 Get screen height
FC0C58 426D099E            clr.w     $99E(A5)                 Left
                                                              and right to zero
```

```
FC0C5C  2B7C00FF824009A4    move.l   #$FF8240,$9A4(A5)      Address of color palette
FC0C64  426D09AC            clr.w    $9AC(A5)               Clear mask pointer
FC0C68  322D0E4A            move.w   $E4A(A5),D1            Get printer configuration
FC0C6C  E649                lsr.w    #3,D1                  Draft/quality mode
FC0C6E  C27C0001            and.w    #1,D1                  Isolate bit
FC0C72  3B4109A2            move.w   D1,$9A2(A5)            and save
FC0C76  322D0E4A            move.w   $E4A(A5),D1            Printer configuration
FC0C7A  3001                move.w   D1,D0
FC0C7C  E848                lsr.w    #4,D0                  Parallel/serial
FC0C7E  C07C0001            and.w    #1,D0                  Isolate bit
FC0C82  3B4009AA            move.w   D0,$9AA(A5)            and save
FC0C86  C27C0007            and.w    #7,D1                  Isolate printer type
FC0C8A  103B1030            move.b   $FC0CBC(PC,D1.w),D0    Get assignment from table
FC0C8E  33C0000009A8        move.w   D0,$9A8                and save for hardcopy
FC0C94  486D0992            pea      $992(A5)               Address of the parameter block
FC0C98  33FC00010000004EE   move.w   #1,$4EE                 dumpflg to one
FC0CA0  6100240C            bsr      $FC30AE                Execute hardcopy
FC0CA4  33FCFFFF000004EE    move.w   #-1,$4EE                dumpflg copy
FC0CAC  584F                addq.w   #4,A7                  Correct stack pointer
FC0CAE  4E75                rts
*************************************************************
FC0CB0  01400280            dc.w     320,640,640            Parameter table for hardcopy
FC0CB2  00C800C80190        dc.w     200,200,400            Screen widths
                                                            Screen heights
*************************************************************
FC0CBC  00                  dc.b     0                      Printer types (-1 = not implemented)
FC0CBD  02                  dc.b     2                      ATARI B/W dot-matrix
FC0CCE  01                  dc.b     1                      ATARI B/W daisy wheel
FC0CCF  FF                  dc.b     -1                     ATARI color dot-matrix
FC0CC0  03                  dc.b     3                      (ATARI color daisy wheel)
FC0CC1  FF                  dc.b     -1                     Epson B/W dot-matrix
                                                            (Epson B/W daisy wheel)
```

```
FC0CC2 FF               dc.b    -1                                      (Epson color dot-matrix)
FC0CC3 FF               dc.b    -1                                      (Epson color daisy wheel)
;*****************************************
FC0CC4 0600             dc.b    %0000011000000000                       "Bomb" bit pattern
FC0CC6 2900             dc.b    %0010100100000000
FC0CC8 0080             dc.b    %0000000010000000
FC0CCA 4840             dc.b    %0100100001000000
FC0CCC 11F0             dc.b    %0001000111110000
FC0CCE 01F0             dc.b    %0000000111110000
FC0CD0 07FC             dc.b    %0000011111111100
FC0CD2 0FFE             dc.b    %0000111111111110
FC0CD4 0FFE             dc.b    %0000111111111110
FC0CD6 1FFF             dc.b    %0001111111111111
FC0CD8 1FEF             dc.b    %0001111111101111
FC0CDA 0FEE             dc.b    %0000111111101110
FC0CDC 0FDE             dc.b    %0000111111011110
FC0CDE 07FC             dc.b    %0000011111111100
FC0CE0 03F8             dc.b    %0000001111111000
FC0CE2 00E0             dc.b    %0000000011100000
;*****************************************
FC0CE4 41F9FFFFFA21     lea     $FFFFFA21,A0                            mfp, Timer B data
FC0CEA 43F9FFFFFA1B     lea     $FFFFFA1B,A1                            mfp, Timer B control
FC0CF0 12BC0010         move.b  #$10,(A1)                               Timer B output low
FC0CF4 7801             moveq.l #1,D4
FC0CF6 12BC0000         move.b  #0,(A1)                                 Stop timer B
FC0CFA 10BC00F0         move.b  #$F0,(A0)                               Load timer B counter with 240
FC0CFE 13FC0008FFFFFA1B move.b  #8,$FFFFFA1B                            Timer B control, delay mode, /50
FC0D06 1010             move.b  (A0),D0                                 Load counter value
FC0D08 B004             cmp.b   D4,D0                                   Same last value?
FC0D0A 66FA             bne     $FC0D06                                 No
```

```
FCOD0C 1810              move.b  (A0),D4              Counter value
FCOD0E 363C0267          move.w  #$267,D3             Loop counter to 616
FCOD12 B810              cmp.b   (A0),D4              Counter value equal?
FCOD14 66F6              bne     $FCOD0C              No, read new value
FCOD16 51CBFFFA          dbra    D3,$FCOD12           Next pass
FCOD1A 12BC0010          move.b  #$10,(A1)            Timer B output low
FCOD1E 4ED6              jmp     (A6)                 Back to call

*****************************************************
FCOD20 20790000042E      move.l  $42E,A0              Execute reset resident programs
FCOD26 90FC0200          sub.w   #$200,A0             phystop
FCOD2A B1FC00000400      cmp.l   #$400,A0             minus $200
FCOD30 672C              beq     $FCOD5E              Exception vectors reached?
FCOD32 0C9012123456      cmp.l   #$12123456,(A0)      Yes, done
FCOD38 66EC              bne     $FCOD26              magic ?
FCOD3A B1E80004          cmp.l   4(A0),A0             No
FCOD3E 66E6              bne     $FCOD26              Address ?
FCOD40 4240              clr.w   D0                   No
FCOD42 2248              move.l  A0,A1                Clear sum
FCOD44 323C00FF          move.w  #$FF,D1              Save address
FCOD48 D059              add.w   (A1)+,D0             256 words
FCOD4A 51C9FFFC          dbra    D1,$FCOD48           sum
FCOD4E B07C5678          cmp.w   #$5678,D0            Next word
FCOD52 66D2              bne     $FCOD26              magic ?
FCOD54 2F08              move.l  A0,-(A7)             No, keep looking
FCOD56 4EA80008          jsr     8(A0)                Save address
FCOD5A 205F              move.l  (A7)+,A0             Execute routine
FCOD5C 60C8              bra     $FCOD26              Restore address
FCOD5E 4E75              rts                          Keep searching

*****************************************************
FCOD60 4E56FFF0          link    A6,#-16              hdv_init, initialize drives
```

303

```
FCOD64  23FC000012C000029B4  move.l  #300,$29B4      maxacctim to 300*20 ms
FCOD6E  4240                 clr.w   D0
FCOD70  33C000004A6          move.w  D0,$4A6         clear _nflops
FCOD76  33C000005622         move.w  D0,$5622        curflop, current drive
FCOD7C  3D40FFFE             move.w  D0,-2(A6)       Start with drive A
FCOD80  604E                 bra     $FCODD0         To loop end
FCOD82  207C00004DB8         move.l  #$4DB8,A0       Address of the DSB (Device Status Block)
FCOD88  326EFFFE             move.w  -2(A6),A1       Drive number
FCOD8C  D1C9                 add.l   A1,A0           as index
FCOD8E  4210                 clr.b   (A0)            Clear DSB
FCOD90  4257                 clr.w   (A7)
FCOD92  4267                 clr.w   -(A7)
FCOD94  4267                 clr.w   -(A7)
FCOD96  3F2EFFFE             move.w  -2(A6),-(A7)    Drive number
FCOD9A  42A7                 clr.l   -(A7)
FCOD9C  42A7                 clr.l   -(A7)
FCOD9E  4EB900FC1556         jsr     $FC1556         flopini
FCODA4  DFFC0000000E         add.l   #$E,A7          Correct stack pointer
FCODAA  3F00                 move.w  D0,-(A7)        Save error code
FCODAC  306EFFFE             move.w  -2(A6),A0       Drive number
FCODB0  D1C8                 add.l   A0,A0           times 2
FCODB2  D1FC000058C0         add.l   #$58C0,A0
FCODB8  309F                 move.w  (A7)+,(A0)      Error code
FCODBA  6610                 bne     $FCODCC         Drive not present?
FCODBC  52790000004A6        addq.w  #1,$4A6         Increment _nflops
FCODC2  00B9000000030000004C2 or.l  #3,$4C2         _drvbits, drive A and B
FCODCC  526EFFFE             addq.w  #1,-2(A6)       Increment drive number
FCODD0  0C6E0002FFFE         cmp.w   #2,-2(A6)       2 drives tested?
FCODD6  6DAA                 blt     $FCOD82         No
FCODD8  4E5E                 unlk    A6
FCODDA  4E75                 rts
```

```
************************************************
FCODDC 4E56FFFC           link    A6,#-4
FCODE0 4280               clr.l   D0                          Zero
FCODE2 4E5E               unlk    A6
FCODE4 4E75               rts
************************************************   getbpb, Get BIOS parameter block
FCODE6 4E56FFF4           link    A6,#-12
FCODEA 48E7070C           movem.l D5-D7/A4-A5,-(A7)            Save registers
FCODEE 0C6E00020008       cmp.w   #2,8(A6)                    Drive number
FCODF4 6D06               blt     $FCODFC                     < 2, OK
FCODF6 4280               clr.l   D0                          else zero
FCODF8 60000192           bra     $FC0F8C
FCODFC 302E0008           move.w  8(A6),D0                    Drive number
FC0E00 EB40               asl.w   #5,D0                       times 32
FC0E02 48C0               ext.l   D0
FC0E04 2A40               move.l  D0,A5                       plus base address
FC0E06 DBFC00004DCE       add.l   #$4DCE,A5                   save
FC0E0C 284D               move.l  A5,A4                       count, read a sector
FC0E0E 3EBC0001           move.w  #1,(A7)                     Side 0
FC0E12 4267               clr.w   -(A7)                       Track 0
FC0E14 4267               clr.w   -(A7)                       Sector 1
FC0E16 3F3C0001           move.w  #1,-(A7)                    Drive number
FC0E1A 3F2E0008           move.w  8(A6),-(A7)                 Filler
FC0E1E 42A7               clr.l   -(A7)                       Address of disk buffer
FC0E20 2F3C0000167A       move.l  #$167A,-(A7)                Read sector
FC0E26 4EB900FC159E       jsr     $FC159E
FC0E2C DFFC00000010       add.l   #$10,A7                     Correct stack pointer
FC0E32 2D40FFF4           move.l  D0,-12(A6)                  Error code
FC0E36 4AAEFFF4           tst.l   -12(A6)                     test
FC0E3A 6C16               bge     $FC0E52                     OK ?
```

```
FC0E3C 3EAE0008        move.w  8(A6),(A7)          Drive number
FC0E40 202EFFF4        move.l  -12(A6),D0          Error code
FC0E44 3F00            move.w  D0,-(A7)            as parameter
FC0E46 4EB900FC073E    jsr     $FC073E             critical error handler
FC0E4C 548F            addq.l  #2,A7                Correct stack pointer
FC0E4E 2D40FFF4        move.l  D0,-12(A6)          Save error code
FC0E52 202EFFF4        move.l  -12(A6),D0          test
FC0E56 B0BC00010000    cmp.l   #$10000,D0
FC0E5C 67B0            beq     $FC0E0E             Retry ?
FC0E5E 4AAEFFF4        tst.l   -12(A6)             Yes, try again
FC0E62 6C06            bge     $FC0E6A             Test error code
FC0E64 4280            clr.l   D0                  OK ?
FC0E66 60000124        bra     $FC0F8C

FC0E6A 2EBC00001685    move.l  #$1685,(A7)         Buffer+11, bytes per sector
FC0E70 610006BE        bsr     $FC1530             u2i, 8086 to 68000 format
FC0E74 3E00            move.w  D0,D7               Save bytes per sector
FC0E76 6F0E            ble     $FC0E86             < = 0, error
FC0E78 1C3900001687    move.b  $1687,D6            Buffer+13, sectors per cluster
FC0E7E 4886            ext.w   D6
FC0E80 CC7C00FF        and.w   #$FF,D6
FC0E84 6E06            bgt     $FC0E8C             > 0, OK
FC0E86 4280            clr.l   D0                  0 as result
FC0E88 60000102        bra     $FC0F8C             Error

FC0E8C 3887            move.w  D7,(A4)             recsize in bpb
FC0E8E 39460002        move.w  D6,2(A4)            clsiz in bpb
FC0E92 2EBC00001690    move.l  #$1690,(A7)         Buffer+22, sectors per FAT
FC0E98 61000696        bsr     $FC1530             u2i, 8086 to 68000 format
FC0E9C 39400008        move.w  D0,8(A4)            fsiz in bpb
FC0EA0 302C0008        move.w  8(A4),D0            fsiz
FC0EA4 5240            addq.w  #1,D0               plus 1
```

```
FC0EA6  3940000A        move.w  D0,10(A4)           as fatrec in bpb
FC0EAA  3014            move.w  (A4),D0             recsize
FC0EAC  C1EC0002        muls.w  2(A4),D0            times clsiz
FC0EB0  39400004        move.w  D0,4(A4)            as clsizb in bpb
FC0EB4  2EBC0000168B    move.l  #$168B,(A7)         Buffer+17, number of director entries
FC0EBA  61000674        bsr     $FC1530             u2i, 8086 to 68000 format
FC0EBE  EB40            asl.w   #5,D0               times 32
FC0EC0  48C0            ext.l   D0
FC0EC2  81D4            divs.w  (A4),D0             by recsiz
FC0EC4  39400006        move.w  D0,6(A4)            as rdlen in bpb
FC0EC8  302C000A        move.w  10(A4),D0           fatrec
FC0ECC  D06C0006        add.w   6(A4),D0            plus rdlen
FC0ED0  D06C0008        add.w   8(A4),D0            plus fsiz
FC0ED4  3940000C        move.w  D0,12(A4)           as datrec in bpb
FC0ED8  2EBC0000168D    move.l  #$168D,(A7)         Buffer+19, number of sectors
FC0EDE  61000650        bsr     $FC1530             u2i, 8086 format to 68000 format
FC0EE2  906C000C        sub.w   12(A4),D0           minus datrec
FC0EE6  48C0            ext.l   D0
FC0EE8  81EC0002        divs.w  2(A4),D0            by clsiz
FC0EEC  3940000E        move.w  D0,14(A4)           as numcl in bpb
FC0EF0  2EBC00001694    move.l  #$1694,(A7)         Buffer+26, number of sides
FC0EF6  61000638        bsr     $FC1530             u2i, 8086 to 68000 format
FC0EFA  3B400014        move.w  D0,20(A5)           as dnsides in bpb
FC0EFE  2EBC00001692    move.l  #$1692,(A7)         Buffer+24, sectors per track
FC0F04  6100062A        bsr     $FC1530             u2i, 8086 to 68000 format
FC0F08  3B400018        move.w  D0,24(A5)           as dspt in bpb
FC0F0C  302D0014        move.w  20(A5),D0           dnsides
FC0F10  C1ED0018        muls.w  24(A5),D0           times dspt
FC0F14  3B400016        move.w  D0,22(A5)           as dspc in bpb
FC0F18  2EBC00001696    move.l  #$1696,(A7)         Buffer+28, number of hidden sectors
FC0F1E  61000610        bsr     $FC1530             u2i, 8086 in 68000 format
FC0F22  3B40001A        move.w  D0,26(A5)           as dhidden in bpb
```

FC0F26 2EBC0000168D	move.l	#$168D,(A7)	Buffer+19, number of sectors on disk
FC0F2C 61000602	bsr	$FC1530	u2i, 8086 to 68000 format
FC0F30 48C0	ext.l	D0	by dspc
FC0F32 81ED0016	divs.w	22(A5),D0	as dntracks in bpb
FC0F36 3B400012	move.w	D0,18(A5)	
FC0F3A 4247	clr.w	D7	Counter to zero
FC0F3C 6016	bra	$FC0F54	Jump to loop end
FC0F3E 204D	move.l	A5,A0	Buffer pointer
FC0F40 3247	move.w	D7,A1	Counter
FC0F42 D1C9	add.l	A1,A0	plus buffer address
FC0F44 3247	move.w	D7,A1	Counter
FC0F46 D3FC0000167A	add.l	#$167A,A1	Address of disk buffer
FC0F4C 11690008001C	move.b	8(A1),28(A0)	Copy byte of serial number
FC0F52 5247	addq.w	#1,D7	Increment counter
FC0F54 BE7C0003	cmp.w	#3,D7	already 3 ?
FC0F58 6DE4	blt	$FC0F3E	No
FC0F5A 207C000009B4	move.l	#$9B4,A0	cdev
FC0F60 326E0008	move.w	8(A6),A1	Drive
FC0F64 D1C9	add.l	A1,A0	
FC0F66 227C000009B2	move.l	#$9B2,A1	wpstatus
FC0F6C 346E0008	move.w	8(A6),A2	Drive
FC0F70 D3CA	add.l	A2,A1	
FC0F72 1091	move.b	(A1),(A0)	
FC0F74 6704	beq	$FC0F7A	
FC0F76 7001	moveq.l	#1,D0	Diskette status uncertain
FC0F78 6002	bra	$FC0F7C	
FC0F7A 4240	clr.w	D0	Status certain
FC0F7C 227C00004DB8	move.l	#$4DB8,A1	
FC0F82 346E0008	move.w	8(A6),A2	Drive
FC0F86 D3CA	add.l	A2,A1	
FC0F88 1280	move.b	D0,(A1)	Save status
FC0F8A 200D	move.l	A5,D0	Address of bpb as result

```
FC0F8C  4A9F            tst.l    (A7)+
FC0F8E  4CDF30C0        movem.l  (A7)+,D6-D7/A4-A5        Restore registers
FC0F92  4E5E            unlk     A6
FC0F94  4E75            rts

*******************************************

FC0F96  4E560000        link     A6,#0                    mediach, disk changed?
FC0F9A  48E70304        movem.l  D6-D7/A5,-(A7)           Save registers
FC0F9E  0C6E00020008    cmp.w    #2,8(A6)                 Drive number < 2 ?
FC0FA4  6D04            blt      $FC0FAA                  Yes
FC0FA6  70F1            moveq.l  #-15,D0                  'unknown device'
FC0FA8  604C            bra      $FC0FF6                  Error exit
FC0FAA  3E2E0008        move.w   8(A6),D7                 Drive number
FC0FAE  3A47            move.w   D7,A5
FC0FB0  DBFC00004DB8    add.l    #$4DB8,A5                plus address of bpb
FC0FB6  0C150002        cmp.b    #2,(A5)
FC0FBA  6604            bne      $FC0FC0
FC0FBC  7002            moveq.l  #2,D0                    media changed, disk was changed
FC0FBE  6036            bra      $FC0FF6                  Error exit
FC0FC0  207C000009B4    move.l   #$9B4,A0                 wplatch
FC0FC6  4A307000        tst.b    0(A0,D7.w)               Test for drive
FC0FCA  6704            beq      $FC0FD0                  OK ?
FC0FCC  1ABC0001        move.b   #1,(A5)                  Status uncertain
FC0FD0  203900004BA     move.l   $4BA,D0                  _hz_200
FC0FD6  3247            move.w   D7,A1
FC0FD8  D3C9            add.l    A1,A1
FC0FDA  D3C9            add.l    A1,A1
FC0FDC  D3FC000009B6    add.l    #$9B6,A1
FC0FE2  2211            move.l   (A1),D1
FC0FE4  9081            sub.l    D1,D0
FC0FE6  B0B9000029B4    cmp.l    $29B4,D0                 maxacctim
FC0FEC  6C04            bge      $FC0FF2
```

```
FC0FEE  4240                    clr.w    D0                    ok, disk wasn't changed
FC0FF0  6004                    bra      $FC0FF6
FC0FF2  1015                    move.b   (A5),D0               Get result
FC0FF4  4880                    ext.w    D0
FC0FF6  4A9F                    tst.l    (A7)+
FC0FF8  4CDF2080                movem.l  (A7)+,D7/A5           Restore registers
FC0FFC  4E5E                    unlk     A6
FC0FFE  4E75                    rts

************************************************
FC1000  4E560000                link     A6,#0                 Test for disk change
FC1004  48E70F04                movem.l  D4-D7/A5,-(A7)        Save registers
FC1008  3C2E0008                move.w   8(A6),D6              Drive number
FC100C  3006                    move.w   D6,D0
FC100E  EB40                    asl.w    #5,D0                 times 32
FC1010  48C0                    ext.l    D0
FC1012  2A40                    move.l   D0,A5
FC1014  DBFC00004DCE            add.l    #$4DCE,A5             plus address bpb
FC101A  3E86                    move.w   D6,(A7)
FC101C  6100FF78                bsr      $FC0F96               test media change
FC1020  3E00                    move.w   D0,D7
FC1022  BE7C0002                cmp.w    #2,D7                 Changed ?
FC1026  660A                    bne      $FC1032
FC1028  3007                    move.w   D7,D0                 No
FC102A  6000009C                bra      $FC10C8
FC102E  60000096                bra      $FC10C6

FC1032  BE7C0001                cmp.w    #1,D7                 Diskette changed?
FC1036  6600008E                bne      $FC10C6               No
FC103A  3EBC0001                move.w   #1,(A7)               Read sector (boot sector)
FC103E  4267                    clr.w    -(A7)                 Side 0
FC1040  4267                    clr.w    -(A7)                 Track 0
```

FC1042	3F3C0001	move.w #1,-(A7)	Sector 1
FC1046	3F06	move.w D6,-(A7)	Drive number
FC1048	42A7	clr.l -(A7)	Filler
FC104A	2F3C0000167A	move.l #$167A,-(A7)	Address of disk buffer
FC1050	4EB900FC159E	jsr $FC159E	floprd
FC1056	DFFC00000010	add.l #$10,A7	Correct stack pointer
FC105C	2A00	move.l D0,D5	Save error number
FC105E	4A85	tst.l D5	OK ?
FC1060	6C10	bge $FC1072	Yes
FC1062	3E86	move.w D6,(A7)	
FC1064	2005	move.l D5,D0	Error number
FC1066	3F00	move.w D0,-(A7)	
FC1068	4EB900FC073E	jsr $FC073E	Pass to critical error handler
FC106E	548F	addq.l #2,A7	Correct stack pointer
FC1070	2A00	move.l D0,D5	Error number
FC1072	BABC00010000	cmp.l #$10000,D5	Retry ?
FC1078	67C0	beq $FC103A	Yes, try again
FC107A	4A85	tst.l D5	Error code
FC107C	6C04	bge $FC1082	OK ?
FC107E	2005	move.l D5,D0	Else error number
FC1080	6046	bra $FC10C8	Error exit
FC1082	4247	clr.w D7	clear media change status
FC1084	601C	bra $FC10A2	
FC1086	207C0000167A	move.l #$167A,A0	Address of disk buffer
FC108C	10307008	move.b 8(A0,D7.w),D0	Serial number
FC1090	4880	ext.w D0	
FC1092	1235701C	move.b 28(A5,D7.w),D1	compare with old value
FC1096	4881	ext.w D1	
FC1098	B041	cmp.w D1,D0	Match ?
FC109A	6704	beq $FC10A0	Yes
FC109C	7002	moveq.l #2,D0	Media changed

311

```
FC109E 6028                    bra     $FC10C8              Error exit

FC10A0 5247                    addq.w  #1,D7                next byte of serial number
FC10A2 BE7C0003                cmp.w   #3,D7                All three bytes tested?
FC10A6 6DDE                    blt     $FC1086              No
FC10A8 3046                    move.w  D6,A0                Drive number
FC10AA D1FC000009B4            add.l   #$9B4,A0             wplatch
FC10B0 3246                    move.w  D6,A1                Drive number
FC10B2 D3FC000009B2            add.l   #$9B2,A1
FC10B8 1091                    move.b  (A1),(A0)            wpstatus
FC10BA 660A                    bne     $FC10C6              accept
FC10BC 3046                    move.w  D6,A0
FC10BE D1FC00004DB8            add.l   #$4DB8,A0
FC10C4 4210                    clr.b   (A0)
FC10C6 4240                    clr.w   D0
FC10C8 4A9F                    tst.l   (A7)+                OK
FC10CA 4CDF20E0                movem.l (A7)+,D5-D7/A5       Restore registers
FC10CE 4E5E                    unlk    A6
FC10D0 4E75                    rts

*********************************************** rwabs, read/write sector(s)

FC10D2 4E560000                link    A6,#0
FC10D6 48E70700                movem.l D5-D7,-(A7)          Save registers
FC10DA 3E2E0012                move.w  18(A6),D7            Drive number
FC10DE 3007                    move.w  D7,D0
FC10E0 B07C0002                cmp.w   #2,D0                Less than 2 ?
FC10E4 6D06                    blt     $FC10EC              yes
FC10E6 70F1                    moveq.l #-15,D0              'unknown device'
FC10E8 60000068                bra     $FC1152              Error exit

FC10EC 4A7900004A6             tst.w   $4A6                 nflops, floppies connected?
FC10F2 6604                    bne     $FC10F8              Yes
```

```
FC10F4  70FE              moveq.l  #-2,D0          'Drive not ready'
FC10F6  605A              bra      $FC1152         Error exit

FC10F8  4AAE000A          tst.l    10(A6)          buffer
FC10FC  6616              bne      $FC1114         Address specified?
FC10FE  302E000E          move.w   14(A6),D0       count, number of sectors
FC1102  227C00004DB8      move.l   #$4DB8,A1       Base address
FC1108  346E0012          move.w   18(A6),A2       Drive number
FC110C  D3CA              add.l    A2,A1           add
FC110E  1280              move.b   D0,(A1)         Sector counter
FC1110  4280              clr.l    D0              OK
FC1112  603E              bra      $FC1152         Done

FC1114  0C6E00020008      cmp.w    #2,8(A6)        rwflag, ignore media change ?
FC111A  6C1C              bge      $FC1138         Yes
FC111C  3E87              move.w   D7,(A7)         Drive number
FC111E  6100FEE0          bsr      $FC1000         was disk changed?
FC1122  48C0              ext.l    D0
FC1124  2C00              move.l   D0,D6           Save error code
FC1126  4A86              tst.l    D6
FC1128  670E              beq      $FC1138         Not changed, OK
FC112A  BCBC00000002      cmp.l    #2,D6           Definitely changed?
FC1130  6602              bne      $FC1134         Yes
FC1132  7CF2              moveq.l  #-14,D6         'Diskette was changed'
FC1134  2006              move.l   D6,D0
FC1136  601A              bra      $FC1152         Error exit

FC1138  3EAE000E          move.w   14(A6),(A7)     count, number of sectors
FC113C  3F07              move.w   D7,-(A7)        Drive number
FC113E  3F2E0010          move.w   16(A6),-(A7)    recno, first sector number
FC1142  2F2E000A          move.l   10(A6),-(A7)    buffer
FC1146  3F2E0008          move.w   8(A6),-(A7)     rwflag, read/write
```

```
FC114A 6110              bsr      $FC115C              floprw
FC114C DFFC0000000A      add.l    #$A,A7               Correct stack pointer
FC1152 4A9F              tst.l    (A7)+
FC1154 4CDF00C0          movem.l  (A7)+,D6-D7          Restore registers
FC1158 4E5E              unlk     A6
FC115A 4E75              rts

************************************************
FC115C 4E56FFFA          link     A6,#-6               floprw, read/write sector(s)
FC1160 48E73F04          movem.l  D2-D7/A5,-(A7)       Restore registers
FC1164 302E0010          move.w   16(A6),D0            Drive number
FC1168 EB40              asl.w    #5,D0                times 32
FC116A 48C0              ext.l    D0
FC116C 2A40              move.l   D0,A5
FC116E DBFC00004DCE      add.l    #$4DCE,A5            plus base address bpb
FC1174 082E0000000D      btst     #0,13(A6)            Buffer address odd?
FC117A 6604              bne      $FC1180              Yes
FC117C 4240              clr.w    D0                   Clear odd flag
FC117E 6002              bra      $FC1182
FC1180 7001              moveq.l  #1,D0                Set odd flag
FC1182 3D40FFFE          move.w   D0,-2(A6)            And save
FC1186 4A6D0016          tst.w    22(A5)               dspc set ?
FC118A 660A              bne      $FC1196              Yes
FC118C 7009              moveq.l  #9,D0                Else use 9
FC118E 3B400016          move.w   D0,22(A5)            as dspt
FC1192 3B400018          move.w   D0,24(A5)            and dspc
FC1196 60000180          bra      $FC1318              to loop end

FC119A 4A6EFFFE          tst.w    -2(A6)               Odd flag set?
FC119E 6708              beq      $FC11A8              No
FC11A0 203C0000167A      move.l   #$167A,D0            Address of disk buffer
FC11A6 6004              bra      $FC11AC
```

314

FC11A8	202E000A	move.l 10(A6),D0	Get buffer address
FC11AC	2D40FFFA	move.l D0,-6(A6)	and save
FC11B0	3C2E000E	move.w 14(A6),D6	recno, logical sector number
FC11B4	48C6	ext.l D6	
FC11B6	8DED0016	divs.w 22(A5),D6	divided by dspc yields track number
FC11BA	382E000E	move.w 14(A6),D4	recno, logical sector number
FC11BE	48C4	ext.l D4	
FC11C0	89ED0016	divs.w 22(A5),D4	divided by dspc, sectors per track
FC11C4	4844	swap D4	Remainder of division as sector number
FC11C6	B86D0018	cmp.w 24(A5),D4	Compare with dspt
FC11CA	6C04	bge $FC11D0	Greater than or equal?
FC11CC	4245	clr.w D5	Side 0
FC11CE	6006	bra $FC11D6	
FC11D0	7A01	moveq.l #1,D5	Side 1
FC11D2	986D0018	sub.w 24(A5),D4	Subtract dspt
FC11D6	4A6EFFFE	tst.w -2(A6)	Odd-flag set?
FC11DA	6704	beq $FC11E0	No
FC11DC	7601	moveq.l #1,D3	Set counter to one
FC11DE	6018	bra $FC11F8	
FC11E0	302D0018	move.w 24(A5),D0	dspt
FC11E4	9044	sub.w D4,D0	minus sector number
FC11E6	B06E0012	cmp.w 18(A6),D0	Compare with number of sectors
FC11EA	6C08	bge $FC11F4	Greater or equal?
FC11EC	362D0018	move.w 24(A5),D3	dspt
FC11F0	9644	sub.w D4,D3	minus sector number equals counter
FC11F2	6004	bra $FC11F8	
FC11F4	362E0012	move.w 18(A6),D3	Number of sectors as counter
FC11F8	5244	addq.w #1,D4	Increment sector number (first sector # = 1)
FC11FA	082E00000009	btst #0,9(A6)	Test rwflag
FC1200	67000080	beq $FC1282	Read ?
FC1204	202EFFFA	move.l -6(A6),D0	Buffer pointer
FC1208	B0AE000A	cmp.l 10(A6),D0	Equals specified buffer address?

FC120C	6710	beq	$FC121E	Yes
FC120E	2EAEFFFA	move.l	-6(A6),(A7)	Source address
FC1212	2F2E000A	move.l	10(A6),-(A7)	Destination address
FC1216	4EB900FC0AD6	jsr	$FC0AD6	Fastcopy, copy sector
FC121C	588F	addq.l	#4,A7	Correct stack pointer
FC121E	3E83	move.w	D3,(A7)	Number of sectors
FC1220	3F05	move.w	D5,-(A7)	Side
FC1222	3F06	move.w	D6,-(A7)	Track
FC1224	3F04	move.w	D4,-(A7)	Sector
FC1226	3F2E0010	move.w	16(A6),-(A7)	Drive
FC122A	42A7	clr.l	-(A7)	Filler
FC122C	2F2EFFFA	move.l	-6(A6),-(A7)	Buffer
FC1230	4EB900FC167C	jsr	$FC167C	flopwr, write sector(s)
FC1236	DFFC00000010	add.l	#$10,A7	Correct stack pointer
FC123C	2E00	move.l	D0,D7	Error code
FC123E	4A87	tst.l	D7	OK ?
FC1240	663E	bne	$FC1280	No
FC1242	4A7900000444	tst.w	$444	_fverify, verify ?
FC1248	6736	beq	$FC1280	No
FC124A	3E83	move.w	D3,(A7)	Number of sectors
FC124C	3F05	move.w	D5,-(A7)	Side
FC124E	3F06	move.w	D6,-(A7)	Track
FC1250	3F04	move.w	D4,-(A7)	Sector
FC1252	3F2E0010	move.w	16(A6),-(A7)	Drive
FC1256	42A7	clr.l	-(A7)	Filler
FC1258	2F3C0000167A	move.l	#$167A,-(A7)	Address of disk buffer
FC125E	4EB900FC18CE	jsr	$FC18CE	flopver, verify sectors
FC1264	DFFC00000010	add.l	#$10,A7	Correct stack pointer
FC126A	2E00	move.l	D0,D7	Error code
FC126C	4A87	tst.l	D7	OK ?

Address	Bytes	Instruction	Operand	Comment
FC126E	6610	bne	$FC1280	No
FC1270	2EBC0000167A	move.l	#$167A,(A7)	Address of the disk buffer
FC1276	610002B8	bsr	$FC1530	u2i, convert 8086 integer to 68000 format
FC127A	4A40	tst.w	D0	Bad sector list
FC127C	6702	beq	$FC1280	No errors during verify?
FC127E	7EF0	moveq.l	#-16,D7	'Bad sectors'
FC1280	603A	bra	$FC12BC	
FC1282	3E83	move.w	D3,(A7)	Number of sectors
FC1284	3F05	move.w	D5,-(A7)	Side
FC1286	3F06	move.w	D6,-(A7)	Track
FC1288	3F04	move.w	D4,-(A7)	Sector
FC128A	3F2E0010	move.w	16(A6),-(A7)	Drive
FC128E	42A7	clr.l	-(A7)	Filler
FC1290	2F2EFFFA	move.l	-6(A6),-(A7)	Buffer
FC1294	4EB900FC159E	jsr	$FC159E	floprd, read sector(s)
FC129A	DFFC00000010	add.l	#$10,A7	Correct stack pointer
FC12A0	2E00	move.l	D0,D7	Error code
FC12A2	202EFFFA	move.l	-6(A6),D0	Buffer used
FC12A6	B0AE000A	cmp.l	10(A6),D0	Equals desired buffer?
FC12AA	6710	beq	$FC12BC	Yes
FC12AC	2EAE000A	move.l	10(A6),(A7)	Source address
FC12B0	2F2EFFFA	move.l	-6(A6),-(A7)	Destination address
FC12B4	4EB900FC0AD6	jsr	$FC0AD6	Fastcopy, copy sector
FC12BA	588F	addq.l	#4,A7	Correct stack pointer
FC12BC	4A87	tst.l	D7	No error?
FC12BE	6C32	bge	$FC12F2	OK
FC12C0	3EAE0010	move.w	16(A6),(A7)	Drive number
FC12C4	2007	move.l	D7,D0	Error code
FC12C6	3F00	move.w	D0,-(A7)	
FC12C8	4EB900FC073E	jsr	$FC073E	critical error handler
FC12CE	548F	addq.l	#2,A7	Correct stack pointer
FC12D0	2E00	move.l	D0,D7	Save error code

317

```
FC12D2  0C6E00020008    cmp.w   #2,8(A6)            rwflag, ignore media change ?
FC12D8  6C18            bge     $FC12F2             Yes
FC12DA  BEBC00010000    cmp.l   #$10000,D7          Retry ?
FC12E0  6610            bne     $FC12F2             No
FC12E2  3EAE0010        move.w  16(A6),(A7)         Drive number
FC12E6  6100FD18        bsr     $FC1000             Diskette change ?
FC12EA  B07C0002        cmp.w   #2,D0               Definitely changed?
FC12EE  6602            bne     $FC12F2             No
FC12F0  7EF2            moveq.l #-14,D7             'media changed'
FC12F2  BEBC00010000    cmp.l   #$10000,D7          Retry ?
FC12F8  6700FF00        beq     $FC11FA             Yes, try again
FC12FC  4A87            tst.l   D7                  Error code
FC12FE  6C04            bge     $FC1304             OK ?
FC1300  2007            move.l  D7,D0               Error code
FC1302  601E            bra     $FC1322             To error exit
FC1304  3003            move.w  D3,D0               Sector counter
FC1306  48C0            ext.l   D0
FC1308  7209            moveq.l #9,D1
FC130A  E3A0            asl.l   D1,D0               times 512
FC130C  D1AE000A        add.l   D0,10(A6)           Increment buffer address
FC1310  D76E000E        add.w   D3,14(A6)           Logical sector number plus sector counter
FC1314  976E0012        sub.w   D3,18(A6)           Decrement number of sectors to process
FC1318  4A6E0012        tst.w   18(A6)              Still sectors to process?
FC131C  6600FE7C        bne     $FC119A             Yes
FC1320  4280            clr.l   D0                  OK
FC1322  4A9F            tst.l   (A7)+
FC1324  4CDF20F8        movem.l (A7)+,D3-D7/A5      Restore registers
FC1328  4E5E            unlk    A6
FC132A  4E75            rts

************************************************  random, generate random numbers

FC132C  4E56FFFC        link    A6,#-4
```

```
FC1330  4AB9000029B8        tst.l    $29B8                      Last random number
FC1336  6616                bne      $FC134E                    Not zero?
FC1338  203900000004BA      move.l   $4BA,D0                    _hz_200
FC133E  7210                moveq.l  #16,D1
FC1340  E3A0                asl.l    D1,D0                      << 16
FC1342  80B9000004BA        or.l     $4BA,D0                    _hz_200
FC1348  23C000029B8         move.l   D0,$29B8                   Use as start value
FC134E  2F3CBB40E62D        move.l   #3141592621,-(A7)
FC1354  2F39000029B8        move.l   $29B8,-(A7)                Last random value
FC135A  4EB900FC4BE4        jsr      $FC4BE4                    Long multiplication
FC1360  508F                addq.l   #8,A7                      Correct stack pointer
FC1362  5280                addq.l   #1,D0                      plus
FC1364  23C000029B8         move.l   D0,$29B8                   as new start value
FC136A  203900029B8         move.l   $29B8,D0                   Result
FC1370  E080                asr.l    #8,D0                      >> 8
FC1372  C0BC00FFFFFF        and.l    #$FFFFFF,D0                Clear bits 24-31
FC1378  4E5E                unlk     A6
FC137A  4E75                rts

************************************************************** hdv_boot, load boot sector
FC137C  4E560000            link     A6,#0
FC1380  48E70300            movem.l  D6-D7,-(A7)                Save registers
FC1384  4EB900FC0AF8        jsr      $FC0AF8                    hdv_init, initialize drive
FC138A  4A79000004A6        tst.w    $4A6                       _nflops
FC1390  6704                beq      $FC1396                    No drive connected?
FC1392  7001                moveq.l  #1,D0                      'couldn't load'
FC1394  6002                bra      $FC1398
FC1396  7002                moveq.l  #2,D0                      'no drive'
FC1398  3E00                move.w   D0,D7                      Save error
FC139A  4A79000004A6        tst.w    $4A6                       _nflops
FC13A0  6744                beq      $FC13E6                    No drive?
FC13A2  0C790002000000446   cmp.w    #2,$446                    _bootdev
```

```
FC13AA  6C3A                    bge       $FC13E6             No diskette?
FC13AC  3EBC0001                move.w    #1,(A7)             One sector
FC13B0  4267                    clr.w     -(A7)               Side 0
FC13B2  4267                    clr.w     -(A7)               Track 0
FC13B4  3F3C0001                move.w    #1,-(A7)            Sector 1
FC13B8  3F39000000446           move.w    $446,-(A7)          _bootdev
FC13BE  42A7                    clr.l     -(A7)               Filler
FC13C0  2F3C0000167A            move.l    #$167A,-(A7)        Address of disk buffer
FC13C6  4EB900FC159E            jsr       $FC159E             floprd, read sector
FC13CC  DFFC00000010            add.l     #$10,A7             Correct stack pointer
FC13D2  4A80                    tst.l     D0                  Error ?
FC13D4  6604                    bne       $FC13DA             Yes
FC13D6  4247                    clr.w     D7                  Clear error code
FC13D8  600C                    bra       $FC13E6
FC13DA  4A39000009B2            tst.b     $9B2                wpstatus
FC13E0  6604                    bne       $FC13E6
FC13E2  7003                    moveq.l   #3,D0               'unreadable'
FC13E4  6024                    bra       $FC140A
FC13E6  4A47                    tst.w     D7                  Error ?
FC13E8  6704                    beq       $FC13EE             No
FC13EA  3007                    move.w    D7,D0               Get error code
FC13EC  601C                    bra       $FC140A
FC13EE  3EBC0100                move.w    #$100,(A7)          $100 words
FC13F2  2F3C0000167A            move.l    #$167A,-(A7)        Address of disk buffer
FC13F8  61000106                bsr       $FC1500             Calculate checksum
FC13FC  588F                    addq.l    #4,A7               Correct stack pointer
FC13FE  B07C1234                cmp.w     #$1234,D0           magic for boot sector?
FC1402  6604                    bne       $FC1408             No
FC1404  4240                    clr.w     D0                  OK
FC1406  6002                    bra       $FC140A
FC1408  7004                    moveq.l   #4,D0               'not valid boot sector'
FC140A  4A9F                    tst.l     (A7)+
```

```
FC140C  4CDF0080              movem.l (A7)+,D7        Restore registers
FC1410  4E5E                  unlk    A6
FC1412  4E75                  rts

*****************************                         proto_bt, generate boot sector
FC1414  4E56FFFA              link    A6,#-6
FC1418  48E70704              movem.l D5-D7/A5,-(A7)  Restore registers
FC141C  4A6E0012              tst.w   18(A6)          Test execflg
FC1420  6C1E                  bge     $FC1440         Preserve executability
FC1422  3EBC0100              move.w  #$100,(A7)      $100 words
FC1426  2F2E0008              move.l  8(A6),-(A7)     Address of the sector buffer
FC142A  610000D4              bsr     $FC1500         Calculate checksum
FC142E  588F                  addq.l  #4,A7           Correct stack pointer
FC1430  B07C1234              cmp.w   #$1234,D0       magic for boot sector?
FC1434  6704                  beq     $FC143A         Yes
FC1436  4240                  clr.w   D0              Not executable
FC1438  6002                  bra     $FC143C
FC143A  7001                  moveq.l #1,D0          Executable
FC143C  3D400012              move.w  D0,18(A6)       execflg
FC1440  4AAE000C              tst.l   12(A6)          Serial number
FC1444  6D3E                  blt     $FC1484         Negative, don't change
FC1446  202E000C              move.l  12(A6),D0       Serial number
FC144A  B0BC00FFFFFF          cmp.l   #$FFFFFF,D0     > $FFFFFF ?
FC1450  6F08                  ble     $FC145A         No
FC1452  6100FED8              bsr     $FC132C         rand, create random number
FC1456  2D40000C              move.l  D0,12(A6)       as serial number
FC145A  4247                  clr.w   D7              Clear counter
FC145C  6020                  bra     $FC147E
FC145E  202E000C              move.l  12(A6),D0       Serial number
FC1462  C0BC000000FF          and.l   #$FF,D0         Bits 0-7
FC1468  3247                  move.w  D7,A1           Pointer to next byte in buffer
FC146A  D3EE0008              add.l   8(A6),A1        plus buffer address
```

Address	Hex	Mnemonic	Operands	Comment
FC146E	13400008	move.b	D0,8(A1)	Byte of the serial number in buffer
FC1472	202E000C	move.l	12(A6),D0	Serial number
FC1476	E080	asr.l	#8,D0	>> 8
FC1478	2D400000C	move.l	D0,12(A6)	
FC147C	5247	addq.w	#1,D7	Increment counter
FC147E	BE7C0003	cmp.w	#3,D7	already 3 ?
FC1482	6DDA	blt	$FC145E	No
FC1484	4A6E0010	tst.w	16(A6)	Disk size
FC1488	6D28	blt	$FC14B2	Negative, don't change
FC148A	3C2E0010	move.w	16(A6),D6	Disk size
FC148E	CDFC0013	muls.w	#$13,D6	times 19 equals pointer to prototype bpb
FC1492	4247	clr.w	D7	Clear counter
FC1494	6016	bra	$FC14AC	
FC1496	3047	move.w	D7,A0	Counter
FC1498	D1EE0008	add.l	8(A6),A0	plus buffer address
FC149C	3246	move.w	D6,A1	Disk size
FC149E	D3FC00FD1B60	add.l	#$FD1B60,A1	plus address of the prototype bpb
FC14A4	1151000B	move.b	(A1),11(A0)	Copy bpb
FC14A8	5246	addq.w	#1,D6	
FC14AA	5247	addq.w	#1,D7	Increment counter
FC14AC	BE7C0013	cmp.w	#$13,D7	already 19 ?
FC14B0	6DE4	blt	$FC1496	No
FC14B2	426EFFFA	clr.w	-6(A6)	
FC14B6	2D6E0008FFFC	move.l	8(A6),-4(A6)	Buffer address
FC14BC	600E	bra	$FC14CC	
FC14BE	206EFFFC	move.l	-4(A6),A0	Buffer address
FC14C2	3010	move.w	(A0),D0	Get word from buffer
FC14C4	D16EFFFA	add.w	D0,-6(A6)	Add to checksum
FC14C8	54AEFFFC	addq.l	#2,-4(A6)	Next word
FC14CC	202E0008	move.l	8(A6),D0	Buffer address
FC14D0	D0BC000001FE	add.l	#$1FE,D0	plus $1FE
FC14D6	B0AEFFFC	cmp.l	-4(A6),D0	Last word?

```
FC14DA 62E2           bhi       $FC14BE              No
FC14DC 303C1234       move.w    #$1234,D0            Checksum for boot sector
FC14E0 906EFFFA       sub.w     -6(A6),D0            subtract from previous value
FC14E4 226EFFFC       move.l    -4(A6),A1
FC14E8 3280           move.w    D0,(A1)              Checksum in buffer
FC14EA 4A6E0012       tst.w     18(A6)               execflg
FC14EE 6606           bne       $FC14F6              Boot sector executable?
FC14F0 206EFFFC       move.l    -4(A6),A0
FC14F4 5250           addq.w    #1,(A0)              Increment checksum, not executable
FC14F6 4A9F           tst.l     (A7)+
FC14F8 4CDF20C0       movem.l   (A7)+,D6-D7/A5       Restore registers
FC14FC 4E5E           unlk      A6
FC14FE 4E75           rts

**********************************************
FC1500 4E560000       link      A6,#0                Calculate checksum
FC1504 48E70300       movem.l   D6-D7,-(A7)          Restore registers
FC1508 4247           clr.w     D7                   Clear sum
FC150A 600C           bra       $FC1518              To loop end
FC150C 206E0008       move.l    8(A6),A0             Address of the buffer
FC1510 3010           move.w    (A0),D0              Get word
FC1512 DE40           add.w     D0,D7                sum
FC1514 54AE0008       addq.l    #2,8(A6)             Increment buffer address
FC1518 302E000C       move.w    12(A6),D0            Number of words
FC151C 536E000C       subq.w    #1,12(A6)            minus 1
FC1520 4A40           tst.w     D0                   All words added?
FC1522 66E8           bne       $FC150C              No
FC1524 3007           move.w    D7,D0                Result to D0
FC1526 4A9F           tst.l     (A7)+
FC1528 4CDF0080       movem.l   (A7)+,D7             Restore registers
FC152C 4E5E           unlk      A6
FC152E 4E75           rts
```

```
;********************************************************  u2i, 8086 integer to 68000 format
FC1530  4E56FFFC       link     A6,#-4
FC1534  206E0008       move.l   8(A6),A0        Address of the number
FC1538  10280001       move.b   1(A0),D0        Hi byte
FC153C  4880           ext.w    D0
FC153E  C07C00FF       and.w    #$FF,D0         Isolate bits 0-7
FC1542  E140           asl.w    #8,D0           Shift to bits 8-15
FC1544  226E0008       move.l   8(A6),A1        Address of the number
FC1548  1211           move.b   (A1),D1         Gte lo-byte
FC154A  4881           ext.w    D1
FC154C  C27C00FF       and.w    #$FF,D1         Isolate bits 0-7
FC1550  8041           or.w     D1,D0           Combine with high byte
FC1552  4E5E           unlk     A6
FC1554  4E75           rts

;********************************************************  flopini, initialize drive
FC1556  43F900000A06   lea      $A06,A1         Address of dsb0
FC155C  4A6F000C       tst.w    12(A7)          Drive A ?
FC1560  6706           beq      $FC1568         Yes
FC1562  43F900000A0A   lea      $A0A,A1         Else address of dsb1
FC1568  33790000400002 move.w   $440,2(A1)      Seek rate in dsb
FC1570  70FF           moveq.l  #-1,D0          Default error number
FC1572  42690000       clr.w    (A1)            Track number to zero
FC1576  610004BC       bsr      $FC1A34         floplock, set parameters
FC157A  61000698       bsr      $FC1C14         select, select drive and side
FC157E  337CFF000000   move.w   #$FF00,(A1)     Track number negative, invalid
FC1584  6100061A       bsr      $FC1BA0         restore, track zero
FC1588  670C           beq      $FC1596         OK, flopok
FC158A  7E0A           moveq.l  #10,D7          Track 10
FC158C  610005A0       bsr      $FC1B2E         hseek, find track
FC1590  6608           bne      $FC159A         Error, flopfail
FC1592  6100060C       bsr      $FC1BA0         restore
```

```
FC1596  67000542                         beq      $FC1ADA                                OK, flopok
FC159A  60000530                         bra      $FC1ACC                                flopfail

*********************************************************************

FC159E  6100071E                         bsr      $FC1CBE                                floprd, read sector(s) from disk
FC15A2  70F5                             moveq.l  #-11,D0                                change, test for disk change
FC15A4  6100048E                         bsr      $FC1A34                                Read error as error number
FC15A8  6100066A                         bsr      $FC1C14                                floplock, set parameters
FC15AC  610005CC                         bsr      $FC1B7A                                select, select drive and side
FC15B0  66000090                         bne      $FC1642                                go2track, find track
FC15B4  33FCFFFF000009E0                 move.w   #-1,$9E0                               Try again if error
FC15BC  3CBC0090                         move.w   #$90,(A6)                              General error
FC15C0  3CBC0190                         move.w   #$190,(A6)
FC15C4  3CBC0090                         move.w   #$90,(A6)                              Clear DMA status, select read
FC15C8  33ED09CAFFFF8604                 move.w   $9CA(A5),$FFFF8604                     ccount, sector counter
FC15D0  3CBC0080                         move.w   #$80,(A6)                              Select 1772
FC15D4  3E3C0090                         move.w   #$90,D7                                Read multiple sectors
FC15D8  610006B6                         bsr      $FC1C90                                wdiskctl, pass D7 to 1772
FC15DC  2E3C00040000                     move.l   #$40000,D7                             Timeout counter
FC15E2  246D09D0                         move.l   $9D0(A5),A2                            edma, end address for DMA
FC15E6  08390005FFFFFA01                 btst     #5,$FFFFFA01                           mfp gpip, 1772 done ?
FC15EE  6734                             beq      $FC1624                                Yes
FC15F0  5387                             subq.l   #1,D7                                  Decrement counter
FC15F2  6724                             beq      $FC1618                                Timeout ?
FC15F4  1B79FFFF860909DB                 move.b   $FFFF8609,$9DB(A5)
FC15FC  1B79FFFF860B09DC                 move.b   $FFFF860B,$9DC(A5)                     DMA address
FC1604  1B79FFFF860D09DD                 move.b   $FFFF860D,$9DD(A5)
FC160C  B5ED09DA                         cmp.l    $9DA(A5),A2                            End address reached?
FC1610  6ED4                             bgt      $FC15E6                                No
FC1612  610005E6                         bsr      $FC1BFA                                reset, end transfer
FC1616  600C                             bra      $FC1624
FC1618  3B7CFFFE09E0                     move.w   #-2,$9E0(A5)                           Drive not ready
```

```
FC161E 610005DA      bsr     $FC1BFA                    reset, end transfer
FC1622 601E          bra     $FC1642
FC1624 3CBC0090      move.w  #$90,(A6)                  Select DMA status register
FC1628 3016          move.w  (A6),D0                    Read status
FC162A 08000000      btst    #0,D0                      DMA error ?
FC162E 6712          beq     $FC1642                    Yes, try again
FC1630 3CBC0080      move.w  #$80,(A6)                  Select 1772
FC1634 6100066E      bsr     $FC1CA4                    rdiskctl, read status register
FC1638 C03C0018      and.b   #$18,D0                    Isolate RNF, CRC and Lost Data
FC163C 6700049C      beq     $FC1ADA                    No error, flopok
FC1640 6118          bsr     $FC165A                    errbits, determine error number
FC1642 0C6D000109B0  cmp.w   #1,$9B0(A5)                retrycnt to second attempt?
FC1648 6604          bne     $FC164E                    No
FC164A 610004FA      bsr     $FC1B46                    ressek, home and seek
FC164E 536D09B0      subq.w  #1,$9B0(A5)                Decrement retrycnt
FC1652 6A00FF54      bpl     $FC15A8                    Another attempt?
FC1656 60000474      bra     $FC1ACC                    No, flopfail
*****************************************************************
FC165A 72F3          moveq.l #-13,D1                    errbits, create floppy error number
FC165C 08000006      btst    #6,D0                      Diskette write-protected
FC1660 6614          bne     $FC1676                    Write protect ?
FC1662 72F8          moveq.l #-8,D1                     Yes
FC1664 08000004      btst    #4,D0                      Sector not found
FC1668 660C          bne     $FC1676                    Sector not found ?
FC166A 72FC          moveq.l #-4,D1                     Yes
FC166C 08000003      btst    #3,D0                      CRC Error
FC1670 6704          beq     $FC1676                    CRC Error ?
FC1672 322D09DE      move.w  $9DE(A5),D1                No
FC1676 3B4109E0      move.w  D1,$9E0(A5)                Default error
FC167A 4E75          rts
```

```
*******************************************************
FC167C  61000640                    bsr     $FC1CBE             flopwr, write sector(s) to disk
FC1680  70F6                        moveq.l #-10,D0             change, test for disk change
FC1682  610003B0                    bsr     $FC1A34             Write error as default error
FC1686  302D09C6                    move.w  $9C6(A5),D0         floplock, set parameters
FC168A  5340                        subq.w  #1,D0               csect, sector number 1 ?
FC168C  806D09C4                    or.w    $9C4(A5),D0         ctrack, track number 0
FC1690  806D09C8                    or.w    $9C8(A5),D0         cside, side 0 ?
FC1694  6606                        bne     $FC169C             No, not boot sector
FC1696  7002                        moveq.l #2,D0               media change
FC1698  6100065C                    bsr     $FC1CF6             Set to 'unsure'
FC169C  61000576                    bsr     $FC1C14             select, select track and side
FC16A0  610004D8                    bsr     $FC1B7A             go2track, find track
FC16A4  6600007E                    bne     $FC1724             Error, try again
FC16A8  3B7CFFFF09E0                move.w  #-1,$9E0(A5)        currerr to default
FC16AE  3CBC0190                    move.w  #$190,(A6)
FC16B2  3CBC0090                    move.w  #$90,(A6)           Clear DMA status, to write
FC16B6  3CBC0190                    move.w  #$190,(A6)
FC16BA  3E3C0001                    move.w  #1,D7               Sector count register
FC16BE  610005D0                    bsr     $FC1C90             wdiskctl, D7 to 1772
FC16C2  3CBC0180                    move.w  #$180,(A6)          Select 1772
FC16C6  3E3C00A0                    move.w  #$A0,D7             Write sector
FC16CA  610005C4                    bsr     $FC1C90             wdiskctl, D7 to 1772
FC16CE  2E3C00040000                move.l  #$40000,D7          Timeout counter
FC16D4  08390005FFFFFA01            btst    #5,$FFFFFA01        mfp gpip, 1772 done ?
FC16DC  670A                        beq     $FC16E8             Yes
FC16DE  5387                        subq.l  #1,D7               Decrement timeout counter
FC16E0  66F2                        bne     $FC16D4             Timeout?
FC16E2  61000516                    bsr     $FC1BFA             reset, terminate transfer
FC16E6  6034                        bra     $FC171C             Next try
FC16E8  3CBC0180                    move.w  #$180,(A6)          Select 1772
```

327

```
FC16EC  610005B6                    bsr     $FC1CA4                 rdiskctl, read status register
FC16F0  6100FF68                    bsr     $FC165A                 errbits, calculate error number
FC16F4  08000006                    btst    #6,D0                   write protect ?
FC16F8  660003D2                    bne     $FC1ACC                 flopfail, no further attempt
FC16FC  C03C005C                    and.b   #$5C,D0                 write protect, RNF, CRC and Lost Data
FC1700  661A                        bne     $FC171C                 Error, try again
FC1702  526D09C6                    addq.w  #1,$9C6(A5)             csect, increment sector number
FC1706  06AD000002C0009CC           add.l   #512,$9CC(A5)           cdma, DMA address to next sector
FC170E  536D09CA                    subq.w  #1,$9CA(A5)             ccount, decrement number of sectors
FC1712  67003C6                     beq     $FC1ADA                 All sectors, done, flopok
FC1716  61000524                    bsr     $FC1C3C                 select1, sector number and DMA pointer
FC171A  608C                        bra     $FC16A8                 Write next sector without seek
FC171C  0C6D000109B0                cmp.w   #1,$9B0(A5)             retrycnt, second try?
FC1722  6604                        bne     $FC1728                 No
FC1724  61000420                    bsr     $FC1B46                 reseek, home and seek
FC1728  536D09B0                    subq.w  #1,$9B0(A5)             retrycnt, decrement try counter
FC172C  6A00FF6E                    bpl     $FC169C                 Another try?
FC1730  6000039A                    bra     $FC1ACC                 No, flopfail
***********************************************************************
FC1734  0CAF876543210016            cmp.l   #$87654321,22(A7)       flopfmt, format track
FC173C  6600038E                    bne     $FC1ACC                 Magic number ?
FC1740  6100057C                    bsr     $FC1CBE                 No, flopfail
FC1744  70FF                        moveq.l #-1,D0                  change, test for disk change
FC1746  610002EC                    bsr     $FC1A34                 Default Error Nummer
FC174A  610004C8                    bsr     $FC1C14                 floplock, set parameters
FC174E  3B6F000E09D4                move.w  14(A7),$9D4(A5)         select, select drive and side
FC1754  3B6F001409D6                move.w  20(A7),$9D6(A5)         spt, sectors per track
FC175A  3B6F001A09D8                move.w  26(A7),$9D8(A5)         interlv, interleave factor
FC1760  7002                        moveq.l #2,D0                   virgin, sector data for formatting
FC1762  61000592                    bsr     $FC1CF6                 'changed'
FC1766  610003C0                    bsr     $FC1B28                 Diskette changed
                                                                    hseek, search for track
```

```
FC176A  66000360           bne     $FC1ACC                        Not found, flopfail
FC176E  336D09C40000       move.w  $9C4(A5),(A1)                  ctrack, write current track in DSB
FC1774  3B7CFFFF09E0       move.w  #-1,$9E0(A5)                   General error
FC177A  6128               bsr     $FC17A4                        Format track
FC177C  6600034E           bne     $FC1ACC                        flopfail, error
FC1780  3B6D09D409CA       move.w  $9D4(A5),$9CA(A5)              spt sectors per track as ccount counter
FC1786  3B7C000109C6       move.w  #1,$9C6(A5)                    csect, start with sector 1
FC178C  6100015C           bsr     $FC18EA                        verify, verify sector
FC1790  246D09CC           move.l  $9CC(A5),A2                    cdma, list with bad sectors
FC1794  4A52               tst.w   (A2)                           Bad sector?
FC1796  67000342           beq     $FC1ADA                        No, flopok
FC179A  3B7CFFF009E0       move.w  #-16,$9E0(A5)                  Bad sectors
FC17A0  6000032A           bra     $FC1ACC                        flopfail, error
*********************************************************         fmtrack, format track
FC17A4  3B7CFFFF609DE      move.w  #-10,$9DE(A5)                  Write error
FC17AA  363C0001           move.w  #1,D3                          Start with sector 1
FC17AE  246D09CC           move.l  $9CC(A5),A2                    cdma, buffer for track data
FC17B2  323C003B           move.w  #$3B,D1                        60 times
FC17B6  103C004E           move.b  #$4E,D0                        $4E, track header
FC17BA  6100010A           bsr     $FC18C6                        wmult, write in buffer
FC17BE  3803               move.w  D3,D4                          Save sector number
FC17C0  323C000B           move.w  #$B,D1                         12 times
FC17C4  4200               clr.b   D0                             0
FC17C6  610000FE           bsr     $FC18C6                        wmult, write in buffer
FC17CA  323C0002           move.w  #2,D1                          3 times
FC17CE  103C00F5           move.b  #$F5,D0                        $F5
FC17D2  610000F2           bsr     $FC18C6                        wmult, write in buffer
FC17D6  14FC00FE           move.b  #$FE,(A2)+                     $FE, address mark
FC17DA  14F9000009C5       move.b  $9C5,(A2)+                     Track
FC17E0  14F9000009C9       move.b  $9C9,(A2)+                     Side
FC17E6  14C4               move.b  D4,(A2)+                       Sector
```

```
FC17E8  14FC0002          move.b   #2,(A2)+              Sector size 512 bytes
FC17EC  14FC00F7          move.b   #$F7,(A2)+            Write checksum
FC17F0  323C0015          move.w   #$15,D1               22 times
FC17F4  103C004E          move.b   #$4E,D0               $4E
FC17F8  610000CC          bsr      $FC18C6               wmult, write in buffer
FC17FC  323C000B          move.w   #$B,D1                12 times
FC1800  4200              clr.b    D0                    0
FC1802  610000C2          bsr      $FC18C6               wmult, write in buffer
FC1806  323C0002          move.w   #2,D1                 3 times
FC180A  103C00F5          move.b   #$F5,D0               $F5
FC180E  610000B6          bsr      $FC18C6               wmult, write in buffer
FC1812  14FC00FB          move.b   #$FB,(A2)+            $FB, data block mark
FC1816  323C00FF          move.w   #$FF,D1               256 times
FC181A  14ED09D8          move.b   $9D8(A5),(A2)+        virgin, initial data in buffer
FC181E  14ED09D9          move.b   $9D9(A5),(A2)+
FC1822  51C9FFF6          dbra     D1,$FC181A            Next word
FC1826  14FC00F7          move.b   #$F7,(A2)+            Write checksum
FC182A  323C0027          move.w   #$27,D1               40 times
FC182E  103C004E          move.b   #$4E,D0               $4E
FC1832  61000092          bsr      $FC18C6               wmult, write in buffer
FC1836  D86D09D6          add.w    $9D6(A5),D4           Add interlv, next sector
FC183A  B86D09D4          cmp.w    $9D4(A5),D4           spt, largest sector number
FC183E  6F80              ble      $FC17C0               No, next sector
FC1840  5243              addq.w   #1,D3                 Start sector plus one
FC1842  B66D09D6          cmp.w    $9D6(A5),D3           interlv
FC1846  6F00FF76          ble      $FC17BE               Next sector
FC184A  323C0578          move.w   #$578,D1              1401 times (until track end)
FC184E  103C004E          move.b   #$4E,D0               $4E
FC1852  6172              bsr      $FC18C6               wmult, write in buffer
FC1854  13ED09CFFFFF860D  move.b   $9CF(A5),$FFFF860D    dmalow
FC185C  13ED09CEFFFF860B  move.b   $9CE(A5),$FFFF860B    dmamid
FC1864  13ED09CDFFFF8609  move.b   $9CD(A5),$FFFF8609    dmahigh
```

```
FC186C  3CBC0190            move.w   #$190,(A6)           Clear DMA status, write
FC1870  3CBC0090            move.w   #$90,(A6)
FC1874  3CBC0190            move.w   #$190,(A6)
FC1878  3E3C001F            move.w   #$1F,D7              Sector counter to 31
FC187C  61000412            bsr      $FC1C90              wdiskctl, send D7 to 1772
FC1880  3CBC0180            move.w   #$180,(A6)           Select 1772
FC1884  3E3C00F0            move.w   #$F0,D7              Format Track command
FC1888  61000406            bsr      $FC1C90              wdiskctl, send D7 to 1772
FC188C  2E3C00040000        move.l   #$40000,D7           Timeout counter
FC1892  0839005FFFFFA01     btst     #5,$FFFFFA01         mfp gpip, 1772 done ?
FC189A  670C                beq      $FC18A8              Yes
FC189C  5387                subq.l   #1,D7                Decrement timeout counter
FC189E  66F2                bne      $FC1892              Run out ?
FC18A0  61000358            bsr      $FC1BFA              Reset, terminate
FC18A4  7E01                moveq.l  #1,D7                Clear Z-bit, error
FC18A6  4E75                rts

FC18A8  3CBC0190            move.w   #$190,(A6)           Select DMA status
FC18AC  3016                move.w   (A6),D0              Read status
FC18AE  08000000            btst     #0,D0                DMA error ?
FC18B2  67F0                beq      $FC18A4              Yes, error
FC18B4  3CBC0180            move.w   #$180,(A6)           Select 1772 status register
FC18B8  610003EA            bsr      $FC1CA4              rdiskctl, read register
FC18BC  6100FD9C            bsr      $FC165A              errbits, calculate error number
FC18C0  C03C0044            and.b    #$44,D0              Test write protect and lost data
FC18C4  4E75                rts

FC18C6  14C0                move.b   D0,(A2)+             Write byte in buffer
FC18C8  51C9FFFC            dbra     D1,$FC18C6           Next byte
FC18CC  4E75                rts

************************************************************  flopver, verify sector(s)
```

```
FC18CE  610003EE                bsr      $FC1CBE                 change, test for disk change
FC18D2  70F5                    moveq.l  #-11,D0                 Read error as default error
FC18D4  6100015E                bsr      $FC1A34                 floplock, set parameter
FC18D8  6100033A                bsr      $FC1C14                 select
FC18DC  6100029C                bsr      $FC1B7A                 go2track, find track
FC18E0  660001EA                bne      $FC1ACC                 flopfail, error
FC18E4  6104                    bsr      $FC18EA                 verify1, verify sectors
FC18E6  600001F2                bra      $FC1ADA                 flopok, done

*****************************************************           verify1
FC18EA  3B7CFFF509DE            move.w   #-11,$9DE(A5)           Read error
FC18F0  246D09CC                move.l   $9CC(A5),A2             cdma, DMA buffer for bad-sector list
FC18F4  06AD000002000 9CC        add.l    #512,$9CC(A5)           cmda to next sector
FC18FC  3B7C000209B0            move.w   #2,$9B0(A5)             retrycnt, 2 tries
FC1902  3CBC0084                move.w   #$84,(A6)               Select sector register
FC1906  3E2D09C6                move.w   $9C6(A5),D7             csect, sector number
FC190A  61000384                bsr      $FC1C90                 wdiskctl, D7 to 1772

FC190E  13ED09CFFFFF860D        move.b   $9CF(A5),$FFFF860D
FC1916  13ED09CEFFFF860B        move.b   $9CE(A5),$FFFF860B
FC191E  13ED09CDFFFF8609        move.b   $9CD(A5),$FFFF8609      Set DMA address
FC1926  3CBC0090                move.w   #$90,(A6)
FC192A  3CBC0190                move.w   #$190,(A6)
FC192E  3CBC0090                move.w   #$90,(A6)               Clar DMA status, read
FC1932  3E3C0001                move.w   #1,D7                   Sector counter to 1
FC1936  61000358                bsr      $FC1C90                 wdiskctl, D7 to 1772
FC193A  3CBC0080                move.w   #$80,(A6)               Select 1772 command register
FC193E  3E3C0080                move.w   #$80,D7                 Read Sector command
FC1942  6100034C                bsr      $FC1C90                 wdiskctl, D7 to 1772
FC1946  2E3C00040000            move.l   #$40000,D7              Timeout counter
FC194C  08390005FFFFFA01        btst     #5,$FFFFFA01            mfp gpip, 1772 done?
FC1954  670A                    beq      $FC1960                 Yes
FC1956  5387                    subq.l   #1,D7                   Decrement timeout counter
```

```
FC1958  66F2                    bne     $FC194C                 Run out?
FC195A  6100029E                bsr     $FC1BFA                 Reset 1772, terminate transfer
FC195E  6036                    bra     $FC1996                 Next try
FC1960  3CBC0090                move.w  #$90,(A6)               Select DMA status register
FC1964  3016                    move.w  (A6),D0                 Read status
FC1966  08000000                btst    #0,D0                   DMA error ?
FC196A  672A                    beq     $FC1996                 Yes, try again
FC196C  3CBC0080                move.w  #$80,(A6)               Select 1772 status register
FC1970  61000332                bsr     $FC1CA4                 rdiskctl, read status
FC1974  6100FCE4                bsr     $FC165A                 errbits, calculate error number
FC1978  C03C001C                and.b   #$1C,D0                 Test RNF, CRC and Lost Data
FC197C  6618                    bne     $FC1996                 Error next try
FC197E  526D09C6                addq.w  #1,$9C6(A5)             csect, next sector
FC1982  536D09CA                subq.w  #1,$9CA(A5)             ccount, decrement sector counter
FC1986  6600FF74                bne     $FC18FC                 Another sector?
FC198A  04AD0000002 0009CC      sub.l   #512,$9CC(A5)           cdma, reset DMA pointer
FC1992  4252                    clr.w   (A2)                    Terminate bad sector list with zero
FC1994  4E75                    rts
FC1996  0C6D0000109B0           cmp.w   #1,$9B0(A5)             retrycnt,2nd try?
FC199C  6604                    bne     $FC19A2                 No
FC199E  610001A6                bsr     $FC1B46                 reseek, home and seek
FC19A2  536D09B0                subq.w  #1,$9B0(A5)             Decrement retrycnt
FC19A6  6A00FF66                bpl     $FC190E                 Another try?
FC19AA  34ED09C6                move.w  $9C6(A5),(A2)+          csect, sector number in bad sector list
FC19AE  60CE                    bra     $FC197E                 Next sector

**********************************************************

FC19B0  9BCD                    sub.l   A5,A5                   flopvbl, Floppy Vertical Blank Handler
FC19B2  4DF9FFFF8606            lea     $FFFF8606,A6            Clear A5
FC19B8  50ED09BE                st      $9BE(A5)                Address of the floppy register
FC19BC  4A6D043E                tst.w   $43E(A5)                Set motor on flag
FC19C0  6670                    bne     $FC1A32                 flock, floppies active ?
                                                                Yes, do nothing
```

FC19C2	20390000000466	move.l $466,D0	_frclock
FC19C8	1200	move.b D0,D1	
FC19CA	C23C0007	and.b #7,D1	Calculate mod 8
FC19CE	6638	bne $FC1A08	8th interrupt ?
FC19D0	3CBC0080	move.w #$80,(A6)	Select 1772 status register
FC19D4	E608	lsr.b #3,D0	Bit 4 as drive number
FC19D6	C07C0001	and.w #1,D0	
FC19DA	41ED09B2	lea $9B2(A5),A0	
FC19DE	D0C0	add.w D0,A0	wpstatus
FC19E0	B079000004A6	cmp.w $4A6,D0	
FC19E6	6602	bne $FC19EA	
FC19E8	4240	clr.w D0	_nflops
FC19EA	5200	addq.b #1,D0	Drive select bit
FC19EC	E308	lsl.b #1,D0	Write in position
FC19EE	0A000007	eor.b #7,D0	Invert for active low
FC19F2	6100026C	bsr $FC1C60	Select drive
FC19F6	3039FFFF8604	move.w $FFFF8604,D0	dskctl, read 1772 status
FC19FC	08000006	btst #6,D0	Test write protect bit
FC1A00	56D0	sne (A0)	and save
FC1A02	1002	move.b D2,D0	Restore previous status
FC1A04	6100025A	bsr $FC1C60	wpstatus
FC1A08	302D09B2	move.w $9B2(A5),D0	Write in wplatch
FC1A0C	816D09B4	or.w D0,$9B4(A5)	
FC1A10	4A6D09C0	tst.w $9C0(A5)	deslflg, floppies already deselected?
FC1A14	6618	bne $FC1A2E	Yes
FC1A16	6100028C	bsr $FC1CA4	Read 1772 status register
FC1A1A	08000007	btst #7,D0	Motor-on bit set?
FC1A1E	6612	bne $FC1A32	Yes, don't deselect
FC1A20	103C0007	move.b #7,D0	Both drives
FC1A24	6100023A	bsr $FC1C60	Deselect
FC1A28	3B7C000109C0	move.w #1,$9C0(A5)	Set deslflg
FC1A2E	426D09BE	clr.w $9BE(A5)	Clear motoron flag

```
FC1A32  4E75              rts

        ********************************************************  floplock
FC1A34  48F978F8000009E2  movem.l D3-D7/A3-A6,$9E2    Save registers
FC1A3C  9BCD              sub.l   A5,A5              Clear A5
FC1A3E  4DF9FFFF8606      lea     $FFFF8606,A6       Address of the floppy register
FC1A44  50F9000009BE      st      $9BE               Set motoron flag
FC1A4A  3B4009DE          move.w  D0,$9DE(A5)        deferror
FC1A4E  3B4009E0          move.w  D0,$9E0(A5)        currerr
FC1A52  3B7C0001043E      move.w  #1,$43E(A5)        flock, disable floppy VBL routine
FC1A58  2B6F000809CC      move.l  8(A7),$9CC(A5)     cdma, buffer address
FC1A5E  3B6F001009C2      move.w  16(A7),$9C2(A5)    cdev, drive
FC1A64  3B6F001209C6      move.w  18(A7),$9C6(A5)    csect, sector
FC1A6A  3B6F001409C4      move.w  20(A7),$9C4(A5)    ctrack, track
FC1A70  3B6F001609C8      move.w  22(A7),$9C8(A5)    cside, side
FC1A76  3B6F001809CA      move.w  24(A7),$9CA(A5)    ccount, number of sectors
FC1A7C  3B7C000209B0      move.w  #2,$9B0(A5)        retrycnt, 2 tries
FC1A82  43ED0A06          lea     $A06(A5),A1        Address dsb0
FC1A86  4A6D09C2          tst.w   $9C2(A5)           cdev, drive A?
FC1A8A  6704              beq     $FC1A90            Yes
FC1A8C  43ED0A0A          lea     $A0A(A5),A1        else address dsb1
FC1A90  7E00              moveq.l #0,D7
FC1A92  3E2D09CA          move.w  $9CA(A5),D7        ccount, number of sectors
FC1A96  E14F              lsl.w   #8,D7              times 512
FC1A98  E34F              lsl.w   #1,D7
FC1A9A  206D09CC          move.l  $9CC(A5),A0        cdma, start DMA address
FC1A9E  D1C7              add.l   D7,A0              plus sector length
FC1AA0  2B4809D0          move.l  A0,$9D0(A5)        edma, yields end DMA address
FC1AA4  4A690000          tst.w   (A1)               dcurtack, current track
FC1AA8  6A20              bpl     $FC1ACA            Valid ?
FC1AAA  61000168          bsr     $FC1C14            select, select drive and side
FC1AAE  42690000          clr.w   (A1)               Track number to zero
```

```
FC1AB2  610000EC                    bsr     $FC1BA0                 restore, find track zero
FC1AB6  6712                        beq     $FC1ACA                 OK ?
FC1AB8  7E0A                        moveq.l #10,D7                  Track 10
FC1ABA  6172                        bsr     $FC1B2E                 hseek, find track
FC1ABC  6606                        bne     $FC1AC4                 Error ?
FC1ABE  610000E0                    bsr     $FC1BA0                 restore, find track 0
FC1AC2  6706                        beq     $FC1ACA                 OK ?
FC1AC4  337CFF000000                move.w  #$FF00,(A1)             Track number invalid
FC1ACA  4E75                        rts

*************************************************
FC1ACC  7001                        moveq.l #1,D0                   flopfail, error in disk routine
FC1ACE  61000226                    bsr     $FC1CF6                 media change to unsure
FC1AD2  302D09E0                    move.w  $9E0(A5),D0             set
FC1AD6  48C0                        ext.l   D0                      currerr, error number
FC1AD8  6002                        bra     $FC1ADC

*************************************************
FC1ADA  4280                        clr.l   D0                      flopok, error-free disk routine
FC1ADC  2F00                        move.l  D0,-(A7)                Clear error number
FC1ADE  3CBC0086                    move.w  #$86,(A6)               Save error number
FC1AE2  3E290000                    move.w  (A1),D7                 Select 1772
FC1AE6  610001A8                    bsr     $FC1C90                 Get track number
FC1AEA  3C3C0010                    move.w  #$10,D6                 wdiskctl, D7 to 1772
FC1AEE  610000C6                    bsr     $FC1BB6                 Seek command
FC1AF2  3039000009C2                move.w  $9C2,D0                 flopcmds
FC1AF8  E548                        lsl.w   #2,D0                   cdev, drive number
FC1AFA  41F9000009B6                lea     $9B6,A0                 times 4
FC1B00  21AD04BA0000                move.l  $4BA(A5),0(A0,D0.w)     acctim
FC1B06  0C790010000004A6            cmp.w   #1,$4A6                 _hz_200 as last access time
FC1B0E  6606                        bne     $FC1B16                 _nflops
FC1B10  216D04BA0004                move.l  $4BA(A5),4(A0)          Only one drive?
                                                                    _hz_200 as last access time
```

```
FC1B16  201F                move.l   (A7)+,D0                 Error number
FC1B18  4CF978F8000009E2    movem.l  $9E2,D3-D7/A3-A6         Restore registers
FC1B20  42790000043E        clr.w    $43E                     flock, release floppy VBL routine
FC1B26  4E75                rts

***********************************************************************

FC1B28  3E3900009C4         move.w   $9C4,D7                  hseek, find track
FC1B2E  33FCFFFA000009E0    move.w   #-6,$9E0                 ctrack, track number
FC1B36  3CBC0086            move.w   #$86,(A6)                Seek error, track not found
FC1B3A  61000154            bsr      $FC1C90                  Select 1772
FC1B3E  3C3C0010            move.w   #$10,D6                  wdiskctl, D7 to 1772
FC1B42  60000072            bra      $FC1BB6                  Seek command
                                                              flopcmds

***********************************************************************

FC1B46  33FCFFFA000009E0    move.w   #-6,$9E0                 reseek, home and seek
FC1B4E  6150                bsr      $FC1BA0                  Seek error, track not found
FC1B50  664C                bne      $FC1B9E                  Restore
FC1B52  42690000            clr.w    (A1)                     Error ?
FC1B56  3CBC0082            move.w   #$82,(A6)                Track number to zero
FC1B5A  4247                clr.w    D7                       Select track register
FC1B5C  61000132            bsr      $FC1C90                  Track zero
FC1B60  3CBC0086            move.w   #$86,(A6)                wdiskctl, D7 to 1772
FC1B64  3E3C0005            move.w   #5,D7                    Select data register
FC1B68  61000126            bsr      $FC1C90                  Track 5
FC1B6C  3C3C0010            move.w   #$10,D6                  wdiskctl, D7 to 1772
FC1B70  6144                bsr      $FC1BB6                  Seek command
FC1B72  662A                bne      $FC1B9E                  flopcmds
FC1B74  337C00050000        move.w   #5,(A1)                  Error ?
                                                              Track number to 5

***********************************************************************

FC1B7A  33FCFFFA000009E0    move.w   #-6,$9E0                 go2track, find track
FC1B82  3CBC0086            move.w   #$86,(A6)                Seek error, track not found
                                                              Select data register
```

```
FC1B86 3E2D09C4          move.w   $9C4(A5),D7      Track number
FC1B8A 61000104          bsr      $FC1C90          wdiskctl, D7 to 1772
FC1B8E 7C14              moveq.l  #$14,D6          Seek with verify command
FC1B90 6124              bsr      $FC1BB6          flopcmds
FC1B92 660A              bne      $FC1B9E          Error ?
FC1B94 336D09C40000      move.w   $9C4(A5),(A1)    Save track number
FC1B9A CE3C0018          and.b    #$18,D7          Test RNF, CRC, Lost Data
FC1B9E 4E75              rts

*********************************************
FC1BA0 4246              clr.w    D6               restore, find track zero
FC1BA2 6112              bsr      $FC1BB6          Restore command
FC1BA4 660E              bne      $FC1BB4          flopcmds
FC1BA6 08070002          btst     #2,D7            Error ?
FC1BAA 0A3C0004          eor.b    #4,SR            Test track-zero bit
FC1BAE 6604              bne      $FC1BB4          Invert Z-flag
FC1BB0 42690000          clr.w    (A1)             Not track zero?
FC1BB4 4E75              rts                       Track number to zero

*********************************************
FC1BB6 30290002          move.w   2(A1),D0         flopcmds
FC1BBA C03C0003          and.b    #3,D0            Seek rate
FC1BBE 8C00              or.b     D0,D6            Bits 0 and 1
FC1BC0 2E3C00040000      move.l   #$40000,D7       OR with command word
FC1BC6 3CBC0080          move.w   #$80,(A6)        Timeout counter
FC1BCA 610000D8          bsr      $FC1CA4          Select 1772
FC1BCE 08000007          btst     #7,D0            rdiskctl
FC1BD2 6606              bne      $FC1BDA          Motor on ?
FC1BD4 2E3C00060000      move.l   #$60000,D7       Yes
FC1BDA 610000AA          bsr      $FC1C86          Else longer timeout
FC1BDE 5387              subq.l   #1,D7            wdiskctl6, write command in D6
FC1BE0 6712              beq      $FC1BF4          Decrement timeout counter
                                                    Run out?
```

```
FC1BE2  08390005FFFFFA01   btst     #5,$FFFFFA01          mfp gpip, disk done?
FC1BEA  66F2                bne      $FC1BDE               No, wait
FC1BEC  610000AC            bsr      $FC1C9A               rdiskctl7, read status
FC1BF0  4246                clr.w    D6                    OK
FC1BF2  4E75                rts

FC1BF4  6104                bsr      $FC1BFA               Reset 1772
FC1BF6  7C01                moveq.l  #1,D6                 Error
FC1BF8  4E75                rts      ¿nl¡¿a3¡

*********************************************
FC1BFA  3CBC0080            move.w   #$80,(A6)             Reset 1772, Reset Floppy Controller
FC1BFE  3E3C00D0            move.w   #$D0,D7               Select command register
FC1C02  6100008C            bsr      $FC1C90               Reset command
FC1C06  3E3C000F            move.w   #$F,D7                wdiskctl, D7 to 1772
FC1C0A  51CFFFFE            dbra     D7,$FC1C0A            Delay counter
FC1C0E  6100008A            bsr      $FC1C9A               Time run out?
FC1C12  4E75                rts                            rdiskctl, read status

*********************************************
FC1C14  426D09C0            clr.w    $9C0(A5)              select, select drive and side
FC1C18  302D09C2            move.w   $9C2(A5),D0           Clear deslflg
FC1C1C  5200                addq.b   #1,D0                 cdev, drive number
FC1C1E  E308                lsl.b    #1,D0                 Calculate bit number
FC1C20  806D09C8            or.w     $9C8(A5),D0           csid, side in bit 0
FC1C24  0A000007            eor.b    #7,D0                 Invert bits for active low
FC1C28  C03C0007            and.b    #7,D0
FC1C2C  6132                bsr      $FC1C60               setporta, set bits
FC1C2E  3CBC0082            move.w   #$82,(A6)             Select track register
FC1C32  3E290000            move.w   (A1),D7               Get track number
FC1C36  6158                bsr      $FC1C90               wdiskctl, D7 to 1772
FC1C38  422D09DA            clr.b    $9DA(A5)              tmpdma, clear bits 24-31
```

```
FC1C3C  3CBC0084            move.w   #$84,(A6)                    Select sector register
FC1C40  3E2D09C6            move.w   $9C6(A5),D7                  csect, get sector number
FC1C44  614A                bsr      $FC1C90                      wdiskct1, D7 to 1772
FC1C46  13ED09CFFFFF860D    move.b   $9CF(A5),$FFFF860D
FC1C4E  13ED09CEFFFF860B    move.b   $9CE(A5),$FFFF860B
FC1C56  13ED09CDFFFF8609    move.b   $9CD(A5),$FFFF8609           Set DMA address
FC1C5E  4E75                rts
*****************************************************
FC1C60  40E7                move.w   SR,-(A7)                     setporta, select drive and side
FC1C62  007C0700            or.w     #$700,SR                     Save status
FC1C66  13FC000EFFFF8800    move.b   #$E,$FFFF8800                IPL 7, no interrupts
FC1C6E  1239FFFF8800        move.b   $FFFF8800,D1                 Select port A
FC1C74  1401                move.b   D1,D2                        Read data from port
FC1C76  C23C00F8            and.b    #$F8,D1                      and save
FC1C7A  8200                or.b     D0,D1                        Clear bits 0-2
FC1C7C  13C1FFFF8802        move.b   D1,$FFFF8802                 Set new bits
FC1C82  46DF                move.w   (A7)+,SR                     Write result in port A
FC1C84  4E75                rts                                   Reset status
*****************************************************
FC1C86  6124                bsr      $FC1CAC                      wdiskct6
FC1C88  33C6FFFF8604        move.w   D6,$FFFF8604                 Delay loop for disk controller
FC1C8E  601C                bra      $FC1CAC                      D6 to disk controller
                                                                  Delay loop for disk controller
*****************************************************
FC1C90  611A                bsr      $FC1CAC                      wdiskct1
FC1C92  33C7FFFF8604        move.w   D7,$FFFF8604                 Delay loop for disk controller
FC1C98  6012                bra      $FC1CAC                      D7 to disk controller
                                                                  Delay loop for disk controller
```

```
*****************************************
FC1C9A 6110              bsr     $FC1CAC                  rdiskct7
FC1C9C 3E39FFFF8604      move.w  $FFFF8604,D7             Delay loop for disk controller
FC1CA2 6008              bra     $FC1CAC                  Disk controller status to D7
                                                          Delay loop for disk controller
*****************************************
FC1CA4 6106              bsr     $FC1CAC                  rdiskctl
FC1CA6 3039FFFF8604      move.w  $FFFF8604,D0             Delay loop for disk controller
FC1CAC 40E7              move.w  SR,-(A7)                 Disk controller status to D0
FC1CAE 3F07              move.w  D7,-(A7)                 Save status
FC1CB0 3E3C0020          move.w  #$20,D7                  Save D7
FC1CB4 51CFFFFE          dbra    D7,$FC1CB4               Counter
FC1CB8 3E1F              move.w  (A7)+,D7                 Delay loop
FC1CBA 46DF              move.w  (A7)+,SR                 D7 back
FC1CBC 4E75              rts                              Status back
*****************************************
FC1CBE 0C7900010000004A6 cmp.w   #1,$4A6                  change, test for disk change
FC1CC6 662C              bne     $FC1CF4                  _nflops
FC1CC8 302F0010          move.w  16(A7),D0                0 or 2 drives, done
FC1CCC B07900005622      cmp.w   $5622,D0                 Drive number
FC1CD2 671C              beq     $FC1CF0                  Same disk number?
FC1CD4 3F00              move.w  D0,-(A7)                 Yes
FC1CD6 3F3CFFEF          move.w  #-17,-(A7)               Drive number
FC1CDA 6100EA62          bsr     $FC073E                  'Insert Disk'
FC1CDE 584F              addq.w  #4,A7                    Critical error handler
FC1CE0 33FCFFFF000009B4  move.w  #-1,$9B4                 Correct stack pointer
FC1CE8 33EF00100005622   move.w  16(A7),$5622             wplatch, status unsure
FC1CF0 426F0010          clr.w   16(A7)                   Save disk number
FC1CF4 4E75              rts                              Drive number to zero
```

341

```
***********************************************************
FC1CF6 41F900004DB8        lea      $4DB8,A0           setdmode, set Drive Change Mode
FC1CFC 1F00                move.b   D0,-(A7)           Address of the bpb
FC1CFE 302D09C2            move.w   $9C2(A5),D0        Save mode
FC1D02 119F0000            move.b   (A7)+,0(A0,D0.w)   cdev, get drive number
FC1D06 4E75                rts                         Set drive mode
***********************************************************
FC1D08 AE                  dc.b     $AE                dskf, disk flags
FC1D09 D6                  dc.b     $D6
FC1D0A 8C                  dc.b     $8C
FC1D0B 17                  dc.b     $17
FC1D0C FB                  dc.b     $FB
FC1D0D 80                  dc.b     $80
FC1D0E 6A                  dc.b     $6A
FC1D0F 2B                  dc.b     $2B
FC1D10 A6                  dc.b     $A6
FC1D11 00                  dc.b     $00
***********************************************************
FC1D12 4BF900000000        lea      $0,A5              Jdostime, IKBD format to DOS format
FC1D18 41ED0E01            lea      $E01(A5),A0        Clear A5
FC1D1C 610000DE            bsr      $FC1DFC            Pointer to clock-time buffer
FC1D20 04000050            sub.b    #80,D0             bcdbin
FC1D24 1400                move.b   D0,D2              Subtract offset of 80
FC1D26 E982                asl.l    #4,D2              Year
FC1D28 610000D2            bsr      $FC1DFC            Write in position
FC1D2C D400                add.b    D0,D2              bcdbin
FC1D2E EB82                asl.l    #5,D2              Add month
                                                       Write in position
```

```
FC1D30  610000CA              bsr     $FC1DFC         bcdbin
FC1D34  D400                  add.b   D0,D2           Add day
FC1D36  EB82                  asl.l   #5,D2           Write in position
FC1D38  610000C2              bsr     $FC1DFC         bcdbin
FC1D3C  D400                  add.b   D0,D2           Add hour
FC1D3E  ED82                  asl.l   #6,D2           Write in position
FC1D40  610000BA              bsr     $FC1DFC         bcdbin
FC1D44  D400                  add.b   D0,D2           Add minute
FC1D46  EB82                  asl.l   #5,D2           Write in position
FC1D48  610000B2              bsr     $FC1DFC         bcdbin
FC1D4C  E208                  lsr.b   #1,D0           2-second resolution
FC1D4E  D400                  add.b   D0,D2           Add seconds
FC1D50  2B420E0A              move.l  D2,$E0A(A5)     Save new time
FC1D54  1B7C00000E4C          move.b  #0,$E4C(A5)     Clear handshake flag
FC1D5A  4E75                  rts

*****************************************************************
FC1D5C  1B7CFFFF0E4C          move.b  #-1,$E4C(A5)    gettime, get current time and date
                                                      Set handshake flag
FC1D62  123C001C              move.b  #$1C,D1         Get time of day command
FC1D66  61000240              bsr     $FC1FA8         Send to IKBD
FC1D6A  4A2D0E4C              tst.b   $E4C(A5)        New time arrived?
FC1D6E  66FA                  bne     $FC1D6A         No, wait
FC1D70  202D0E0A              move.l  $E0A(A5),D0     Put time in D0
FC1D74  4E75                  rts

*****************************************************************
FC1D76  2B6F00040E0E          move.l  4(A7),$E0E(A5)  settime, set time and data
                                                      Pass time

*****************************************************************
FC1D7C  41F900000E18          lea     $E18,A0         ikbdtime
                                                      Pointer to end of time buffer
```

```
FC1D82  242D0E0E        move.l  $E0E(A5),D2     Get time to convert
FC1D86  1002            move.b  D2,D0              in D0
FC1D88  0200001F        and.b   #$1F,D0         Bits 0-4, seconds
FC1D8C  E300            asl.b   #1,D0           2-second resolution
FC1D8E  6154            bsr     $FC1DE4         convert
FC1D90  EA8A            lsr.l   #5,D2           Minutes
FC1D92  1002            move.b  D2,D0
FC1D94  0200003F        and.b   #$3F,D0         Bits 0-5
FC1D98  614A            bsr     $FC1DE4         convert
FC1D9A  EC8A            lsr.l   #6,D2           Hours
FC1D9C  1002            move.b  D2,D0
FC1D9E  0200001F        and.b   #$1F,D0         Bits 0-4
FC1DA2  6140            bsr     $FC1DE4         convert
FC1DA4  EA8A            lsr.l   #5,D2           Day
FC1DA6  1002            move.b  D2,D0
FC1DA8  0200001F        and.b   #$1F,D0         Bits 0-4
FC1DAC  6136            bsr     $FC1DE4         convert
FC1DAE  EA8A            lsr.l   #5,D2           Month
FC1DB0  1002            move.b  D2,D0
FC1DB2  0200000F        and.b   #$F,D0          Bits 0-3
FC1DB6  612C            bsr     $FC1DE4         convert
FC1DB8  E88A            lsr.l   #4,D2           Year
FC1DBA  1002            move.b  D2,D0
FC1DBC  0200007F        and.b   #$7F,D0         Bits 0-6
FC1DC0  6122            bsr     $FC1DE4         convert
FC1DC2  06100080        add.b   #$80,(A0)       Add offset
FC1DC6  123C001B        move.b  #$1B,D1         Set time of day command
FC1DCA  610001DC        bsr     $FC1FA8         Send to IKBD
```

```
FC1DCE  7605              moveq.l  #5,D3              Number of bytes minus 1
FC1DD0  45F900000E12      lea      $E12,A2            Address of the string
FC1DD6  610001F0          bsr      $FC1FC8            ikbdws, send string
FC1DDA  123C001C          move.b   #$1C,D1            Get time of day command
FC1DDE  610001C8          bsr      $FC1FA8            Send to IKBD
FC1DE2  4E75              rts

*************************************************

FC1DE4  7200              moveq.l  #0,D1              binbcd, convert byte to BCD
FC1DE6  760A              moveq.l  #10,D3             Ten's counter
FC1DE8  9003              sub.b    D3,D0              Subtract 10
FC1DEA  6B04              bmi      $FC1DF0
FC1DEC  5201              addq.b   #1,D1              Increment ten's counter
FC1DEE  60F8              bra      $FC1DE8
FC1DF0  0600000A          add.b    #10,D0             Generate one's place
FC1DF4  E901              asl.b    #4,D1              Tens in upper nibble
FC1DF6  D001              add.b    D1,D0              plus ones
FC1DF8  1100              move.b   D0,-(A0)           Write in buffer
FC1DFA  4E75              rts

*************************************************

FC1DFC  7000              moveq.l  #0,D0              bcdbin, convert BCD to binary
FC1DFE  1010              move.b   (A0),D0            BCD byte
FC1E00  E808              lsr.b    #4,D0              Tens place
FC1E02  E308              lsl.b    #1,D0              times 2
FC1E04  1200              move.b   D0,D1
FC1E06  E500              asl.b    #2,D0              times 4
FC1E08  D001              add.b    D1,D0
FC1E0A  1218              move.b   (A0)+,D1           One's place
```

```
FC1E0C  0241000F         and.w    #$F,D1              isolate
FC1E10  D041             add.w    D1,D0               and add
FC1E12  4E75             rts

*********************************************************
FC1E14  70FF             moveq.l  #-1,D0              midiost, MIDI output status
FC1E16  1439FFFFFC04     move.b   $FFFFFC04,D2        Default to OK
FC1E1C  08020001         btst     #1,D2               Read MIDI ACIA status
FC1E20  6602             bne      $FC1E24             and test
FC1E22  7000             moveq.l  #0,D0               OK
FC1E24  4E75             rts                          Not OK, ACIA is sending

*********************************************************
FC1E26  322F0006         move.w   6(A7),D1            midiwc, output character to MIDI
FC1E2A  43F9FFFFFC04     lea      $FFFFFC04,A1        Get character
FC1E30  14290000         move.b   (A1),D2             MIDI ACIA control
FC1E34  08020001         btst     #1,D2               Get MIDI status
FC1E38  67F6             beq      $FC1E30             OK ?
FC1E3A  13410002         move.b   D1,2(A1)            No, wait
FC1E3E  4E75             rts                          Output byte

*********************************************************
FC1E40  7600             moveq.l  #0,D3               midiws, send string to MIDI
FC1E42  362F0004         move.w   4(A7),D3            (unnecessary!)
FC1E46  246F0006         move.l   6(A7),A2            Length of the string - 1
FC1E4A  121A             move.b   (A2)+,D1            Address of the string
FC1E4C  61DC             bsr      $FC1E2A             Get byte
FC1E4E  51CBFFFA         dbra     D3,$FC1E4A          and send
FC1E52  4E75             rts                          Next byte
```

```
***********************************
FC1E54 41ED0DBE          lea      $DBE(A5),A0              midstat, MIDI receiver status
FC1E58 43F9FFFFFC04      lea      $FFFFFC04,A1             iorec for MIDI
FC1E5E 70FF              moveq.l  #-1,D0                   MIDI ACIA control
FC1E60 45E80006          lea      6(A0),A2                 Default to OK
FC1E64 47E80008          lea      8(A0),A3                 Head index
FC1E68 B54B              cmpm.w   (A3)+,(A2)+              Tail index
FC1E6A 6602              bne      $FC1E6E                  Characters in buffer?
FC1E6C 7000              moveq.l  #0,D0                    Yes
FC1E6E 4E75              rts                               Character ready

***********************************
FC1E70 61E2              bsr      $FC1E54                  midin, get character from MIDI
FC1E72 4A40              tst.w    D0                       midstat, character ready?
FC1E74 67FA              beq      $FC1E70                  No, wait
FC1E76 40E7              move.w   SR,-(A7)                 Save status
FC1E78 007C0700          or.w     #$700,SR                 IPL 7, disable interrupts
FC1E7C 32280006          move.w   6(A0),D1                 Head index
FC1E80 B2680008          cmp.w    8(A0),D1                 Compare with tail index
FC1E84 6716              beq      $FC1E9C                  Buffer empty
FC1E86 5241              addq.w   #1,D1                    Increment head index
FC1E88 B2680004          cmp.w    4(A0),D1                 Larger buffer size?
FC1E8C 6502              bcs      $FC1E90                  No
FC1E8E 7200              moveq.l  #0,D1                    Start again beginning of buffer
FC1E90 22680000          move.l   (A0),A1                  Buffer address
FC1E94 10311000          move.b   0(A1,D1.w),D0            Get character from buffer
FC1E98 31410006          move.w   D1,6(A0)                 Save new head index
FC1E9C 46DF              move.w   (A7)+,SR                 Get status
FC1E9E 4E75              rts
```

```
*********************************************
FC1EA0 082D00040E4A  btst    #4,$E4A(A5)        lstout, printer output
FC1EA6 660000DE      bne     $FC1F86            RS 232 printer?
FC1EAA 242D04BA      move.l  $4BA(A5),D2        Yes, output to RS 232
FC1EAE 94AD0E3E      sub.l   $E3E(A5),D2        _hz_200, 200 Hz counter
FC1EB2 0C82000003E8  cmp.l   #1000,D2           minus last time
FC1EB8 6518          bcs     $FC1ED2            Less than 10 seconds
FC1EBA 242D04BA      move.l  $4BA(A5),D2        Yes
FC1EBE 6174          bsr     $FC1F34            _hz_200
FC1EC0 4A40          tst.w   D0                 lstostat, printer ready?
FC1EC2 6618          bne     $FC1EDC
FC1EC4 262D04BA      move.l  $4BA(A5),D3        Yes, output character
FC1EC8 9682          sub.l   D2,D3              _hz_200, 200 Hz counter
FC1ECA 0C8300001770  cmp.l   #6000,D3           minus last time
FC1ED0 6DEC          blt     $FC1EBE            More than 30 seconds?
FC1ED2 7000          moveq.l #0,D0              No, wait
FC1ED4 2B6D04BA0E3E  move.l  $4BA(A5),$E3E(A5)  Character not sent
FC1EDA 4E75          rts                        Save _hz_200 as new time
*********************************************
FC1EDC 40C3          move.w  SR,D3              Output character to parallel port
FC1EDE 007C0700      or.w    #$700,SR           Save status
FC1EE2 7207          moveq.l #7,D1              IPL 7, no interrupts
FC1EE4 61000E6E      bsr     $FC2D54            Register 7
FC1EE8 00000080      or.b    #$80,D0            select
FC1EEC 7287          moveq.l #$87,D1            Port B
FC1EEE 61000E64      bsr     $FC2D54            Write register 7
FC1EF2 46C3          move.w  D3,SR              Port B to output
FC1EF4 302F0006      move.w  6(A7),D0           Save status
FC1EF8 728F          moveq.l #$8F,D1            Character to output
                                                Write port B
```

348

```
FC1EFA 61000E58        bsr      $FC2D54            Output character
FC1EFE 610E            bsr      $FC1F0E            Strobe low
FC1F00 610C            bsr      $FC1F0E            Strobe low
FC1F02 6104            bsr      $FC1F08            Strobe high
FC1F04 70FF            moveq.l  #-1,D0             OK
FC1F06 4E75            rts

***********************************************
FC1F08 7420            moveq.l  #$20,D2            Strobe 5
FC1F0A 60000E8A        bra      $FC2D96            Bit 5
                                                   set in port A
***********************************************
FC1F0E 74DF            moveq.l  #$DF,D2            Strobe low
FC1F10 60000EAA        bra      $FC2DBC            Bit 5
                                                   clear in port A
***********************************************
FC1F14 7207            moveq.l  #7,D1              lstin, get character from parallel port
FC1F16 61000E3C        bsr      $FC2D54            Mixer
FC1F1A 0200007F        and.b    #$7F,D0            Select register in PSG
FC1F1E 7287            moveq.l  #$87,D1            Port B to input
FC1F20 61000E32        bsr      $FC2D54            Write register 7
                                                   giacces
FC1F24 61E2            bsr      $FC1F08            Strobe high = receiver ready
FC1F26 610C            bsr      $FC1F34            lstostat, character arrived?
FC1F28 4A40            tst.w    D0
FC1F2A 66FA            bne      $FC1F26            No, wait
FC1F2C 61E0            bsr      $FC1F0E            Strobe low = receiver busy
```

```
FC1F2E  720F                moveq.l  #15,D1              Select port B
FC1F30  60000E22            bra      $FC2D54             Read byte from port
*****************************************************************
FC1F34  41F9FFFFFA01        lea      $FFFFFA01,A0        lstostat, printer output status
FC1F3A  70FF                moveq.l  #-1,D0              mfp gpip
FC1F3C  0828000000000       btst     #0,(A0)             Default to ok
FC1F42  6702                beq      $FC1F46             Busy to low ?
FC1F44  7000                moveq.l  #0,D0               Yes
FC1F46  4E75                rts                          Printer not ready
*****************************************************************
FC1F48  41ED0D8E            lea      $D8E(A5),A0         auxistat, RS 232 input status
FC1F4C  70FF                moveq.l  #-1,D0              iorec for rs232
FC1F4E  45E80006            lea      6(A0),A2            Default to OK
FC1F52  47E80008            lea      8(A0),A3            Head index
FC1F56  B54B                cmpm.w   (A3)+,(A2)+         Tail index
FC1F58  6602                bne      $FC1F5C             Buffer empty?
FC1F5A  7000                moveq.l  #0,D0               No
FC1F5C  4E75                rts                          No characters ready
*****************************************************************
FC1F5E  61E8                bsr      $FC1F48             auxin, RS 232 input
FC1F60  4A40                tst.w    D0                  auxistat, character ready?
FC1F62  67FA                beq      $FC1F5E             No, wait
FC1F64  610005D6            bsr      $FC253C             rs232get, get character
```

```
FC1F68  024000FF           and.w    #$FF,D0                    Isolate bits 0-7
FC1F6C  4E75               rts

*****************************************************
FC1F6E  41ED0D8E           lea      $D8E(A5),A0                auxostat, RS 232 output status
FC1F72  70FF               moveq.l  #-1,D0                     iorec for RS 232
FC1F74  34280016           move.w   22(A0),D2                  Default to OK
FC1F78  61000896           bsr      $FC2810                    Tail index
FC1F7C  B4680014           cmp.w    20(A0),D2                  Compare with head index
FC1F80  6602               bne      $FC1F84                    OK
FC1F82  7000               moveq.l  #0,D0                      No space in buffer
FC1F84  4E75               rts

*****************************************************
FC1F86  322F0006           move.w   6(A7),D1                   auxout, RS 232 output
FC1F8A  61000554           bsr      $FC24E0                    Get byte
FC1F8E  65F6               bcs      $FC1F86                    rs232put, write in buffer
FC1F90  4E75               rts                                 Not sent, try again

*****************************************************
FC1F92  70FF               moveq.l  #-1,D0                     ikbdost, IKBD output status
FC1F94  1439FFFFFC00       move.b   $FFFFFC00,D2               Default to ok
FC1F9A  08020001           btst     #1,D2                      Keyboard ACIA status
FC1F9E  6602               bne      $FC1FA2                    ACIA ready ?
FC1FA0  7000               moveq.l  #0,D0                      Yes
FC1FA2  4E75               rts                                 Not used

*****************************************************
FC1FA4  322F0006           move.w   6(A7),D1                   ikbdwc, send byte to IKBD
FC1FA8  43F9FFFFFC00       lea      $FFFFFC00,A1               Get byte
FC1FAE  14290000           move.b   (A1),D2                    Keyboard ACIA control
FC1FB2  08020001           btst     #1,D2                      Get ACIA status
                                                               Ready?
```

```
FC1FB6  67F6           beq     $FC1FAE                 No, wait
FC1FB8  13410002       move.b  D1,2(A1)                Send byte
FC1FBC  4E75           rts

;*********************************************************
FC1FBE  7600           moveq.l #0,D3                   ikbdws, send string to keyboard
FC1FC0  362F0004       move.w  4(A7),D3                unnecessary!
                                                       Number of characters minus 1
FC1FC4  246F0006       move.l  6(A7),A2                Address of the string
FC1FC8  121A           move.b  (A2)+,D1                Get byte
FC1FCA  61DC           bsr     $FC1FA8                 Send to keyboard
FC1FCC  51CBFFFA       dbra    D3,$FC1FC8              Next byte
FC1FD0  4E75           rts

;*********************************************************
FC1FD2  41ED0DB0       lea     $DB0(A5),A0             constat, keyboard input status
FC1FD6  70FF           moveq.l #-1,D0                  iorec for keyboard
                                                       Default for OK
FC1FD8  45E80006       lea     6(A0),A2                Head index
FC1FDC  47E80008       lea     8(A0),A3                Tail index
FC1FE0  B54B           cmpm.w  (A3)+,(A2)+             Buffer empty?
FC1FE2  6602           bne     $FC1FE6                 No, OK
FC1FE4  7000           moveq.l #0,D0                   No characters there
FC1FE6  4E75           rts

;*********************************************************
FC1FE8  61E8           bsr     $FC1FD2                 conin, get character from keyboard
FC1FEA  4A40           tst.w   D0                      constat, key pressed?
FC1FEC  67FA           beq     $FC1FE8                 No, wait
FC1FEE  40E7           move.w  SR,-(A7)                Save status
FC1FF0  007C0700       or.w    #$700,SR                IPL 7, disable interrupts
FC1FF4  32280006       move.w  6(A0),D1                Head index
FC1FF8  B2680008       cmp.w   8(A0),D1                Compare with tail index
FC1FFC  6716           beq     $FC2014                 Buffer empty?
```

```
FC1FFE  5841                        addq.w   #4,D1                      Increment head index
FC2000  B2680004                    cmp.w    4(A0),D1                   Greater or equal to buffer size?
FC2004  6502                        bcs      $FC2008                    No
FC2006  7200                        moveq.l  #0,D1                      Buffer point back to start
FC2008  22680000                    move.l   (A0),A1                    Buffer address
FC200C  20311000                    move.l   0(A1,D1.w),D0              Get character
FC2010  31410006                    move.w   D1,6(A0)                   Save new head index
FC2014  46DF                        move.w   (A7)+,SR                   Get status
FC2016  4E75                        rts

************************************************   conoutst, console output status
FC2018  70FF                        moveq.l  #-1,D0                     Status always OK
FC201A  4E75                        rts

************************************************   ringbel, tone after CTRL G
FC201C  082D00020484                btst     #2,$484(A5)                conterm, sound enabled ?
FC2022  670E                        beq      $FC2032                    No
FC2024  2B7C00FC30760E44            move.l   #$FC3076,$E44(A5)          Pointer to sound table for ell
FC202C  1B7C00000E48                move.b   #0,$E48(A5)                Start sound timer
FC2032  4E75                        rts

************************************************   Keyboard table, unshifted
FC2034  001B31323334353          dc.b  $00,esc,'1','2','3','4','5','6'
FC203C  3738393039E270809           dc.b  '7','8','9','0','u','',bs,tab
FC2044  7177657274747A7569          dc.b  'q','w','e','r','t','z','u','i'
FC204C  6F70812B0D006173            dc.b  'o','p','Ä','+',cr,$00,'a','s'
FC2054  64666768686A6B6C94          dc.b  'd','f','g','h','j','k','l','ì'
FC205C  8423007E79786376            dc.b  'Ñ','#',$00,'~','y','x','c','v'
FC2064  626E6D2C2E2D0000            dc.b  'b','n','m',',','.','-',$00,$00
FC206C  0020000000000000            dc.b  $00,' ',$00,$00,$00,$00,$00,$00
FC2074  0000000000000000            dc.b  $00,$00,$00,$00,$00,$00,$00,$00
FC207C  00002D0000002B00            dc.b  $00,$00,'-',$00,$00,$00,'+',$00
```

```
FC2084  0000007F00000000        dc.b    $00,$00,$00,del,$00,$00,$00,$00
FC208C  0000000000000000        dc.b    $00,$00,$00,$00,$00,$00,$00,$00
FC2094  3C00002892F2A37         dc.b    '<',$00,$00,'(',')','/','*','7'
FC209C  3839343536313233        dc.b    '8','9','4','5','6','1','2','3'
FC20A4  302E0D0000000000        dc.b    '0','.',cr,$00,$00,$00,$00,$00
FC20AC  0000000000000000        dc.b    $00,$00,$00,$00,$00,$00,$00,$00
*************************************************** Keyboard table, shifted
FC20B4  001B2122DD242526        dc.b    $00,esc,'!','"',£','$','%','&'
FC20BC  2F28293D3F600809        dc.b    '/','(',')','=','?','`',bs,tab
FC20C4  5157455254455549        dc.b    'Q','W','E','R','T','Z','U','I'
FC20CC  4F509A2A0D004153        dc.b    'O','P','ö','*',cr,$00,'A','S'
FC20D4  444647484A4B4C99        dc.b    'D','F','G','H','J','K','L','ö'
FC20DC  8E5E007C59584356        dc.b    'é','^',$00,'|','Y','X','C','V'
FC20E4  424E4D3B3A5F0000        dc.b    'B','N','M',';',':','_',$00,$00
FC20EC  0200000000000000        dc.b    $00,' ',$00,$00,$00,$00,$00,$00
FC20F4  0000000000000037        dc.b    $00,$00,$00,$00,$00,$00,$00,'7'
FC20FC  38002D3400362B00        dc.b    '8',$00,'-','4',$00,'6','+',$00
FC2104  3200307F00000000        dc.b    '2',$00,'0',del,$00,$00,$00,$00
FC210C  0000000000000000        dc.b    $00,$00,$00,$00,$00,$00,$00,$00
FC2114  3E000028292F2A37        dc.b    '>',$00,'(',')','/','*','7'
FC211C  3839343536313233        dc.b    '8','9','4','5','6','1','2','3'
FC2124  302E0D0000000000        dc.b    '0','.',cr,$00,$00,$00,$00,$00
FC212C  0000000000000000        dc.b    $00,$00,$00,$00,$00,$00,$00,$00
*************************************************** Keyboard table, Caps lock
FC2134  001B3132333435386       dc.b    $00,esc,'1','2','3','4','5','6'
FC213C  3738393909E270809       dc.b    '7','8','9','0','''',bs,tab
FC2144  5157455254455549        dc.b    'Q','W','E','R','T','Z','U','I'
FC214C  4F509A2B0D004153        dc.b    'O','P','ö','+',cr,$00,'A','S'
FC2154  444647484A4B4C99        dc.b    'D','F','G','H','J','K','L','ö'
FC215C  8E23007E59584356        dc.b    'é','#',$00,'~','Y','X','C','V'
FC2164  424E4D2C2E2D0000        dc.b    'B','N','M',',','.','-',$00,$00
FC216C  0200000000000000        dc.b    $00,' ',$00,$00,$00,$00,$00,$00
```

```
FC2174 00000000000000000      dc.b    $00,$00,$00,$00,$00,$00,$00,$00
FC217C 00002D0000002B00        dc.b    $00,$00,'-',$00,$00,$00,'+',$00
FC2184 0000007F00000000        dc.b    $00,$00,$00,del,$00,$00,$00,$00
FC218C 00000000000000000      dc.b    '<',$00,$00,'(',')','/','*','7'
FC2194 3C000028292F2A37        dc.b    '8','9','4','5','6','1','2','3'
FC219C 383934353631323 33      dc.b    $00,$00,$00,$00,$00,$00,$00,$00
FC21A4 302E0D0000000000        dc.b    '0','.',$00,$00,$00,$00,$00,$00
FC21AC 00000000000000000      dc.b    $00,$00,$00,$00,$00,$00,$00,$00
*****************************************************   initmfp, initialize MFP 68901
FC21B4 41F9FFFFFA01            lea     $FFFFFA01,A0                  Address of mfp
FC21BA 7000                    moveq.l #0,D0                         Initialize register with zero
FC21BC 01C80000                movep.l D0,0(A0)                      gpip to iera
FC21C0 01C80008                movep.l D0,8(A0)                      ierb to isra
FC21C4 01C80010                movep.l D0,16(A0)                     isrb to vr
FC21C8 117C00480016            move.b  #$48,22(A0)                   MFP non-autovector number to $40, set S-bit
FC21CE 3B7C11110E42            move.w  #$1111,$E42(A5)               Timer C bit map to every 4th IRQ
FC21D4 3B7C00140442            move.w  #$14,$442(A5)                 _timer_ms to 20 ms
FC21DA 7002                    moveq.l #2,D0                         Select timer C
FC21DC 7250                    moveq.l #80,D1                        /64 for 200 Hz
FC21DE 343C00C0                move.w  #$C0,D2                       192
FC21E2 61000182                bsr     $FC2366                       Initialize timer and interrupt vector
FC21E6 45F900FC2F78            lea     $FC2F78,A2                    Timer C interrupt routine
FC21EC 7005                    moveq.l #5,D0                         Timer C interrupt number
FC21EE 6100022C                bsr     $FC241C                       initint, initialize interrupt
FC21F2 7003                    moveq.l #3,D0                         Select timer D
FC21F4 7201                    moveq.l #1,D1                         /4 for 9600 baud
FC21F6 7402                    moveq.l #2,D2                         9600 baud
FC21F8 6100016C                bsr     $FC2366                       Initialize timer and interrupt vector
FC21FC 203C00980101            move.l  #$980101,D0                   $00, $98, $01, $01
FC2202 01C80026                movep.l D0,$26(A0)                    to scr, ucr, rsr, tsr
FC2206 61000B84                bsr     $FC2D8C                       DTR on
```

355

```
FC220A  61000B78                    bsr       $FC2D84                        RTS on
FC220E  41ED0D8E                    lea       $D8E(A5),A0                    Pointer to iorec for RS 232
FC2212  43F900FC2334                lea       $FC2334,A1                     Start data for iorec
FC2218  7021                        moveq.l   #33,D0                         34 bytes
FC221A  610000F0                    bsr       $FC230C                        Copy to RAM
FC221E  41ED0DBE                    lea       $DBE(A5),A0                    Pointer to iorec for MIDI
FC2222  43F900FC2326                lea       $FC2326,A1                     Start data for iorec
FC2228  700D                        moveq.l   #13,D0                         14 bytes
FC222A  610000E0                    bsr       $FC230C                        Copy to RAM
FC222E  203C00FC288E                move.l    #$FC288E,D0                    Keyboard and MIDI error vector
FC2234  2B400DD0                    move.l    D0,$DD0(A5)                    Pointer to keyboard error routine
FC2238  2B400DD4                    move.l    D0,$DD4(A5)                    Pointer to MIDI error routine
FC223C  2B7C00FC2CE20DCC            move.l    #$FC2CE2,$DCC(A5)              sysmidi vector
FC2244  2B7C00FC284A0DE8            move.l    #$FC284A,$DE8(A5)              midisys vector
FC224C  2B7C00FC285A0DEC            move.l    #$FC285A,$DEC(A5)              ikbdsys vector
FC2254  13FC0003FFFFFC04            move.b    #3,$FFFFFC04                   MIDI ACIA control, master reset
FC225C  13FC0095FFFFFC04            move.b    #$95,$FFFFFC04                 /16, 8 Bit, 1 stop bit, no parity
FC2264  1B7C00070484                move.b    #7,$484(A5)                    conterm, keyclick, repeat und bell enable
FC226A  2B7C00FC1D120DE0            move.l    #$FC1D12,$DE0(A5)              Jdostime, time vector
FC2272  203C00FC230A                move.l    #$FC230A,D0                    Pointer to rts
FC2278  2B400DD8                    move.l    D0,$DD8(A5)                    statvec, IKBD status package
FC227C  2B400DDC                    move.l    D0,$DDC(A5)                    mousevec, mouse action
FC2280  2B400DE4                    move.l    D0,$DE4(A5)                    joyvec, joystick action
FC2284  7000                        moveq.l   #0,D0                          Clear sound variables
FC2286  2B400E44                    move.l    D0,$E44(A5)                    Sound pointer
FC228A  1B400E48                    move.b    D0,$E48(A5)                    Delay timer
FC228E  1B400E49                    move.b    D0,$E49(A5)                    Temp value
FC2292  2B400E3E                    move.l    D0,$E3E(A5)                    Printer timeout
FC2296  6100FC70                    bsr       $FC1F08                        Strobe to high
FC229A  1B7C000F0E3C                move.b    #$F,$E3C(A5)                   Keyboard delay 1
FC22A0  1B7C00020E3D                move.b    #2,$E3D(A5)                    Keyboard delay 2
FC22A6  41ED0DB0                    lea       $DB0(A5),A0                    Pointer to iorec keyboard
```

```
FC22AA  43F900FC2318      lea      $FC2318,A1              Start data for iorec
FC22B0  700D              moveq.l  #13,D0                  14 bytes
FC22B2  6158              bsr      $FC230C                 Copy to RAM
FC22B4  61000C58          bsr      $FC2F0E                 Pointer to BIOS keyboard table
FC22B8  13FC0003FFFFFC00  move.b   #3,$FFFFFC00            Keyboard ACIA control, master reset
FC22C0  13FC0096FFFFFC00  move.b   #$96,$FFFFFC00          /64, 8 Bit, 1 stop bit, no parity
FC22C8  267C00FC2356      move.l   #$FC2356,A3             Pointer to MFP interrupt vectors
FC22CE  7203              moveq.l  #3,D1                   Initialize 4 vectors
FC22D0  2401              move.l   D1,D2
FC22D2  2001              move.l   D1,D0                   Interrupt number
FC22D4  06000009          add.b    #9,D0                   plus offset
FC22D8  E582              asl.l    #2,D2
FC22DA  24732000          move.l   0(A3,D2.w),A2           Get vector from table
FC22DE  6100013C          bsr      $FC241C                 initint, install interrupt
FC22E2  51C9FFEC          dbra     D1,$FC22D0              Next vector
FC22E6  45F900FC281C      lea      $FC281C,A2              MIDI and keyboard vector
FC22EC  7006              moveq.l  #6,D0                   Vector number 6
FC22EE  6100012C          bsr      $FC241C                 initint, install interrupt
FC22F2  45F900FC26B2      lea      $FC26B2,A2              CTS interrupt routine
FC22F8  7002              moveq.l  #2,D0                   Vector number 2
FC22FA  61000120          bsr      $FC241C                 initint, install interrupt
FC22FE  247C00FC2314      move.l   #$FC2314,A2             Pointer to init data for IKBD
FC2304  7603              moveq.l  #3,D3                   4 bytes
FC2306  6100FCC0          bsr      $FC1FC8                 Send string to IKBD
FC230A  4E75              rts

*****************************************************
FC230C  10D9              move.b   (A1)+,(A0)+             Block move
FC230E  51C8FFFC          dbra     D0,$FC230C              Next byte
FC2312  4E75              rts

*****************************************************
FC2314  8001121A          dc.b     $80,$01,$12,$1A         Reset Keyboard, disable mouse + joystick
```

```
;*****************************************
FC2318 00000C0E    dc.l    $C0E        ; iorec for keyboard
FC231C 0100        dc.w    $100        ; Buffer address
FC231E 0000        dc.w    0           ; Buffer size
FC2320 0000        dc.w    0           ; Head index
FC2322 0040        dc.w    $40         ; Tail index
FC2322 00C0        dc.w    $C0         ; Low-water mark
                                       ; High-water mark
;*****************************************
FC2326 00000D0E    dc.l    $D0E        ; iorec for MIDI
FC232A 0080        dc.w    $80         ; Buffer address
FC232C 0000        dc.w    0           ; Buffer size
FC232E 0000        dc.w    0           ; Head index
FC2330 0020        dc.w    $20         ; Tail index
FC2332 0060        dc.w    $60         ; Low-water mark
                                       ; High-water mark
;*****************************************
FC2334 00000A0E    dc.l    $A0E        ; iorec for RS 232 input
FC2338 0100        dc.w    $100        ; Buffer address
FC233A 0000        dc.w    0           ; Buffer size
FC233C 0000        dc.w    0           ; Head index
FC233E 0040        dc.w    $40         ; Tail index
FC2340 00C0        dc.w    $C0         ; Low-water mark
                                       ; High-water mark
;*****************************************
FC2342 00000B0E    dc.l    $B0E        ; iorec for RS 232 output
FC2346 0100        dc.w    $100        ; Buffer address
FC2348 0000        dc.w    0           ; Buffer size
FC234A 0000        dc.w    0           ; Head index
FC234C 0040        dc.w    $40         ; Tail index
FC234E 00C0        dc.w    $C0         ; Low-water mark
FC2350 00          dc.b    0           ; High-water mark
                                       ; rsrbyte, receiver status
```

```
FC2351  00                        dc.b     0                              tsrbyte, transmitter status
FC2352  00                        dc.b     0                              rxoff
FC2353  00                        dc.b     0                              txoff
FC2354  01                        dc.b     1                              rsmode, XON/XOFF mode
FC2355  00                        dc.b     0                              filler
*****************************************************                     Interrupt vectors for MFP
FC2356  00FC2718                  dc.l     $FC2718                        #9, transmitter error
FC235A  00FC2666                  dc.l     $FC2666                        #10, transmitter interrupt
FC235E  00FC26FA                  dc.l     $FC26FA                        #11, receiver error
FC2362  00FC2596                  dc.l     $FC2596                        #12, receiver interrupt
*****************************************************                     setimer, initialize timer in MFP
FC2366  48E7F8F0                  movem.l  D0-D4/A0-A3,-(A7)              Save registers
FC236A  207CFFFFFA01              move.l   #$FFFFFA01,A0                  Address of MFP
FC2370  267C00FC23FA              move.l   #$FC23FA,A3                    Timer interrupt mask bit
FC2376  247C00FC23FE              move.l   #$FC23FE,A2
FC237C  615A                      bsr      $FC23D8                        mskreg
FC237E  267C00FC23EE              move.l   #$FC23EE,A3                    Timer interrupt enable bit
FC2384  247C00FC23FE              move.l   #$FC23FE,A2
FC238A  614C                      bsr      $FC23D8                        mskreg
FC238C  267C00FC23F2              move.l   #$FC23F2,A3                    Timer interrupt pending bit
FC2392  247C00FC23FE              move.l   #$FC23FE,A2
FC2398  613E                      bsr      $FC23D8                        mskreg
FC239A  267C00FC23F6              move.l   #$FC23F6,A3                    Timer interrupt in-service bit
FC23A0  247C00FC23FE              move.l   #$FC23FE,A2
FC23A6  6130                      bsr      $FC23D8                        mskreg
FC23A8  267C00FC2402              move.l   #$FC2402,A3                    Timer control bit
FC23AE  247C00FC2406              move.l   #$FC2406,A2
FC23B4  6122                      bsr      $FC23D8                        mskreg
FC23B6  C749                      exg      A3,A1                          Save A3
FC23B8  47F900FC240A              lea      $FC240A,A3                     Address of timer data register
```

359

```
FC23BE 7600              moveq.l  #0,D3
FC23C0 16330000          move.b   0(A3,D0.w),D3        Get register number
FC23C4 11823000          move.b   D2,0(A0,D3.w)        Write data in MFP
FC23C8 B4303000          cmp.b    0(A0,D3.w),D2
FC23CC 66F6              bne      $FC23C4              and read
FC23CE C749              exg      A3,A1                until match
FC23D0 8313              or.b     D1,(A3)              Restore A3
FC23D2 4CDF0F1F          movem.l  (A7)+,D0-D4/A0-A3    Mask timer control register
FC23D6 4E75              rts                           Restore registers

*******************************************
FC23D8 6106              bsr      $FC23E0              mskreg
FC23DA 1612              move.b   (A2),D3              getmask
FC23DC C713              and.b    D3,(A3)              Load mask
FC23DE 4E75              rts                           and clear bit(s)

*******************************************
FC23E0 7600              moveq.l  #0,D3                getmask
FC23E2 D6C0              add.w    D0,A3
FC23E4 1613              move.b   (A3),D3              Base plus register number
FC23E6 D688              add.l    A0,D3                yields address offset in MFP
FC23E8 2643              move.l   D3,A3                plus address of MFP
FC23EA D4C0              add.w    D0,A2                to A3
FC23EC 4E75              rts                           Pointer to the mask

*******************************************
FC23EE 06060808          dc.b     6,6,8,8              MFP register numbers
FC23F2 0A0A0C0C          dc.b     10,10,12,12          iera, iera, ierb, ierb
FC23F6 0E0E1010          dc.b     14,14,16,16          ipra, ipra, iprb, iprb
FC23FA 12121414          dc.b     18,18,20,20          isra, isra, isrb, isrb
                                                       imra, imra, imrb, imrb
```

```
*********************************************
*                                            * Masks for MFP registers
FC23FE DFFEDFEF          dc.b    $DF,$FE,$DF,$EF   Clear bits 5, 0, 5, 0
FC2402 181A1C1C          dc.b    $18,$1A,$1C,$1C   Set bits 3+4, bits 1,3+4, bits 2-4, bits 2-4
FC2406 00008FF8          dc.b    0,0,$8F,$F8       none, none, clear bits 5-7, bits 0-2
FC240A 1E202224          dc.b    $1E,$20,$22,$24   Set bits 2-4, bits 5, bits 1+5, bits 2+5

*********************************************
*                                            * mfpint, set MFP interrupt vector
FC240E 302F0004          move.w  4(A7),D0          Interrupt number
FC2412 246F0006          move.l  6(A7),A2          Interrupt vector
FC2416 0280000000F       and.l   #15,D0            Number 0-15, long word

*********************************************
*                                            * initint, set MFP interrupt vector
FC241C 48E7E0E0          movem.l D0-D2/A0-A2,-(A7) Save registers
FC2420 6120              bsr     $FC2442           Disable interrupts
FC2422 2400              move.l  D0,D2             Vector number
FC2424 E542              asl.w   #2,D2             As index for long word
FC2426 06820000100       add.l   #$100,D2          Plus base address of the MFP vectors
FC242C 2242              move.l  D2,A1             Vector address
FC242E 228A              move.l  A2,(A1)           Set new vector
FC2430 614A              bsr     $FC247C           Enable interrupts
FC2432 4CDF0707          movem.l (A7)+,D0-D2/A0-A2 Restore registers
FC2436 4E75              rts

*********************************************
*                                            * disint, disable MFP interrupt
FC2438 302F0004          move.w  4(A7),D0          Get interrupt number
FC243C 0280000000F       and.l   #15,D0            as long word index
FC2442 48E7C0C0          movem.l D0-D1/A0-A1,-(A7) Save registers
FC2446 41F9FFFFFA01      lea     $FFFFFA01,A0      Address of mfp
FC244C 43E80012          lea     18(A0),A1         Address of imra
FC2450 614A              bsr     $FC249C           Calculate bit number to clear
FC2452 0391              bclr    D1,(A1)           And clear bit
FC2454 43E80006          lea     6(A0),A1          Address of iera
```

```
FC2458 6142            bsr     $FC249C             Calculate bit number to clear
FC245A 0391            bclr    D1,(A1)             And clear bit
FC245C 43E8000A        lea     10(A0),A1           Address of ipra
FC2460 613A            bsr     $FC249C             Calculate bit number to clear
FC2462 0391            bclr    D1,(A1)             And clear bit
FC2464 43E8000E        lea     14(A0),A1           Address of isra
FC2468 6132            bsr     $FC249C             Calculate bit number to clear
FC246A 0391            bclr    D1,(A1)             and clear bit
FC246C 4CDF0303        movem.l (A7)+,D0-D1/A0-A1   Restore registers
FC2470 4E75            rts
;**************************************************
FC2472 302F0004        move.w  4(A7),D0            jenabint, enable MFP interrupt
FC2476 02800000000F    and.l   #15,D0              Vector number
FC247C 48E7C0C0        movem.l D0-D1/A0-A1,-(A7)   as long word index
                                                   Save registers
FC2480 41F9FFFFFA01    lea     $FFFFFA01,A0        Address of the MFP
FC2486 43E80006        lea     6(A0),A1            Address of iera
FC248A 6110            bsr     $FC249C             Calculate bit number to set
FC248C 03D1            bset    D1,(A1)             and set bit
FC248E 43E80012        lea     18(A0),A1           Address of imra
FC2492 6108            bsr     $FC249C             Calculate bit number to set
FC2494 03D1            bset    D1,(A1)             and set bit
FC2496 4CDF0303        movem.l (A7)+,D0-D1/A0-A1   Restire registers
FC249A 4E75            rts
;**************************************************
FC249C 1200            move.b  D0,D1               bselect, determine bit and register number
FC249E 0C000008        cmp.b   #8,D0               Save interrupt number
FC24A2 6D02            blt     $FC24A6             Greater than 8 ?
FC24A4 5141            subq.w  #8,D1               No
FC24A6 0C000008        cmp.b   #8,D0               Else subtract offset
FC24AA 6C02            bge     $FC24AE             Greater than 8 ?
                                                   Yes
```

```
FC24AC 5449              addq.w  #2,A1                    Pointer from A to B register
FC24AE 4E75              rts

*************************************************************
                                                            rs232ptr
FC24B0 41F900000D8E      lea     $D8E,A0                  Pointer to RS 232 iorec
FC24B6 43F9FFFFFA01      lea     $FFFFFA01,A1             Address of the MFP
FC24BC 4E75              rts

*************************************************************
                                                            rs232ibuf, determine buffer contents
FC24BE 34280008          move.w  8(A0),D2                 Tail index
FC24C2 36280006          move.w  6(A0),D3                 Head index
FC24C6 B443              cmp.w   D3,D2                    Head > tail ?
FC24C8 6204              bhi     $FC24CE                  No
FC24CA D4680004          add.w   4(A0),D2                 Add buffer size
FC24CE 9443              sub.w   D3,D2                    Determine buffer contents
FC24D0 4E75              rts

*************************************************************
                                                            rtschk
FC24D2 082800010020      btst    #1,32(A0)                RTS/CTS mode ?
FC24D8 6704              beq     $FC24DE                  No
FC24DA 610008A8          bsr     $FC2D84                  rtson
FC24DE 4E75              rts

*************************************************************
                                                            rs232put, RS 232 output
FC24E0 40E7              move.w  SR,-(A7)                 Save status
FC24E2 007C0700          or.w    #$700,SR                 IPL 7, disable interrupts
FC24E6 61C8              bsr     $FC24B0                  rs232ptr, get RS 232 buffer pointer
FC24E8 082800000020      btst    #0,32(A0)                XON/XOFF mode?
FC24EE 6706              beq     $FC24F6                  No
FC24F0 4A28001F          tst.b   31(A0)                   XON active ?
FC24F4 6618              bne     $FC250E                  Yes
FC24F6 08290007002C      btst    #7,44(A1)                Is MFP still sending ?
```

```
FC24FC 6710              beq     $FC250E             Yes
FC24FE 34280014          move.w  20(A0),D2           Head index
FC2502 B4680016          cmp.w   22(A0),D2           Compare with tail index
FC2506 6606              bne     $FC250E             Characters still in buffer
FC2508 1341002E         .move.b  D1,46(A1)           Byte into MFP transmitter register
FC250C 601A              bra     $FC2528
FC250E 34280016          move.w  22(A0),D2           Tail index
FC2512 610002FC          bsr     $FC2810             Test for wrap around
FC2516 B4680014          cmp.w   20(A0),D2           Compare with head index
FC251A 6716              beq     $FC2532             Buffer full?
FC251C 2268000E          move.l  14(A0),A1           Pointer to send buffer
FC2520 13812000          move.b  D1,0(A1,D2.w)       Write byte in buffer
FC2524 31420016          move.w  D2,22(A0)           Save new tail index
FC2528 61A8              bsr     $FC24D2             rtschk, set RTS ?
FC252A 46DF              move.w  (A7)+,SR            Restore status
FC252C 023C00FE          and.b   #$FE,SR             OK, clear carry flag
FC2530 4E75              rts

FC2532 619E              bsr     $FC24D2             rtschk, set RTS?
FC2534 46DF              move.w  (A7)+,SR            Restore status
FC2536 003C0001          or.b    #1,SR               No output, set carry flag
FC253A 4E75              rts

****************************************************
FC253C 40E7              move.w  SR,-(A7)            rs232get, RS 232 input
FC253E 007C0700          or.w    #$700,SR            Save status
FC2542 6100FF6C          bsr     $FC24B0             IPL 7, disable interrupts
FC2546 32280006          move.w  6(A0),D1            rs232ptr, get RS 232 pointer
FC254A B2680008          cmp.w   8(A0),D1            Head index
FC254E 671A              beq     $FC256A             Compare with tail index
FC2550 610002B2          bsr     $FC2804             Receiver buffer empty?
FC2554 22680000          move.l  (A0),A1             Test for wrap around
                                                      Get buffer address
```

FC2558	7000		moveq.l	#0,D0	Get character from buffer
FC255A	10311000		move.b	0(A1,D1.w),D0	Save new head index
FC255E	31410006		move.w	D1,6(A0)	Restore status
FC2562	46DF		move.w	(A7)+,SR	Character there, clear carry flag
FC2564	023C00FE		and.b	#$FE,SR	
FC2568	6006		bra	$FC2570	
FC256A	46DF		move.w	(A7)+,SR	Restore status
FC256C	003C0001		or.b	#1,SR	No character, set carry flag
FC2570	082800000020		btst	#0,32(A0)	XON/XOFF mode?
FC2576	671C		beq	$FC2594	No
FC2578	4A28001E		tst.b	30(A0)	XON active ?
FC257C	6716		beq	$FC2594	No
FC257E	6100FF3E		bsr	$FC24BE	Get input buffer length
FC2582	B468000A		cmp.w	10(A0),D2	Equals low-water mark?
FC2586	660C		bne	$FC2594	No
FC2588	123C0011		move.b	#$11,D1	XON
FC258C	6100FF52		bsr	$FC24E0	Send
FC2590	4228001E		clr.b	30(A0)	Clear XON flag
FC2594	4E75		rts		

****

FC2596	48E7F0E0		movem.l	D0-D3/A0-A2,-(A7)	rcvint, RS 232 receiver interrupt
FC259A	6100FF14		bsr	$FC24B0	Save registers
FC259E	1169002A001C		move.b	42(A1),28(A0)	rs232ptr, get RS 232 pointer
FC25A4	08280007001C		btst	#7,28(A0)	Save receiver status register
FC25AA	670000AE		beq	$FC265A	Interrupt through receiver buffer full ?
FC25AE	082800010020		btst	#1,32(A0)	No, ignore interrupt
FC25B4	6704		beq	$FC25BA	RTS/CTS mode?
FC25B6	610007C8		bsr	$FC2D80	No
FC25BA	1029002E		move.b	46(A1),D0	rtsoff
FC25BE	082800010020		btst	#1,32(A0)	Read received byte
FC25C4	6640		bne	$FC2606	RTS/CTS mode?
					Yes

365

```
FC25C6 082800000020  btst    #0,32(A0)          XON/XOFF mode?
FC25CC 6738          beq     $FC2606            No
FC25CE 0C000011      cmp.b   #17,D0             XON received?
FC25D2 6624          bne     $FC25F8            No
FC25D4 117C0000001F  move.b  #0,31(A0)          Clear XOFF flag
FC25DA 34280014      move.w  20(A0),D2          Head index sender
FC25DE B4680016      cmp.w   22(A0),D2          Compare with tail index sender
FC25E2 6776          beq     $FC265A            Send buffer empty?
FC25E4 6100022A      bsr     $FC2810            Test for wrap around
FC25E8 2468000E      move.l  14(A0),A2          Pointer to send buffer
FC25EC 137220000002E move.b  0(A2,D2.w),46(A1)  Byte in MFP transmitter register
FC25F2 31420014      move.w  D2,20(A0)          Save new head index
FC25F6 6062          bra     $FC265A
FC25F8 0C000013      cmp.b   #19,D0             XOFF received ?
FC25FC 6608          bne     $FC2606            No
FC25FE 117C00FF001F  move.b  #$FF,31(A0)        Set XOFF flag
FC2604 6054          bra     $FC265A
FC2606 32280008      move.w  8(A0),D1           Tail index
FC260A 610001F8      bsr     $FC2804            Test for wrap around
FC260E B2680006      cmp.w   6(A0),D1           Receiver buffer full?
FC2612 6746          beq     $FC265A            Yes, ignore characters
FC2614 24680000      move.l  (A0),A2            Pointer to input buffer
FC2618 15801000      move.b  D0,0(A2,D1.w)      Received character in buffer
FC261C 31410008      move.w  D1,8(A0)           Save new tail index
FC2620 6100FE9C      bsr     $FC24BE            Get input buffer length used
FC2624 B468000C      cmp.w   12(A0),D2          Same as high-water mark?
FC2628 6624          bne     $FC264E            No
FC262A 082800010020  btst    #1,32(A0)          RTS/CTS mode?
FC2630 6628          bne     $FC265A            No
FC2632 082800000020  btst    #0,32(A0)          XON/XOFF mode?
FC2638 6714          beq     $FC264E            No
FC263A 4A28001E      tst.b   30(A0)             XOFF already sent?
```

```
FC263E 660E              bne     $FC264E                        Yes
FC2640 117C00FF001E      move.b  #$FF,30(A0)                    Flag for setting XOFF
FC2646 123C0013          move.b  #$13,D1                        XOFF
FC264A 6100FE94          bsr     $FC24E0                        send
FC264E 082800010020      btst    #1,32(A0)                      RTS/CTS mode?
FC2654 6704              beq     $FC265A                        No
FC2656 6100072C          bsr     $FC2D84                        rtson
FC265A 08A90004000E      bclr    #4,14(A1)                      Clear interrupt service bit
FC2660 4CDF070F          movem.l (A7)+,D0-D3/A0-A2              Restore registers
FC2664 4E73              rte

************************************************

FC2666 48E720E0          movem.l D2/A0-A2,-(A7)                 txrint, transmitter buffer empty
FC266A 6100FE44          bsr     $FC24B0                        Save registers
FC266E 082800010020      btst    #1,32(A0)                      rs232ptr, get RS 232 pointer
FC2674 6630              bne     $FC26A6                        RTS/CTS mode?
FC2676 082800000020      btst    #0,32(A0)                      Yes, then use this interrupt
FC267C 6706              beq     $FC2684                        XON/XOFF mode?
FC267E 4A28001F          tst.b   31(A0)                         No
FC2682 6622              bne     $FC26A6                        XOFF active ?
FC2684 1169002C001D      move.b  44(A1),29(A0)                  Yes, do nothing
FC268A 34280014          move.w  20(A0),D2                      Save transmitter status register
FC268E B468016           cmp.w   22(A0),D2                      Head index
FC2692 6712              beq     $FC26A6                        Compare with tail index
FC2694 6100017A          bsr     $FC2810                        Send buffer empty?
FC2698 2468000E          move.l  14(A0),A2                      Test for wrap around
FC269C 13722000002E      move.b  0(A2,D2.w),46(A1)              Pointer to send buffer
FC26A2 31420014          move.w  D2,20(A0)                      Byte in MFP transmitter register
FC26A6 08A90002000E      bclr    #2,14(A1)                      Save new head index
FC26AC 4CDF0704          movem.l (A7)+,D2/A0-A2                 Clear interrupt service bit
FC26B0 4E73              rte                                    Restore registers
```

```
*************************************               ctsint, CTS interrupt routine
FC26B2 48E720E0         movem.l  D2/A0-A2,-(A7)      Save registers
FC26B6 6100FDF8         bsr      $FC24B0             rs232ptr, get RS 232 pointer
FC26BA 082800010020     btst     #1,32(A0)           RTS/CTS mode?
FC26C0 672A             beq      $FC26EC             No, ignore interrupt
FC26C2 1169002C001D     move.b   44(A1),29(A0)       Save transmitter status
FC26C8 08280007001D     btst     #7,29(A0)           Transmitter buffer empty ?
FC26CE 67F8             beq      $FC26C8             No, wait (must jump to $FC26C2!)
FC26D0 34280014         move.w   20(A0),D2           Head index
FC26D4 B468016          cmp.w    22(A0),D2           Compare with tail index
FC26D8 671E             beq      $FC26F8             Send buffer empty
FC26DA 61000134         bsr      $FC2810             Test for wrap around
FC26DE 2468000E         move.l   14(A0),A2           Pointer to send buffer
FC26E2 13722000002E     move.b   0(A2,D2.w),46(A1)   Byte in MFP transmitter register
FC26E8 31420014         move.w   D2,20(A0)           Save new head index
FC26EC 08A900020010     bclr     #2,16(A1)           Clear interrupt service bit
FC26F2 4CDF0704         movem.l  (A7)+,D2/A0-A2      Restore registers
FC26F6 4E73             rte

FC26F8 60F2             bra      $FC26EC             Send buffer empty
*************************************               rxerror, RS 232 receiver error
FC26FA 48E780C0         movem.l  D0/A0-A1,-(A7)      Save registers
FC26FE 6100FDB0         bsr      $FC24B0             rs232ptr, get RS 232 pointer
FC2702 1169002A001C     move.b   42(A1),28(A0)       Save receiver status
FC2708 1029002E         move.b   46(A1),D0           Read data register (clear status)
FC270C 08A90003000E     bclr     #3,14(A1)           Clear interrupt service bit
FC2712 4CDF0301         movem.l  (A7)+,D0/A0-A1      Restore registers
FC2716 4E73             rte

*************************************               txerror, RS 232 send error
FC2718 48E700C0         movem.l  A0-A1,-(A7)         Save registers
FC271C 6100FD92         bsr      $FC24B0             rs232ptr, get RS 232 pointer
```

```
FC2720  1169002C001D          move.b    44(A1),29(A0)       Save transmitter status
FC2726  08A90001000E          bclr      #1,14(A1)           Clear interrupt service bit
FC272C  4CDF0300              movem.l   (A7)+/A0-A1         Restore registers
FC2730  4E73                  rte

************************************************
                                                            get iorec
FC2732  7200                  moveq.l   #0,D1               Device number
FC2734  322F0004              move.w    4(A7),D1
FC2738  40E7                  move.w    SR,-(A7)            Save status
FC273A  007C0700              or.w      #$700,SR            IPL 7, disable interrupts
FC273E  45F900FC274E          lea       $FC274E,A2          Address of the table
FC2744  E581                  asl.l     #2,D1               Long access
FC2746  20321800              move.l    0(A2,D1.l),D0       Get pointer to iorec
FC274A  46DF                  move.w    (A7)+,SR            Restore status
FC274C  4E75                  rts

************************************************
                                                            iorec table
FC274E  00000D8E              dc.l      $D8E                RS 232
FC2752  00000DB0              dc.l      $DB0                IKBD
FC2756  00000DBE              dc.l      $DBE                MIDI

************************************************
                                                            rsconf, configure RS 232
FC275A  007C0700              or.w      #$700,SR            IPL 7, disable interrupts
FC275E  6100FD50              bsr       $FC24B0             rs232ptr, get RS 232 pointer
FC2762  0F490028              movep.l   $28(A1),D7          Save ucr, rsr, tsr and scr
FC2766  4A6F0006              tst.w     6(A7)               Mode
FC276A  6B0A                  bmi       $FC2776             Negative, don't reset
FC276C  116F00070020          move.b    7(A7),32(A0)        Reset rsmode
FC2772  7000                  moveq.l   #0,D0
FC2774  7400                  moveq.l   #0,D2
FC2776  4A6F0004              tst.w     4(A7)               Baud rate
FC277A  6B34                  bmi       $FC27B0             Negative, don't change
```

```
FC277C  7000                    moveq.l  #0,D0              Disable receiver
FC277E  1340002A                move.b   D0,42(A1)          Disable sender
FC2782  1340002C                move.b   D0,44(A1)          Get new baud rate
FC2786  322F0004                move.w   4(A7),D1
FC278A  45F900FC27E4            lea      $FC27E4,A2         Table of timer values, control registers
FC2790  10321000                move.b   0(A2,D1.w),D0      Get value
FC2794  45F900FC27F4            lea      $FC27F4,A2         Table of timer values, data registers
FC279A  14321000                move.b   0(A2,D1.w),D2      Get value
FC279E  2200                    move.l   D0,D1
FC27A0  7003                    moveq.l  #3,D0              Pointer to timer D
FC27A2  6100FBC2                bsr      $FC2366            Set timer D for new baud rate
FC27A6  7001                    moveq.l  #1,D0
FC27A8  1340002A                move.b   D0,42(A1)          Enable receiver
FC27AC  1340002C                move.b   D0,44(A1)          Enable sender
FC27B0  4A6F0008                tst.w    8(A7)              Set ucr ?
FC27B4  6B06                    bmi      $FC27BC            No
FC27B6  136F00090028            move.b   9(A7),40(A1)       New ucr value
FC27BC  4A6F000A                tst.w    10(A7)             Set rsr ?
FC27C0  6B06                    bmi      $FC27C8            No
FC27C2  136F000B002A            move.b   11(A7),42(A1)      New rsr value
FC27C8  4A6F000C                tst.w    12(A7)             Set tsr?
FC27CC  6B06                    bmi      $FC27D4            No
FC27CE  136F000D002C            move.b   13(A7),44(A1)      New tsr value
FC27D4  4A6F000E                tst.w    14(A7)             Set scr?
FC27D8  6B06                    bmi      $FC27E0            No
FC27DA  136F000F0026            move.b   15(A7),38(A1)      Set scr
FC27E0  2007                    move.l   D7,D0              old value for control register
FC27E2  4E75                    rts

*******************************************************
FC27E4  0101010101010101        dc.b     1,1,1,1,1,1,1,1    Timer values for RS 232 baud rate
FC27EC  0101010101010202        dc.b     1,1,1,1,1,1,2,2    Control register
                                                            1 = /4, 2 = /10
```

```
FC27F4 0102040508080A0B10      dc.b     1,2,4,5,8,10,11,16          Data register
FC27FC 20406080808FAFF4060     dc.b     32,64,96,128,143,175,64,96

*****************************************************************
                                                                   wrapin, test for wrap around
FC2804 5241                    addq.w   #1,D1                      Head index + 1
FC2806 B2680004                cmp.w    4(A0),D1                   Equals buffer size?
FC280A 6502                    bcs      $FC280E                    No
FC280C 7200                    moveq.l  #0,D1                      Else begin with zero
FC280E 4E75                    rts

*****************************************************************
                                                                   wrapout, test for wrap around
FC2810 5242                    addq.w   #1,D2                      Tail index + 1
FC2812 B4680012                cmp.w    18(A0),D2                  Equals buffer size?
FC2816 6502                    bcs      $FC281A                    No
FC2818 7200                    moveq.l  #0,D2                      Else begin with zero
FC281A 4E75                    rts

*****************************************************************
                                                                   midikey, keyboard and MIDI interrupt
FC281C 48E7F0F4                movem.l  D0-D3/A0-A3/A5,-(A7)       Save registers
FC2820 4BF900000000            lea      $0,A5                      Clear A5
FC2826 246D0DE8                move.l   $DE8(A5),A2                mbufrec, MIDI
FC282A 4E92                    jsr      (A2)                       Interrupt from MIDI ACIA ?
FC282C 246D0DEC                move.l   $DEC(A5),A2                kbufrec, keyboard
FC2830 4E92                    jsr      (A2)                       Interrupt from keyboard ACIA ?
FC2832 0839004FFFFFA01         btst     #4,$FFFFFA01               mfp gpip, still an interrupt there?
FC283A 67EA                    beq      $FC2826                    Yes, proces
FC283C 08B90006FFFFFA11        bclr     #6,$FFFFFA11               Clear interrupt service bit
FC2844 4CDF2F0F                movem.l  (A7)+,D0-D3/A0-A3/A5       Restore registers
FC2848 4E73                    rte

*****************************************************************
                                                                   midisys, MIDI interrupt
FC284A 41ED0DBE                lea      $DBE(A5),A0                iorec for MIDI
```

```
FC284E  43F9FFFFFC04       lea      $FFFFFC04,A1           MIDI ACIA control
FC2854  246D0DD4           move.l   $DD4(A5),A2            MIDI error routine
FC2858  600E               bra      $FC2868

*********************************************************
FC285A  41ED0DB0           lea      $DB0(A5),A0            ikbdsys, keyboard interrupt
FC285E  43F9FFFFFC00       lea      $FFFFFC00,A1           1orec for keyboard
FC2864  246D0DD0           move.l   $DD0(A5),A2            Keyboard ACIA control
FC2868  14290000           move.b   (A1),D2                Keyboard error routine
FC286C  08020007           btst     #7,D2                  Get ACIA status
FC2870  671C               beq      $FC288E                Interrupt request ?
FC2872  08020000           btst     #0,D2                  No
FC2876  670A               beq      $FC2882                Receiver buffer full?
FC2878  48E720E0           movem.l  D2/A0-A2,-(A7)         No
FC287C  6112               bsr      $FC2890                Save registers
FC287E  4CDF0704           movem.l  (A7)+,D2/A0-A2         arcvint, get byte
FC2882  02020020           and.b    #$20,D2                Restore registers
FC2886  6706               beq      $FC288E                Clear tested bit
FC2888  10290002           move.b   2(A1),D0               No error
FC288C  4ED2               jmp      (A2)                   Read data again, clear status
FC288E  4E75               rts                             Execute error routine

*********************************************************
FC2890  10290002           move.b   2(A1),D0               arcvint, get byte from ACIA
FC2894  B1FC00000DB0       cmp.l    #$DB0,A0               get data from ACIA
FC289A  66000440           bne      $FC2CDC                Keyboard ACIA ?
FC289E  4A2D0DF0           tst.b    $DF0(A5)               No, MIDI
FC28A2  6660               bne      $FC2904                Keyboard state
FC28A4  0C0000F6           cmp.b    #$F6,D0                Keypress ?
FC28A8  65000100           bcs      $FC29AA                yes
FC28AC  040000F6           sub.b    #$F6,D0                Subtract offset
FC28B0  028000000FF        and.l    #$FF,D0
```

```
FC28B6  47F90FC28F0         lea      $FC28F0,A3              Pointer to IKBD code table
FC28BC  1B7300000DF0        move.b   0(A3,D0.w),$DF0(A5)     Save IKBD
FC28C2  47F900FC28FA        lea      $FC28FA,A3              Pointer to IKBD length table
FC28C8  1B7300000DF1        move.b   0(A3,D0.w),$DF1(A5)     IKBD index
FC28CE  064000F6            add.w    #$F6,D0                 Add offset again
FC28D2  0C0000F8            cmp.b    #$F8,D0                 Mouse position record ?
FC28D6  6D0C                blt      $FC28E4                 No
FC28D8  0C0000FB            cmp.b    #$FB,D0                 Mouse position record ?
FC28DC  6E06                bgt      $FC28E4                 No
FC28DE  1B400DFE            move.b   D0,$DFE(A5)             Save mouse position
FC28E2  4E75                rts
FC28E4  0C0000FD            cmp.b    #$FD,D0                 Joystick record ?
FC28E8  6D04                blt      $FC28EE                 No
FC28EA  1B400E07            move.b   D0,$E07(A5)             Save joystick data
FC28EE  4E75                rts
*************************************************************************
FC28F0  01020303030304050607 dc.b    1,2,3,3,3,4,5,6,7       IKBD parameters
FC28FA  0705020202060020101 dc.b     7,5,2,2,2,6,2,1,1       Status code for $F6-$FF
                                                             Length-1 for $F6-$FF
*************************************************************************
FC2904  0C2D00060DF0        cmp.b    #6,$DF0(A5)             Joystick record ?
FC290A  64000084            bcc      $FC2990                 Yes
FC290E  45F900FC2954        lea      $FC2954,A2              Pointer to IKBD parameter table
FC2914  7400                moveq.l  #0,D2
FC2916  142D0DF0            move.b   $DF0(A5),D2             Kstate
FC291A  5302                subq.b   #1,D2                   1-5 => 0-4
FC291C  E342                asl.w    #1,D2                   times 2
FC291E  D42D0DF0            add.b    $DF0(A5),D2             plus once
FC2922  5302                subq.b   #1,D2
FC2924  E542                asl.w    #2,D2
FC2926  20722000            move.l   0(A2,D2.w),A0           IKBD record pointer
```

```
FC292A  22722004     move.l    4(A2,D2.w),A1       IKBD index base
FC292E  24722008     move.l    8(A2,D2.w),A2       IKBD interrupt routine
FC2932  2452         move.l    (A2),A2             Get interrupt vector
FC2934  7400         moveq.l   #0,D2
FC2936  142D0DF1     move.b    $DF1(A5),D2         Get IKBD index
FC293A  93C2         sub.l     D2,A1               minus base
FC293C  1280         move.b    D0,(A1)
FC293E  532D0DF1     subq.b    #1,$DF1(A5)         IKBD index minus 1
FC2942  4A2D0DF1     tst.b     $DF1(A5)            Test index
FC2946  660A         bne       $FC2952
FC2948  2F08         move.l    A0,-(A7)            Pass record pointer
FC294A  4E92         jsr       (A2)                Execute interrupt routine
FC294C  584F         addq.w    #4,A7               Correct stack pointer
FC294E  422D0DF0     clr.b     $DF0(A5)            Clear IKBD state
FC2952  4E75         rts
*****************************************
FC2954  00000DF2     dc.l      $DF2                Parameter table for IKBD
FC2958  00000DF9     dc.l      $DF9
FC295C  00000DD8     dc.l      $DD8
FC2960  00000DF9     dc.l      $DF9
FC2964  00000DFE     dc.l      $DFE
FC2968  00000DDC     dc.l      $DDC
FC296C  00000DFE     dc.l      $DFE
FC2970  00000E01     dc.l      $E01
FC2974  00000DDC     dc.l      $DDC
FC2978  00000E01     dc.l      $E01
FC297C  00000E07     dc.l      $E07
FC2980  00000DE0     dc.l      $DE0
FC2984  00000E07     dc.l      $E07
FC2988  00000E09     dc.l      $E09
FC298C  00000DE4     dc.l      $DE4
```

```
*****************************************
FC2990  223C0000E08   move.l  #$E08,D1                    Joystick 0 and 1
FC2996  D22D0DF0      add.b   $DF0(A5),D1
FC299A  5D01          subq.b  #6,D1
FC299C  2441          move.l  D1,A2
FC299E  1480          move.b  D0,(A2)
FC29A0  246D0DE4      move.l  $DE4(A5),A2                 Joystick interrupt routine
FC29A4  41ED0E07      lea     $E07(A5),A0                 Address of joystick data
FC29A8  609E          bra     $FC2948
*****************************************
FC29AA  122D0E1B      move.b  $E1B(A5),D1                 Process keypress
FC29AE  0C00002A      cmp.b   #$2A,D0                     Shift status
FC29B2  6606          bne     $FC29BA                     Left shift key pressed?
FC29B4  08C10001      bset    #1,D1                       No
FC29B8  6074          bra     $FC2A2E                     Set bit for left shift key
FC29BA  0C0000AA      cmp.b   #$AA,D0                     Left shift key released?
FC29BE  6606          bne     $FC29C6                     No
FC29C0  08810001      bclr    #1,D1                       Clear bit for left shift key
FC29C4  6068          bra     $FC2A2E
FC29C6  0C000036      cmp.b   #$36,D0                     Right shift key pressed?
FC29CA  6606          bne     $FC29D2                     No
FC29CC  08C10000      bset    #0,D1                       Set bit for right shift key
FC29D0  605C          bra     $FC2A2E
FC29D2  0C0000B6      cmp.b   #$B6,D0                     Right shift key released?
FC29D6  6606          bne     $FC29DE                     No
FC29D8  08810000      bclr    #0,D1                       Clear bit for right shift key
FC29DC  6050          bra     $FC2A2E
FC29DE  0C00001D      cmp.b   #$1D,D0                     CTRL key pressed?
FC29E2  6606          bne     $FC29EA                     No
FC29E4  08C10002      bset    #2,D1                       Set bit for CTRL key
FC29E8  6044          bra     $FC2A2E
```

```
FC29EA  0C00009D              cmp.b   #$9D,D0                CTRL key released?
FC29EE  6606                  bne     $FC29F6                No
FC29F0  08810002              bclr    #2,D1                  Clear bit for CTRL key
FC29F4  6038                  bra     $FC2A2E
FC29F6  0C000038              cmp.b   #$38,D0                ALT key pressed?
FC29FA  6606                  bne     $FC2A02                No
FC29FC  08C10003              bset    #3,D1                  Set bit for ALT key
FC2A00  602C                  bra     $FC2A2E
FC2A02  0C0000B8              cmp.b   #$B8,D0                ALT key released?
FC2A06  6606                  bne     $FC2A0E                No
FC2A08  08810003              bclr    #3,D1                  Clear bit for ALT key
FC2A0C  6020                  bra     $FC2A2E
FC2A0E  0C00003A              cmp.b   #$3A,D0                CAPS LOCK pressed ?
FC2A12  6620                  bne     $FC2A34                No
FC2A14  082D00000484          btst    #0,$484(A5)            conterm, key click ?
FC2A1A  670E                  beq     $FC2A2A                No
FC2A1C  2B7C00FC30940E44      move.l  #$FC3094,$E44(A5)      Addres of key click sound table
FC2A24  1B7C00000E48          move.b  #0,$E48(A5)            Start sound
FC2A2A  08410004              bchg    #4,D1                  Invert CAPS LOCK status
FC2A2E  1B410E1B              move.b  D1,$E1B(A5)            Save new shift status
FC2A32  4E75                  rts

FC2A34  08000007              btst    #7,D0                  Was key released?
FC2A38  662A                  bne     $FC2A64                Yes
FC2A3A  4A2D0E39              tst.b   $E39(A5)               Repeat ?
FC2A3E  6616                  bne     $FC2A56                Yes
FC2A40  1B400E39              move.b  D0,$E39(A5)            Save key code for repeat
FC2A44  1B7900000E3C0E3A      move.b  $E3C,$E3A(A5)          Delay 1
FC2A4C  1B7900000E3D0E3B      move.b  $E3D,$E3B(A5)          Delay 2
FC2A54  603A                  bra     $FC2A90
```

```
FC2A56  1B7C00000E3A     move.b    #0,$E3A(A5)              Clear counter for delay 1
FC2A5C  1B7C00000E3B     move.b    #0,$E3B(A5)              Clear counter for delay 2
FC2A62  602C             bra       $FC2A90
FC2A64  4A2D0E39         tst.b     $E39(A5)                 Key for repeat?
FC2A68  670E             beq       $FC2A78                  No
FC2A6A  7200             moveq.l   #0,D1
FC2A6C  1B410E39         move.b    D1,$E39(A5)              Clear key code for repeat
FC2A70  1B410E3A         move.b    D1,$E3A(A5)              Clear delay 1
FC2A74  1B410E3B         move.b    D1,$E3B(A5)              Clear delay 2
FC2A78  0C0000C7         cmp.b     #$C7,D0                  HOME key released?
FC2A7C  6708             beq       $FC2A86                  Yes
FC2A7E  0C0000D2         cmp.b     #$D2,D0                  INSERT key released?
FC2A82  66000256         bne       $FC2CDA                  No
FC2A86  082D00030E1B     btst      #3,$E1B(A5)              ALT key still pressed?
FC2A8C  6700024C         beq       $FC2CDA                  No
FC2A90  082D00000484     btst      #0,$484(A5)              conterm, key click ?
FC2A96  670E             beq       $FC2AA6                  No
FC2A98  2B7C00FC30940E44 move.l    #$FC3094,$E44(A5)        Address of sound table for key click
FC2AA0  1B7C00000E48     move.b    #0,$E48(A5)              Start sound
FC2AA6  2F08             move.l    A0,-(A7)                 Save iorec for keyboard
FC2AA8  7200             moveq.l   #0,D1
FC2AAA  1200             move.b    D0,D1                    Scancode to D1
FC2AAC  206D0E1C         move.l    $E1C(A5),A0              Address of the standard keyboard table
FC2AB0  0240007F         and.w     #$7F,D0                  Clear bit for released
FC2AB4  082D00040E1B     btst      #4,$E1B(A5)              CAPS LOCK active ?
FC2ABA  6704             beq       $FC2AC0                  No
FC2ABC  206D0E24         move.l    $E24(A5),A0              Address of CAPS LOCK keyboard table
FC2AC0  082D00000E1B     btst      #0,$E1B(A5)              Right shift key pressed?
FC2AC6  6608             bne       $FC2AD0                  Yes
FC2AC8  082D00010E1B     btst      #1,$E1B(A5)              Left shift key pressed?
FC2ACE  671A             beq       $FC2AEA                  No
FC2AD0  0C00003B         cmp.b     #$3B,D0                  Function key ? (F1)
```

```
FC2AD4 6510              bcs      $FC2AE6              No
FC2AD6 0C000044          cmp.b    #$44,D0              Function key ? (F10)
FC2ADA 620A              bhi      $FC2AE6              No
FC2ADC 06410019          add.w    #$19,D1              Add offset to GSX standard
FC2AE0 7000              moveq.l  #0,D0                ASCII code equals zero
FC2AE2 600001B2          bra      $FC2C96
FC2AE6 206D0E20          move.l   $E20(A5),A0          Address of the shift keyboard table
FC2AEA 10300000          move.b   0(A0,D0.w),D0        Get ASCII code from table
FC2AEE 082D00020E1B      btst     #2,$E1B(A5)          CTRL key table?
FC2AF4 6760              beq      $FC2B56              No
FC2AF6 0C00000D          cmp.b    #13,D0               Carriage return?
FC2AFA 6604              bne      $FC2B00              No
FC2AFC 700A              moveq.l  #10,D0               Convert to linefeed
FC2AFE 672A              beq      $FC2B2A
FC2B00 0C010047          cmp.b    #$47,D1              CTRL HOME?
FC2B04 6608              bne      $FC2B0E              No
FC2B06 06410030          add.w    #$30,D1              Add offset to GSX standard
FC2B0A 6000018A          bra      $FC2C96
FC2B0E 0C01004B          cmp.b    #$4B,D1              CTRL cursor left?
FC2B12 6608              bne      $FC2B1C              No
FC2B14 7273              moveq.l  #$73,D1              GSX standard
FC2B16 7000              moveq.l  #0,D0                ASCII code zero
FC2B18 6000017C          bra      $FC2C96
FC2B1C 0C01004D          cmp.b    #$4D,D1              CTRL cursor right ?
FC2B20 6608              bne      $FC2B2A              No
FC2B22 7274              moveq.l  #$74,D1              GSX standard
FC2B24 7000              moveq.l  #0,D0                ASCII code zero
FC2B26 6000016E          bra      $FC2C96
FC2B2A 0C000032          cmp.b    #$32,D0              CTRL M ?
FC2B2E 6606              bne      $FC2B36
FC2B30 7000              moveq.l  #0,D0                ASCII code zero
FC2B32 60000162          bra      $FC2C96
```

```
FC2B36  0C000036         cmp.b    #$36,D0                        CTRL Shift ?
FC2B3A  6606             bne      $FC2B42
FC2B3C  701E             moveq.l  #$1E,D0                        ASCI code RS
FC2B3E  60000156         bra      $FC2C96
FC2B42  0C00002D         cmp.b    #$2D,D0                        CTRL C ?
FC2B46  6606             bne      $FC2B4E
FC2B48  701F             moveq.l  #$1F,D0                        ASCII code US
FC2B4A  6000014A         bra      $FC2C96
FC2B4E  0240001F         and.w    #$1F,D0                        Convert code to CTRL code
FC2B52  60000142         bra      $FC2C96
FC2B56  082D00030E1B     btst     #3,$E1B(A5)                    ALT key pressed?
FC2B5C  67000138         beq      $FC2C96                        No
FC2B60  0C01001A         cmp.b    #26,D1                         Key 'Ü' ?
FC2B64  6618             bne      $FC2B7E
FC2B66  103C0040         move.b   #$40,D0                        '@'
FC2B6A  142D0E1B         move.b   $E1B(A5),D2                    Shift status
FC2B6E  02020003         and.b    #3,D2                          One of the shift keys pressed?
FC2B72  67000122         beq      $FC2C96                        No
FC2B76  103C005C         move.b   #$5C,D0                        '\'
FC2B7A  6000011A         bra      $FC2C96
FC2B7E  0C010027         cmp.b    #39,D1                         Key 'Ö' ?
FC2B82  6618             bne      $FC2B9C
FC2B84  103C005B         move.b   #$5B,D0                        '['
FC2B88  142D0E1B         move.b   $E1B(A5),D2                    Shift status
FC2B8C  02020003         and.b    #3,D2                          One of the shift keys pressed?
FC2B90  67000104         beq      $FC2C96                        No
FC2B94  103C007B         move.b   #$7B,D0                        '{'
FC2B98  600000FC         bra      $FC2C96
FC2B9C  0C010028         cmp.b    #40,D1                         Key 'Ä' ?
FC2BA0  6618             bne      $FC2BBA
FC2BA2  103C005D         move.b   #$5D,D0                        ']'
FC2BA6  142D0E1B         move.b   $E1B(A5),D2                    Shift status
```

FC2BAA 02020003	and.b	#3,D2	One of the shift keys pressed?
FC2BAE 670000E6	beq	$FC2C96	No
FC2BB2 103C007D	move.b	#$7D,D0	'}'
FC2BB6 600000DE	bra	$FC2C96	
FC2BBA 0C010062	cmp.b	#98,D1	ALT HELP ?
FC2BBE 660A	bne	$FC2BCA	No
FC2BC0 526D04EE	addq.w	#1,$4EE(A5)	_dumpflg for hardcopy
FC2BC4 205F	move.l	(A7)+,A0	Restore keyboard iorec
FC2BC6 60000112	bra	$FC2CDA	
FC2BCA 45F900FC2D48	lea	$FC2D48,A2	Pointer to mouse scancode table
FC2BD0 7403	moveq.l	#3,D2	Test four values
FC2BD2 B2322000	cmp.b	0(A2,D2.w),D1	Value found?
FC2BD6 6700012C	beq	$FC2D04	Yes
FC2BDA 51CAFFF6	dbra	D2,$FC2BD2	Next value
FC2BDE 0C010048	cmp.b	#$48,D1	Cursor up?
FC2BE2 661C	bne	$FC2C00	No
FC2BE4 123C0000	move.b	#0,D1	X-offset for cursor up
FC2BE8 143CFFF8	move.b	#-8,D2	Y-offset for cursor up
FC2BEC 102D0E1B	move.b	$E1B(A5),D0	Get shift status
FC2BF0 02000003	and.b	#3,D0	One of the shift keys pressed?
FC2BF4 6700012C	beq	$FC2D22	No
FC2BF8 143CFFFF	move.b	#-1,D2	Y-offset, only one pixel high
FC2BFC 60000124	bra	$FC2D22	
FC2C00 0C01004B	cmp.b	#$4B,D1	Cursor left ?
FC2C04 661C	bne	$FC2C22	No
FC2C06 143C0000	move.b	#0,D2	Y-offset for cursor left
FC2C0A 123CFFF8	move.b	#-8,D1	X-offset for cursor left
FC2C0E 102D0E1B	move.b	$E1B(A5),D0	Get shift status
FC2C12 02000003	and.b	#3,D0	One of the shift keys pressed?
FC2C16 6700010A	beq	$FC2D22	No
FC2C1A 123CFFFF	move.b	#-1,D1	X-offset, only one pixel left

```
FC2C1E  60000102              bra     $FC2D22
FC2C22  0C01004D              cmp.b   #$4D,D1              Cursor right ?
FC2C26  661C                  bne     $FC2C44              No
FC2C28  123C0008              move.b  #8,D1                X-offset for cursor right
FC2C2C  143C0000              move.b  #0,D2                Y-offset for cursor right
FC2C30  102D0E1B              move.b  $E1B(A5),D0          Get shift status
FC2C34  02000003              and.b   #3,D0                One of the shift keys pressed?
FC2C38  670000E8              beq     $FC2D22              No
FC2C3C  123C0001              move.b  #1,D1                X-offset, only one pixel right
FC2C40  600000E0              bra     $FC2D22
FC2C44  0C010050              cmp.b   #$50,D1              Cursor down ?
FC2C48  661C                  bne     $FC2C66              No
FC2C4A  123C0000              move.b  #0,D1                X-offset for cursor down
FC2C4E  143C0008              move.b  #8,D2                Y-offset for cursor down
FC2C52  102D0E1B              move.b  $E1B(A5),D0          Shift status
FC2C56  02000003              and.b   #3,D0                One of the shift keys pressed?
FC2C5A  670000C6              beq     $FC2D22              No
FC2C5E  143C0001              move.b  #1,D2                Y-offset, only one pixel down
FC2C62  600000BE              bra     $FC2D22
FC2C66  0C010002              cmp.b   #2,D1
FC2C6A  650C                  bcs     $FC2C78
FC2C6C  0C01000D              cmp.b   #13,D1               '1'
FC2C70  6206                  bhi     $FC2C78
FC2C72  06010076              add.b   #118,D1
FC2C76  600C                  bra     $FC2C84
FC2C78  0C000041              cmp.b   #65,D0               '='
FC2C7C  650A                  bcs     $FC2C88
FC2C7E  0C00005A              cmp.b   #90,D0               'A'
FC2C82  6204                  bhi     $FC2C88
FC2C84  7000                  moveq.l #0,D0
FC2C86  600E                  bra     $FC2C96              'Z'
FC2C88  0C000061              cmp.b   #97,D0               'a'
```

```
FC2C8C  6508             bcs       $FC2C96
FC2C8E  0C00007A         cmp.b     #122,D0             'z'
FC2C92  6202             bhi       $FC2C96
FC2C94  60EE             bra       $FC2C84
FC2C96  E141             asl.w     #8,D1               Scancode to bits 8-15
FC2C98  D041             add.w     D1,D0               plus ASCII code
FC2C9A  205F             move.l    (A7)+,A0            iorec pointer to keyboard
FC2C9C  32280008         move.w    8(A0),D1            Tail index
FC2CA0  5841             addq.w    #4,D1               plus 4
FC2CA2  B2680004         cmp.w     4(A0),D1            End of buffer reached?
FC2CA6  6502             bcs       $FC2CAA             No
FC2CA8  7200             moveq.l   #0,D1               Start over again
FC2CAA  B2680006         cmp.w     6(A0),D1            Buffer full?
FC2CAE  672A             beq       $FC2CDA             Yes, ignore data
FC2CB0  24680000         move.l    (A0),A2             Address of the buffer
FC2CB4  4840             swap      D0                  ASCII code to bits 16-23
FC2CB6  303C0000         move.w    #0,D0
FC2CBA  102D0E1B         move.b    $E1B(A5),D0         Shift status
FC2CBE  4840             swap      D0                  in upper word
FC2CC0  E188             lsl.l     #8,D0               in bits 24-31
FC2CC2  E048             lsr.w     #8,D0               ASCII code to bits 0-7
FC2CC4  082D00030484     btst      #3,$484(A5)         conterm, accept shift status?
FC2CCA  6606             bne       $FC2CD2             Yes
FC2CCC  028000FFFFFF     and.l     #$00FFFFFF,D0       Clear shift status
FC2CD2  25801000         move.l    D0,0(A2,D1.w)       Write data in keyboard buffer
FC2CD6  31410008         move.w    D1,8(A0)            Update buffer pointer
FC2CDA  4E75             rts

;****************************************************

FC2CDC  246D0DCC         move.l    $DCC(A5),A2         midibyte
                                                       Pointer to MIDI interrupt handler
FC2CE0  4ED2             jmp       (A2)                Execute routine
```

```
*****************************************              sysmidi
FC2CE2 32280008           move.w   8(A0),D1             Tail index
FC2CE6 5241               addq.w   #1,D1                Increment
FC2CE8 B2680004           cmp.w    4(A0),D1             End of buffer reached?
FC2CEC 6502               bcs      $FC2CF0              No
FC2CEE 7200               moveq.l  #0,D1                Buffer pointer back to buffer start
FC2CF0 B2680006           cmp.w    6(A0),D1             Head equals tail ?
FC2CF4 670C               beq      $FC2D02              Yes, buffer full
FC2CF6 24680000           move.l   (A0),A2              Buffer address
FC2CFA 15801000           move.b   D0,0(A2,D1.w)        Write byte in buffer
FC2CFE 31410008           move.w   D1,8(A0)             New tail index
FC2D02 4E75               rts

*****************************************              keymaus1
FC2D04 7605               moveq.l  #5,D3                Accept right button
FC2D06 08010004           btst     #4,D1
FC2D0A 6702               beq      $FC2D0E              is right button ($47/$C7)
FC2D0C 7606               moveq.l  #6,D3                Left button
FC2D0E 08010007           btst     #7,D1                Pressed or released?
FC2D12 6706               beq      $FC2D1A              pressed
FC2D14 07AD0E1B           bclr     D3,$E1B(A5)          Clear bit for button
FC2D18 6004               bra      $FC2D1E
FC2D1A 07ED0E1B           bset     D3,$E1B(A5)          Set bit for button
FC2D1E 7200               moveq.l  #0,D1                X to 0
FC2D20 7400               moveq.l  #0,D2                Y to 0

*****************************************              keymouse
FC2D22 41ED0E18           lea      $E18(A5),A0          Pointer to mouse emulator buffer
FC2D26 246D0DDC           move.l   $DDC(A5),A2          Mouse interrupt vector
FC2D2A 4280               clr.l    D0
FC2D2C 102D0E1B           move.b   $E1B(A5),D0          Get status of the "mouse" buttons
FC2D30 EA08               lsr.b    #5,D0                Bit for right/left to bits 0/1
```

```
FC2D32  060000F8         add.b    #$F8,D0                      plus relative mouse header
FC2D36  11400000         move.b   D0,(A0)                      in buffer
FC2D3A  11410001         move.b   D1,1(A0)                     Store X-value
FC2D3E  11420002         move.b   D2,2(A0)                     Store Y-value
FC2D42  4E92             jsr      (A2)                         Call mouse interrupt routine
FC2D44  205F             move.l   (A7)+,A0                     iorec for keyboard back
FC2D46  4E75             rts

;*****************************************************
FC2D48  47C752D2         dc.b     $47,$C7,$52,$D2              mousekey1
                                                               Scancode for pseudo mouse
;*****************************************************
FC2D4C  302F0004         move.w   4(A7),D0                     giaccess,read write sound chip
FC2D50  322F0006         move.w   6(A7),D1                     Data
FC2D54  40E7             move.w   SR,-(A7)                     Register number plus read/write
FC2D56  007C0700         or.w     #$700,SR                     Save status
FC2D5A  48E76080         movem.l  D1-D2/A0,-(A7)               IPL 7, disable interrupts
FC2D5E  41F9FFFF8800     lea      $FFFF8800,A0                 Save registers
FC2D64  1401             move.b   D1,D2                        Address of the sound chip
FC2D66  0201000F         and.b    #$F,D1                       Get register number
FC2D6A  1081             move.b   D1,(A0)                      Registers 0-15
FC2D6C  E302             asl.b    #1,D2                        Select register
FC2D6E  6404             bcc      $FC2D74                      Test read/write bit
FC2D70  11400002         move.b   D0,2(A0)                     Read
FC2D74  7000             moveq.l  #0,D0                        Write data byte in sound chip register
FC2D76  1010             move.b   (A0),D0                      Read byte from sound chip
FC2D78  4CDF0106         movem.l  (A7)+,D1-D2/A0               Restore registers
FC2D7C  46DF             move.w   (A7)+,SR                     Restore status
FC2D7E  4E75             rts
```

```
***********************************************
FC2D80  7408              moveq.l  #8,D2              rtsoff, turn RTS off
FC2D82  6012              bra      $FC2D96            Bit 3
                                                      Set in port A

***********************************************
FC2D84  74F7              moveq.l  #$F7,D2            rtson, turn RTS on
FC2D86  6034              bra      $FC2DBC            Bit 3
                                                      Clear in port A

***********************************************
FC2D88  7410              moveq.l  #$10,D2            dtroff, turn DTR off
FC2D8A  600A              bra      $FC2D96            Bit 4
                                                      Set in port A

***********************************************
FC2D8C  74EF              moveq.l  #$EF,D2            dtron, turn DTR on
FC2D8E  602C              bra      $FC2DBC            Bit 4
                                                      Clear in port A

***********************************************
FC2D90  7400              moveq.l  #0,D2              ongibit, set bit(s) in sound chip port A
FC2D92  342F0004          move.w   4(A7),D2           Get bit pattern
FC2D96  48E7E000          movem.l  D0-D2,-(A7)        Save registers
FC2D9A  40E7              move.w   SR,-(A7)           Save status
FC2D9C  007C0700          or.w     #$700,SR           IPL 7, disable interrupts
FC2DA0  720E              moveq.l  #$E,D1             Read port A
FC2DA2  2F02              move.l   D2,-(A7)           Save bit pattern
FC2DA4  61AE              bsr      $FC2D54            Read port A
FC2DA6  241F              move.l   (A7)+,D2           Restore bit pattern
FC2DA8  8002              or.b     D2,D0              OR bits to old value
FC2DAA  728E              moveq.l  #$8E,D1            Write port A
FC2DAC  61A6              bsr      $FC2D54            Write new value
FC2DAE  46DF              move.w   (A7)+,SR           Restore status
FC2DB0  4CDF0007          movem.l  (A7)+,D0-D2        Restore registers
FC2DB4  4E75              rts
```

```
*******************************************************  offgibit, clear bits in sound chip port A
FC2DB6  7400                moveq.l  #0,D2                Bit pattern
FC2DB8  342F0004            move.w   4(A7),D2
FC2DBC  48E7E000            movem.l  D0-D2,-(A7)          Save registers
FC2DC0  40E7                move.w   SR,-(A7)             Save status
FC2DC2  007C0700            or.w     #$700,SR             IPL 7, disable interrupts
FC2DC6  720E                moveq.l  #$E,D1               Read port A
FC2DC8  2F02                move.l   D2,-(A7)             Save bit pattern
FC2DCA  6188                bsr      $FC2D54              Read port A
FC2DCC  241F                move.l   (A7)+,D2             Restore bit pattern
FC2DCE  C002                and.b    D2,D0                Clear bits
FC2DD0  728E                moveq.l  #$8E,D1              Write to port A
FC2DD2  6180                bsr      $FC2D54              Write new value
FC2DD4  46DF                move.w   (A7)+,SR             Restore status
FC2DD6  4CDF0007            movem.l  (A7)+,D0-D2          Restore registers
FC2DDA  4E75                rts

*******************************************************  initmouse
FC2DDC  4A6F0004            tst.w    4(A7)                Turn mouse off?
FC2DE0  6726                beq      $FC2E08              Yes, disable mouse
FC2DE2  2B6F000A0DDC        move.l   10(A7),$DDC(A5)      Mouse interrpt vector
FC2DE8  266F0006            move.l   6(A7),A3             Address of the parameter block
FC2DEC  0C6F00010004        cmp.w    #1,4(A7)             Relative mouse ?
FC2DF2  6724                beq      $FC2E18              Yes
FC2DF4  0C6F00020004        cmp.w    #2,4(A7)             Absolute mouse ?
FC2DFA  6736                beq      $FC2E32              Yes
FC2DFC  0C6F00040004        cmp.w    #4,4(A7)             Keycode mouse ?
FC2E02  6770                beq      $FC2E74              Yes
FC2E04  7000                moveq.l  #0,D0                Error, invalid
FC2E06  4E75                rts
```

```
*****************************************
FC2E08  7212                    moveq.l  #$12,D1              disable mouse
FC2E0A  6100F19C                bsr      $FC1FA8              Disable mouse command
FC2E0E  2B7C00FC2EDC00DC        move.l   #$FC2EDC,$DDC(A5)    Send to IKBD
FC2E16  6070                    bra      $FC2E88              Mouse interrpt vector to rts
*****************************************
FC2E18  45ED0E28                lea      $E28(A5),A2          relative mouse
FC2E1C  14FC0008                move.b   #8,(A2)+             Transfer buffer pointer
FC2E20  14FC000B                move.b   #$B,(A2)+            Relative mouse
FC2E24  6166                    bsr      $FC2E8C              Relative mouse threshold x, y
FC2E26  7606                    moveq.l  #6,D3                Set mouse parameters
FC2E28  45ED0E28                lea      $E28(A5),A2          Length of string - 1
FC2E2C  6100F19A                bsr      $FC1FC8              Transfer buffer pointer
FC2E30  6056                    bra      $FC2E88              Send string to IKBD
*****************************************
FC2E32  45ED0E28                lea      $E28(A5),A2          absolute mouse
FC2E36  14FC0009                move.b   #9,(A2)+             Transfer buffer pointer
FC2E3A  14EB0004                move.b   4(A3),(A2)+          Absolute mouse
FC2E3E  14EB0005                move.b   5(A3),(A2)+          xmax msb
FC2E42  14EB0006                move.b   6(A3),(A2)+          xmax lsb
FC2E46  14EB0007                move.b   7(A3),(A2)+          ymax msb
FC2E4A  14FC000C                move.b   #$C,(A2)+            ymax lsb
FC2E4E  613C                    bsr      $FC2E8C              Absolute mouse scale
FC2E50  14FC000E                move.b   #$E,(A2)+            Set mouse parameters
FC2E54  14FC0000                move.b   #0,(A2)+             Initial absolute mouse position
FC2E58  14EB0008                move.b   8(A3),(A2)+          Fill byte
FC2E5C  14EB0009                move.b   9(A3),(A2)+          Start position x msb
FC2E60  14EB000A                move.b   10(A3),(A2)+         Start position x lsb
FC2E64  14EB000B                move.b   11(A3),(A2)+         Start position y msb
FC2E68  7610                    moveq.l  #16,D3               Start position y lsb
                                                              String length - 1
```

```
FC2E6A 45ED0E28        lea      $E28(A5),A2         Transfer buffer pointer
FC2E6E 6100F158        bsr      $FC1FC8             Send string to IKBD
FC2E72 6014            bra      $FC2E88

;********************************************
FC2E74 45ED0E28        lea      $E28(A5),A2         Keycode mouse
FC2E78 14FC000A        move.b   #$A,(A2)+           Transfer buffer pointer
FC2E7C 610E            bsr      $FC2E8C             Mouse keycode mode
FC2E7E 7605            moveq.l  #5,D3               Set mouse parameters
FC2E80 45ED0E28        lea      $E28(A5),A2         Length of string - 1
FC2E84 6100F142        bsr      $FC1FC8             Transfer buffer pointer
FC2E88 70FF            moveq.l  #-1,D0              Send string to IKBD
FC2E8A 4E75            rts                          Flag for OK

;********************************************
FC2E8C 14EB0002        move.b   2(A3),(A2)+         setmouse, set mouse parameters
FC2E90 14EB0003        move.b   3(A3),(A2)+         x threshold, scale, delta
FC2E94 7210            moveq.l  #16,D1              y threshold, scale, delta
FC2E96 922B0000        sub.b    (A3),D1             top/bottom ?
FC2E9A 14C1            move.b   D1,(A2)+
FC2E9C 14FC0007        move.b   #7,(A2)+
FC2EA0 14EB0001        move.b   1(A3),(A2)+
FC2EA4 4E75            rts

;********************************************
FC2EA6 7000            moveq.l  #0,D0               xbtimer, initialize timer
FC2EA8 7200            moveq.l  #0,D1
FC2EAA 7400            moveq.l  #0,D2               Clear registers
FC2EAC 302F0004        move.w   4(A7),D0            Timer number (0-3 => A-D)
FC2EB0 322F0006        move.w   6(A7),D1            Value for control register
FC2EB4 342F0008        move.w   8(A7),D2            Value for date register
FC2EB8 6100F4AC        bsr      $FC2366             Set timer values
```

```
FC2EBC  4AAF000A        tst.l    10(A7)              Corresponding interrupt vector
FC2EC0  6B1A            bmi      $FC2EDC             not used?
FC2EC2  246F000A        move.l   10(A7),A2           Get vector
FC2EC6  7200            moveq.l  #0,D1
FC2EC8  43F900FC2EDE    lea      $FC2EDE,A1          Table for determining interrupt number
FC2ECE  0280000000FF    and.l    #$FF,D0
FC2ED4  10310000        move.b   0(A1,D0.w),D0       Get interrupt number
FC2ED8  6100F542        bsr      $FC241C             initint, install interrupt
FC2EDC  4E75            rts

****************************************************
FC2EDE  0D080504        dc.b     13,8,5,4            Interrupt numbers of the MFP timer
****************************************************

FC2EE2  4AAF0004        tst.l    4(A7)               keytrans, set keyboard tables
FC2EE6  6B06            bmi      $FC2EEE             Change standard table?
FC2EE8  2B6F00040E1C    move.l   4(A7),$E1C(A5)      No
FC2EEE  4AAF0008        tst.l    8(A7)               Address of the standard table
FC2EF2  6B06            bmi      $FC2EFA             Change shift table?
FC2EF4  2B6F00080E20    move.l   8(A7),$E20(A5)      No
FC2EFA  4AAF000C        tst.l    12(A7)              Address of the shift table
FC2EFE  6B06            bmi      $FC2F06             Change Caps Lock table
FC2F00  2B6F000C0E24    move.l   12(A7),$E24(A5)     No
FC2F06  203C00000E1C    move.l   #$E1C,D0            Address of the Caps Lock table
FC2F0C  4E75            rts                          Pointer to addresses of the tables

****************************************************
FC2F0E  2B7C00FC20340E1C move.l  #$FC2034,$E1C(A5)   bioskeys, standard keyboard table
FC2F16  2B7C00FC20B40E20 move.l  #$FC20B4,$E20(A5)   Standard table
FC2F1E  2B7C00FC21340E24 move.l  #$FC2134,$E24(A5)   Shift table
FC2F26  4E75            rts                          Caps Lock table
```

```
*****************************************************
FC2F28  202D0E44       move.l   $E44(A5),D0    dosound, start sound
FC2F2C  222F0004       move.l   4(A7),D1       Get sound status
FC2F30  6B08           bmi      $FC2F3A        Address of the sound table
FC2F32  2B410E44       move.l   D1,$E44(A5)    Don't set
FC2F36  422D0E48       clr.b    $E48(A5)       New sound table
FC2F3A  4E75           rts                     Start sound timer

*****************************************************
FC2F3C  302D0E4A       move.w   $E4A(A5),D0    setprt, set/get printer configuration
FC2F40  4A6F0004       tst.w    4(A7)          Old printer configuration
FC2F44  6B06           bmi      $FC2F4C        New value negative?
FC2F46  3B6F00040E4A   move.w   4(A7),$E4A(A5) Yes, don't set
FC2F4C  4E75           rts                     Set new value

*****************************************************
FC2F4E  302D0E3C       move.w   $E3C(A5),D0    kbrate, set/get keyboard repeat
FC2F52  4A6F0004       tst.w    4(A7)          Delay before key repeat
FC2F56  6B16           bmi      $FC2F6E        new value negative?
FC2F58  322F0004       move.w   4(A7),D1       Yes, don't set
FC2F5C  1B410E3C       move.b   D1,$E3C(A5)    Get new value
FC2F60  4A6F0006       tst.w    6(A7)          and save
FC2F64  6B08           bmi      $FC2F6E        Repeat rate
FC2F66  322F0006       move.w   6(A7),D1       Negative, don't set
FC2F6A  1B410E3D       move.b   D1,$E3D(A5)    Get new value
FC2F6E  4E75           rts                     and save

*****************************************************
FC2F70  203C00000DCC   move.l   #$DCC,D0       ikbdvecs, pointer to IKBD + MIDI vectors
FC2F76  4E75           rts                     Address of the vector table
```

```
************************************************  timercint, timer C interrupt
FC2F78  52B90000004BA   addq.l  #1,$4BA             _hz_200, increment 200 Hz counter
FC2F7E  E7F900000E42    rol.w   $E42                Rotate bit map
FC2F84  6A4E            bpl     $FC2FD4             Not fourth interrupt, then done
FC2F86  48E7FFFE        movem.l D0-D7/A0-A6,-(A7)   Save registers
FC2F8A  4BF900000000    lea     $0,A5               Clear A5
FC2F90  614C            bsr     $FC2FDE             Process sound
FC2F92  082D00010484    btst    #1,$484(A5)         conterm, key repeat enabled ?
FC2F98  672A            beq     $FC2FC4             No
FC2F9A  4A2D0E39        tst.b   $E39(A5)            Key pressed ?
FC2F9E  6724            beq     $FC2FC4             No
FC2FA0  4A2D0E3A        tst.b   $E3A(A5)            Counter for start delay
FC2FA4  6706            beq     $FC2FAC             Not active
FC2FA6  532D0E3A        subq.b  #1,$E3A(A5)         decrement counter
FC2FAA  6618            bne     $FC2FC4             Not run out?
FC2FAC  532D0E3B        subq.b  #1,$E3B(A5)         Decrement counter for repeat rate
FC2FB0  6612            bne     $FC2FC4             Not run out?
FC2FB2  1B6D0E3D0E3B    move.b  $E3D(A5),$E3B(A5)   Reload counter
FC2FB8  102D0E39        move.b  $E39(A5),D0         Key to repeat
FC2FBC  41ED0DB0        lea     $DB0(A5),A0         Pointer to iorec keyboard
FC2FC0  6100FACE        bsr     $FC2A90             Key code in keyboard buffer
FC2FC4  3F2D0442        move.w  $442(A5),-(A7)      _timer_ms
FC2FC8  206D0400        move.l  $400(A5),A0         etv_timer
FC2FCC  4E90            jsr     (A0)                Execute routine
FC2FCE  544F            addq.w  #2,A7               Correct stack pointer
FC2FD0  4CDF7FFF        movem.l (A7)+,D0-D7/A0-A6   Restore register
FC2FD4  08B90005FFFFFA11 bclr   #5,$FFFFFA11        Clear interrupt service bit
FC2FDC  4E73            rte

************************************************  sndirq, sound interrupt routine
FC2FDE  48E7C080        movem.l D0-D1/A0,-(A7)      Save registers
FC2FE2  202D0E44        move.l  $E44(A5),D0         Pointer to sound table
```

```
FC2FE6  67000088         beq      $FC3070              No sound active?
FC2FEA  2040             move.l   D0,A0                Pointer to A0
FC2FEC  102D0E48         move.b   $E48(A5),D0          Load timer value
FC2FF0  6708             beq      $FC2FFA              New sound started?
FC2FF2  5300             subq.b   #1,D0                Else decrement timer
FC2FF4  1B400E48         move.b   D0,$E48(A5)          and store again
FC2FF8  6076             bra      $FC3070              Done
FC2FFA  1018             move.b   (A0)+,D0             Get sound command
FC2FFC  6B2E             bmi      $FC302C              Bit 7 set, special command
FC2FFE  13C0FFFF8800     move.b   D0,$FFFF8800         Select register in sound chip
FC3004  0C000007         cmp.b    #7,D0                Mixer ?
FC3008  661A             bne      $FC3024              No
FC300A  1218             move.b   (A0)+,D1             Data for mixer
FC300C  0201003F         and.b    #$3F,D1              Isolate bits 0-5
FC3010  1039FFFF8800     move.b   $FFFF8800,D0         Read mixer
FC3016  020000C0         and.b    #$C0,D0              Isolate bits 6-7
FC301A  8001             or.b     D1,D0                OR with sound data
FC301C  13C0FFFF8802     move.b   D0,$FFFF8802         and write in register
FC3022  60D6             bra      $FC2FFA              Next sound command
FC3024  13D8FFFF8800     move.b   (A0)+,$FFFF8800      Write byte directly in sound chip
FC302A  60CE             bra      $FC2FFA              Next sound command
FC302C  5200             addq.b   #1,D0                Was command $FF ?
FC302E  6A32             bpl      $FC3062              Yes
FC3030  0C000081         cmp.b    #$81,D0              Was command $80 ?
FC3034  6606             bne      $FC303C              No
FC3036  1B580E49         move.b   (A0)+,$E49(A5)       Save byte for later
FC303A  60BE             bra      $FC2FFA              Next sound command
FC303C  0C000082         cmp.b    #$82,D0              Was command $81 ?
FC3040  6620             bne      $FC3062              No
FC3042  13D8FFFF8800     move.b   (A0)+,$FFFF8800      Select register
FC3048  1018             move.b   (A0)+,D0             Increment value
FC304A  D12D0E49         add.b    D0,$E49(A5)          Add
```

```
FC304E 1018              move.b   (A0)+,D0              End value
FC3050 13ED0E49FFFF8802  move.b   $E49(A5),$FFFF8802    Write temp value in sound chip
FC3058 B02D0E49          cmp.b    $E49(A5),D0           End value reached?
FC305C 670E              beq      $FC306C               Yes
FC305E 5948              subq.w   #4,A0                 Sound back to same command
FC3060 600A              bra      $FC306C
FC3062 1B580E48          move.b   (A0)+,$E48(A5)        Next value as delay timer
FC3066 6604              bne      $FC306C
FC3068 307C0000          move.w   #0,A0                 Clear sound pointer
FC306C 2B480E44          move.l   A0,$E44(A5)           Save current sound pointer
FC3070 4CDF0103          movem.l  (A7)+,D0-D1/A0        Restore registers
FC3074 4E75              rts

*******************************************   bellsnd, sound for CTRL G

FC3076 0034              dc.b     0,$34
FC3078 0100              dc.b     1,0
FC307A 0200              dc.b     2,0
FC307C 0300              dc.b     3,0
FC307E 0400              dc.b     4,0
FC3080 0500              dc.b     5,0
FC3082 0600              dc.b     6,0
FC3084 07FE              dc.b     7,$FE
FC3086 0810              dc.b     8,10
FC3088 0900              dc.b     9,0
FC308A 0A00              dc.b     10,0
FC308C 0B00              dc.b     11,0
FC308E 0C10              dc.b     12,16
FC3090 0D09              dc.b     13,9
FC3092 FF00              dc.b     $FF,0
```

```
*****************************************  keyclick, sound on key click
FC3094 003B         dc.b    0,$3B
FC3096 0100         dc.b    1,0
FC3098 0200         dc.b    2,0
FC309A 0300         dc.b    3,0
FC309C 0400         dc.b    4,0
FC309E 0500         dc.b    5,0
FC30A0 0600         dc.b    6,0
FC30A2 07FE         dc.b    7,$FE
FC30A4 0810         dc.b    8,16
FC30A6 0D03         dc.b    13,3
FC30A8 0B80         dc.b    11,$80
FC30AA 0C01         dc.b    12,1
FC30AC FF00         dc.b    $FF,0

*****************************************  prtblk, hardcopy
FC30AE 4E560000     link    A6,#0
FC30B2 48E7070C     movem.l D5-D7/A4-A5,-(A7)   Save registers
FC30B6 2A6E0008     move.l  8(A6),A5            Address of the parameter block
FC30BA 287C000029BE move.l  #$29BE,A4           Address of the working memory
FC30C0 7E1E         moveq.l #30,D7              30 bytes
FC30C2 6004         bra     $FC30C8
FC30C4 18DD         move.b  (A5)+,(A4)+         Copy parameters in working memory
FC30C6 5347         subq.w  #1,D7
FC30C8 4A47         tst.w   D7
FC30CA 6EF8         bgt     $FC30C4
FC30CC 0C790001000029D6 cmp.w #1,$29D6          Next byte
FC30D4 630E         bls     $FC30E4             p_port
FC30D6 33FCFFFF000004EE move.w #-1,$4EE         0 or 1 ?
FC30DE 70FF         moveq.l #-1,D0              Clear _dumpflg
FC30E0 60000F6C     bra     $FC404E             Flag for error
                                                Terminate
```

Address	Bytes	Instruction	Operands	Comment
FC30E4	4A7900002 9D6	tst.w	$29D6	p_port
FC30EA	6704	beq		Centronics ?
FC30EC	4240	clr.w	D0	0 = RS 232
FC30EE	6002	bra	$FC30F2	
FC30F0	7001	moveq.l	#1,D0	1 = Centronics
FC30F2	13C00000 29BC	move.b	D0,$29BC	Save printer port
FC30F8	4A7900002 9C6	tst.w	$29C6	p_height
FC30FE	6654	bne	$FC3154	Not zero?
FC3100	6032	bra	$FC3134	Else just dump p_width bytes
FC3102	0C790001 000004EE	cmp.w	#1,$4EE	_dumpflg to one?
FC310A	663A	bne	$FC3146	Terminate hardcopy?
FC310C	20790000 29BE	move.l	$29BE,A0	p_blkptr, screen address
FC3112	1010	move.b	(A0),D0	Get byte
FC3114	4880	ext.w	D0	
FC3116	3E80	move.w	D0,(A7)	on the stack
FC3118	61000F3E	bsr	$FC4058	Output character
FC311C	52B90000 29BE	addq.l	#1,$29BE	Increment p_blkptr
FC3122	4A40	tst.w	D0	Output OK ?
FC3124	670E	beq	$FC3134	Yes
FC3126	33FCFFFF 000004EE	move.w	#-1,$4EE	Clear _dumpflg
FC312C	70FF	moveq.l	#-1,D0	Flag for error
FC3130	60000F1C	bra	$FC404E	Terminate
FC3134	4240	clr.w	D0	
FC3136	30390000 29C4	move.w	$29C4,D0	p_width
FC313C	53790000 29C4	subq.w	#1,$29C4	Decrement p_width
FC3142	4A40	tst.w	D0	Not zero yet?
FC3144	66BC	bne	$FC3102	Output next character
FC3146	33FCFFFF 000004EE	move.w	#-1,$4EE	Clear _dumpflg
FC314E	4240	clr.w	D0	OK
FC3150	60000EFC	bra	$FC404E	Terminate

```
FC3154  0C790003000029D4    cmp.w    #3,$29D4      p_type
FC315C  630E                bls      $FC316C       OK ?
FC315E  33FCFFFF000004EE    move.w   #-1,$4EE      Clear _dumpflg
FC3166  70FF                moveq.l  #-1,D0        Flag for error
FC3168  60000EE4            bra      $FC404E       Terminate

FC316C  0C790001000029CE    cmp.w    #1,$29CE      p_destres, printer resolution
FC3174  630E                bls      $FC3184       OK ?
FC3176  33FCFFFF000004EE    move.w   #-1,$4EE      Clear _dumpflg
FC317E  70FF                moveq.l  #-1,D0        Flag for error
FC3180  60000ECC            bra      $FC404E       Terminate

FC3184  0C790002000029CC    cmp.w    #2,$29CC      p_srcres, screen resolution
FC318C  630E                bls      $FC319C       OK ?
FC318E  33FCFFFF000004EE    move.w   #-1,$4EE      Clear _dumpflg
FC3196  70FF                moveq.l  #-1,D0        Flag for error
FC3198  60000EB4            bra      $FC404E       Terminate

FC319C  0C790007000029C2    cmp.w    #7,$29C2      p_offset
FC31A4  630E                bls      $FC31B4       OK ?
FC31A6  33FCFFFF000004EE    move.w   #-1,$4EE      Clear _dumpflg
FC31AE  70FF                moveq.l  #-1,D0        Flag for error
FC31B0  60000E9C            bra      $FC404E       Terminate

FC31B4  4A79000029CC        tst.w    $29CC         p_srcres, screen resolution
FC31BA  6704                beq      $FC31C0       Low resolution ?
FC31BC  4240                clr.w    D0
FC31BE  6002                bra      $FC31C2
FC31C0  7001                moveq.l  #1,D0
FC31C2  13C00000609A        move.b   D0,$609A      Flag for low resolution
FC31C8  0C790001000029CC    cmp.w    #1,$29CC      p_srcres, screen resolution
FC31D0  6704                beq      $FC31D6       Medium resolution ?
```

```
FC31D2  4240              clr.w    D0
FC31D4  6002              bra      $FC31D8
FC31D6  7001              moveq.l  #1,D0                Flag for medium resolution
FC31D8  13C000005FE4      move.b   D0,$5FE4             p_srcres, screen resolution
FC31DE  0C7900020000029CC cmp.w    #2,$29CC             High resolution ?
FC31E6  6704              beq      $FC31EC
FC31E8  4240              clr.w    D0
FC31EA  6002              bra      $FC31EE
FC31EC  7001              moveq.l  #1,D0                Flag for high resolution
FC31EE  13C000005FE6      move.b   D0,$5FE6             p_destres, printer resolution
FC31F4  4A79000029CE      tst.w    $29CE                Test mode?
FC31FA  6704              beq      $FC3200              Quality mode
FC31FC  4240              clr.w    D0
FC31FE  6002              bra      $FC3202
FC3200  7001              moveq.l  #1,D0                Flag for mode
FC3202  13C000005FFE      move.b   D0,$5FFE             p_type, ATARI color dot-matrix printer?
FC3208  0C7900010000029D4 cmp.w    #1,$29D4
FC3210  6704              beq      $FC3216              Yes
FC3212  4240              clr.w    D0
FC3214  6002              bra      $FC3218
FC3216  7001              moveq.l  #1,D0                Flag for ATARI color dot-matrix printer
FC3218  13C00000575E      move.b   D0,$575E             p_type, ATARI daisy-wheel printer?
FC321E  0C7900020000029D4 cmp.w    #2,$29D4
FC3226  6704              beq      $FC322C
FC3228  4240              clr.w    D0
FC322A  6002              bra      $FC322E
FC322C  7001              moveq.l  #1,D0                Flag for ATARI daisy-wheel printer
FC322E  13C00000609C      move.b   D0,$609C             p_type, Epson B/W dot-matrix printer?
FC3234  0C7900030000029D4 cmp.w    #3,$29D4
FC323C  6704              beq      $FC3242              Yes
FC323E  4240              clr.w    D0                   Else ATARI B/W matrix printer
FC3240  6002              bra      $FC3244
```

```
FC3242  7001                  moveq.l  #1,D0                Flag for Epson B/W dot matrix printer
FC3244  13C000005780          move.b   D0,$5780             ATARI daisy wheel?
FC324A  4A390000609C          tst.b    $609C
FC3250  670E                  beq      $FC3260              No
FC3252  33FCFFFF000004EE      move.w   #-1,$4EE             Clear _dumpflg
FC325A  70FF                  moveq.l  #-1,D0               Flag for error
FC325C  60000DF0              bra      $FC404E              Terminate

FC3260  4A3900005780          tst.b    $5780                Epson B/W dot-matrix?
FC3266  670C                  beq      $FC3274              No
FC3268  4A3900005FFE          tst.b    $5FFE                Quality mode?
FC326E  6604                  bne      $FC3274              No
FC3270  7001                  moveq.l  #1,D0
FC3272  6008                  bra      $FC327C
FC3274  103900005FFE          move.b   $5FFE,D0
FC327A  4880                  ext.w    D0                   Quality mode
FC327C  13C000005FFE          move.b   D0,$5FFE             Quality mode
FC3282  4A390000609A          tst.b    $609A                Low resolution ?
FC3288  6726                  beq      $FC32B0              No
FC328A  0C7901400000029C4     cmp.w    #320,$29C4           p_width
FC3292  631C                  bls      $FC32B0
FC3294  4240                  clr.w    D0
FC3296  303900000029C4        move.w   $29C4,D0             p_width
FC329C  D07CFEC0              add.w    #-320,D0
FC32A0  D179000029CA          add.w    D0,$29CA             p_right
FC32A6  33FC01400000029C4     move.w   #320,$29C4           p_width
FC32AE  6024                  bra      $FC32D4
FC32B0  0C7902800000029C4     cmp.w    #640,$29C4           p_width
FC32B8  631A                  bls      $FC32D4
FC32BA  4240                  clr.w    D0
FC32BC  303900000029C4        move.w   $29C4,D0             p_width
FC32C2  D07CFD80              add.w    #-640,D0
```

```
FC32C6  D179000029CA              add.w    D0,$29CA              p_right
FC32CC  33FC028000029C4           move.w   #640,$29C4            p_width
FC32D4  4AB9000029D8              tst.l    $29D8                 p_masks, half-tone mask
FC32DA  6614                      bne      $FC32F0
FC32DC  23FC00FD1BAC000029D8      move.l   #$FD1BAC,$29D8        Use default mask
FC32E6  13FC000100004DBA          move.b   #1,$4DBA
FC32EE  6006                      bra      $FC32F6
FC32F0  4239000004DBA             clr.b    $4DBA
FC32F6  4A3900005FE6              tst.b    $5FE6                 High resolution ?
FC32FC  6718                      beq      $FC3316               No
FC32FE  2079000029D0              move.l   $29D0,A0              p_colpal
FC3304  4240                      clr.w    D0
FC3306  3010                      move.w   (A0),D0               Get color
FC3308  C07C0001                  and.w    #1,D0
FC330C  33C00000608C              move.w   D0,$608C
FC3312  60000290                  bra      $FC35A4
FC3316  4247                      clr.w    D7                    Clear counter for running color
FC3318  60000282                  bra      $FC359C               To loop end

FC331C  2079000029D0              move.l   $29D0,A0              colpal, address of color palette
FC3322  4240                      clr.w    D0
FC3324  3010                      move.w   (A0),D0               Get color
FC3326  C07C0777                  and.w    #$777,D0              Mask irrelevant bits
FC332A  33C000000574A             move.w   D0,$574A              Mask color
FC3330  54B9000029D0              addq.l   #2,$29D0              Poiner to next color
FC3336  0C790777000574A           cmp.w    #$777,$574A           Color equals white?
FC333E  67000230                  beq      $FC3570               Yes
FC3342  30390000574A              move.w   $574A,D0              Load color
FC3348  C07C0007                  and.w    #7,D0                 Isolate blue level
FC334C  33C000004150              move.w   D0,$4150              And save
FC3352  30390000574A              move.w   $574A,D0              Load color
FC3358  E840                      asr.w    #4,D0
```

399

```
FC335A C07C0007        and.w    #7,D0              Isolate green level
FC335E 33C000005FE8    move.w   D0,$5FE8           and save
FC3364 303900000574A   move.w   $574A,D0           Load color
FC336A E040            asr.w    #8,D0
FC336C C07C0007        and.w    #7,D0              Isolate red level
FC3370 33C000005624    move.w   D0,$5624           and save
FC3376 4A390000575E    tst.b    $575E              ATARI color dot-matrix printer?
FC337C 670001A0        beq      $FC351E            No
FC3380 3047            move.w   D7,A0
FC3382 D1C8            add.l    A0,A0
FC3384 D1FC00005760    add.l    #$5760,A0
FC338A 30B900005624    move.w   $5624,(A0)
FC3390 3047            move.w   D7,A0
FC3392 D1C8            add.l    A0,A0
FC3394 227C00005760    move.l   #$5760,A1
FC339A 30309800        move.w   0(A0,A1.1),D0
FC339E B07900005FE8    cmp.w    $5FE8,D0
FC33A4 6C08            bge      $FC33AE            Red level
FC33A6 303900005FE8    move.w   $5FE8,D0
FC33AC 600E            bra      $FC33BC
FC33AE 3047            move.w   D7,A0
FC33B0 D1C8            add.l    A0,A0
FC33B2 227C00005760    move.l   #$5760,A1
FC33B8 30309800        move.w   0(A0,A1.1),D0
FC33BC 3247            move.w   D7,A1
FC33BE D3C9            add.l    A1,A1
FC33C0 D3FC00005760    add.l    #$5760,A1          Green level
FC33C6 3280            move.w   D0,(A1)
FC33C8 3047            move.w   D7,A0
FC33CA D1C8            add.l    A0,A0
FC33CC 227C00005760    move.l   #$5760,A1          Green level
FC33D2 30309800        move.w   0(A0,A1.1),D0
```

```
FC33D6 B07900004150        cmp.w    $4150,D0            Blue level
FC33DC 6C08                bge      $FC33E6
FC33DE 30390004150         move.w   $4150,D0            Blue level
FC33E4 600E                bra      $FC33F4
FC33E6 3047                move.w   D7,A0
FC33E8 D1C8                add.l    A0,A0
FC33EA 227C00005760        move.l   #$5760,A1
FC33F0 30309800            move.w   0(A0,A1.1),D0
FC33F4 3247                move.w   D7,A1
FC33F6 D3C9                add.l    A1,A1
FC33F8 D3FC00005760        add.l    #$5760,A1
FC33FE 3280                move.w   D0,(A1)
FC3400 3047                move.w   D7,A0
FC3402 D1C8                add.l    A0,A0
FC3404 D1FC00005760        add.l    #$5760,A0
FC340A 5250                addq.w   #1,(A0)
FC340C 3047                move.w   D7,A0
FC340E D1C8                add.l    A0,A0
FC3410 D1FC00006002        add.l    #$6002,A0           Red level
FC3416 30B900005624        move.w   $5624,(A0)
FC341C 3047                move.w   D7,A0
FC341E D1C8                add.l    A0,A0
FC3420 227C00006002        move.l   #$6002,A1
FC3426 30309800            move.w   0(A0,A1.1),D0
FC342A B07900005FE8        cmp.w    $5FE8,D0            Green level
FC3430 6F08                ble      $FC343A
FC3432 30390005FE8         move.w   $5FE8,D0            Green level
FC3438 600E                bra      $FC3448
FC343A 3047                move.w   D7,A0
FC343C D1C8                add.l    A0,A0
FC343E 227C00006002        move.l   #$6002,A1
FC3444 30309800            move.w   0(A0,A1.1),D0
```

```
FC3448  3247              move.w   D7,A1
FC344A  D3C9              add.l    A1,A1
FC344C  D3FC00006002      add.l    #$6002,A1
FC3452  3280              move.w   D0,(A1)
FC3454  3047              move.w   D7,A0
FC3456  D1C8              add.l    A0,A0
FC3458  227C00006002      move.l   #$6002,A1
FC345E  30309800          move.w   0(A0,A1.1),D0
FC3462  B0790004150       cmp.w    $4150,D0           Green level
FC3468  6F08              ble      $FC3472
FC346A  30390004150       move.w   $4150,D0           Green level
FC3470  600E              bra      $FC3480
FC3472  3047              move.w   D7,A0
FC3474  D1C8              add.l    A0,A0
FC3476  227C00006002      move.l   #$6002,A1
FC347C  30309800          move.w   0(A0,A1.1),D0
FC3480  3247              move.w   D7,A1
FC3482  D3C9              add.l    A1,A1
FC3484  D3FC00006002      add.l    #$6002,A1
FC348A  3280              move.w   D0,(A1)
FC348C  30390005624       move.w   $5624,D0           Red level
FC3492  3247              move.w   D7,A1
FC3494  D3C9              add.l    A1,A1
FC3496  D3FC00006002      add.l    #$6002,A1
FC349C  3211              move.w   (A1),D1
FC349E  5241              addq.w   #1,D1
FC34A0  9041              sub.w    D1,D0
FC34A2  6E04              bgt      $FC34A8
FC34A4  4240              clr.w    D0
FC34A6  6002              bra      $FC34AA
FC34A8  7001              moveq.l  #1,D0
FC34AA  33C000005624      move.w   D0,$5624           Red level
```

```
FC34B0  30390005FE8    move.w   $5FE8,D0         Green level
FC34B6  3247           move.w   D7,A1
FC34B8  D3C9           add.l    A1,A1
FC34BA  D3FC00006002   add.l    #$6002,A1
FC34C0  3211           move.w   (A1),D1
FC34C2  5241           addq.w   #1,D1
FC34C4  9041           sub.w    D1,D0
FC34C6  6E04           bgt      $FC34CC
FC34C8  4240           clr.w    D0
FC34CA  6002           bra      $FC34CE
FC34CC  7001           moveq.l  #1,D0
FC34CE  33C000005FE8   move.w   D0,$5FE8         Green level
FC34D4  30390004150    move.w   $4150,D0         Blue level
FC34DA  3247           move.w   D7,A1
FC34DC  D3C9           add.l    A1,A1
FC34DE  D3FC00006002   add.l    #$6002,A1
FC34E4  3211           move.w   (A1),D1
FC34E6  5241           addq.w   #1,D1
FC34E8  9041           sub.w    D1,D0
FC34EA  6E04           bgt      $FC34F0
FC34EC  4240           clr.w    D0
FC34EE  6002           bra      $FC34F2
FC34F0  7001           moveq.l  #1,D0
FC34F2  33C000004150   move.w   D0,$4150         Blue level
FC34F8  30390005624    move.w   $5624,D0         Red level
FC34FE  E540           asl.w    #2,D0            times 4
FC3500  32390005FE8    move.w   $5FE8,D1         Green level
FC3506  E341           asl.w    #1,D1            times 2
FC3508  D041           add.w    D1,D0            Add to red level
FC350A  D0790004150    add.w    $4150,D0         Add blue level
FC3510  3247           move.w   D7,A1
FC3512  D3C9           add.l    A1,A1
```

```
FC3514 D3FC00005628   add.l    #$5628,A1
FC351A 3280           move.w   D0,(A1)
FC351C 6050           bra      $FC356E
FC351E 30390000562 4  move.w   $5624,D0       Red level
FC3524 C1FC001E       muls.w   #$1E,D0        times 30, weighting 30 %
FC3528 323900005FE8   move.w   $5FE8,D1       Green level
FC352E C3FC003B       muls.w   #$3B,D1        times 59, weighting 59 %
FC3532 D041           add.w    D1,D0
FC3534 323900004150   move.w   $4150,D1       Blue level
FC353A C3FC000B       muls.w   #$B,D1         times 11, weighting 11 %
FC353E D041           add.w    D1,D0
FC3540 48C0           ext.l    D0
FC3542 81FC0064       divs.w   #$64,D0        divided by 100, scaling
FC3546 3247           move.w   D7,A1
FC3548 D3C9           add.l    A1,A1
FC354A D3FC00006002   add.l    #$6002,A1
FC3550 3280           move.w   D0,(A1)
FC3552 3047           move.w   D7,A0
FC3554 D1C8           add.l    A0,A0
FC3556 D1FC00005628   add.l    #$5628,A0
FC355C 30BC0007       move.w   #7,(A0)
FC3560 3047           move.w   D7,A0
FC3562 D1C8           add.l    A0,A0
FC3564 D1FC00005760   add.l    #$5760,A0
FC356A 30BC0008       move.w   #8,(A0)
FC356E 602A           bra      $FC359A
FC3570 3047           move.w   D7,A0
FC3572 D1C8           add.l    A0,A0
FC3574 D1FC00006002   add.l    #$6002,A0
FC357A 30BC0008       move.w   #8,(A0)
FC357E 3047           move.w   D7,A0
FC3580 D1C8           add.l    A0,A0
```

```
FC3582  D1FC00005628    add.l    #$5628,A0
FC3588  30BC0007        move.w   #7,(A0)
FC358C  3047            move.w   D7,A0
FC358E  D1C8            add.l    A0,A0
FC3590  D1FC00005760    add.l    #$5760,A0
FC3596  30BC0008        move.w   #8,(A0)
FC359A  5247            addq.w   #1,D7             Next color
FC359C  BE7C0010        cmp.w    #$10,D7           16 colors?
FC35A0  6D00FD7A        blt      $FC331C           No, next color
FC35A4  4A390000609A    tst.b    $609A             Low resolution ?
FC35AA  6716            beq      $FC35C2           No
FC35AC  7004            moveq.l  #4,D0             Four points per screen point
FC35AE  33C000006022    move.w   D0,$6022
FC35B4  33C000005FF8    move.w   D0,$5FF8
FC35BA  33C000056F8     move.w   D0,$56F8
FC35C0  6038            bra      $FC35FA
FC35C2  4A3900005FE4    tst.b    $5FE4             Medium resolution ?
FC35C8  6718            beq      $FC35E2           No
FC35CA  7002            moveq.l  #2,D0             2 points per screen point
FC35CC  33C000006022    move.w   D0,$6022
FC35D2  33C000056F8     move.w   D0,$56F8
FC35D8  33FC000400005FF8 move.w  #4,$5FF8
FC35E0  6018            bra      $FC35FA
FC35E2  33FC0001000056F8 move.w  #1,$56F8
FC35EA  33FC000800005FF8 move.w  #8,$5FF8
FC35F2  33FC000200006022 move.w  #2,$6022
FC35FA  4A3900005780    tst.b    $5780             Epson B/W dot matrix printer?
FC3600  6706            beq      $FC3608           No
FC3602  3F3C0002        move.w   #2,-(A7)
FC3606  6004            bra      $FC360C
FC3608  3F3C0001        move.w   #1,-(A7)
FC360C  303900006022    move.w   $6022,D0
```

405

```
FC3612  48C0                  ext.l    D0
FC3614  81DF                  divs.w   (A7)+,D0
FC3616  33C000006022          move.w   D0,$6022
FC361C  4240                  clr.w    D0
FC361E  303900002 9C8         move.w   $29C8,D0              p_left
FC3624  D0790000 29C4         add.w    $29C4,D0              p_width
FC362A  D0790000 29CA         add.w    $29CA,D0              p_right
FC3630  C0F9000056F8          mulu.w   $56F8,D0
FC3636  E848                  lsr.w    #4,D0                 divided by 16
FC3638  33C000005626          move.w   D0,$5626
FC363E  303900005626          move.w   $5626,D0
FC3644  C1F900005FF8          muls.w   $5FF8,D0
FC364A  33C000004E10          move.w   D0,$4E10
FC3650  203900002 9BE         move.l   $29BE,D0
FC3656  C0BCFFFFFFFE          and.l    #$FFFFFFFE,D0
FC365C  23C000005648          move.l   D0,$5648
FC3662  203900002 9BE         move.l   $29BE,D0
FC3668  B0B900005648          cmp.l    $5648,D0
FC366E  660A                  bne      $FC367A
FC3670  4240                  clr.w    D0
FC3672  303900002 9C2         move.w   $29C2,D0
FC3678  600A                  bra      $FC3684
FC367A  4240                  clr.w    D0
FC367C  303900002 9C2         move.w   $29C2,D0
FC3682  5040                  addq.w   #8,D0
FC3684  33C00000574C          move.w   D0,$574C
FC368A  13FC0001000060A0      move.b   #1,$60A0
FC3692  427900001 6A8         clr.w    $16A8
FC3698  60000976              bra      $FC4010
FC369C  0C790001000004EE      cmp.w    #1,$4EE
FC36A4  6600097C              bne      $FC4022
FC36A8  4A3900004DBA          tst.b    $4DBA
```

p_blkptr, screen address
Even address
save
p_blkptr

p_offset

p_offset

_dumpflg at one?

```
FC36AE 6700018E              beq       $FC383E
FC36B2 13FC00010000041B6     move.b    #1,$41B6
FC36BA 4240                  clr.w     D0
FC36BC 30390000029C4         move.w    $29C4,D0         p_width
FC36C2 C0F900056F8           mulu.w    $56F8,D0
FC36C8 E848                  lsr.w     #4,D0
FC36CA 90790000056F8         sub.w     $56F8,D0
FC36D0 E348                  lsl.w     #1,D0
FC36D2 4840                  swap      D0
FC36D4 4240                  clr.w     D0
FC36D6 4840                  swap      D0
FC36D8 D0B900005648          add.l     $5648,D0
FC36DE 23C000005FEA          move.l    D0,$5FEA
FC36E4 700F                  moveq.l   #15,D0
FC36E6 4241                  clr.w     D1
FC36E8 32390000029C4         move.w    $29C4,D1         p_width
FC36EE C27C000F              and.w     #$F,D1
FC36F2 9041                  sub.w     D1,D0
FC36F4 33C000006028          move.w    D0,$6028
FC36FA 33F9000029C400004DBC  move.w    $29C4,$4DBC      p_width
FC3704 6000012C              bra       $FC3832
FC3708 4240                  clr.w     D0
FC370A 30390000029C6         move.w    $29C6,D0         p_height
FC3710 90790000016A8         sub.w     $16A8,D0
FC3716 4840                  swap      D0
FC3718 4240                  clr.w     D0
FC371A 4840                  swap      D0
FC371C 80F900005FF8          divu.w    $5FF8,D0
FC3722 6708                  beq       $FC372C
FC3724 30390000005FF8        move.w    $5FF8,D0
FC372A 600E                  bra       $FC373A
```

```
FC372C 4240                    clr.w    D0
FC372E 303900002906            move.w   $29C6,D0          p_height
FC3734 907900001A8             sub.w    $16A8,D0
FC373A 33C000005FE0            move.w   D0,$5FE0
FC3740 23F900005FEA00005BEC    move.l   $5FEA,$58EC
FC374A 4247                    clr.w    D7
FC374C 600000A6                bra      $FC37F4
FC3750 427900006030            clr.w    $6030
FC3756 33FC000100006024        move.w   #1,$6024
FC375E 23F900005BEC0000574E    move.l   $58EC,$574E
FC3768 4246                    clr.w    D6
FC376A 6030                    bra      $FC379C
FC376C 20790000574E            move.l   $574E,A0
FC3772 3010                    move.w   (A0),D0
FC3774 720F                    moveq.l  #15,D1
FC3776 927900006028            sub.w    $6028,D1
FC377C E260                    asr.w    D1,D0
FC377E C07C0001                and.w    #1,D0
FC3782 C1F900006024            muls.w   $6024,D0
FC3788 D17900006030            add.w    D0,$6030
FC378E 54B90000574E            addq.l   #2,$574E
FC3794 E1F900006024            asl.w    $6024
FC379A 5246                    addq.w   #1,D6
FC379C BC7900056F8              cmp.w    $56F8,D6
FC37A2 6DC8                    blt      $FC376C
FC37A4 4A3900005FE6            tst.b    $5FE6
FC37AA 671A                    beq      $FC37C6          High resolution ?
FC37AC 303900006030            move.w   $6030,D0         No
FC37B2 32390000608C            move.w   $608C,D1
FC37B8 B340                    eor.w    D1,D0
FC37BA 6608                    bne      $FC37C4
FC37BC 42390000418B6           clr.b    $41B6
```

```
FC37C2  603A                      bra       $FC37FE
FC37C4  601C                      bra       $FC37E2
FC37C6  30790000603O              move.w    $6030,A0
FC37CC  D1C8                      add.l     A0,A0
FC37CE  D1FC00006002              add.l     #$6002,A0
FC37D4  0C500008                  cmp.w     #8,(A0)
FC37D8  6708                      beq       $FC37E2
FC37DA  42390000041B6             clr.b     $41B6
FC37E0  601C                      bra       $FC37FE
FC37E2  30390005626               move.w    $5626,D0
FC37E8  E340                      asl.w     #1,D0
FC37EA  48C0                      ext.l     D0
FC37EC  D1B9000058EC              add.l     D0,$58EC
FC37F2  5247                      addq.w    #1,D7
FC37F4  BE7900005FE0              cmp.w     $5FE0,D7
FC37FA  6D00FF54                  blt       $FC3750
FC37FE  4A39000041B6              tst.b     $41B6
FC3804  6736                      beq       $FC383C
FC3806  53790006028               subq.w    #1,$6028
FC380C  4A7900006028              tst.w     $6028
FC3812  6C18                      bge       $FC382C
FC3814  30390056F8                move.w    $56F8,D0
FC381A  E340                      asl.w     #1,D0
FC381C  48C0                      ext.l     D0
FC381E  91B900005FEA              sub.l     D0,$5FEA
FC3824  33FC000F00006028          move.w    #$F,$6028
FC382C  537900004DBC              subq.w    #1,$4DBC
FC3832  4A7900004DBC              tst.w     $4DBC
FC3838  6E00FECE                  bgt       $FC3708
FC383C  600A                      bra       $FC3848
FC383E  33F9000029C400004DBC      move.w    $29C4,$4DBC      p_width
FC3848  3E3900004DBC              move.w    $4DBC,D7
```

```
FC384E  CFF900006022    muls.w  $6022,D7            Epson B/W dot-matrix printer?
FC3854  4A3900005780    tst.b   $5780
FC385A  670A            beq     $FC3866             No
FC385C  3007            move.w  D7,D0
FC385E  48C0            ext.l   D0
FC3860  81FC0002        divs.w  #2,D0
FC3864  6002            bra     $FC3868
FC3866  4240            clr.w   D0
FC3868  DE40            add.w   D0,D7
FC386A  3007            move.w  D7,D0               Number of points
FC386C  48C0            ext.l   D0
FC386E  81FC0100        divs.w  #$100,D0            divided by 256
FC3872  4840            swap    D0                  remainder
FC3874  13C000004E16    move.b  D0,$4E16            Number of points, low byte
FC387A  3007            move.w  D7,D0               Number of points
FC387C  48C0            ext.l   D0
FC387E  81FC0100        divs.w  #$100,D0            divided by 256
FC3882  13C000004E18    move.b  D0,$4E18            Number of points, high byte
FC3888  427900005782    clr.w   $5782
FC388E  6000066         bra     $FC3EE6
FC3892  427900006042    clr.w   $60A2
FC3898  600005F0        bra     $FC3E8A
FC389C  4A39000005575E  tst.b   $575E               ATARI color dot-matrix printer?
FC38A2  67000076        beq     $FC391A             No
FC38A6  4A3900005FE6    tst.b   $5FE6               High resolution ?
FC38AC  6600006C        bne     $FC391A             Yes
FC38B0  4A79000060A2    tst.w   $60A2
FC38B6  661E            bne     $FC38D6
FC38B8  2EBC00FD1BBE    move.l  #$FD1BBE,(A7)       ESC 'X', 6
FC38BE  610007E4        bsr     $FC40A4             Send string to printer
FC38C2  4A40            tst.w   D0                  Output OK?
```

```
FC38C4  670E                    beq       $FC38D4                       Yes
FC38C6  33FCFFFF000004EE        move.w    #-1,$4EE                      Clear _dumpflg
FC38CE  70FF                    moveq.l   #-1,D0                        Flag for error
FC38D0  6000077C                bra       $FC404E                       Terminate

FC38D4  6044                    bra       $FC391A

FC38D6  0C7900010000060A2       cmp.w     #1,$60A2
FC38DE  661E                    bne       $FC38FE
FC38E0  2EBC00FD1BC3            move.l    #$FD1BC3,(A7)
FC38E6  610007BC                bsr       $FC40A4                       Send string to printer
FC38EA  4A40                    tst.w     D0                            Output OK?
FC38EC  670E                    beq       $FC38FC                       Yes
FC38EE  33FCFFFF000004EE        move.w    #-1,$4EE                      Clear _dumpflg
FC38F6  70FF                    moveq.l   #-1,D0                        Flag for error
FC38F8  60000754                bra       $FC404E                       Terminate

FC38FC  601C                    bra       $FC391A

FC38FE  2EBC00FD1BC8            move.l    #$FD1BC8,(A7)                 ESC 'X', 3
FC3904  6100079E                bsr       $FC40A4                       Send string to printer
FC3908  4A40                    tst.w     D0                            Output OK?
FC390A  670E                    beq       $FC391A                       Yes
FC390C  33FCFFFF000004EE        move.w    #-1,$4EE                      Clear _dumpflg
FC3914  70FF                    moveq.l   #-1,D0                        Flag for error
FC3916  60000736                bra       $FC404E                       Terminate

FC391A  4A3900005780            tst.b     $5780                         Epson B/W dot-matrix printer?
FC3920  6708                    beq       $FC392A                       No
FC3922  2EBC00FD1BCD            move.l    #$FD1BCD,(A7)                 ESC 'L', bit image 960 dots/line
FC3928  6006                    bra       $FC3930
```

```
FC392A 2EBC00FD1BD1      move.l    #$FD1BD1,(A7)      ESC 'Y', bit image 1280 dots/line
FC3930 61000772          bsr       $FC40A4            Send string to printer
FC3934 4A40              tst.w     D0                 Output OK?
FC3936 670E              beq       $FC3946            Yes
FC3938 33FCFFFF000004EE  move.w    #-1,$4EE           Clear _dumpflg
FC3940 70FF              moveq.l   #-1,D0             Flag for error
FC3942 6000070A          bra       $FC404E            Terminate

FC3946 10390004E16       move.b    $4E16,D0           Number of points, low-byte
FC394C 4880              ext.w     D0
FC394E 3E80              move.w    D0,(A7)
FC3950 61000706          bsr       $FC4058            Output character
FC3954 4A40              tst.w     D0                 Output OK?
FC3956 670E              beq       $FC3966            Yes
FC3958 33FCFFFF000004EE  move.w    #-1,$4EE           Clear _dumpflg
FC3960 70FF              moveq.l   #-1,D0             Flag for error
FC3962 600006EA          bra       $FC404E            Terminate

FC3966 10390004E18       move.b    $4E18,D0           Number of points, high-byte
FC396C 4880              ext.w     D0
FC396E 3E80              move.w    D0,(A7)
FC3970 610006E6          bsr       $FC4058            Output character
FC3974 4A40              tst.w     D0                 Output OK?
FC3976 670E              beq       $FC3986            Yes
FC3978 33FCFFFF000004EE  move.w    #-1,$4EE           Clear _dumpflg
FC3980 70FF              moveq.l   #-1,D0             Flag for error
FC3982 600006CA          bra       $FC404E            Terminate

FC3986 13FC000100006000  move.b    #1,$6000
FC398E 23F9000056480005FEA move.l  $5648,$5FEA
FC3998 33F90000574C0006028 move.w  $574C,$6028
```

```
FC39A2  42790000016A6        clr.w   $16A6
FC39A8  600004B0             bra     $FC3E5A

FC39AC  4247                 clr.w   D7
FC39AE  600C                 bra     $FC39BC

FC39B0  3047                 move.w  D7,A0
FC39B2  D1FC00005784         add.l   #$5784,A0
FC39B8  4210                 clr.b   (A0)
FC39BA  5247                 addq.w  #1,D7
FC39BC  BE7C0008             cmp.w   #8,D7
FC39C0  6DEE                 blt     $FC39B0
FC39C2  4247                 clr.w   D7
FC39C4  601E                 bra     $FC39E4

FC39C6  3047                 move.w  D7,A0
FC39C8  D1C8                 add.l   A0,A0
FC39CA  D1FC00004E1A         add.l   #$4E1A,A0
FC39D0  30BC0007             move.w  #7,(A0)
FC39D4  3047                 move.w  D7,A0
FC39D6  D1C8                 add.l   A0,A0
FC39D8  D1FC00005FEE         add.l   #$5FEE,A0
FC39DE  30BC0008             move.w  #8,(A0)
FC39E2  5247                 addq.w  #1,D7
FC39E4  BE7C0004             cmp.w   #4,D7
FC39E8  6DDC                 blt     $FC39C6
FC39EA  4240                 clr.w   D0
FC39EC  303900002 9C6        move.w  $29C6,D0     p_height
FC39F2  907900 0016A8        sub.w   $16A8,D0
FC39F8  4840                 swap    D0
FC39FA  4240                 clr.w   D0
FC39FC  4840                 swap    D0
```

```
FC39FE  80F900005FF8           divu.w  $5FF8,D0
FC3A04  6708                   beq     $FC3A0E
FC3A06  303900005FF8           move.w  $5FF8,D0
FC3A0C  600E                   bra     $FC3A1C

FC3A0E  4240                   clr.w   D0
FC3A10  303900029C6            move.w  $29C6,D0         p_height
FC3A16  907900016A8            sub.w   $16A8,D0
FC3A1C  33C000005FE0           move.w  D0,$5FE0
FC3A22  4240                   clr.w   D0
FC3A24  303900029C6            move.w  $29C6,D0         p_height
FC3A2A  907900016A8            sub.w   $16A8,D0
FC3A30  4840                   swap    D0
FC3A32  4240                   clr.w   D0
FC3A34  4840                   swap    D0
FC3A36  80F900005FF8           divu.w  $5FF8,D0
FC3A3C  670C                   beq     $FC3A4A
FC3A3E  33F900005FF800005FE0   move.w  $5FF8,$5FE0
FC3A48  601A                   bra     $FC3A64

FC3A4A  4240                   clr.w   D0
FC3A4C  303900029C6            move.w  $29C6,D0
FC3A52  907900016A8            sub.w   $16A8,D0
FC3A58  33C000005FE0           move.w  D0,$5FE0
FC3A5E  423900060A0            clr.b   $60A0
FC3A64  23F900005FEA00058EC    move.l  $5FEA,$58EC
FC3A6E  4247                   clr.w   D7
FC3A70  6000011C               bra     $FC3B8E

FC3A74  427900006030           clr.w   $6030
FC3A7A  33FC00010006024        move.w  #1,$6024
FC3A82  23F90058EC00005748E    move.l  $58EC,$574E
```

```
FC3A8C  4246                clr.w    D6
FC3A8E  6030                bra      $FC3AC0

FC3A90  20790000574E        move.l   $574E,A0
FC3A96  3010                move.w   (A0),D0
FC3A98  720F                moveq.l  #15,D1
FC3A9A  92790000602B        sub.w    $6028,D1
FC3AA0  E260                asr.w    D1,D0
FC3AA2  C07C0001            and.w    #1,D0
FC3AA6  C1F900006024        muls.w   $6024,D0
FC3AAC  D179000006030       add.w    D0,$6030
FC3AB2  54B90000574E        addq.l   #2,$574E
FC3AB8  E1F900006024        asl.w    $6024
FC3ABE  5246                addq.w   #1,D6
FC3AC0  BC790000056F8       cmp.w    $56F8,D6
FC3AC6  6DC8                blt      $FC3A90
FC3AC8  4A3900005FE6        tst.b    $5FE6                    High resolution ?
FC3ACE  672C                beq      $FC3AFC                  No
FC3AD0  30390000 6030       move.w   $6030,D0
FC3AD6  3239000006080       move.w   $6080,D1
FC3ADC  B340                eor.w    D1,D0
FC3ADE  660C                bne      $FC3AEC
FC3AE0  207900000 29D8      move.l   $29D8,A0
FC3AE6  1010                move.b   (A0),D0
FC3AE8  4880                ext.w    D0
FC3AEA  6002                bra      $FC3AEE

FC3AEC  4240                clr.w    D0
FC3AEE  3247                move.w   D7,A1
FC3AF0  D3FC00005784        add.l    #$5784,A1                p_masks, address of half-tone mask
FC3AF6  1280                move.b   D0,(A1)
FC3AF8  60000082            bra      $FC3B7C
```

```
FC3AFC  3047              move.w  D7,A0
FC3AFE  D0C8              add.w   A0,A0
FC3B00  D1FC00005784      add.l   #$5784,A0
FC3B06  32790006030       move.w  $6030,A1
FC3B0C  D3C9              add.l   A1,A1
FC3B0E  D3FC00006002      add.l   #$6002,A1
FC3B14  3251              move.w  (A1),A1
FC3B16  D2C9              add.w   A1,A1
FC3B18  D3F9000029D8      add.l   $29D8,A1        plus p_masks
FC3B1E  1091              move.b  (A1),(A0)
FC3B20  3047              move.w  D7,A0
FC3B22  D0C8              add.w   A0,A0
FC3B24  D1FC00005784      add.l   #$5784,A0
FC3B2A  32790006030       move.w  $6030,A1
FC3B30  D3C9              add.l   A1,A1
FC3B32  D3FC00006002      add.l   #$6002,A1
FC3B38  3251              move.w  (A1),A1
FC3B3A  D2C9              add.w   A1,A1
FC3B3C  D3F9000029D8      add.l   $29D8,A1        plus p_masks
FC3B42  11690010001       move.b  1(A1),1(A0)
FC3B48  3047              move.w  D7,A0
FC3B4A  D1C8              add.l   A0,A0
FC3B4C  D1FC00004E1A      add.l   #$4E1A,A0
FC3B52  32790006030       move.w  $6030,A1
FC3B58  D3C9              add.l   A1,A1
FC3B5A  D3FC00005628      add.l   #$5628,A1
FC3B60  3091              move.w  (A1),(A0)
FC3B62  3047              move.w  D7,A0
FC3B64  D1C8              add.l   A0,A0
FC3B66  D1FC00005FEE      add.l   #$5FEE,A0
FC3B6C  32790006030       move.w  $6030,A1
FC3B72  D3C9              add.l   A1,A1
```

```
FC3B74  D3FC00005760        add.l    #$5760,A1
FC3B7A  3091                move.w   (A1),(A0)
FC3B7C  30390005626         move.w   $5626,D0
FC3B82  E340                asl.w    #1,D0
FC3B84  48C0                ext.l    D0
FC3B86  D1B90058EC          add.l    D0,$58EC
FC3B8C  5247                addq.w   #1,D7
FC3B8E  BE7900005FE0        cmp.w    $5FE0,D7
FC3B94  6D00FEDE            blt      $FC3A74
FC3B98  4A39000575E         tst.b    $575E            ATARI color dot-matrix printer?
FC3B9E  670001BE            beq      $FC3D5E          No
FC3BA2  4A3900005FE6        tst.b    $5FE6            High resolution ?
FC3BA8  660001B4            bne      $FC3D5E          Yes
FC3BAC  4247                clr.w    D7
FC3BAE  600001A4            bra      $FC3D54
FC3BB2  423900005FF6        clr.b    $5FF6
FC3BB8  4A7900060A2         tst.w    $60A2
FC3BBE  6626                bne      $FC3BE6
FC3BC0  3047                move.w   D7,A0
FC3BC2  D1C8                add.l    A0,A0
FC3BC4  227C00004E1A        move.l   #$4E1A,A1
FC3BCA  30309800            move.w   0(A0,A1.l),D0
FC3BCE  48C0                ext.l    D0
FC3BD0  81FC0002            divs.w   #2,D0
FC3BD4  4840                swap     D0
FC3BD6  4A40                tst.w    D0
FC3BD8  6708                beq      $FC3BE2
FC3BDA  13FC000100005FF6    move.b   #1,$5FF6
FC3BE2  600000F0            bra      $FC3CD4
FC3BE6  0C7900010000060A2   cmp.w    #1,$60A2
```

```
FC3BEE  6600008C            bne     $FC3C7C
FC3BF2  3047                move.w  D7,A0
FC3BF4  D1C8                add.l   A0,A0
FC3BF6  D1FC00004E1A        add.l   #$4E1A,A0
FC3BFC  0C500006            cmp.w   #6,(A0)
FC3C00  6630                bne     $FC3C32
FC3C02  3047                move.w  D7,A0
FC3C04  D1C8                add.l   A0,A0
FC3C06  D1FC00005FEE        add.l   #$5FEE,A0
FC3C0C  0C500008            cmp.w   #8,(A0)
FC3C10  6C20                bge     $FC3C32
FC3C12  3047                move.w  D7,A0
FC3C14  D0C8                add.w   A0,A0
FC3C16  D1FC00005784        add.l   #$5784,A0
FC3C1C  02100001            and.b   #1,(A0)
FC3C20  3047                move.w  D7,A0
FC3C22  D0C8                add.w   A0,A0
FC3C24  D1FC00005784        add.l   #$5784,A0
FC3C2A  02280040001         and.b   #4,1(A0)
FC3C30  6048                bra     $FC3C7A

FC3C32  3047                move.w  D7,A0
FC3C34  D1C8                add.l   A0,A0
FC3C36  D1FC00004E1A        add.l   #$4E1A,A0
FC3C3C  0C500002            cmp.w   #2,(A0)
FC3C40  6730                beq     $FC3C72
FC3C42  3047                move.w  D7,A0
FC3C44  D1C8                add.l   A0,A0
FC3C46  D1FC00004E1A        add.l   #$4E1A,A0
FC3C4C  0C500003            cmp.w   #3,(A0)
FC3C50  6720                beq     $FC3C72
FC3C52  3047                move.w  D7,A0
```

```
FC3C54 D1C8                    add.l    A0,A0
FC3C56 D1FC00004E1A            add.l    #$4E1A,A0
FC3C5C 0C500006                cmp.w    #6,(A0)
FC3C60 6710                    beq      $FC3C72
FC3C62 3047                    move.w   D7,A0
FC3C64 D1C8                    add.l    A0,A0
FC3C66 D1FC00004E1A            add.l    #$4E1A,A0
FC3C6C 0C500007                cmp.w    #7,(A0)
FC3C70 6608                    bne      $FC3C7A
FC3C72 13FC000100005FF6        move.b   #1,$5FF6
FC3C7A 6058                    bra      $FC3CD4

FC3C7C 3047                    move.w   D7,A0
FC3C7E D1C8                    add.l    A0,A0
FC3C80 D1FC00004E1A            add.l    #$4E1A,A0
FC3C86 0C500006                cmp.w    #6,(A0)
FC3C8A 6630                    bne      $FC3CBC
FC3C8C 3047                    move.w   D7,A0
FC3C8E D1C8                    add.l    A0,A0
FC3C90 D1FC00005FEE            add.l    #$5FEE,A0
FC3C96 0C500008                cmp.w    #8,(A0)
FC3C9A 6C20                    bge      $FC3CBC
FC3C9C 3047                    move.w   D7,A0
FC3C9E D0C8                    add.w    A0,A0
FC3CA0 D1FC00005784            add.l    #$5784,A0
FC3CA6 02100004                and.b    #4,(A0)
FC3CAA 3047                    move.w   D7,A0
FC3CAC D0C8                    add.w    A0,A0
FC3CAE D1FC00005784            add.l    #$5784,A0
FC3CB4 02280010001             and.b    #1,1(A0)
FC3CBA 6018                    bra      $FC3CD4
```

```
FC3CBC 3047               move.w    D7,A0
FC3CBE D1C8               add.l     A0,A0
FC3CC0 D1FC00004E1A       add.l     #$4E1A,A0
FC3CC6 0C500003           cmp.w     #3,(A0)
FC3CCA 6F08               ble       $FC3CD4
FC3CCC 13FC00010005FF6    move.b    #1,$5FF6
FC3CD4 4A3900005FF6       tst.b     $5FF6
FC3CDA 671A               beq       $FC3CF6
FC3CDC 3047               move.w    D7,A0
FC3CDE D0C8               add.w     A0,A0
FC3CE0 D1FC00005784       add.l     #$5784,A0
FC3CE6 4210               clr.b     (A0)
FC3CE8 3047               move.w    D7,A0
FC3CEA D0C8               add.w     A0,A0
FC3CEC D1FC00005784       add.l     #$5784,A0
FC3CF2 42280001           clr.b     1(A0)
FC3CF6 2079000029D8       move.l    $29D8,A0        p_masks
FC3CFC 3247               move.w    D7,A1
FC3CFE D3C9               add.l     A1,A1
FC3D00 D3FC00005FEE       add.l     #$5FEE,A1
FC3D06 3251               move.w    (A1),A1
FC3D08 D2C9               add.w     A1,A1
FC3D0A 10309000           move.b    0(A0,A1.w),D0
FC3D0E 4880               ext.w     D0
FC3D10 3F00               move.w    D0,-(A7)
FC3D12 3047               move.w    D7,A0
FC3D14 D0C8               add.w     A0,A0
FC3D16 D1FC00005784       add.l     #$5784,A0
FC3D1C 1010               move.b    (A0),D0
FC3D1E 805F               or.w      (A7)+,D0
FC3D20 1080               move.b    D0,(A0)
FC3D22 2079000029D8       move.l    $29D8,A0        p_masks
```

```
FC3D28  3247              move.w    D7,A1
FC3D2A  D3C9              add.l     A1,A1
FC3D2C  D3FC00005FEE      add.l     #$5FEE,A1
FC3D32  3251              move.w    (A1),A1
FC3D34  D2C9              add.w     A1,A1
FC3D36  10309001          move.b    1(A0,A1.w),D0
FC3D3A  4880              ext.w     D0
FC3D3C  3F00              move.w    D0,-(A7)
FC3D3E  3047              move.w    D7,A0
FC3D40  D0C8              add.w     A0,A0
FC3D42  D1FC00005784      add.l     #$5784,A0
FC3D48  10280001          move.b    1(A0),D0
FC3D4C  805F              or.w      (A7)+,D0
FC3D4E  11400001          move.b    D0,1(A0)
FC3D52  5247              addq.w    #1,D7
FC3D54  BE7900005FE0      cmp.w     $5FE0,D7
FC3D5A  6D00FE56          blt       $FC3BB2
FC3D5E  7E04              moveq.l   #4,D7
FC3D60  6000008E          bra       $FC3DF0
FC3D64  42390000414C      clr.b     $414C
FC3D6A  33FC008000006026  move.w    #$80,$6026
FC3D72  4246              clr.w     D6
FC3D74  603E              bra       $FC3DB4
FC3D76  207C00005784      move.l    #$5784,A0
FC3D7C  10306000          move.b    0(A0,D6.w),D0
FC3D80  4880              ext.w     D0
FC3D82  7207              moveq.l   #7,D1
FC3D84  9247              sub.w     D7,D1
FC3D86  E260              asr.w     D1,D0
FC3D88  C07C0001          and.w     #1,D0
```

```
FC3D8C  C1F900006026         muls.w   $6026,D0
FC3D92  12390000414C         move.b   $414C,D1
FC3D98  D200                  add.b    D0,D1
FC3D9A  13C10000414C         move.b   D1,$414C
FC3DA0  30390000602 6        move.w   $6026,D0
FC3DA6  48C0                  ext.l    D0
FC3DA8  81FC0002              divs.w   #2,D0
FC3DAC  33C000006026         move.w   D0,$6026
FC3DB2  5246                  addq.w   #1,D6
FC3DB4  BC7C0008              cmp.w    #8,D6
FC3DB8  6DBC                  blt      $FC3D76
FC3DBA  10390000414C         move.b   $414C,D0
FC3DC0  4880                  ext.w    D0
FC3DC2  3E80                  move.w   D0,(A7)
FC3DC4  61000292              bsr      $FC4058       Output character
FC3DC8  4A40                  tst.w    D0            Output OK?
FC3DCA  670E                  beq      $FC3DDA       Yes
FC3DCC  33FCFFFF000004EE     move.w   #-1,$4EE      Clear _dumpflg
FC3DD4  70FF                  moveq.l  #-1,D0        Flag for error
FC3DD6  60000276              bra      $FC404E       Terminate

FC3DDA  4A39000060 00        tst.b    $6000
FC3DE0  6704                  beq      $FC3DE6
FC3DE2  4240                  clr.w    D0
FC3DE4  6002                  bra      $FC3DE8

FC3DE6  7001                  moveq.l  #1,D0
FC3DE8  13C000006000         move.b   D0,$6000
FC3DEE  5247                  addq.w   #1,D7
FC3DF0  30390000602 2        move.w   $6022,D0
FC3DF6  5840                  addq.w   #4,D0
FC3DF8  BE40                  cmp.w    D0,D7
```

```
FC3DFA  6D00FF68              blt       $FC3D64
FC3DFE  4A3900005780          tst.b     $5780              Epson B/W dot-matrix printer?
FC3E04  6728                  beq       $FC3E2E            No
FC3E06  4A3900006000          tst.b     $6000
FC3E0C  6720                  beq       $FC3E2E
FC3E0E  10390000414C          move.b    $414C,D0
FC3E14  4880                  ext.w     D0
FC3E16  3E80                  move.w    D0,(A7)            Output character
FC3E18  6100023E              bsr       $FC4058            Output OK?
FC3E1C  4A40                  tst.w     D0                 Yes
FC3E1E  670E                  beq       $FC3E2E
FC3E20  33FCFFFF000004EE      move.w    #-1,$4EE           Clear _dumpflg
FC3E28  70FF                  moveq.l   #-1,D0             Flag for error
FC3E2A  60000222              bra       $FC404E            Terminate
FC3E2E  52790006028           addq.w    #1,$6028
FC3E34  0C790000F00006028     cmp.w     #15,$6028
FC3E3C  6F16                  ble       $FC3E54
FC3E3E  30390000056F8         move.w    $56F8,D0
FC3E44  E340                  asl.w     #1,D0
FC3E46  48C0                  ext.l     D0
FC3E48  D1B900005FEA          add.l     D0,$5FEA
FC3E4E  42790006028           clr.w     $6028
FC3E54  52790000016A6         addq.w    #1,$16A6
FC3E5A  30390000016A6         move.w    $16A6,D0
FC3E60  B07900004DBC          cmp.w     $4DBC,D0
FC3E66  6D00FB44              blt       $FC39AC
FC3E6A  3EBC000D              move.w    #$D,(A7)           Carriage Return
FC3E6E  610001E8              bsr       $FC4058            Output character
FC3E72  4A40                  tst.w     D0                 Output OK?
FC3E74  670E                  beq       $FC3E84            Yes
FC3E76  33FCFFFF000004EE      move.w    #-1,$4EE           Clear _dumpflg
```

```
FC3E7E  70FF                  moveq.l  #-1,D0               Flag for error
FC3E80  600001CC              bra      $FC404E              Terminate

FC3E84  527900000060A2        addq.w   #1,$60A2             ATARI color dot-matrix printer?
FC3E8A  4A390000575E          tst.b    $575E
FC3E90  670C                  beq      $FC3E9E              No
FC3E92  4A3900005FE6          tst.b    $5FE6                High resolution ?
FC3E98  6604                  bne      $FC3E9E
FC3E9A  7003                  moveq.l  #3,D0                Yes
FC3E9C  6002                  bra      $FC3EA0

FC3E9E  7001                  moveq.l  #1,D0
FC3EA0  B07900000060A2        cmp.w    $60A2,D0
FC3EA6  6E00F9F4              bgt      $FC389C
FC3EAA  2EBC00FD1BD5          move.l   #$FD1BD5,(A7)        ESC '3', 1, 1/216" line spacing
FC3EB0  610001F2              bsr      $FC40A4              Send string to printer
FC3EB4  4A40                  tst.w    D0                   Output OK?
FC3EB6  670E                  beq      $FC3EC6              Yes
FC3EB8  33FCFFFF000004EE      move.w   #-1,$4EE             Clear _dumpflg
FC3EC0  70FF                  moveq.l  #-1,D0               Flag for error
FC3EC2  6000018A              bra      $FC404E              Terminate

FC3EC6  3EBC000A              move.w   #$A,(A7)             Linefeed
FC3ECA  6100018C              bsr      $FC4058              Output character
FC3ECE  4A40                  tst.w    D0                   Output OK?
FC3ED0  670E                  beq      $FC3EE0              Yes
FC3ED2  33FCFFFF000004EE      move.w   #-1,$4EE             Clear _dumpflg
FC3EDA  70FF                  moveq.l  #-1,D0               Flag for error
FC3EDC  60000170              bra      $FC404E              Terminate

FC3EE0  527900005782          addq.w   #1,$5782             Quality mode?
FC3EE6  4A3900005FFE          tst.b    $5FFE
```

FC3EEC	6704	beq	$FC3EF2	Yes
FC3EEE	7001	moveq.l	#1,D0	
FC3EF0	6002	bra	$FC3EF4	
FC3EF2	7002	moveq.l	#2,D0	
FC3EF4	B07900005782	cmp.w	$5782,D0	Quality mode?
FC3EFA	6E00F996	bgt	$FC3892	
FC3EFE	4A3900005FFE	tst.b	$5FFE	
FC3F04	674E	beq	$FC3F54	Yes
FC3F06	4247	clr.w	D7	
FC3F08	6038	bra	$FC3F42	
FC3F0A	2EBC00FD1BDA	move.l	#$FD1BDA,(A7)	ESC '3', 1, 1/216" line spacing
FC3F10	61000192	bsr	$FC40A4	Send string to printer
FC3F14	4A40	tst.w	D0	Output OK?
FC3F16	670E	beq	$FC3F26	Yes
FC3F18	33FCFFFF000004EE	move.w	#-1,$4EE	Clear _dumpflg
FC3F20	70FF	moveq.l	#-1,D0	Flag for error
FC3F22	6000012A	bra	$FC404E	Terminate
FC3F26	3EBC000A	move.w	#$A,(A7)	Linefeed
FC3F2A	6100012C	bsr	$FC4058	Output character
FC3F2E	4A40	tst.w	D0	Output OK?
FC3F30	670E	beq	$FC3F40	Yes
FC3F32	33FCFFFF000004EE	move.w	#-1,$4EE	Clear _dumpflg
FC3F3A	70FF	moveq.l	#-1,D0	Flag for error
FC3F3C	60000110	bra	$FC404E	Terminate
FC3F40	5247	addq.w	#1,D7	
FC3F42	4A3900005780	tst.b	$5780	Epson B/W dot-matrix printer?
FC3F48	6704	beq	$FC3F4E	No

```
FC3F4A  7002                    moveq.l  #2,D0
FC3F4C  6002                    bra      $FC3F50

FC3F4E  7001                    moveq.l  #1,D0
FC3F50  BE40                    cmp.w    D0,D7
FC3F52  6DB6                    blt      $FC3F0A
FC3F54  4A39000060A0            tst.b    $60A0
FC3F5A  6738                    beq      $FC3F94
FC3F5C  2EBC00FD1BDF            move.l   #$FD1BDF,(A7)   ESC '1', 7/72" line spacing
FC3F62  61000140                bsr      $FC40A4         Send string to printer
FC3F66  4A40                    tst.w    D0              Output OK?
FC3F68  670E                    beq      $FC3F78         Yes
FC3F6A  33FCFFFF000004EE        move.w   #-1,$4EE        Clear _dumpflg
FC3F72  70FF                    moveq.l  #-1,D0          Flag for error
FC3F74  600000D8                bra      $FC404E         Terminate

FC3F78  3EBC000A                move.w   #$A,(A7)        Linefeed
FC3F7C  610000DA                bsr      $FC4058         Output character
FC3F80  4A40                    tst.w    D0              Output OK?
FC3F82  670E                    beq      $FC3F92         Yes
FC3F84  33FCFFFF000004EE        move.w   #-1,$4EE        Clear _dumpflg
FC3F8C  70FF                    moveq.l  #-1,D0          Flag for error
FC3F8E  600000BE                bra      $FC404E         Terminate

FC3F92  6060                    bra      $FC3FF4

FC3F94  4247                    clr.w    D7
FC3F96  6038                    bra      $FC3FD0

FC3F98  2EBC00FD1BE3            move.l   #$FD1BE3,(A7)   ESC '3', 1, 1/216" line spacing
FC3F9E  61000104                bsr      $FC40A4         Send string to printer
```

```
FC3FA2  4A40                    tst.w     D0                  Output OK?
FC3FA4  670E                    beq       $FC3FB4             Yes
FC3FA6  33FCFFFF000004EE        move.w    #-1,$4EE            Clear _dumpflg
FC3FAE  70FF                    moveq.l   #-1,D0              Flag for error
FC3FB0  6000009C                bra       $FC404E             Terminate

FC3FB4  3EBC000A                move.w    #$A,(A7)            Linefeed
FC3FB8  6100009E                bsr       $FC4058             Output character
FC3FBC  4A40                    tst.w     D0                  Output OK?
FC3FBE  670E                    beq       $FC3FCE             Yes
FC3FC0  33FCFFFF000004EE        move.w    #-1,$4EE            Clear _dumpflg
FC3FC8  70FF                    moveq.l   #-1,D0              Flag for error
FC3FCA  60000082                bra       $FC404E             Terminate

FC3FCE  5247                    addq.w    #1,D7
FC3FD0  4A3900005780            tst.b     $5780               Epson B/W dot-matrix printer?
FC3FD6  670E                    beq       $FC3FE6             No
FC3FD8  303900005FE0            move.w    $5FE0,D0
FC3FDE  C1FC0006                muls.w    #6,D0
FC3FE2  5740                    subq.w    #3,D0
FC3FE4  600A                    bra       $FC3FF0

FC3FE6  303900005FE0            move.w    $5FE0,D0
FC3FEC  E540                    asl.w     #2,D0
FC3FEE  5540                    subq.w    #2,D0
FC3FF0  BE40                    cmp.w     D0,D7
FC3FF2  6DA4                    blt       $FC3F98
FC3FF4  303900004E10            move.w    $4E10,D0
FC3FFA  E340                    asl.w     #1,D0
FC3FFC  48C0                    ext.l     D0
FC3FFE  D1B900005648            add.l     D0,$5648
FC4004  303900005FF8            move.w    $5FF8,D0
```

```
FC400A D179000016A8    add.w    D0,$16A8
FC4010 4240            clr.w    D0
FC4012 303900029C6     move.w   $29C6,D0           p_height
FC4018 B079000016A8    cmp.w    $16A8,D0
FC401E 6200F67C        bhi      $FC369C
FC4022 2EBC00FD1BE8    move.l   #$FD1BE8,(A7)      ESC '2', 1/6" line spacing
FC4028 6100007A        bsr      $FC40A4            Send string to printer
FC402C 4A3900005758E   tst.b    $575E              ATARI color dot-matrix printer?
FC4032 6710            beq      $FC4044            No
FC4034 4A3900005FE6    tst.b    $5FE6              High resolution ?
FC403A 6608            bne      $FC4044            Yes
FC403C 2EBC00FD1BEC    move.l   #$FD1BEC,(A7)      ESC 'X', 0
FC4042 6160            bsr      $FC40A4            Send string to printer
FC4044 33FCFFFF000004EE move.w  #-1,$4EE           Clear _dumpflg
FC404C 4240            clr.w    D0                 OK
FC404E 4A9F            tst.l    (A7)+
FC4050 4CDF30C0        movem.l  (A7)+,D6-D7/A4-A5  Restore registers
FC4054 4E5E            unlk     A6
FC4056 4E75            rts

;**************************************************

FC4058 4E56FFFC        link     A6,#-4             Output character to printer
FC405C 4A39000029BC    tst.b    $29BC
FC4062 6722            beq      $FC4086            Printer port
FC4064 102E0009        move.b   9(A6),D0           RS 232 ?
FC4068 4880            ext.w    D0                 Get character
FC406A 3E80            move.w   D0,(A7)
FC406C 102E0009        move.b   9(A6),D0           on the stack
FC4070 4880            ext.w    D0
FC4072 3F00            move.w   D0,-(A7)           (again ?)
FC4074 4EB900FC40E4    jsr      $FC40E4            Output character to printer
FC407A 548F            addq.l   #2,A7
```

```
FC407C  4A40            tst.w    D0                  OK ?
FC407E  6604            bne      $FC4084             Yes
FC4080  70FF            moveq.l  #-1,D0              Flag for error
FC4082  601C            bra      $FC40A0             Terminate

FC4084  6018            bra      $FC409E             OK
FC4086  102E0009        move.b   9(A6),D0            Get character
FC408A  4880            ext.w    D0
FC408C  3E80            move.w   D0,(A7)             on stack
FC408E  102E0009        move.b   9(A6),D0
FC4092  4880            ext.w    D0
FC4094  3F00            move.w   D0,-(A7)            (again ?)
FC4096  4EB900FC4112    jsr      $FC4112             RS 232 output
FC409C  548F            addq.l   #2,A7
FC409E  4240            clr.w    D0                  OK
FC40A0  4E5E            unlk     A6
FC40A2  4E75            rts

************************************************   Send string to printer

FC40A4  4E56FFFC        link     A6,#-4
FC40A8  6018            bra      $FC40C2

FC40AA  206E0008        move.l   8(A6),A0            String address
FC40AE  1010            move.b   (A0),D0             Character of the string
FC40B0  4880            ext.w    D0
FC40B2  3E80            move.w   D0,(A7)             on stack
FC40B4  61A2            bsr      $FC4058             Output character
FC40B6  52AE0008        addq.l   #1,8(A6)            Pointer to next character
FC40BA  4A40            tst.w    D0                  Output OK?
FC40BC  6704            beq      $FC40C2             Yes
FC40BE  70FF            moveq.l  #-1,D0              Flag for error
FC40C0  600C            bra      $FC40CE
```

```
FC40C2  206E0008           move.l    8(A6),A0                String address
FC40C6  0C1000FF           cmp.b     #$FF,(A0)               End criterium reached?
FC40CA  66DE               bne       $FC40AA                 No
FC40CC  4240               clr.w     D0                      OK
FC40CE  4E5E               unlk      A6
FC40D0  4E75               rts
*********************************************
FC40D2  48E71F1E           movem.l   D3-D7/A3-A6,-(A7)       Get printer status
FC40D6  9BCD               sub.l     A5,A5                   Save registers
FC40D8  206D0506           move.l    $506(A5),A0             Clear A5
FC40DC  4E90               jsr       (A0)                    prt_stat
FC40DE  4CDF78F8           movem.l   (A7)+,D3-D7/A3-A6       Jump via vector
FC40E2  4E75               rts                               Restore registers
*********************************************
FC40E4  302F0006           move.w    6(A7),D0                Printer output
FC40E8  48E71F1E           movem.l   D3-D7/A3-A6,-(A7)       Character to output
FC40EC  3F00               move.w    D0,-(A7)                Save registers
FC40EE  3F00               move.w    D0,-(A7)                Character on stack
FC40F0  9BCD               sub.l     A5,A5                   (again ?)
FC40F2  206D050A           move.l    $50A(A5),A0             Clear A5
FC40F6  4E90               jsr       (A0)                    prt_vec
FC40F8  584F               addq.w    #4,A7                   Jump via vector
FC40FA  4CDF78F8           movem.l   (A7)+,D3-D7/A3-A6       Correct stack pointer
FC40FE  4E75               rts                               Restore registers
*********************************************
FC4100  48E71F1E           movem.l   D3-D7/A3-A6,-(A7)       RS 232 output status
FC4104  9BCD               sub.l     A5,A5                   Save regisers
FC4106  206D050E           move.l    $50E(A5),A0             Clear A5
FC410A  4E90               jsr       (A0)                    aux_stat
                                                             Jump via vector
```

```
FC410C  4CDF78F8          movem.l (A7)+,D3-D7/A3-A6          Restore registers
FC4110  4E75              rts

*****************************************

FC4112  302F0006          move.w  6(A7),D0                   RS 232 output
FC4116  48E71F1E          movem.l D3-D7/A3-A6,-(A7)          Character to output
FC411A  3F00              move.w  D0,-(A7)                   Save registers
FC411C  3F00              move.w  D0,-(A7)                   Character on stack
FC411E  9BCD              sub.l   A5,A5                      (again ?)
FC4120  206D0512          move.l  $512(A5),A0                Clear A5
FC4124  4E90              jsr     (A0)                       aux_vec
FC4126  584F              addq.w  #4,A7                      Jump via vector
FC4128  4CDF78F8          movem.l (A7)+,D3-D7/A3-A6          Correct stack pointer
FC412C  4E75              rts                                Restore registers

*****************************************

FC412E  20790000293E      move.l  $293E,A0                   VDI ESCAPE functions
FC4134  3028000A          move.w  10(A0),D0                  Address of the CONTRL array
FC4138  B07C0013          cmp.w   #$13,D0                    Function number
FC413C  6236              bhi     $FC4174                    Greater than 19 ?
FC413E  E340              asl.w   #1,D0                      Yes
FC4140  307B000A          move.w  $FC414C(PC,D0.w),A0        Get relative address from the table
FC4144  D1FC00FC4348      add.l   #$FC4348,A0                Add base address
FC414A  4ED0              jmp     (A0)                       Execute routine

*****************************************

FC414C  0000              dc.w    $FC4348-$FC4348            Address of the VDI escape functions
FC414E  FFD8              dc.w    $FC4320-$FC4348            0, rts
FC4150  0012              dc.w    $FC435A-$FC4348            1, Inquire addressable alpha character cells
FC4152  000C              dc.w    $FC4354-$FC4348            2, Exit alpha mode
FC4154  001A              dc.w    $FC4362-$FC4348            3, Enter alpha mode
FC4156  002E              dc.w    $FC4376-$FC4348            4, Alpha cursor up
                                                             5, Alpha cursor down
```

431

```
FC4158 0048                dc.w    $FC4390-$FC4348        6, Alpha cursor right
FC415A 0062                dc.w    $FC43AA-$FC4348        7, Alpha cursor left
FC415C 0076                dc.w    $FC436E-$FC4348        8, Home alpha cursor
FC415E 007E                dc.w    $FC43C6-$FC4348        9, Erase to end of alpha screen
FC4160 00AA                dc.w    $FC43F2-$FC4348        10, Erase to end of alpha text line
FC4162 0114                dc.w    $FC445C-$FC4348        11, Direct alpha cursor address
FC4164 0128                dc.w    $FC4470-$FC4348        12, Output cursor addressable alpha text
FC4166 014E                dc.w    $FC4496-$FC4348        13, Reverse video on
FC4168 0158                dc.w    $FC44A0-$FC4348        14, Reverse video off
FC416A 0162                dc.w    $FC44AA-$FC4348        15, Inquire current alpha cursor address
FC416C 018C                dc.w    $FC44D4-$FC4348        16, Inquire tablet status
FC416E 0002                dc.w    $FC434A-$FC4348        17, Hardcopy
FC4170 01A4                dc.w    $FC44EC-$FC4348        18, Place graphic cursor at location
FC4172 01B4                dc.w    $FC44FC-$FC4348        19, Remove last graphic cursor

;****************************************************************
FC4174 B07C065             cmp.w   #$65,D0                VDI ESC 101 ?
FC4178 670A                beq     $FC4178                Yes
FC417A B07C0066            cmp.w   #$66,D0                VDI ESC 102 ?
FC417E 6700096A            beq     $FC4AEA                Yes, select font
FC4182 4E75                rts

;****************************************************************
FC4184 6100043C            bsr     $FC45C2
FC4188 207900002942        move.l  $2942,A0               VDI ESC 101, character offset from screen start
FC418E 3010                move.w  (A0),D0                Cursor off
FC4190 C0F90000293C        mulu.w  $293C,D0               Address of INTIN array
FC4196 33C00000291C        move.w  D0,$291C               INTIN[0], offset in raster lines
FC419C 60000412            bra     $FC45B0                times bytes per screen line
                                                          equals offset in bytes
                                                          Turn cursor on again

;****************************************************************
FC41A0 322F0006            move.w  6(A7),D1               ascout
                                                          Get character from stack
```

```
FC41A4  024100FF           and.w   #$FF,D1                         Bits 0-7
FC41A8  600005D2           bra     $FC477C                         Output character
*******************************************************************************
FC41AC  322F0006           move.w  6(A7),D1                        Character from stack
FC41B0  024100FF           and.w   #$FF,D1                         Bits 0-7
FC41B4  207900004A8        move.l  $4A8,A0                         con_state vector
FC41BA  4ED0               jmp     (A0)                            Execute routine
*******************************************************************************
FC41BC  B27C0020           cmp.w   #$20,D1                         Standard conout
FC41C0  6C0005BA           bge     $FC477C                         Control code ?
FC41C4  B23C001B           cmp.b   #$1B,D1                         No, output character
FC41C8  660C               bne     $FC41D6                         ESC ?
FC41CA  23FC00FC421800004A8 move.l #$FC4218,$4A8                   No, different control codes
FC41D4  4E75               rts                                     con_state to ESC processing
*******************************************************************************
FC41D6  5F41               subq.w  #7,D1                           Process CTRL codes
FC41D8  6B22               bmi     $FC41FC                         Less than 7 ?
FC41DA  B27C0006           cmp.w   #6,D1                           ignore
FC41DE  6E1C               bgt     $FC41FC                         Greater than 13 ?
FC41E0  E349               lsl.w   #1,D1                           ignore
FC41E2  307B100A           move.w  $FC41EE(PC,D1.w),A0             as word index
FC41E6  D1FC00FC41FE       add.l   #$FC41FE,A0                     Get relative address from table
FC41EC  4ED0               jmp     (A0)                            Add base address
                                                                   Execute routine
*******************************************************************************
FC41EE  0000               dc.w    $FC41FE-$FC41FE                 Jump table for CTRL codes
FC41F0  01AC               dc.w    $FC43AA-$FC41FE                 7, BEL
FC41F2  0004               dc.w    $FC4202-$FC41FE                 8, BS
FC41F4  049E               dc.w    $FC469C-$FC41FE                 9, TAB
                                                                   10, LF
```

```
FC41F6  049E                    dc.w    $FC469C-$FC41FE       11, VT
FC41F8  049E                    dc.w    $FC469C-$FC41FE       12, FF
FC41FA  0492                    dc.w    $FC4690-$FC41FE       13, CR

;*********************************************************
FC41FC  4E75                    rts                           rts for dummy routine
;*********************************************************
FC41FE  6000DE1C                bra     $FC201C               BEL
                                                              Output sound
;*********************************************************
FC4202  30390000291E            move.w  $291E,D0              TAB
FC4208  0240FFF8                and.w   #$FFF8,D0             Current cursor column
FC420C  5040                    addq.w  #8,D0                 Convert to number divisable by 8
FC420E  32390000292O            move.w  $2920,D1              plus 8
FC4214  60000764                bra     $FC497A               Current cursor line
                                                              Reposition cursor
;*********************************************************
FC4218  23FC00FC41BC000004A8    move.l  #$FC41BC,$4A8         Process character as ESC
FC4222  927C0041                sub.w   #$41,D1               con_state back to standard
FC4226  6BD4                    bmi     $FC41FC               minus 'A'
FC4228  B27C000C                cmp.w   #$C,D1                less, ignore
FC422C  6F50                    ble     $FC427E               'M'
FC422E  B27C0018                cmp.w   #$18,D1               To escape table for uppercase letters
FC4232  663C                    bne     $FC4270               'Y' for set cursor?
FC4234  23FC00FC424000004A8     move.l  #$FC4240,$4A8         No, test for lowercase letters
FC423E  4E75                    rts                           con_state for ESC Y
;*********************************************************
FC4240  927C0020                sub.w   #$20,D1               Process line under ESC Y
FC4244  33C1000004AC            move.w  D1,$4AC               Subtract offset
                                                              save_row, save line
```

```
FC424A 23FC00FC425600004A8  move.l  #$FC4256,$4A8         con_state to column process
FC4254 4E75                 rts

************************************************************
FC4256 927C0020             sub.w   #$20,D1               Process column under ESC Y
FC425A 3001                 move.w  D1,D0                 Subtract offset
FC425C 32390000004AC        move.w  $4AC,D1               Column
FC4262 23FC00FC41BC00004A8  move.l  #$FC41BC,$4A8         save_row, line
FC426C 6000070C             bra     $FC497A               con_state to standard
                                                          Set cursor
************************************************************
FC4270 927C0021             sub.w   #$21,D1               Test for ESC lowercase letters
FC4274 6B86                 bmi     $FC41FC               Subtract offset
FC4276 B27C0015             cmp.w   #$15,D1               less than 'b' ignore
FC427A 6F10                 ble     $FC428C               'w'
FC427C 4E75                 rts                           less than or equal, process sequence
************************************************************
FC427E E349                 lsl.w   #1,D1                 ESC uppercase letters
FC4280 307B1058             move.w  $FC42DA(PC,D1.w),A0   Word access
FC4284 D1FC00FC41FC         add.l   #$FC41FC,A0           Get relative address from table
FC428A 4ED0                 jmp     (A0)                  Add base address
                                                          Execute routine
************************************************************
FC428C E349                 lsl.w   #1,D1                 ESC lowercase letters
FC428E 307B1064             move.w  $FC42F4(PC,D1.w),A0   Word access
FC4292 D1FC00FC41FC         add.l   #$FC41FC,A0           Get relative address from table
FC4298 4ED0                 jmp     (A0)                  Add base address
                                                          Execute routine
************************************************************
FC429A 23FC00FC42A600004A8  move.l  #$FC42A6,$4A8         ESC b, set type color
FC42A4 4E75                 rts                           Set con_state
```

```
          ;**********************************
FC42A6 23FC00FC41BC000004A8  move.l  #$FC41BC,$4A8
FC42B0 927C0020              sub.w   #$20,D1           ;con_state to standard
FC42B4 3001                  move.w  D1,D0             ;Subtract offset
FC42B6 60000290              bra     $FC4548           ;Set type color
          ;**********************************
FC42BA 23FC00FC42C6000004A8  move.l  #$FC42C6,$4A8     ;ESC c, set background color
FC42C4 4E75                  rts                       ;Set con_state
          ;**********************************
FC42C6 23FC00FC41BC000004A8  move.l  #$FC41BC,$4A8     ;Set background color
FC42D0 927C0020              sub.w   #$20,D1           ;con_state to standard
FC42D4 3001                  move.w  D1,D0             ;Subtract offset
FC42D6 6000027C              bra     $FC4554           ;Set background color
          ;**********************************
FC42DA 0166                  dc.w    $FC4362-$FC41FC   ;Address table for ESC uppercase
FC42DC 017A                  dc.w    $FC4376-$FC41FC   ;ESC A
FC42DE 0194                  dc.w    $FC4390-$FC41FC   ;ESC B
FC42E0 01AE                  dc.w    $FC43AA-$FC41FC   ;ESC C
FC42E2 0162                  dc.w    $FC435E-$FC41FC   ;ESC D
FC42E4 0000                  dc.w    $FC41FC-$FC41FC   ;ESC E
FC42E6 0000                  dc.w    $FC41FC-$FC41FC   ;ESC F, rts
FC42E8 01C2                  dc.w    $FC436E-$FC41FC   ;ESC G, rts
FC42EA 0306                  dc.w    $FC4502-$FC41FC   ;ESC H
FC42EC 01CA                  dc.w    $FC43C6-$FC41FC   ;ESC I
FC42EE 01F6                  dc.w    $FC43F2-$FC41FC   ;ESC J
FC42F0 0320                  dc.w    $FC451C-$FC41FC   ;ESC K
FC42F2 033C                  dc.w    $FC4538-$FC41FC   ;ESC L
                                                       ;ESC M
```

```
***********************************   Address table for ESC lowercase
FC42F4  009E            dc.w    $FC429A-$FC41FC     ESC b
FC42F6  00BE            dc.w    $FC42BA-$FC41FC     ESC c
FC42F8  0364            dc.w    $FC4560-$FC41FC     ESC d
FC42FA  0380            dc.w    $FC457C-$FC41FC     ESC e
FC42FC  03C6            dc.w    $FC45C2-$FC41FC     ESC f
FC42FE  0000            dc.w    $FC41FC-$FC41FC     ESC g, rts
FC4300  0000            dc.w    $FC41FC-$FC41FC     ESC h, rts
FC4302  0000            dc.w    $FC41FC-$FC41FC     ESC i, rts
FC4304  03E6            dc.w    $FC45E2-$FC41FC     ESC j
FC4306  0402            dc.w    $FC45FE-$FC41FC     ESC k
FC4308  041C            dc.w    $FC4618-$FC41FC     ESC l
FC430A  0000            dc.w    $FC41FC-$FC41FC     ESC m, rts
FC430C  0000            dc.w    $FC41FC-$FC41FC     ESC n, rts
FC430E  043A            dc.w    $FC4636-$FC41FC     ESC o
FC4310  029A            dc.w    $FC4496-$FC41FC     ESC p
FC4312  02A4            dc.w    $FC44A0-$FC41FC     ESC q
FC4314  0000            dc.w    $FC41FC-$FC41FC     ESC r, rts
FC4316  0000            dc.w    $FC41FC-$FC41FC     ESC s, rts
FC4318  0000            dc.w    $FC41FC-$FC41FC     ESC t, rts
FC431A  0000            dc.w    $FC41FC-$FC41FC     ESC u, rts
FC431C  0480            dc.w    $FC467C-$FC41FC     ESC v
FC431E  048A            dc.w    $FC4686-$FC41FC     ESC w
***********************************
FC4320  20790000293E    lea     $293E,A0            VDI ESC 1, get screen size
FC4326  317C00020008    move.w  #2,8(A0)            Address of CONTRL array
FC432C  20790000294A    move.l  $294A,A0            2 result values
FC4332  30390000290E    move.w  $290E,D0            Address of INTOUT array
FC4338  5240            addq.w  #1,D0               Maximum cursor column
FC433A  31400002        move.w  D0,2(A0)            plus 1 equals number of columns
FC433E  303900002910    move.w  $2910,D0            as INTOUT[1]
                                                    Maximum cursor line
```

437

```
FC4344 5240            addq.w   #1,D0           plus 1 equals number of lines
FC4346 3080            move.w   D0,(A0)         as INTOUT[0]
FC4348 4E75            rts
*****************************************
FC434A 3F3C0014        move.w   #$14,-(A7)      VDI ESC 17, hardcopy
FC434E 4E4E            trap     #14             Hardcopy
FC4350 548F            addq.l   #2,A7           XBIOS
FC4352 4E75            rts                      Correct stack pointer
*****************************************
FC4354 6108            bsr      $FC435E         VDI ESC 3, Enter alpha mode
FC4356 60000224        bra      $FC457C         ESC E, Clear home, clear screen
                                                ESC e, Cursor on
*****************************************
FC435A 61000266        bsr      $FC45C2         VDI ESC 2, Exit alpha mode
                                                ESC f, Cursor off
*****************************************
FC435E 615E            bsr      $FC43BE         ESC E, Clear home
FC4360 6064            bra      $FC43C6         ESC H, Cursor home
                                                ESC J, Clear rest of screen
*****************************************
FC4362 32390002920     move.w   $2920,D1        ESC A, VDI ESC 4, Cursor up
FC4368 67DE            beq      $FC4348         Current cursor line
FC436A 5341            subq.w   #1,D1           Zero, done
FC436C 30390000291E    move.w   $291E,D0        Subtract one
FC4372 60000606        bra      $FC497A         Current cursor column
                                                Set cursor
*****************************************
FC4376 32390002920     move.w   $2920,D1        ESC B, VDI ESC 5, Cursor down
FC437C B27900002910    cmp.w    $2910,D1        Current cursor line
FC4382 67C4            beq      $FC4348         Maximum cursor line
                                                Already in lowest line?
```

```
FC4384  5241                 addq.w  #1,D1              Increment by one
FC4386  30390000291E         move.w  $291E,D0           Current cursor column
FC438C  600005EC             bra     $FC497A            Set cursor

*********************************************************

FC4390  30390000291E         move.w  $291E,D0           ESC C, VDI ESC 6, Cursor right
FC4396  B0790000290E         cmp.w   $290E,D0           Current cursor column
                                                        Maximum cursor column
FC439C  67AA                 beq     $FC4348            Already in last column?
FC439E  5240                 addq.w  #1,D0              Increment by one
FC43A0  32390000292A0        move.w  $2920,D1           Current cursor line
FC43A6  600005D2             bra     $FC497A            Set cursor

*********************************************************

FC43AA  30390000291E         move.w  $291E,D0           ESC D, BS, VDI ESC 7, Cursor left
                                                        Current cursor column
FC43B0  6796                 beq     $FC4348            Cursor already in first column?
FC43B2  5340                 subq.w  #1,D0              Subtract one
FC43B4  32390000292A0        move.w  $2920,D1           Current cursor line
FC43BA  600005BE             bra     $FC497A            Set cursor

*********************************************************

FC43BE  7000                 moveq.l #0,D0              ESC H, VDI ESC 8, Cursor home
                                                        Column 0
FC43C0  3200                 move.w  D0,D1              Line 0
FC43C2  600005B6             bra     $FC497A            Set cursor

*********************************************************

FC43C6  612A                 bsr     $FC43F2            ESC J, VDI ESC 9, Clear rest of screen
FC43C8  32390000292A0        move.w  $2920,D1           ESC K, Clear rest of line
                                                        Current cursor line
FC43CE  B27900002910         cmp.w   $2910,D1           Maximum cursor line
FC43D4  6700FF72             beq     $FC4348
FC43D8  5241                 addq.w  #1,D1
FC43DA  4841                 swap    D1
FC43DC  323C0000             move.w  #0,D1
```

```
FC43E0  34390002910              move.w   $2910,D2            Maximum cursor line
FC43E6  4842                     swap     D2
FC43E8  3439000290E              move.w   $290E,D2            Maximum cursor column
FC43EE  60000436                 bra      $FC4826             Clear screen area

*************************************************************
FC43F2  08B900030002934          bclr     #3,$2934            ESC K, VDI ESC 10, Clear rest of line
FC43FA  40E7                     move.w   SR,-(A7)            Cursorflag, clear wrap
FC43FC  610001C4                 bsr      $FC45C2             Save old value
FC4400  610001E0                 bsr      $FC45E2             ESC f, Cursor off
FC4404  32390000291E             move.w   $291E,D1            ESC j, Store cursor position
FC440A  08010000                 btst     #0,D1               Current cursor column
FC440E  6716                     beq      $FC4426
FC4410  B2790000290E             cmp.w    $290E,D1
FC4416  673A                     beq      $FC4452
FC4418  323C0020                 move.w   #$20,D1             Maximum cursor column
FC441C  6100035E                 bsr      $FC477C             Blank
FC4420  32390000291E             move.w   $291E,D1            Output
FC4426  4841                     swap     D1                  Current cursor column
FC4428  32390002920              move.w   $2920,D1
FC442E  3401                     move.w   D1,D2               Current cursor line
FC4430  4841                     swap     D1
FC4432  4842                     swap     D2
FC4434  3439000290E              move.w   $290E,D2            Maximum cursor column
FC443A  610003EA                 bsr      $FC4826             Clear screen area
FC443E  44DF                     move.w   (A7)+,CCR           Restore flag
FC4440  6708                     beq      $FC444A             Not set?
FC4442  08F900030002934          bset     #3,$2934            Cursorflag, set wrap
FC444A  610001B2                 bsr      $FC45FE             ESC k, Restore cursor position
FC444E  60000160                 bra      $FC45B0             Turn cursor back on
FC4452  323C0020                 move.w   #$20,D1             Blank
FC4456  61000324                 bsr      $FC477C             output
```

```
FC445A 60E2                    bra       $FC443E

************************************************************
FC445C 20790000 2942           move.l    $2942,A0           VDI ESC 11, Set cursor
                                                            Address of the INTIN array
FC4462 3210                    move.w    (A0),D1            Get line
FC4464 5341                    subq.w    #1,D1              Subtract offset
FC4466 30280002                move.w    2(A0),D0           Get column
FC446A 5340                    subq.w    #1,D0              Subtract offset
FC446C 6000050C                bra       $FC497A            Set cursor

************************************************************
FC4470 20790000 293E           move.l    $293E,A0           VDI ESC 12, Text output
                                                            Address of the CONTRL array
FC4476 30280006                move.w    6(A0),D0           Number of characters
FC447A 20790000 2942           move.l    $2942,A0           Address of the INTIN array
FC4480 600E                    bra       $FC4490            To end of loop
FC4482 3218                    move.w    (A0)+,D1           Get characters in D1
FC4484 48E78080                movem.l   D0/A0,-(A7)        Save registers
FC4488 6100FD26                bsr       $FC41B0            Output character in D1
FC448C 4CDF0101                movem.l   (A7)+,D0/A0        Restore registers
FC4490 51C8FFF0                dbra      D0,$FC4482         Output next character
FC4494 4E75                    rts

************************************************************
FC4496 08F90004 00002934       bset      #4,$2934           ESC p, VDI ESC 13, Reverse on
                                                            Cursor flag, set reverse
FC449E 4E75                    rts

************************************************************
FC44A0 08B90004 00002934       bclr      #4,$2934           ESC q, VDI ESC 14, Reverse off
                                                            Cursor flag, clear reverse
FC44A8 4E75                    rts

************************************************************
FC44AA 20790000 293E           move.l    $293E,A0           VDI ESC 15, Get cursor position
                                                            Address of the CONTRL array
```

```
FC44B0  317C00020008       move.w    #2,8(A0)         2 result values
FC44B6  20790000294A       move.l    $294A,A0         Address of the INTOUT array
FC44BC  30390002920        move.w    $2920,D0         Current cursor line
FC44C2  5240                addq.w    #1,D0            plus offset
FC44C4  3080                move.w    D0,(A0)          as INTOUT[0]
FC44C6  3039000291E        move.w    $291E,D0         Current cursor column
FC44CC  5240                addq.w    #1,D0            plus offset
FC44CE  31400002           move.w    D0,2(A0)         as INTOUT[1]
FC44D2  4E75                rts
******************************************
FC44D4  20790000293E       move.l    $293E,A0         VDI ESC 16, Inquire tablet status
FC44DA  317C00010008       move.w    #1,8(A0)         Address of CONTRL array
FC44E0  20790000294A       move.l    $294A,A0         One result value
FC44E6  30BC0001           move.w    #1,(A0)          Address of the INTOUT array
FC44EA  4E75                rts                        Tablet available
******************************************
FC44EC  207900002942       move.l    $2942,A0         VDI ESC 18, Set graphic cursor
FC44F2  30BC0000           move.w    #0,(A0)          Address of the INTIN array
FC44F6  4EF900FCAFCA       jmp       $FCAFCA          No result value
                                                      Turn mouse cursor off
******************************************
FC44FC  4EF900FCAFF2       jmp       $FCAFF2          VDI ESC 19, Clear graphic cursor
                                                      Turn mouse cursor off
******************************************
FC4502  323900002920       move.w    $2920,D1         ESC I, Cursor up, scroll if necessary
FC4508  6600FE60           bne       $FC436A          Current cursor line
FC450C  3F3900000291E      move.w    $291E,-(A7)      Not in line 0, cursor up
FC4512  6108                bsr       $FC451C          Save current cursor column
FC4514  301F                move.w    (A7)+,D0         ESC L, insert line
FC4516  7200                moveq.l   #0,D1            Restore cursor column
FC4518  60000460           bra       $FC497A          Line 0
                                                      Set cursor
```

```
*********************************************
FC451C 610000A4        bsr      $FC45C2         ESC L, Insert line
FC4520 32390000292O    move.w   $2920,D1        ESC f, Cursor off
FC4526 6100058A        bsr      $FC4AB2         Current cursor line
FC452A 4240            clr.w    D0              Scroll rest of screen down
FC452C 3239000029O0    move.w   $2920,D1        Column 0
FC4532 61000446        bsr      $FC497A         Current cursor line
FC4536 6078            bra      $FC45B0         Set cursor
                                                Turn cursor on again
*********************************************
FC4538 61000088        bsr      $FC45C2         ESC M, Delete line
FC453C 32390000292O    move.w   $2920,D1        ESC f, Cursor off
FC4542 61000526        bsr      $FC4A6A         Current cursor line
FC4546 60E2            bra      $FC452A         Move rest of screen up
*********************************************
FC4548 C07C000F        and.w    #$F,D0          Set background color
FC454C 33C000002916    move.w   D0,$2916        Color 0-15
FC4552 4E75            rts                      Type color
*********************************************
FC4554 C07C000F        and.w    #$F,D0          Set background color
FC4558 33C000002914    move.w   D0,$2914        Color 0-15
FC455E 4E75            rts                      Background color
*********************************************
FC4560 610000D4        bsr      $FC4636         ESC d, Clear screen to cursor
FC4564 3439000029O0    move.w   $2920,D2        ESC o, Clear line to cursor
FC456A 67F2            beq      $FC455E         Current cursor line
FC456C 5342            subq.w   #1,D2           Zero, done
FC456E 4842            swap     D2
```

```
FC4570 34390000290E        move.w   $290E,D2            Maximum cursor column
FC4576 7200                moveq.l  #0,D1
FC4578 600002AC            bra      $FC4826             Clear screen area
;********************************************************
FC457C 4A79000027E0        tst.w    $27E0               ESC e, Turn cursor on
FC4582 67DA                beq      $FC455E             Cursor already on?
FC4584 427900002 7E0       clr.w    $27E0               Yes, done
FC458A 41F900002934        lea      $2934,A0            Clear number of hide calls
FC4590 08100000            btst     #0,(A0)             Cursor flag
FC4594 660E                bne      $FC45A4
FC4596 08D00002            bset     #2,(A0)
FC459A 227900002918        move.l   $2918,A1            Screen address of the cursor
FC45A0 60000456            bra      $FC49F8             Invert character at cursor position
FC45A4 61F4                bsr      $FC459A             Invert character at cursor position
FC45A6 08D00001            bset     #1,(A0)
FC45AA 08D00002            bset     #2,(A0)
FC45AE 4E75                rts
;********************************************************
FC45B0 4A79000027E0        tst.w    $27E0               Cursor on ?
FC45B6 67A6                beq      $FC455E             Yes, rts
FC45B8 537900002 7E0       subq.w   #1,$27E0            Decrement number of hide calls
FC45BE 67CA                beq      $FC458A             Turn on again
FC45C0 4E75                rts
;********************************************************
FC45C2 527900002 7E0       addq.w   #1,$27E0            ESC f, Cursor off
FC45C8 41F900002934        lea      $2934,A0            Increment number of hide calls
FC45CE 08900002            bclr     #2,(A0)             Cursor flag
FC45D2 678A                beq      $FC455E             Cursor not visible
FC45D4 08100000            btst     #0,(A0)             Cursor was already off
                                                        Cursor flashing ?
```

```
FC45D8  67C0                    beq     $FC459A                 No
FC45DA  08900001                bclr    #1,(A0)                 Cursor not visible
FC45DE  66BA                    bne     $FC459A                 Invert character at cursor position
FC45E0  4E75                    rts
***********************************************************
FC45E2  08F9000500002934        bset    #5,$2934                ESC j, Save cursor position
FC45EA  41F9000027EC            lea     $27EC,A0                Cursor flag, position saved
FC45F0  30F900000291E           move.w  $291E,(A0)+             Address of the save area
FC45F6  30B900000002920         move.w  $2920,(A0)              Current cursor column
FC45FC  4E75                    rts                             Current cursor line
***********************************************************
FC45FE  08B9000500002934        bclr    #5,$2934                ESC k, Cursor to saved position
FC4606  6700FDB6                beq     $FC43BE                 Cursor flag, position saved?
FC460A  41F9000027EC            lea     $27EC,A0                No, Cursor home
FC4610  3018                    move.w  (A0)+,D0                Address of the save area
FC4612  3210                    move.w  (A0),D1                 Cursor column
FC4614  60000364                bra     $FC497A                 Cursor line
                                                                Set cursor
***********************************************************
FC4618  61A8                    bsr     $FC45C2                 ESC l, Delete line
FC461A  323900002920            move.w  $2920,D1                ESC f, Turn cursor off
FC4620  3401                    move.w  D1,D2                   Current cursor line
FC4622  4841                    swap    D1
FC4624  4241                    clr.w   D1
FC4626  4842                    swap    D2
FC4628  343900000290E           move.w  $290E,D2                Maximum cursor column
FC462E  610001F6                bsr     $FC4826                 Clear screen area
FC4632  6000FEF6                bra     $FC452A                 Cursor in colun zero
***********************************************************                                ESC o, Clear line to cursor
```

445

```
FC4636  618A                         bsr      $FC45C2           ESC f, Turn cursor off
FC4638  61A8                         bsr      $FC45E2           ESC j, Save cursor position
FC463A  3439 0000 291E               move.w   $291E,D2          Current cursor column
FC4640  6730                         beq      $FC4672           Zero, done
FC4642  0802 0000                    btst     #0,D2
FC4646  6610                         bne      $FC4658
FC4648  323C 0020                    move.w   #$20,D1           Blank
FC464C  6100 012E                    bsr      $FC477C           output
FC4650  3439 0000 291E               move.w   $291E,D2          Current cursor column
FC4656  5542                         subq.w   #2,D2
FC4658  4842                         swap     D2
FC465A  3439 0000 2920               move.w   $2920,D2          Current cursor line
FC4660  3202                         move.w   D2,D1
FC4662  4842                         swap     D2
FC4664  4841                         swap     D1
FC4666  4241                         clr.w    D1
FC4668  6100 01BC                    bsr      $FC4826           Clear screen area
FC466C  6190                         bsr      $FC45FE           ESC k, Cursor to saved position
FC466E  6000 FF40                    bra      $FC45B0           and turn cursor back on
FC4672  323C 0020                    move.w   #$20,D1           Blank
FC4676  6100 0104                    bsr      $FC477C           output
FC467A  60F0                         bra      $FC466C
*****************************************************************
FC467C  08F9 0003 0000 2934          bset     #3,$2934          ESC v, Turn line-wrap off
                                                                Cursor flag, flag for new line
FC4684  4E75                         rts
*****************************************************************
FC4686  08B9 0003 0000 2934          bclr     #3,$2934          ESC w, Turn line-wrap on
                                                                Cursor flag, clear flag
FC468E  4E75                         rts
*****************************************************************
                                                                CR, Cursor to column zero
```

```
FC4690  32390000 2920    move.w  $2920,D1         Current cursor line
FC4696  4240             clr.w   D0               Column zero
FC4698  600002E0         bra     $FC497A          Set cursor

*********************************************************************
FC469C  30390000 2920    move.w  $2920,D0         LF, (VT, FF), Cursor down
FC46A2  B0790000 2910    cmp.w   $2910,D0         Current cursor line
                                                  Maximum cursor line
FC46A8  6600FCCC         bne     $FC4376          Not in lowest line, just cursor down
FC46AC  6100FF14         bsr     $FC45C2          ESC f, Turn cursor off
FC46B0  4241             clr.w   D1
FC46B2  610003B6         bsr     $FC4A6A          Scroll screen up
FC46B6  6000FEF8         bra     $FC45B0          and turn cursor back on

*********************************************************************
FC46BA  41F90000 2934    lea     $2934,A0         Flash cursor
FC46C0  08100006         btst    #6,(A0)          Cursor flag
FC46C4  662A             bne     $FC46F0          Update flag set ?
                                                  Yes, do nothing
FC46C6  08100002         btst    #2,(A0)          Cursor turned on ?
FC46CA  6724             beq     $FC46F0          No
FC46CC  08100000         btst    #0,(A0)          Cursor flashing ?
FC46D0  671E             beq     $FC46F0          No
FC46D2  43F90000 2923    lea     $2923,A1         Cursor flash counter
FC46D8  5311             subq.b  #1,(A1)          decrement
FC46DA  6614             bne     $FC46F0          Run out?
FC46DC  12B90000 2922    move.b  $2922,(A1)       Reload cursor flash rate
FC46E2  08500001         bchg    #1,(A0)          Invert cursor phase
FC46E6  22790000 2918    move.l  $2918,A1         Screen address of the cursor
FC46EC  6000030A         bra     $FC49F8          Invert character at cursor position
FC46F0  4E75             rts

*********************************************************************
FC46F2  302F0004         move.w  4(A7),D0         Cursor configuration
                                                  Function number
```

```
FC46F6 6BF8              bmi     $FC46F0                      Negative, ignore
FC46F8 B07C0005          cmp.w   #5,D0                        Greater than 5 ?
FC46FC 6EF2              bgt     $FC46F0                      Yes
FC46FE E340              asl.w   #1,D0                        Word access
FC4700 41F900FC4718      lea     $FC4718,A0                   Base address of the table
FC4706 D0FB0004          add.w   $FC470C(PC,D0.w),A0          plus relative address
FC470A 4ED0              jmp     (A0)                         Execute routine

;*********************************************                Jump table for cursor configuration
FC470C 0000              dc.w    $FC4718-$FC4718
FC470E 0004              dc.w    $FC471C-$FC4718
FC4710 0008              dc.w    $FC4720-$FC4718
FC4712 0016              dc.w    $FC472E-$FC4718
FC4714 0024              dc.w    $FC473C-$FC4718
FC4716 002C              dc.w    $FC4744-$FC4718
;*********************************************                0
FC4718 6000FEA8          bra     $FC45C2                      ESC f, Turn cursor on
;*********************************************                1
FC471C 6000FE5E          bra     $FC457C                      ESC e, Turn cursor on
;*********************************************                2
FC4720 6100FEA0          bsr     $FC45C2                      ESC f, Turn cursor off
FC4724 08ED00C02934      bset    #0,$2934(A5)                 Cursor flag
FC472A 6000FE84          bra     $FC45B0                      And back on
;*********************************************                3
FC472E 6100FE92          bsr     $FC45C2                      ESC f, Turn cursor off
FC4732 08AD00002934      bclr    #0,$2934(A5)                 Cursor flag
FC4738 6000FE76          bra     $FC45B0                      And back on
;*********************************************                4
```

```
FC473C  1B6F00072922            move.b   7(A7),$2922(A5)     Set cursor flash rate
FC4742  4E75                    rts
*******************************************************
FC4744  7000                    moveq.l  #0,D0               5
FC4746  102D2922                move.b   $2922(A5),D0        Load cursor flash rate
FC474A  4E75                    rts
*******************************************************
FC474C  3639000002922A          move.w   $292A,D3            Calculate font data for character in D1
FC4752  B243                    cmp.w    D3,D1               Smallest ASCII code in font
FC4754  6522                    bcs      $FC4778             Compare with character to output
                                                             Character not in font
FC4756  B279000002928           cmp.w    $2928,D1            Largest ASCII code in font
FC475C  621A                    bhi      $FC4778             Character not in font
FC475E  2079000002930           move.l   $2930,A0            Pointer to offset data
FC4764  D241                    add.w    D1,D1               Code times 2
FC4766  32301000                move.w   0(A0,D1.w),D1       Yields bit number in font
FC476A  E649                    lsr.w    #3,D1               Divided by 8 equals byte number
FC476C  2079000002924           move.l   $2924,A0            Pointer to font data
FC4772  D0C1                    add.w    D1,A0               Yields pointer to data for this character
FC4774  4243                    clr.w    D3                  Flag for character present
FC4776  4E75                    rts
FC4778  7601                    moveq.l  #1,D3               Character not in font
FC477A  4E75                    rts
*******************************************************
FC477C  61CE                    bsr      $FC474C             ascout, ignore control codes
FC477E  6702                    beq      $FC4782             Character in font?
FC4780  4E75                    rts                          Yes
FC4782  227900002918            move.l   $2918,A1            Screen address of the cursor
FC4788  3E39000002914           move.w   $2914,D7            Background color
```

FC478E 4847	swap	D7	In upper word
FC4790 3E3900002916	move.w	$2916,D7	Type color in lower word
FC4796 083900040000002934	btst	#4,$2934	Cursor flag, reverse ?
FC479E 6702	beq	$FC47A2	No
FC47A0 4847	swap	D7	Exchange colors
FC47A2 08B90002000002934	bclr	#2,$2934	Cursor flag, character in flash phase?
FC47AA 40E7	move.w	SR,-(A7)	Save status
FC47AC 61000160	bsr	$FC490E	Write character to the screen
FC47B0 22790002918	move.l	$2918,A1	Screen address of the cursor
FC47B6 30390000291E	move.w	$291E,D0	Current cursor column
FC47BC 32390002920	move.w	$2920,D1	Current cursor line
FC47C2 6100026E	bsr	$FC4A32	Increment cursor position
FC47C6 6732	beq	$FC47FA	No CR/LF needed ?
FC47C8 303900002912	move.w	$2912,D0	Bytes per character line
FC47CE C0C1	mulu.w	D1,D0	times lines
FC47D0 2279000044E	move.l	$44E,A1	_v_bs_ad
FC47D6 D3C0	add.l	D0,A1	Yields address of the character
FC47D8 4240	clr.w	D0	Column 0
FC47DA B2790002910	cmp.w	$2910,D1	Cursor in lowest line?
FC47E0 640A	bcc	$FC47EC	Yes
FC47E2 D2F900002912	add.w	$2912,A1	Bytes per character line, next line
FC47E8 5241	addq.w	#1,D1	Increment line
FC47EA 600E	bra	$FC47FA	
FC47EC 48E7C040	movem.l	D0-D1/A1,-(A7)	Save registers
FC47F0 7200	moveq.l	#0,D1	to line 0
FC47F2 61000276	bsr	$FC4A6A	Scroll screen up
FC47F6 4CDF0203	movem.l	(A7)+,D0-D1/A1	Restore registers
FC47FA 23C900002918	move.l	A1,$2918	Screen address of the cursor
FC4800 33C000000291E	move.w	D0,$291E	Current cursor column
FC4806 33C100002920	move.w	D1,$2920	Current cursor line
FC480C 44DF	move.w	(A7)+,CCR	Restore status
FC480E 6714	beq	$FC4824	Flag not set?

```
FC4810 610001E6          bsr     $FC49F8              Invert character at cursor position
FC4814 08F9000100002934  bset    #1,$2934             Cursor flag, cursor visible
FC481C 08F9000200002934  bset    #2,$2934             Cursor flag, cursor in flash phase
FC4824 4E75              rts
*******************************************************
FC4826 9481              sub.l   D1,D2                Clear screen area
FC4828 3001              move.w  D1,D0                Cursor column
FC482A 4841              swap    D1                   Cursor line
FC482C 61000098          bsr     $FC48C6              Calculate cursor position
FC4830 E242              asr.w   #1,D2
FC4832 36390000293A      move.w  $293A,D3             Number of screen planes
FC4838 0C430004          cmp.w   #4,D3                Low resolution ?
FC483C 6602              bne     $FC4840              No
FC483E 5343              subq.w  #1,D3                minus 1, yields 1, 2, 3
FC4840 3202              move.w  D2,D1
FC4842 5241              addq.w  #1,D1
FC4844 E761              asl.w   D3,D1
FC4846 34790000293C      move.w  $293C,A2             Number of bytes per screen line
FC484C 94C1              sub.w   D1,A2
FC484E 3202              move.w  D2,D1
FC4850 4842              swap    D2
FC4852 5242              addq.w  #1,D2
FC4854 C4F900000290C     mulu.w  $290C,D2             times height of a character
FC485A 5342              subq.w  #1,D2                als dbra counter
FC485C 4280              clr.l   D0
FC485E 3A3900002914      move.w  $2914,D5             Background color
FC4864 0C7900020000293A  cmp.w   #2,$293A             Number of screen planes
FC486C 6B44              bmi     $FC48B2              High resolution ?
FC486E 6728              beq     $FC4898              Medium resolution ?
*******************************************************
FC4870 E245              asr.w   #1,D5                Background color, bit 0 into carry
```

```
FC4872 4040          negx.w   D0              Bit set, invert word
FC4874 4840          swap     D0
FC4876 E245          asr.w    #1,D5           Background color, bit 1 into color
FC4878 4040          negx.w   D0              Bit set, invert word
FC487A 4283          clr.l    D3              planes three and four
FC487C E245          asr.w    #1,D5           Background color, bit 2 into carry
FC487E 4043          negx.w   D3              Bit set, invert word
FC4880 4843          swap     D3
FC4882 E245          asr.w    #1,D5           Background color, bit 3 into carry
FC4884 4043          negx.w   D3              Bit set, invert word
FC4886 3A01          move.w   D1,D5           Number of long words per line
FC4888 22C0          move.l   D0,(A1)+        Color planes one and two
FC488A 22C3          move.l   D3,(A1)+        Color planes three and four
FC488C 51CDFFFA      dbra     D5,$FC4888      Next long word
FC4890 D3CA          add.l    A2,A1           Pointer to next raster line
FC4892 51CAFFF2      dbra     D2,$FC4886      Next raster line
FC4896 4E75          rts

*************************************************
FC4898 E245          asr.w    #1,D5           Medium resolution
FC489A 4040          negx.w   D0              Background color, bit 0 into carry
FC489C 4840          swap     D0              Bit set, invert word
FC489E E245          asr.w    #1,D5           Background color, bit 1 into carry
FC48A0 4040          negx.w   D0              Bit set, invert word
FC48A2 3A01          move.w   D1,D5           Number of long words per line
FC48A4 22C0          move.l   D0,(A1)+        Color planes one and two
FC48A6 51CDFFFC      dbra     D5,$FC48A4      Next long word
FC48AA D3CA          add.l    A2,A1           Pointer to next raster line
FC48AC 51CAFFF4      dbra     D2,$FC48A2      Next raster line
FC48B0 4E75          rts
```

```
*************************************************
FC48B2  E245              asr.w    #1,D5           high resolution
FC48B4  4040              negx.w   D0              Background color, bit 0 in carry
FC48B6  3A01              move.w   D1,D5           Bit set, invert word
FC48B8  32C0              move.w   D0,(A1)+        Number of long words per line
FC48BA  51CDFFFC          dbra     D5,$FC48B8      Color plane one
FC48BE  D3CA              add.l    A2,A1           Next long word
FC48C0  51CAFFF4          dbra     D2,$FC48B6      Pointer to next raster line
FC48C4  4E75              rts                      Next raster line
*************************************************
FC48C6  36390000290E      move.w   $290E,D3        Calculate cursor position (D0/D1)
FC48CC  B640              cmp.w    D0,D3           Maximum cursor column
FC48CE  6A02              bpl      $FC48D2         Column value too large?
FC48D0  3003              move.w   D3,D0           No
FC48D2  3639000002910     move.w   $2910,D3        Replace with maximum value
FC48D8  B641              cmp.w    D1,D3           Maximum cursor line
FC48DA  6A02              bpl      $FC48DE         Line value too large?
FC48DC  3203              move.w   D3,D1           No
FC48DE  3639000002293A    move.w   $293A,D3        Replace with maximum value
FC48E4  3A00              move.w   D0,D5           Number of screen planes
FC48E6  08850000          bclr     #0,D5           Column
FC48EA  C6C5              mulu.w   D5,D3           Round to even value
FC48EC  08000000          btst     #0,D0           Number of screen planes times cursor column
FC48F0  6702              beq      $FC48F4         Odd column?
FC48F2  5283              addq.l   #1,D3           No
FC48F4  3A3900002912      move.w   $2912,D5        Add one
FC48FA  CAC1              mulu.w   D1,D5           Bytes per character line
FC48FC  227900000044E     move.l   $44E,A1         Times cursor line
FC4902  D3C5              add.l    D5,A1           _v_bs_ad
FC4904  D3C3              add.l    D3,A1           plus line offset
FC4906  D2F90000291C      add.w    $291C,A1        plus column offset
                                                   plus offset from screen start
```

```
FC490C  4E75              rts

************************

FC490E  3479 0000 292C    move.w  $292C,A2        Character from font on the screen
FC4914  3679 0000 293C    move.w  $293C,A3        Width of font, formwidth
FC491A  3839 0000 290C    move.w  $290C,D4        Number of bytes per screen line
FC4920  5344              subq.w  #1,D4           Height of a character
FC4922  3C39 0000 293A    move.w  $293A,D6                as dbra counter
FC4928  5346              subq.w  #1,D6           Number of screen planes
FC492A  3A04              move.w  D4,D5                   as dbra counter
FC492C  2848              move.l  A0,A4           Counter for raster lines
FC492E  2A49              move.l  A1,A5           Font address of the character
FC4930  E287              asr.l   #1,D7           Screen address of the character
FC4932  0807 000F         btst    #15,D7          Next bit back- and foreground color
FC4936  6706              beq     $FC493E         Bit set in background color?
FC4938  642A              bcc     $FC4964         No
FC493A  76FF              moveq.l #-1,D3          Foreground color not set?
FC493C  6004              bra     $FC4942         Fore- and background colors set

FC493E  6512              bcs     $FC4952         Foreground color set?
FC4940  7600              moveq.l #0,D3           Fore and background cleared
FC4942  1A83              move.b  D3,(A5)         Set byte in video RAM
FC4944  DACB              add.w   A3,A5           Pointer to next raster line
FC4946  51CD FFFA         dbra    D5,$FC4942      Next raster line
FC494A  5449              addq.w  #2,A1           Pointer to next color plane
FC494C  51CE FFDC         dbra    D6,$FC492A      Next color plane
FC4950  4E75              rts

************************

FC4952  1A94              move.b  (A4),(A5)       Set foreground color only
FC4954  DACB              add.w   A3,A5           Copy byte in font in video RAM
FC4956  D8CA              add.w   A2,A4           Next raster line of the screen
                                                  Next raster line in font
```

```
FC4958  51CDFFF8            dbra    D5,$FC4952          Write next raster line
FC495C  5449                addq.w  #2,A1               Pointer to next color plane
FC495E  51CEFFCA            dbra    D6,$FC492A          Next color plane
FC4962  4E75                rts

;*********************************************

FC4964  1614                move.b  (A4),D3             Set background color only
FC4966  4603                not.b   D3                  Get byte from font
FC4968  1A83                move.b  D3,(A5)             Invert
FC496A  DACB                add.w   A3,A5               and to screen
FC496C  D8CA                add.w   A2,A4               Next raster line on the screen
FC496E  51CDFFF4            dbra    D5,$FC4964          Next raster line in font
FC4972  5449                addq.w  #2,A1               Display next raster line
FC4974  51CEFFB4            dbra    D6,$FC492A          Pointer to next color plane
FC4978  4E75                rts                         Next color plane

;*********************************************

FC497A  B07900000290E       cmp.w   $290E,D0            Set cursor
FC4980  6306                bls     $FC4988             Compare column with maximum value
FC4982  30390000290E        move.w  $290E,D0            Smaller ?
FC4988  B27900002910        cmp.w   $2910,D1            Maximum cursor column
FC498E  6306                bls     $FC4996             Compare line with maximum value
FC4990  32390002910         move.w  $2910,D1            Smaller ?
FC4996  33C00000291E        move.w  D0,$291E            Maximum cursor line
FC499C  33C100002920        move.w  D1,$2920            Current cursor column
FC49A2  41F900002934        lea     $2934,A0            Current cursor line
FC49A8  08100002            btst    #2,(A0)             Cursor flag
FC49AC  673E                beq     $FC49EC             Cursor in flash phase?
FC49AE  08100000            btst    #0,(A0)             No
FC49B2  670A                beq     $FC49BE             Cursor flashing ?
FC49B4  08900002            bclr    #2,(A0)             No
FC49B8  08100001            btst    #1,(A0)             Clear flag for flash phase
                                                        Cursor visible ?
```

```
FC49BC  671E                    beq     $FC49DC         No
FC49BE  22790000 2918           move.l  $2918,A1        Screen address of the old cursor
FC49C4  6132                    bsr     $FC49F8         Invert character at cursor position
FC49C6  6100FEFE                bsr     $FC48C6         Calculate new cursor position
FC49CA  23C90000 2918           move.l  A1,$2918        Screen address of the new cursor
FC49D0  6126                    bsr     $FC49F8         Invert character at cursor position
FC49D2  08F90002 00002934       bset    #2,$2934        Cursor flag
FC49DA  4E75                    rts
FC49DC  6100FEE8                bsr     $FC48C6         Calculate cursor position
FC49E0  23C90000 2918           move.l  A1,$2918        Screen address of the cursor
FC49E6  08D00002                bset    #2,(A0)         Cursor in flash phase
FC49EA  4E75                    rts
FC49EC  6100FED8                bsr     $FC48C6         Calculate cursor position
FC49F0  23C90000 2918           move.l  A1,$2918        Screen addres of the cursor
FC49F6  4E75                    rts
;**************************************************************
FC49F8  34790000 293C           move.w  $293C,A2        Invert character at cursor position
FC49FE  38390000 290C           move.w  $290C,D4        Number of bytes per screen line
FC4A04  5344                    subq.w  #1,D4           Height of a character
                                                        as dbra counter
FC4A06  3C390000 293A           move.w  $293A,D6        Number of screen planes
FC4A0C  5346                    subq.w  #1,D6           as dbra as counter
FC4A0E  08F90006 00002934       bset    #6,$2934        Set cursor flag for update
FC4A16  3A04                    move.w  D4,D5           Counter for raster lines
FC4A18  2849                    move.l  A1,A4           Screen address of the cursor
FC4A1A  4614                    not.b   (A4)            Invert byte
FC4A1C  D8CA                    add.w   A2,A4           Pointer to next raster line
FC4A1E  51CDFFFA                dbra    D5,$FC4A1A      Next raster line
FC4A22  5449                    addq.w  #2,A1           Pointer to next color plane
FC4A24  51CEFFF0                dbra    D6,$FC4A16      Next color plane
FC4A28  08B90006 00002934       bclr    #6,$2934        Clear cursor flag for update
FC4A30  4E75                    rts
```

```
*******************************************************
FC4A32  B0790000290E    cmp.w     $290E,D0         Increment cursor position (D0/D1)
FC4A38  6612            bne       $FC4A4C          Cursor in last column?
FC4A3A  08390003000290  btst      #3,$2934         No
FC4A42  6604            bne       $FC4A48          Cursor flag, overflow in next line?
FC4A44  4243            clr.w     D3               Yes
FC4A46  4E75            rts                        Cursor still in same line

FC4A48  7601            moveq.l   #1,D3            CR/LF necessary
FC4A4A  4E75            rts

FC4A4C  5240            addq.w    #1,D0            Next column
FC4A4E  08000000        btst      #0,D0            Even column number?
FC4A52  6706            beq       $FC4A5A          Yes, not in same word
FC4A54  5249            addq.w    #1,A1            Increment addres by one
FC4A56  4243            clr.w     D3               Cursor still in same line
FC4A58  4E75            rts

FC4A5A  3639000000293A  move.w    $293A,D3         Number of screen planes
FC4A60  E343            asl.w     #1,D3            times 2
FC4A62  5343            subq.w    #1,D3            minus 1
FC4A64  D2C3            add.w     D3,A1            Address of next position
FC4A66  4243            clr.w     D3               Cursor still in same line
FC4A68  4E75            rts

*******************************************************
FC4A6A  267900000044E   move.l    $44E,A3          Scroll screen up at line D1
FC4A70  3639000002912   move.w    $2912,D3         _v_bs_ad
FC4A76  C6C1            mulu.w    D1,D3            Bytes per character line
FC4A78  47F33000        lea       0(A3,D3.w),A3    multiply by number of lines
FC4A7C  4441            neg.w     D1               Address of the current line
FC4A7E  D2790000002910  add.w     $2910,D1         Current line
                                                   Maximum cursor line - current line
```

```
FC4A84  363900002912  move.w  $2912,D3          Bytes per character line
FC4A8A  45F33000      lea     0(A3,D3.w),A2     Address of the last line
FC4A8E  C6C1          mulu.w  D1,D3             Number of bytes to move
FC4A90  E443          asr.w   #2,D3             Divided by four, equals number of longs
FC4A92  6002          bra     $FC4A96
FC4A94  26DA          move.l  (A2)+,(A3)+       Copy screen lines
FC4A96  51CBFFFC      dbra    D3,$FC4A94        Next long word
FC4A9A  323900002910  move.w  $2910,D1          Maximum cursor line
FC4AA0  3401          move.w  D1,D2
FC4AA2  4841          swap    D1
FC4AA4  4842          swap    D2
FC4AA6  4241          clr.w   D1
FC4AA8  34390000290E  move.w  $290E,D2          Maximum cursor column
FC4AAE  6000FD76      bra     $FC4826           Clear last line
**************************************************
FC4AB2  26790000044E  move.l  $44E,A3           Scroll screen down at line D1
                                                _v_bs_ad
FC4AB8  363900002910  move.w  $2910,D3          Maximum cursor line
FC4ABE  C6F900002912  mulu.w  $2912,D3          Bytes per character line
FC4AC4  47F33000      lea     0(A3,D3.w),A3     Address of the last line
FC4AC8  363900002912  move.w  $2912,D3          Bytes per character line
FC4ACE  45F33000      lea     0(A3,D3.w),A2     Address of the first line
FC4AD2  3001          move.w  D1,D0             Current line
FC4AD4  4440          neg.w   D0
FC4AD6  D07900002910  add.w   $2910,D0          Maximum cursor line
FC4ADC  C6C0          mulu.w  D0,D3             times bytes per character line
FC4ADE  E443          asr.w   #2,D3             Divided by 4 for long word counter
FC4AE0  6002          bra     $FC4AE4
FC4AE2  2523          move.l  -(A3),-(A2)       Copy screen lines
FC4AE4  51CBFFFC      dbra    D3,$FC4AE2        Next long word
FC4AE8  60B6          bra     $FC4AA0           Clear top line
```

```
*****************************   VDI ESC 102, Initialize font parameters
FC4AEA  207900002942   move.l   $2942,A0       Address of INTIN array
FC4AF0  2050           move.l   (A0),A0        Address of the font header
FC4AF2  30280052       move.w   82(A0),D0      formhight, height of a character
FC4AF6  33C00000290C   move.w   D0,$290C       save
FC4AFC  323900002 93C  move.w   $293C,D1       Number of bytes per screen line
FC4B02  C2C0           mulu.w   D0,D1          times height of a character
FC4B04  33C100002912   move.w   D1,$2912       yields bytes per character line
FC4B0A  7200           moveq.l  #0,D1
FC4B0C  323900002936   move.w   $2936,D1       Screen height in bits
FC4B12  82C0           divu.w   D0,D1          Divided by font height
FC4B14  5341           subq.w   #1,D1          minus 1
FC4B16  33C100002910   move.w   D1,$2910       yields maximum cursor line
FC4B1C  7200           moveq.l  #0,D1
FC4B1E  32390000292E   move.w   $292E,D1       Screen width in bits
FC4B24  82E80034       divu.w   52(A0),D1      Divide by maximum character width
FC4B28  5341           subq.w   #1,D1          minus 1
FC4B2A  33C10000290E   move.w   D1,$290E       yields maximum cursor column
FC4B30  33E80050000292C move.w  80(A0),$292C   Width of the font, formwidth
FC4B38  33E800240000292A move.w 36(A0),$292A   Smallest ASCII code in font
FC4B40  33E800260000292 8 move.w 38(A0),$2928  Largest ASCII code in font
FC4B48  23E8004C00002924 move.l 76(A0),$2924   Pointer to font data
FC4B50  23E800480000293 0 move.l 72(A0),$2930  Pointer to offset data
FC4B58  4E75           rts

*****************************   Initialize screen output
FCA7C4  10390000044C   move.b   $44C,D0        sshiftmd, screen resolution
FCA7CA  C07C0003       and.w    #3,D0          Isolate bits 0 and 1
FCA7CE  B07C0003       cmp.w    #3,D0          3 ?
FCA7D2  6604           bne      $FCA7D8        No
FCA7D4  303C0002       move.w   #2,D0          Replace with 2 (high resolution)
FCA7D8  3F00           move.w   D0,-(A7)       Save resolution
```

```
FCA7DA  6100007E                          bsr       $FCA85A                      Set parameters for screen resolution
FCA7DE  301F                              move.w    (A7)+,D0                     Restore resolution
FCA7E0  41F900FD2D00                      lea       $FD2D00,A0                   Address of the 8x8 system-font header
FCA7E6  B07C0002                          cmp.w     #2,D0                        High resolution ?
FCA7EA  6606                              bne       $FCA7F2                      No
FCA7EC  41F900FD375C                      lea       $FD375C,A0                   Else address of the 8x16 system-font header
FCA7F2  6100A2FE                          bsr       $FC4AF2                      Initialize font data
FCA7F6  33FCFFFF00002916                  move.w    #$FFFF,$2916                 Type color to black
FCA7FE  7000                              moveq.l   #0,D0
FCA800  33C000002914                      move.w    D0,$2914                     Background color white
FCA806  33C000002911E                     move.w    D0,$2911E                    Cursor column zero
FCA80C  33C000002920                      move.w    D0,$2920                     Cursor line zero
FCA812  33C000002911C                     move.w    D0,$2911C                    Line offset zero
FCA818  20790000044E                      move.l    $44E,A0                      _v_bs_ad, screen address
FCA81E  23C800002918                      move.l    A0,$2918                     as cursor address
FCA824  13FC000100002934                  move.b    #1,$2934                     Set cursor flag
FCA82C  13FC001E00002923                  move.b    #$1E,$2923                   Cursor flash counter to 30
FCA834  13FC001E00002922                  move.b    #$1E,$2922                   Cursor flash rate to 30
FCA83C  33FC000100002F7E0                 move.w    #1,$27E0                     Cursor not visible
FCA844  323C1F3F                          move.w    #$1F3F,D1
FCA848  20C0                              move.l    D0,(A0)+                     8000 long words
FCA84A  51C9FFFC                          dbra      D1,$FCA848                   Clear screen
FCA84E  23FC00FC41BC000004A8              move.l    #$FC41BC,$4A8                constate vector to standard
FCA858  4E75                              rts

***********************************************************************
FCA85A  7200                              moveq.l   #0,D1                        Set parameters for screen resolution
FCA85C  123B0030                          move.b    $FCA88E(PC,D0.w),D1          Get number of screen planes
FCA860  33C10000293A                      move.w    D1,$293A                     and save
FCA866  123B0029                          move.b    $FCA891(PC,D0.w),D1          Get bytes per screen line
FCA86A  33C10000293C                      move.w    D1,$293C                     and save
FCA870  33C100002938                      move.w    D1,$2938
```

```
FCA876 E340                asl.w     #1,D0                  Resolution as word index
FCA878 323B001A            move.w    $FCA894(PC,D0.w),D1    Get screen height
FCA87C 33C100002936        move.w    D1,$2936               and save
FCA882 323B0016            move.w    $FCA89A(PC,D0.w),D1    Get screen width
FCA886 33C10000292E        move.w    D1,$292E               and save
FCA88C 4E75                rts
*******************************************
FCA88E 040201              dc.b      4,2,1                  Screen parameters
FCA891 A0A050              dc.b      160,160,80             Number of screen planes
FCA894 00C800C80190        dc.w      200,200,400            Number of bytes per screen line
FCA89A 01400280            dc.w      320,640,640            Screen height
                                                            Screen width
```

Chapter Four

Appendix

4.1 The System Fonts
4.2 Alphabetical listing of GEMDOS functions

4.1 The System Fonts

The operating system contains three different fonts for character output.

The 6x6 font is used by the icons, the 8x8 font is used as the standard output on a color monitor, and the 8x16 font is used for the monochrome monitor output. The chart on the next page includes the characters with the ASCII codes 1 to 255.

6X6 System Font

8X8 System Font

8X16 System Font

4.2 Alphabetical listing of GEMDOS functions

Name	Opcode (hex)	Page Number
Cauxin	03	108
Cauxis	12	115
Cauxos	13	115
Cauxout	04	109
Cconin	01	107
Cconis	0B	113
Cconos	10	114
Cconout	02	108
Cconrs	0A	112
Cconws	09	111
Cnecin	08	111
Cprnos	11	115
Cprnout	05	109
Crawcin	07	110
Crawio	06	110
Dcreate	39	123
Ddelete	3A	124
Dfree	36	122
Dgetdrv	19	116
Dgetpath	47	135
Dsetdrv	0E	114
Dsetpath	3B	125
Fattrib	43	132
Fclose	3E	128
Fcreate	3C	126
Fdatime	57	143
Fdelete	41	130
Fdup	45	134
Fforce	46	134
Fgetdta	2F	120
Fopen	3D	127
Fread	3F	129
Frename	56	143
Fseek	42	131
Fsetdta	1A	116
Fsfirst	4E	140
Fsnext	4F	142
Fwrite	40	130

Malloc	48	135
Mfree	49	137
Mshrink	4A	137
Pexec	4B	138
Pterm	4C	140
Pterm0	00	107
Ptermres	31	121
Super	20	117
Sversion	30	121
Tgetdate	2A	118
Tgettime	2C	119
Tsetdate	2B	119
Tsettime	2D	120

4.3 The blitter chip

Anyone who has followed the development of the ST has surely heard the word *blitter*. More than two years were spent developing the blitter chip. The main advantage of this chip is its speed, working with data in the DMA register. The blitter uses a memory range independent of the 68000 microprocessor. Without the blitter chip, you need several kilobytes of program code to realize graphics through software.

The basic graphic routines of the ST are accessed by software through line-A opcodes. The blitter can take on parts of these routines and execute them faster than the 68000 could handle them. That is first taken by the BITBLT function, shifting the established pixel-oriented memory range. However, the fill can be taken up in any memory range. The details of the blitter options follow later. First let's look at chip design.

Figure 4.3-1 BLITTER

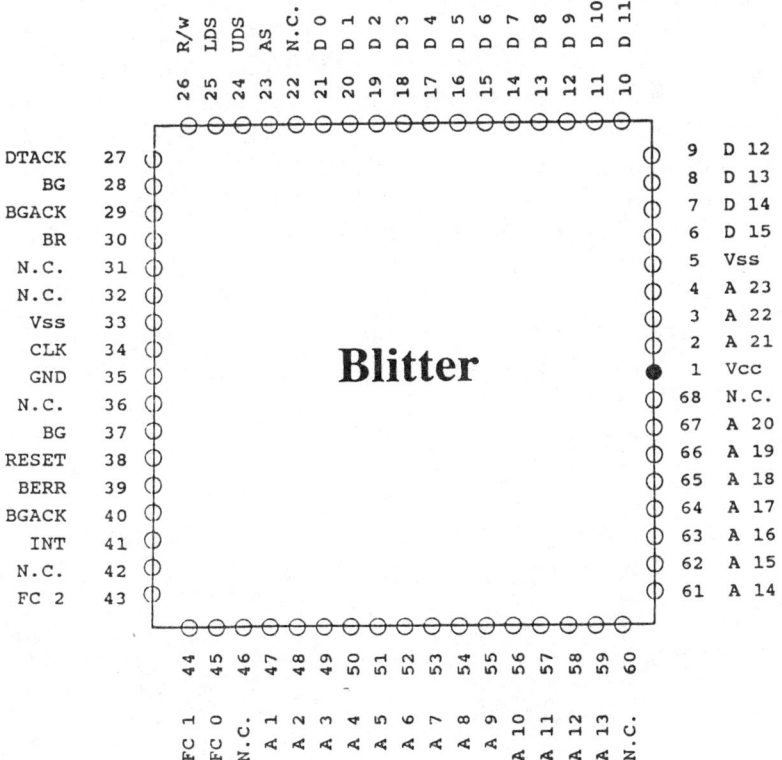

Since the blitter is a DMA device, it must be able to transfer the processor in an idle state. The processor needs the 68000 pins BR (Bus Request), BG (Bus Grant) and BGACK (Bus Grant Acknowledge). The BG pin conveys everything needed for the address and data bus. If the processor recognizes a Bus Request, BG tells the attached device that there is now a bus available for the DMA device. Now a short delay loop executes until the 68000 stops its activity in the different pins (see Section 1.2). As long as the DMA entry has established that the processor is no longer active, then it restarts with the help of BGACK. After data transfer finishes, BGACK clears, and the processor receives control of the bus.

The blitter chip can use the entire address range of the 68000 (16 megabytes). In order to manipulate the data in memory through programming, the processor cannot produce any control signals. These controlled by the READ/WRITE pin, which determines which data is read and which is written to memory. Other important signals for accessing memory are AS (Address Strobe), LDS (Lower Data Strobe) and UDS (Upper Data Strobe).

The DTACK signal (Data Transfer Acknowledge) invokes the blitter chip only, when the processor displays the transfer of data. It cannot do the DMA transfer itself, since the RAM chip timing is set by the blitter or the CLK signal. Like the other onboard DMA channels (floppy disk and DMA port) and the ACIAs, the blitter is also capable of performing interrupts. This means that it can create its own interrupts to end data transfers. Therefore, it uses the free bit 3 of the MFP interrupt entry (GPIP). This option is not usually used by the ST operatng system. However, other interrupt-oriented operating systems like RTOS, OS9 or UNIX should have blitter integration.

The last group of blitter connections belong to the power connections. In addition to the usual 5 volt current and ground, the blitter needs a time signal of 8 mHz.

4.3.1 The blitter registers

The ST blitter chip is the hardware implementation of the BITBLT algorithm used in the line-A opcodes.

Figure 4.3.1-1 shows a block diagram of the blitter functions. The blitter can basically set up a source range which can be combined with a current raster, a destination range of 16 different logical operands, and a destination range in which it stores the result. Both source and destination ranges can be stored in the same area of RAM. Unlike the processor, which can only operate in bytes and words, the blitter is bit-oriented. This makes the blitter ideal for handling bitmapped graphics. It is also practical for normal copy and transfer commands, e.g., high-speed RAM disk operations without hard disk interrupts.

The following is a look at the individual registers used by the blitter:

Figure 4.3.1-1 BLITTER BLOCK DIAGRAM

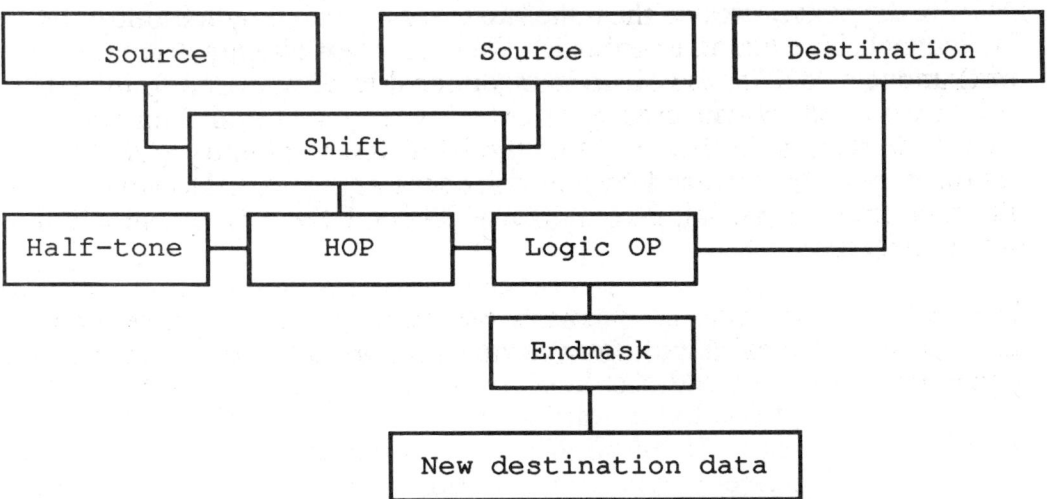

The first 16 registers are marked as half-tone RAM, and contain the raster used in half-tone operations. The registers are each 16 bits wide. When the raster is used, a proportional register for a lin is used. The raster repeats over all 16 lines. The Line Number register (see below) determines which half-tone register is used next.

	Bit	F E D C B A 9 8 7 6 5 4 3 2 1 0	
$FF8A00	R/W	X X X X X X X X X X X X X X X X	Half-tone RAM 0
$FF8A02	R/W	X X X X X X X X X X X X X X X X	Half-tone RAM 1
$FF8A04	R/W	X X X X X X X X X X X X X X X X	Half-tone RAM 2
$FF8A06	R/W	X X X X X X X X X X X X X X X X	Half-tone RAM 3
$FF8A08	R/W	X X X X X X X X X X X X X X X X	Half-tone RAM 4
$FF8A0A	R/W	X X X X X X X X X X X X X X X X	Half-tone RAM 5
$FF8A0C	R/W	X X X X X X X X X X X X X X X X	Half-tone RAM 6
$FF8A0E	R/W	X X X X X X X X X X X X X X X X	Half-tone RAM 7
$FF8A10	R/W	X X X X X X X X X X X X X X X X	Half-tone RAM 8
$FF8A12	R/W	X X X X X X X X X X X X X X X X	Half-tone RAM 9
$FF8A14	R/W	X X X X X X X X X X X X X X X X	Half-tone RAM 10
$FF8A16	R/W	X X X X X X X X X X X X X X X X	Half-tone RAM 11
$FF8A18	R/W	X X X X X X X X X X X X X X X X	Half-tone RAM 12
$FF8A1A	R/W	X X X X X X X X X X X X X X X X	Half-tone RAM 13
$FF8A1C	R/W	X X X X X X X X X X X X X X X X	Half-tone RAM 14
$FF8A1E	R/W	X X X X X X X X X X X X X X X X	Half-tone RAM 15

The next register is called X Increment. This is a leading character dependent 15-bit register. The lowest bit is ignored and constantly registers 0. This makes only even numbers possible. The register gives the offset in bytes in the next source word in the same line. Normally, the Atari gives a 2 for monochrome mode. This is also the case when all planes are copied in color mode. If a plane is copied in medium-res or low-res mode, then 4 or 8 must exist in this register.

```
         Bit F E D C B A 9 8 7 6 5 4 3 2 1 0
$FF8A20  R/W X X X X X X X X X X X X X X X 0   Source X
                                           |   Increment
              (always zero, even increments only)
```

The Source Y Increment register determines how many bytes must be added to the current source address, in order to figure out the distance from the end of the current line to the start of the next line. In monochrome mode, a set of pixels measures 80 bytes: When only a segment of 20 bytes is copied, the Source Y Increment gives a value of 60.

```
         Bit F E D C B A 9 8 7 6 5 4 3 2 1 0
$FF8A22  R/W X X X X X X X X X X X X X X X 0   Source Y
                                           |   Increment
              (always zero, even increments only)
```

The Source Address register determines the starting address at the beginning of the copy. It can read or write long word accesses. Bits 0 and 24-31 are used only for even 24- bit addresses. The contents of this register are incremented as part of the operation with the help of the above mentioned increment register (or decremented, depending on the leading character of the increment register). By reading the source address register, the address of the source word used next is received.

```
           Bit F E D C B A 9 8 7 6 5 4 3 2 1 0
$FF8A24 R/W    - - - - - - - - X X X X X X X 0   Source Address
                                                  High    Word
           (unused)        (24-bit addresses only)

           Bit F E D C B A 9 8 7 6 5 4 3 2 1 0
$FF8A26 R/W    X X X X X X X X X X X X X X X 0   Source Address
                                             |    Low word
                         (always zero, even increments only)
```

The next three registers contain the endmask, which states which bits are changed and which are unchanged. Since the blitter is pixel oriented, but the bus accesses RAM in words, the first and the last word are read as bits. To write 16 bits over the processor bus, the destination word must first read then change the allowable bits, and transfer the result (Read-Modify-Write). Endmask 1 does this for the beginning of a line, endmask 3 applies to the end of a line. Endmask 2 is used by all other words. It is normally set to $FFFF (all bits are altered by it). Thus, a previous reading of the destination word is unnecessary.

```
           Bit F E D C B A 9 8 7 6 5 4 3 2 1 0
$FF8A28 R/W    X X X X X X X X X X X X X X X X   Endmask 1
$FF8A2A R/W    X X X X X X X X X X X X X X X X   Endmask 2
$FF8A2C R/W    X X X X X X X X X X X X X X X X   Endmask 3
```

The next three registers are Destination X Increment, Destination Y Increment and Destination Address. They have the same uses as the above-mentioned source registers, except that these three apply to the destination.

```
           Bit F E D C B A 9 8 7 6 5 4 3 2 1 0
$FF8A2E R/W    X X X X X X X X X X X X X X X 0   Destination X
                                             |    Increment
                         (always zero, even increments only)
```

```
          Bit  F E D C B A 9 8 7 6 5 4 3 2 1 0
$FF8A30 R/W   X X X X X X X X X X X X X X X 0  Destination Y
                                            |  Increment
                       (always zero, even increments only)


          Bit  F E D C B A 9 8 7 6 5 4 3 2 1 0
$FF8A32 R/W   - - - - - - - - X X X X X X X X  Destination
                                                Address High Word
              (unused)      (24-bit addresses only)


          Bit  F E D C B A 9 8 7 6 5 4 3 2 1 0
$FF8A34 R/W   X X X X X X X X X X X X X X X 0  Destination
                                            |  Address Low Word
                       (always zero, even increments only)
```

The X Count register informs you how many words are in a destination line. The minimum value is 1; the highest is 65536 ($0000). Reading the register gives the number of values in this line as words are transferred. When the X Count register is loaded with 1, the values in Destination X Increment, as well as Source X Increment, are unused. Since the line after a word is already the end, and the corresponding Y Increment is used direct.

The Y Count register determines the number of lines. The smallest value is again one, and values of zero are interpreted as 65536. Reading this register gives you the number of lines which need copying. After every transferred line, the value decrements by one until it reaches 0, ending the transfer.

```
          Bit  F E D C B A 9 8 7 6 5 4 3 2 1 0
$FF8A36 R/W   X X X X X X X X X X X X X X X X  X-Count
$FF8A38 R/W   X X X X X X X X X X X X X X X X  Y-Count
```

All the abovementioned registers can only be read as words or long words; byte access is not allowed.

The HOP register determines the combination of source and half-tone RAM. The two lowest bits have the following meanings:

```
     HOP    Combination
     0      All 1-bits
     1      Half-tone RAM
     2      Source
     3      Source and half-tone RAM
```

You can therefore determine whether the source can be used unaltered (HOP = 2), whether the half-tone RAM is combined with the logical AND (HOP = 3) or whether only the half-tone RAM is used (HOP =1). This is useful, for example, when filling an area with a raster pattern. Furthermore, it is still possible to fill the destination with 1-bits (HOP = 0). When half-tone RAM is used, another register determines which half-tone registers are used.

```
              Bit   7 6 5 4 3 2 1 0
$FF8A3A       R/W   - - - - - - X X      HOP
                                         Half-tone operation
```

The next register determines the receiver of the new destination value, after logical operations between destination and source. Here are 16 different options in the following table.

(~s&~d)	(~s&d)	(s&~d)	(s&d)	Operation	New destination
0	0	0	0	0	all 0 bits
0	0	0	1	1	source AND destination
0	0	1	0	2	source AND NOT destination
0	0	1	1	3	source
0	1	0	0	4	NOT source AND destination
0	1	0	1	5	destination
0	1	1	0	6	source XOR destination
0	1	1	1	7	source OR destination
1	0	0	0	8	NOT source AND NOT destination
1	0	0	1	9	NOT source XOR destination
1	0	1	0	10	NOT destination
1	0	1	1	11	source OR NOT destination
1	1	0	0	12	NOT source
1	1	0	1	13	NOT source OR destination
1	1	1	0	14	NOT source OR NOT destination
1	1	1	1	15	all 1 bits

The most important operations are the following three (Replace mode, Source replaces and destination), 6 (XOR mode; overlapping of destination and source) and and 7 (OR mode).

```
              Bit   7 6 5 4 3 2 1 0
$FF8A3B       R/W   - - - - X X X X      OP
                                         Logical operation
```

```
              Bit    7 6 5 4 3 2 1 0
$FF8A3C       R/W    X X X - X X X X
                             |_|_|_|_____Line number
                           |_____Unused
                         |_____SMUDGE
                       |_____HOG
                     |_____Busy
```

The next register combines several functions. The lowest 4 bits determine which of the 16 half-tone RAM registers are even used. The value is incremented or decremented after a line, depending on the leading character in the Destination Y Register. When the SMUDGE bit is set, the number of the half-tone RAM register is determined by the four lowest bits of the above mentioned source data. The selected half-tone operation (HOP) stays active. This allows special effects.

The next bit in this register determines the method of bus access in the blitter. When the HOG bit clears, the blitter and processor share the same bus. After 64 bus cycles, the blitter stops and the processor takes over the bus for 64 bus cycles. When the HOG bit is set, the processor stops until the blitter finishes its operations. In either case, other DMA devices (floppy and harddisk) have priority over the blitter. The Prefetch mechanism of the 68000 processor lets you bypass HOG mode, so after the start of the blitter the next processor command executes when the blitter is ready.

The BUSY bit is set, initializing all other blitter registers, in order to start the blitter. It waits until the blitter ends its operation. Since the interrupt output mirrors the status of the blitter, blitter operations can be ended by an interrupt taken from the third bit of the GPIP within the MFP 68901.

```
              Bit    7 6 5 4 3 2 1 0
$FF8A3D       R/W    X X - - X X X X
                             |_|_|_|_____SKEW
                         |_|_____Unused
                       |_____NFSR
                     |_____FXSR
```

The last blitter register also has several functions. The lowest four bits determine the source operand shifts, to protect the destination operations. Since the blitter is bit-oriented, but bus access is word-oriented, the source data must move to set the bit positions of half-tone masks and destination data. Therefore, two source data words are read, shifting the relevant bits for calling in a 16-bit source register (see Figure 4.3.1-1).

FXSR and NFSR are abbreviations for Force eXtra Source Read and No Final Source Read. When the FXSR bit is set, the beginning of each line is read as an additional source word. The NFSR bit is set when the last word of the source line cannot be read. The use of these bits require changes to Source Y Increment and Source Address Register.

Normally you can access the blitter directly through the operating system. When you use the line-A or VDI functions, the operating system can tell whether the function is produced by software or by the blitter (see XBIOS function $64).

4.4 The Mega ST realtime clock

When the ST was initially released, GEMDOS set the software-run clock in two-second increments. In addition, the clock and date needed resetting every time the user switched on the computer.

To get around this, the ROM circuits, keyboard processor and clock IC offered some solutions. The Mega ST's clock IC is a permanent solution to the problem. Its timekeeping registers are as follows:

	Bit	7 6 5 4 3 2 1 0	(bits 4-7 unused)
$FFFC21	R/W	- - - - X X X X	one second
$FFFC23	R/W	- - - - X X X X	ten seconds
$FFFC25	R/W	- - - - X X X X	one minute
$FFFC27	R/W	- - - - X X X X	ten minutes
$FFFC29	R/W	- - - - X X X X	one hour
$FFFC2B	R/W	- - - - X X X X	ten hours
$FFFC2D	R/W	- - - - X X X X	weekday
$FFFC2F	R/W	- - - - X X X X	one day
$FFFC31	R/W	- - - - X X X X	tenth day
$FFFC33	R/W	- - - - X X X X	one month
$FFFC35	R/W	- - - - X X X X	tenth month
$FFFC35	R/W	- - - - X X X X	one year
$FFFC37	R/W	- - - - X X X X	tenth year
$FFFC39	R/W	- - - - X X X X	control register
$FFFC3B	R/W	- - - - X X X X	control register
$FFFC3D	R/W	- - - - X X X X	control register

The RP 5 C 15 appears to be the same as most clock ICs. It has a four-bit-wide data and address bus, which addresses a total of 16 registers. All of these registers had data width of 4 bits, and contain areas of date and time in BCD format. The next three registers ($FFFC3B to $FFFC3F) are unknown. They describe some registers of setting the clock, but disassembly doesn't give any further information. Clock timing counts through a quartz oscillator running at a frequency of 32,768 kHz. This relatively slow IC is controlled through a PAL (programmable logic array).

All clock registers lie in the address area of the processor, offering a simple to read and accurate clock. The Mega ST's operating system and XBIOS functions determine theimselves whether the clock time is taken from the keyboard processor, or whether the hardware clock is available at all.

4.5 Blitter chip demonstration programs

This section contains programs demonstrating some of the blitter chip's abilities.

This sample program moves the screen memory to another location. The function blit is universal, however, you can blit any RAM. Try the program as a test only. The main purpose of this program is to show how to establish screen areas (forms) and pixel coordinates for the individual registers of the blitter. This program directly accesses the blitter, and must run in 68000 supervisor mode. If you attempt to run the program in user mode, a bus error occurs.

```
blitter    equ       $ff8a00

;          blitter register offsets

halftone   equ       0
src_xinc   equ       $20
src_yinc   equ       $22
src_addr   equ       $24
ENDMASK1   EQU       $28
endmask2   equ       $2a
endmask3   equ       $2c
dst_xinc   equ       $2e
dst_yinc   equ       $30
dst_addr   equ       $32
x_count    equ       $36
y_count    equ       $38
hop        equ       $3a
op         equ       $3b
line_num   equ       $3c
skew       equ       $3d

;          blitter register flags

flinebusy  equ       7           ;busy bit

;          mask blitter register bit

mhop_src   equ       $02         ;half-tone operation: source

mskewfxsr  equ       $80         ;fxsr mask
mskewnfsr  equ       $40         ;nfsr mask
```

```
mlinebusy  equ        $80         ;busy mask


physbase   equ        2           ;get screen address
xbios      equ        14

demo:
           lea        para,a4

           move       #physbase,-(sp)
           trap       #xbios
           addq.l     #2,sp                   ;get screen address

           move.l     d0,src_form(a4)         ;screen acts as
           move.l     d0,dst_form(a4)         ;source and destination

           moveq      #2,d0                   ;2 bytes offset
           move       d0,src_nxwd(a4)         ;to next word in
           move       d0,dst_nxwd(a4)         ;same color plane

           moveq      #80,d0                  ;one line is 80 bytes long
           move       d0,src_nxln(a4)         ;(monochrome mode)
           move       d0,dst_nxln(a4)

           moveq      #2,d0                   ;offset to next color plane
           move       d0,src_nxpl(a4)         ;not used in
           move       d0,dst_nxpl(a4)         ;monochrome mode

           move       #25,src_xmin(a4)        ;x1-coordinate source
           move       #34,src_ymin(a4)        ;y1-coordinate source

           move       #220,dst_xmin(a4)       ;x1-coordinate destination
           move       #234,dst_ymin(a4)       ;y1-coordinate destination

           move       #77,width(a4)           ;width in pixels
           move       #50,height(a4)          ;height-pixels (number of lines)
           move       #1,planes(a4)           ;monochrome

           jsr        blit_it                 ;access blitter

           rts                                ;ready
para       dc.w       17                      ;room for parameter block

;          end maskn

lf_endmask:
```

```
              dc.w      $ffff

rt_endmask:
              dc.w      $7fff
              dc.w      $3fff
              dc.w      $1fff
              dc.w      $0fff
              dc.w      $07ff
              dc.w      $03ff
              dc.w      $01ff
              dc.w      $00ff
              dc.w      $007f
              dc.w      $003f
              dc.w      $001f
              dc.w      $000f
              dc.w      $0007
              dc.w      $0003
              dc.w      $0001
              dc.w      $0000

;
;             input: pointer to 34-byte parameter block in a4
;

src_form      equ       0         ;base address source memory form
src_nxwd      equ       4         ;offset next word in source
src_nxln      equ       6         ;source form width
src_nxpl      equ       8         ;offset between source planes
src_xmin      equ       10        ;source x1
src_ymin      equ       12        ;source y1

dst_form      equ       14        ;base address dest memory form
dst_nxwd      equ       18        ;offset next word in dest
dst_nxln      equ       20        ;dest form width
dst_nxpl      equ       22        ;offset between dst planes
dst_xmin      equ       24        ;dest x1
dst_ymin      equ       26        ;dest y1

width         equ       28        ;width in pixels
height        equ       30        ;height in pixels
planes        equ       32        ;number of planes

blit_it:
              lea       blitter,a5
```

```
;       compute xmax from xmin and width

        move        width(a4),d6
        subq        #1,d6                   ;width -1

        move        src_xmin(a4),d0
        move        d0,d1
        add         d6,d1                   ;src_xmax

        move        dst_xmin(a4),d2
        move        d2,d3
        add         d6,d3                   ;dst_xmax

        moveq       #$f,d6                  ;mod 16 mask

        move        d2,d4                   ;dst_xmin
        and         d6,d4                   ;dst_xmin mod 16
        add         d4,d4                   ;pointer to left end mask table
        move        lf_endmask(pc,d4),d4    ;left end mask

        move        d3,d5                   ;dst_xmax
        and         d6,d5                   ;dst_xmax mod 16
        add         d5,d5                   ;pointer to right end mask
                                            ;table
        move        rt_endmask(pc,d5),d5    ;inverted left end mask
        not         d5                      ;right end mask
;       calculate skew
;       ((dst_xmin mod 16) - (src_xmin mod 16)) mod 16
;
;       determine FXSR and NFSR
;
;       3 bit index in table
;
;       bit 0       0 src_xmin mod 16 >= dst_xmin mod 16
;                   1 src_xmin mod 16 >  dst_xmin mod 16
;
;       bit 1       0 src_xmax/16 - src_xmin/16 <> dst_xmax/16 -
;                   dst_xmin/16
;                   0 src_xmax/16 - src_xmin/16 <> dst_xmax/16 -
;                   dst_xmin/16
;
;       bit 2       0 dst_span equals several words
;                   1 dst_span equals one word
;

        move        d2,d7       ;dst_xmin
```

```
            and         d6,d7           ;dst_xmin mod 16
            and         d0,d6           ;src_xmin mod 16
            sub         d6,d7           ;dst_xmin mod 16 - src_xmin mod 16
;                                       > ? cy = 1 : cy = 0
            clr         d6              ;delete index in table
            addx        d6,d6           ;cy after bit 0

            lsr         #4,d0           ;src_xmin / 16
            lsr         #4,d1           ;src_xmax / 16
            sub         d0,d1           ;src_span - 1

            lsr         #4,d2           ;dst_xmin / 16
            lsr         #4,d3           ;dst_xmax / 16
            sub         d2,d3           ;dst_span - 1

            bne         set_endmask

;           if
;           if dst_span = one word, both endmasks stand in endmask 1
;           the blitter ignores endmask 2

            and         d5,d4
            addq        #4,d6           ;d6 bit 2 = 1 one word destination

set_endmask:
            move        d4,endmask1(a5)     ;left endmask
            move        #$ffff,endmask2(a5) ;middle endmask
            move        d5,endmask3(a5)     ;right endmask

            cmp         d1,d3           ;number of source und dest words
                                        ;equal?
            bne         set_count       ;no

            addq        #2,d6           ;d6 bit 1 = 1 equal number of
                                        ;words

set_count:
            move        d3,d4
            addq        #1,d4           ;number of words in dest line
            move        d4,x_count(a5)

;
;           determine source start address
;
;           src_form + (src_ymin * src_nxln) * (src_xmin/16 * src_nxwd)
```

```
        move.l      src_form(a4),a0        ;a0 -> start src form
        move        src_ymin(a4),d4        ;offset in lines to ymin
        move        src_nxln(a4),d5        ;length src line
        mulu        d5,d4
        add.l       d4,a0                  ;a0 -> (0, ymin)

        move        src_nxwd(a4),d4        ;offset of next word
        move        d4,src_xinc(a5)

        mulu        d4,d0
        add.l       d0,a0                  ;a0 -> first word (xmin, ymin)

        mulu        d4,d1                  ;source line length in bytes
        sub         d1,d5
        move        d5,src_yinc(a5)        ;offset next end line beginning

;       compute destination start address

        move.l      dst_form(a4),a1        ;a1 -> start dst form
        move        dst_ymin(a4),d4
        move        dst_nxln(a4),d5

        mulu        d5,d4
        add.l       d4,a1

        move        dst_nxwd(a4),d4
        move        d4,dst_xinc(a5)

        mulu        d4,d2
        add.l       d2,d1

;       compute dst yinc

        mulu        d4,d3
        sub         d3,d5
        move        d5,dst_yinc(a5)        ;destination y increment

        and.b       #$f,d7
        or.b        skew_flags(pc,d6),d7   ;skew-flags from table

        move.b      d7,skew(a5)            ;in blitter

        move.b      #mhop_src,hop(a5)      ;half-tone operation: source only
        move.b      #3,op(a5)              ;replace mode

        lea         line_num(a5),a2        ;pointer to line number register
```

```
            move.b      #flinebusy,d2         ;busy bit after d2
            move        planes(a4),d7         ;number of bitplanes
            bra         begin

skew_flags:
            dc.b        mskewnfsr
            dc.b        mskewfxsr
            dc.b        0
            dc.b        mskewnfsr+mskewfxsr

            dc.b        0
            dc.b        mskewfxsr
            dc.b        0
            dc.b        0

next_plane:
            move.l      a0,src_addr(a5)       ;load source address
            move.l      a1,dst_addr(a5)       ;load destination address
            move        height(a4),y_count(a5) ;number of lines

            move.b      #mlinebusy,(a2)       ;start blitter
            add         src_nxpl(a4),a0       ;start next src plane
            add         dst_nxpl(a4),a1       ;start next dst plane

restart:
            bset        d2,(a2)               ;restart blitter
            nop
            bne         restart               ;not ready yet?

begin       dbra        d7,next_plane         ;next bitplane

            rts
end
```

Here are some extremely interesting sample programs for the BITBLT line-A command.

The first example defines a monochrome picture and copies it to a monchrome screen. The picture should appear on the screen starting at the coordinates X = 200 and Y = 100. This replaces the original screen contents using the replace mode. No raster is used, so the raster address is set to zero. The program looks like this:

```
;***********************************************************************
;              bitblt demo                                              *
;              copy one-color source range to monochrome screen         *
;***********************************************************************

          bitblt    equ       $a007          ;op code

          b_width   equ       0              ;width in pixel
          b_height  equ       2              ;height in pixel
          planes    equ       4              ;number of colorplanes
          fg_col    equ       6              ;foreground color
          bg_col    equ       8              ;background color
          op_tab    equ       10             ;logical operations

          s_xmin    equ       14             ;x-coordinate in source
          s_ymin    equ       16             ;y-coordinate in source
          s_form    equ       18             ;address of source
          s_nxwd    equ       22             ;offset of next word in source
          s_nxln    equ       24             ;offset of next line in source
          s_nxpl    equ       26             ;offset of next colorplane in source

          d_xmin    equ       28             ;x-coordinate in destination
          d_ymin    equ       30             ;y-coordinate in destination
          d_form    equ       32             ;address of destination
          d_nxwd    equ       36             ;offset of next word in destination
          d_nxln    equ       38             ;offset of next line in destination
          d_nxpl    equ       40             ;offset of next colorplane in
                                             ;destination

          p_addr    equ       42             ;address of raster used
          p_nxln    equ       46             ;offset of next line in raster
          p_nxpl    equ       48             ;offset of next colorplane in raster
          p_mask    equ       50             ;raster index mask (number of lines)

          physbase  equ       2
          xbios     equ       14

          do_blit   lea       para(pc),a6           ;pointer to parameter block

                    move      #92,b_width(a6)       ;width in pixel
                    move      #52,b_height(a6)      ;height in pixel

                    move      #1,planes(a6)         ;monochrome

                    move      #1,fg_col(a6)         ;foreground color
                    move      #0,bg_col(a6)         ;background color
```

```
            move.l    #$03030303,op_tab(a6)  ;replace mode

;                                            transfer source data
            move      #0,s_xmin(a6)          ;upper left corner of source
            move      #0,s_ymin(a6)
            move.l    #source,s_form(a6)     ;source address

            move      #2,22(a6)              ;2 byte offset of next word
            move      #12,s_nxln(a6)         ;80 byte offset of next
                                             ;line
            move      #2,s_nxpl(a6)          ;2 byte offset of next
                                             ;colorplane

;                                            screen is destination

            move      #200,d_xmin(a6)        ;x-coordinate of screen
            move      #100,d_ymin(a6)        ;y-coordinate of screen

            move      #physbase,-(sp)
            trap      #xbios                 ;get screen address
            addq.l    #2,sp

            move.l    d0,d_form(a6)          ;as destination address

            move      #2,d_nxwd(a6)          ;2 byte offset of next word
            move      #80,d_nxln(a6)         ;80 byte offset of next line
            move      #2,d_nxpl(a6)          ;2 byte offset of next
                                             ;colorplane

            clr.l     p_addr(a6)             ;no raster used

            dc.w      bitblt                 ;execute bitblt
            rts

            align
para:       ds.b      76                     ;76 byte parameter block

;           width  = 92       width of source in pixels
;           height = 52       height of source in pixels


source      dc.w      $AAAA,$AAAA,$AAAA,$AAAA,$AAAA,$AAA0
            dc.w      $5555,$5555,$5555,$5555,$5555,$5550
            dc.w      $AAAA,$AAAA,$AAAA,$AAAA,$AAAA,$AAA0
            dc.w      $5555,$5555,$5555,$5555,$5555,$5550
            dc.w      $AAAA,$AAAA,$AAAA,$AAAA,$AAAA,$AAA0
            dc.w      $5555,$5555,$5555,$5FD5,$5555,$5550
```

```
        dc.w    $AAAA,$AAAA,$AAAA,$B06A,$AAAA,$AAA0
        dc.w    $5555,$5555,$55FF,$E03D,$5555,$5550
        dc.w    $AAAA,$AAAA,$AB83,$000A,$AAAA,$AAA0
        dc.w    $D555,$5555,$5701,$FFEF,$5555,$5550
        dc.w    $EAAA,$AAAA,$AC00,$002A,$AAAA,$AAA0
        dc.w    $F555,$5555,$5FF7,$F7A7,$5555,$5550
        dc.w    $FAAA,$AAAA,$B00C,$18AE,$AAAA,$AAA0
        dc.w    $FD55,$5555,$7FF8,$0E9B,$5555,$5550
        dc.w    $E0AA,$AAAA,$C000,$02B2,$AAAA,$AAA0
        dc.w    $6555,$5555,$FFFF,$FC63,$5555,$5550
        dc.w    $B2AA,$AAAB,$0000,$04C6,$AAAA,$AAA0
        dc.w    $3555,$5555,$0700,$058B,$5555,$5550
        dc.w    $9AAA,$AAAB,$0880,$0712,$AAAA,$AAA0
        dc.w    $5955,$5555,$0F80,$0627,$5555,$5550
        dc.w    $A2AA,$AAAB,$0880,$044A,$AAAA,$AAA0
        dc.w    $5555,$5555,$0880,$0493,$5555,$5550
        dc.w    $AAAA,$AAAB,$0000,$0522,$AAAA,$AAA0
        dc.w    $5555,$5555,$03FC,$0647,$5555,$5550
        dc.w    $AAAA,$AAAB,$0204,$048C,$AAAA,$AAA0
        dc.w    $5555,$5555,$0204,$0519,$5555,$5550
        dc.w    $AAAA,$AAAB,$03FC,$0632,$AAAA,$AAA0
        dc.w    $5555,$5555,$0000,$0465,$5555,$5550
        dc.w    $AAAA,$AAAB,$0000,$04CA,$AAAA,$AAA0
        dc.w    $5555,$5555,$060C,$0595,$5555,$5550
        dc.w    $AAAA,$AAAB,$0FF8,$072A,$AAAA,$AAA0
        dc.w    $5555,$5555,$0000,$0655,$5555,$5550
        dc.w    $AAAA,$AAAB,$0000,$04AA,$AAAA,$AAA0
        dc.w    $5555,$5555,$0000,$0555,$5555,$5550
        dc.w    $AAAA,$AAAB,$FFFF,$FEAA,$AAAA,$AAA0
        dc.w    $5540,$0000,$0000,$0000,$0000,$1550
        dc.w    $AAA0,$0000,$0000,$0000,$0000,$0AA0
        dc.w    $5543,$C71E,$49EF,$9CF9,$C722,$1550
        dc.w    $AAA2,$2220,$5202,$2220,$88B2,$0AA0
        dc.w    $5542,$221C,$61C2,$3E20,$88AA,$1550
        dc.w    $AAA2,$2202,$5022,$2220,$88A6,$0AA0
        dc.w    $5543,$C73C,$4BC2,$2221,$C722,$1550
        dc.w    $AAA0,$0000,$0000,$0000,$0000,$0AA0
        dc.w    $5540,$0000,$0000,$0000,$0000,$1550
        dc.w    $AAA0,$0000,$0000,$0000,$0000,$0AA0
        dc.w    $5555,$5555,$5555,$5555,$5555,$5550
        dc.w    $AAAA,$AAAA,$AAAA,$AAAA,$AAAA,$AAA0
        dc.w    $5555,$5555,$5555,$5555,$5555,$5550
        dc.w    $AAAA,$AAAA,$AAAA,$AAAA,$AAAA,$AAA0
        dc.w    $5555,$5555,$5555,$5555,$5555,$5550
        dc.w    $AAAA,$AAAA,$AAAA,$AAAA,$AAAA,$AAA0
        dc.w    $5555,$5555,$5555,$5555,$5555,$5550
end
```

The next example tests out raster use. A raster is basically a graphic area which combines with a source range through a logical AND, and the desired logical operation is copied to the destination range. The comparison of the source range with the raster naturally occurs within the BITBLT function. The source range itself stays independent.

p_mask and p_addr correspond to the variables _patptr and _patmsk through the function $A004, HORIZONTAL LINE. The variable p_nxln gives the offset for the next line of the raster, and must be an even number, so a line from any number of 16 bit words must coincide, as well as source and destination.

A raster can usually be multicolor. The individual bitplanes must then be overlapped word for word as described in the beginning of this chapter. The raster index mask (p_mask) gives which raster line should be combined with the source line. From the source line the number of raster line comes from AND and p_mask. This is the usual count:

Raster Lines	p_mask
2	1
4	3
8	7
16	15

The blitter has 16 registers of 16 bits into which a raster can be loaded.

This sample program is almost identical to the earlier BITBLT demo. Just replace the material at the do_blit and raster labels with the coding below. Then save the new version of BITBLT under another name.

```
;*****************************************************************
;                                                                *
;        bitblt demo changes                                     *
;        copy one-color range to monchrome screen using a raster *
;                                                                *
;*****************************************************************
do_blit  lea     para(pc),a6         ;pointer to parameter block

         move    #92,b_width(a6)     ;width in pixels
         move    #52,b_height(a6)    ;height in pixels

         move    #1,planes(a6)       ;monochrome
```

```
        move      #1,fg_col(a6)         ;foreground color
        move      #0,bg_col(a6)         ;background color

        move.l    #$03030303,op_tab(a6) ;replace mode

;                                       transfer source data
        move      #0,s_xmin(a6)         ;source from upper left corner
        move      #0,s_ymin(a6)
        move.l    #source,s_form(a6)    ;source address

        move      #2,s_nxwd(a6)         ;2 byte offset to next word
        move      #12,s_nxln(a6)        ;80 byte offset to next line
        move      #2,s_nxpl(a6)         ;2 byte offset - next color plane
;                                       dest is screen

        move      #200,d_xmin(a6)       ;x-coordinate on screen
        move      #100,d_ymin(a6)       ;y-coordinate on screen

        move      #physbase,-(sp)
        trap      #xbios                ;get screen address
        addq.l    #2,sp

        move.l    d0,d_form(a6)         ;use as dest address

        move      #2,d_nxwd(a6)         ;2 byte offset of next word
        move      #80,d_nxln(a6)        ;80 byte offset to next line
        move      #2,d_nxpl(a6)         ;2 byte offset of next color
                                        ;plane

        move.l    #raster,p_addr(a6)    ;use raster
        move      #2,p_nxln(a6)         ;offset of next raster line
        move      #0,p_nxpl(a6)         ;single color raster
        move      #1,p_mask(a6)         ;raster index mask

        dc.w      bitblt                ;execute bitblt
        rts

        align

raster  dc.w      %1010101010101010     ;first raster line
        dc.w      %0101010101010101     ;second raster line

para:   ds.b      76            ;76-byte parameter block

;  source and rest of original program follow....
```

Every other pixel is deleted, giving us a raster.

Index

address bus	7,8
asynchronous bus control	8-9
ADDRESS STROBE (AS)	8
DTACK	9-12
LOWER DATA STROBE (LDS)	8
READ/WRITE (R/W)	8
UPPER DATA STROBE (UDS)	8
Asynchronous Communications Interface Adapter (ACIA)	41-47,62-63
pins	41-44
registers	45-47
BANK	55
Basic Input Output System (BIOS)	152-163,245,250
listing	271-461
BCD—see Binary Coded Decimal	
BERR	11-15
BG—see Bus Grant	
BGACK—see Bus Grant Acknowledge	
BGO—see Bus Grant Out	
Binary Coded Decimal (BCD)	4
BIOS—see Basic Input Output System	
BLANK	15
Blitter chip	204-205,469-476,484-496
Bus Grant (BG)	10,13
Bus Grant Acknowledge (BGACK)	10,13
Bus Grant Out (BGO)	13
Bus Request (BR)	1013
cartridge slot	96-98
Centronics interface	88-89
CLK	11
data bus	7
data registers	4
Data Request (DR)	22
DE—see Display Enable	
Digital Research	105
Direct Memory Access (DMA)	8-9,12-13,18-19,25,58-59,101-102
Display Enable (DE)	15
DMA—see Direct Memory Access	
DR—see Data Request	

exception vectors	235-237
FDC—see Floppy Disk Controller	
Floppy Disk Controller (FDC)	20-27
Command Register (CR)	24
Data Register (DR)	24
Sector Register (SR)	24
Status Register (STR)	24
Track Register (TR)	24
floppy disk interface	99-100
GEM graphics	206-234
high-res	207-210
line-A opcodes	227-234
line-A variables	224-226
lo-res	206-209
medium-res	205-207
GEM graphic commands	211-224
BITBLT	215-217
COPY RASTER FORM	224-225
CONTOUR FILL	223-224
DRAW SPRITE	222-223
FILLED POLYGON	214-215
FILLED RECTANGLE	213-214
GET PIXEL	211
HIDE CURSOR	221
HORIZONTAL LINE	213
Initialize	211
LINE	212
PUT PIXEL	211
SHOW MOUSE	220
TEXTBLT	217-222,232-235
TRANSFORM MOUSE	221,230-231
UNDRAW SPRITE	221-222,221-222
GEMDOS	105-151, 245
functions	106-151
error messages	151
GLUE	13-15, 18,69
HALT	11,12
HSYNC	15

IACK	13
integrated circuits	3-63
INTEL	3
interrupts	7,10,240-244
I/O registers	55-63
ACIAs	62
DMA/Disk Controller	58-59
keyboard	62
MFP 68901	60-61
MIDI	62
sound chip	59-60
Video Display Register	56-58
keyboard control	67-71,74-84
line-F emulator	238-239
longword	7
Memory Management Unit(MMU)	11,13,15-16,18,55
memory maps	62-63
MFP 68901—see Multi-Function Peripheral	
MFPINT	13
MIDI—see Musicial Instrument Digital Interface	
MMU—see Memory Management Unit	
Motorola 68000 microprocessor	3-12,258-270
instruction set	258-270
mouse	71-74
MS-DOS	106, 186
Multi-Function Peripheral(MFP 68901)	28-40,60-61,90,171,242-244
Active Edge Register(AER)	32
connections	28-32
Data Direction Register(DDR)	32
General Purpose I/O Interrupt Port(GPIP)	32
Interrupt Enable Register(IERA,IERB)	33
Interrupt In-Service Register(ISRA,ISRB)	34
Interrupt Mask Register(IMRA,IMRB)	34
Interrupt Pending Register(IPRA,IPRB)	33-34
Receiver Status Register(RSR)	38-39
registers	32-40
Synchronous Character Register(SCR)	37
Timer A/B Control Register(TACR,TBCR)	35
Timers C and D Control Register(TCDCR)	36

Timer Data Registers (TADR,TBDR,TCDR,TDDR)	37
Transmitter Status Register(TSR)	39-40
UCR/USART	37-38
UDR/USART	40
Vector Register(VR)	34
Musical Instrument Digital Interface(MIDI)	93-95,177
NMI—see Non-Maskable Interrupt	
Non-Maskable Interrupt (NMI)	6,13,240
operating system	105
PSG (Programmable Sound Generator)—see YM-2149 Sound Generator	
RESET	11-12
RS-232 interface	90-92,243-244
SHIFTER	13,15,17,18
status register	6
supervisor mode	4,6,7,235
synchronous bus control	9
E	9
Valid Memory Address (VMA)	9
Valid Peripheral Address (VPA)	9,10
system fonts	465-466
system variables	250-257
Tramiel Operating System (TOS)	105
UNIX	106
user mode	4,6,7,235
video interface	85-87
VSYNC	15
VT52 emulator	245-249
WD 1772	20-27
word	7
word access	8
XBIOS	164-205
YM-2149 Sound Generator	48-54

Optional Diskette

For your convenience, the program listings contained in this book are available on an SF354 formatted floppy disk. You should order the diskette if you want to use the programs, but don't want to type them in from the listings in the book.

All programs on the diskette have been fully tested. You can change the programs for your particular needs. The diskette is available for $14.95 plus $2.00 ($5.00 foreign) for postage and handling.

When ordering, please give your name and shipping address. Enclose a check, money order or credit card information. Mail your order to:

Abacus Software
P.O. Box 318
Grand Rapids, MI 49588

Or for fast service, call **616-698-0330**.

Selected Books from our ATARI ST Reference Library

3D Graphics

Teaches how to create impressive, lightning-fast three-dimensional graphics on the Atari ST in 68000 machine language. **Atari ST 3D Graphics** covers introductory concepts and background materials, graphic animation, using the assembler and much more.

Learn real-time animation with dozens of graphic routines. 3D Graphics is an amazing book for all programmers interested in advanced level graphics.

Some of the topics covered include:

- Mathematical basis for 3D graphics
- Coordinate systems
- Scaling the axis
- Two- and three-dimensional transformations
- Hidden lines & surfaces
- Data structure for 3D objects
- Object animation
- Spatial projection
- Rotation of objects
- Light and shadows
- Introduction to 3D computer-aided design (CAD)

A must for all serious ST programmers. **Atari ST 3D Graphics** includes complete listings for a fascinating 3D pattern-maker and animator. 351 pages.

Atari ST 3D Graphics   Suggested Retail Price: **$24.95**
Optional Diskette   Suggested Retail Price: **$14.95**

The programs are clearly printed, well commented, planned in a sensible modular fashion, and contain many invaluable assembly-language 'tips and tricks.' And they work. ST programmers are fortunate to have this book."

—Douglas Weir
ST-Log

ST Disk Drives: Inside and Out

The latest title in the widely-acclaimed *Abacus Atari ST Reference Library* is the exclusive **Atari ST Disk Drives: Inside and Out**. This outstanding technical reference is <u>the</u> definitive source of information for the ST disk drives—it thoroughly discusses the floppy disk, the hard disk and RAM disk from both a programming and a technical perspective. In addition, the reader will find several full-length utilities and programming tools that enables him to further explore the ST disk drives' operations and capabilities. Topics include:

- Information of sequential and random access file structures
- Access to data files from BASIC, Pascal, C, and FORTRAN
- Data structures and management
- The boot sector and BIOS parameter bloc (BPB)
- The directory and File Allocation Table (FAT)
- Relocation table
- Hard disk format
- Details of drive construction: (DMA chip, disk controller, connector layout, and organization, etc.
- Command description, status interpretation, floppy interface, hard disk partition analyzer

Atari ST Disk Drives: Inside and Out is literally packed with utility programs. The book includes a complete listing for an easy-to-use RAM disk, BASIC/TOS interface, BASIC/FDC interface, BASIC loaders, Floppy-to-RAM disk copy, creating standard and foreign formats, and many more timesaving programs. **Available April '87.**

ST Disk Drives: Inside and Out   Suggested Retail Price: **$24.95**
Optional Diskette   Suggested Retail Price: **$14.95**

Atari ST, 520ST, 1040ST, TOS, ST BASIC and ST LOGO are trademarks or registered trademarks of Atari Corp. GEM is a registered trademark of Digital Research Inc.

Selected Abacus Products for the ATARI ST

AssemPro

Machine language development system for the Atari ST

"...I wish I had (AssemPro) a year and a half ago... it could have saved me hours and hours and hours."
—Kurt Madden
ST World

"The whole system is well designed and makes the rapid development of 68000 assembler programs very easy."
—Jeff Lewis
Input

AssemPro is a complete machine language development package for the Atari ST. It offers the user a single, comprehensive package for writing high speed ST programs in machine language, all at a very reasonable price.

AssemPro is completely GEM-based—this makes it easy to use. The powerful integrated editor is a breeze to use and even has helpful search, replace, block, upper/lower case conversion functions and user definable function keys. AssemPro's extensive help menus summarizes hundreds of pages of reference material.

The fast macro assembler <u>assembles object code to either disk or memory.</u> If it finds an error, it lets you correct it (if possible) and continue. This feature alone can save the programmer countless hours of debugging.

The debugger is a pleasure to work with. It features single-step, breakpoint, disassembly, reassembly and 68020 emulation. It lets users thoroughly and conveniently test their programs immediately after assembly.

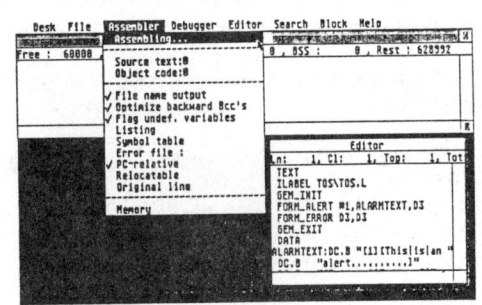

AssemPro Features:

- Full screen editor with dozens of powerful features
- Fast 68000 macro assembler assembles to disk or memory
- Powerful debugger with single-step, breakpoint, 68020 emulator, more
- Helpful tools such as disassembler and reassembler
- Includes comprehensive 175-page manual

AssemPro   Suggested retail price: **$59.95**

Atari ST, 520ST, 1040ST, TOS, ST BASIC and ST LOGO are trademarks or registered trademarks of Atari Corp.
GEM is a registered trademark of Digital Research Inc.

Selected Abacus Products for the ATARI ST

Chartpak ST

Professional-quality charts and graphs on the Atari ST

In the past few years, Roy Wainwright has earned a deserved reputation as a topnotch software author. **Chartpak ST** may well be his best work yet. **Chartpak ST** combines the features of his **Chartpak** programs for Commodore computers with the efficiency and power of GEM on the Atari ST.

Chartpak ST is a versatile package for the ST that lets the user make professional quality charts and graphs fast. Since it takes advantage of the ST's GEM functions, **Chartpak ST** combines speed and ease of use that was unimaginable til now.

The user first inputs, saves and recalls his data using **Chartpak ST**'s menus, then defines the data positioning, scaling and labels. **Chartpak ST** also has routines for standard deviation, least squares and averaging if they are needed. Then, with a single command, your chart is drawn instantly in any of 8 different formats—and the user can change the format or resize it immediately to draw a different type of chart.

In addition to direct data input, **Chartpak ST** interfaces with ST spreadsheet programs spreadsheet programs (such as **PowerLedger ST**). Artwork can be imported from **PaintPro ST** or DEGAS. Hardcopy of the finshed graphic can be sent most dot-matrix printers. The results on both screen and paper are documents of truly professional quality.

Your customers will be amazed by the versatile, powerful graphing and charting capabilities of **Chartpak ST** .

Chartpak ST works with Atari ST systems with one or more single- or double-sided disk drives. Works with either monochrome or color ST monitors. Works with most popular dot-matrix printers (optional).

Chartpak ST   Suggested Retail Price: **$49.95**

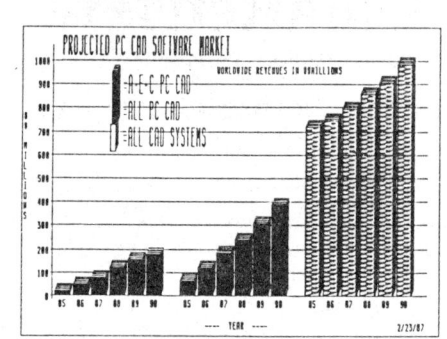

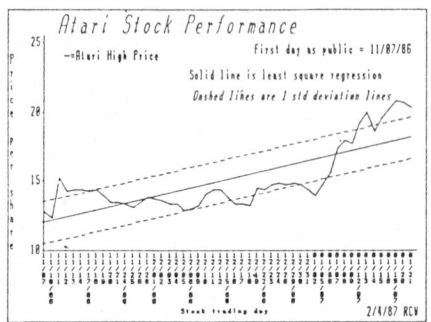

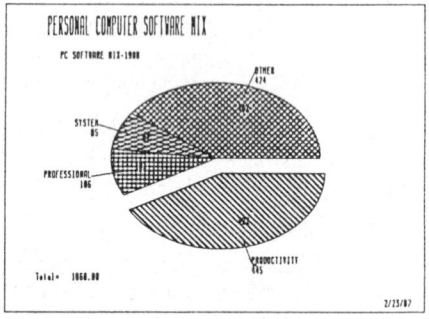

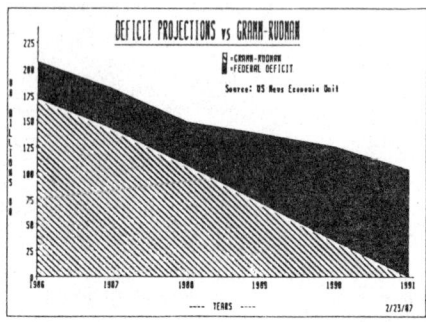

Selected Abacus Products for the ATARI ST

DataRetrieve

(formerly FilePro ST)

Database management package for the Atari ST

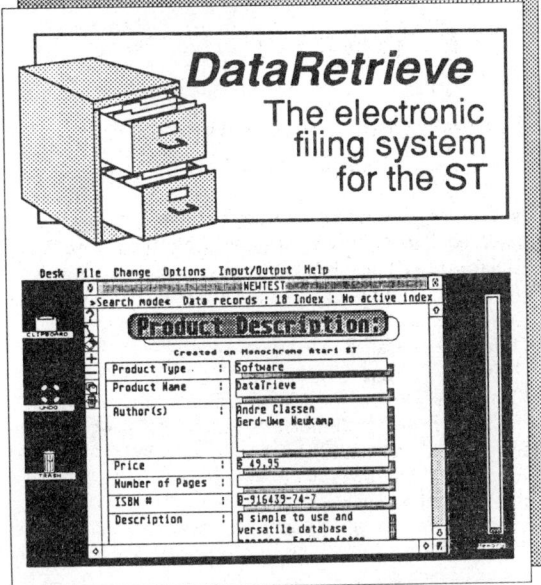

"DataRetrieve is the most versatile, and yet simple, data base manager available for the Atari 520ST/1040ST on the market to date."

—Bruce Mittleman
Atari Journal

DataRetrieve is one of Abacus' best-selling software packages for the Atari ST computers—it's received highest ratings from many leading computer magazines. **DataRetrieve** is perfect for your customers who need a powerful, yet easy to use database system at a moderate price of $49.95.

DataRetrieve's drop-down menus let the user quickly and easily define a file and enter information through screen templates. But even though it's easy to use, **DataRetrieve** is also powerful. **DataRetrieve** has fast search and sorting capabilities, a capacity of up to 64,000 records, and allows numeric values with up to 15 significant digits. **DataRetrieve** lets the user access data from up to four files simultaneously, indexes up to 20 different fields per file, supports multiple files, and has an integral editor for complete reporting capabilities.

DataRetrieve's screen templates are paintable for enhanced appearance on the screen and when printed, and data items may be displayed in multiple type styles and font sizes.

The package includes six predefined databases for mailing list, record/video albums, stamp and coin collection, recipes, home inventory and auto maintenance that users can customize to their own requirements. The templates may be printed on Rolodex cards, as well as 3 x 5 and 4 x 5 index cards. **DataRetrieve**'s built-in RAM disks support lightning-fast operation on the 1040ST. **DataRetrieve** interfaces to **TextPro** files, features easy printer control, many help screens, and a complete manual.

DataRetrieve works with Atari ST systems with one or more single- or double-sided disk drives. Works with either monochrome or color monitors. Printer optional.

DataRetrieve   Suggested Retail Price: **$49.95**

DataRetrieve Features:

- Easily define your files using drop-down menus
- Design screen mask size to 5000 by 5000 pixels
- Choose from six font sizes and six text styles
- Add circles, boxes and lines to screen masks
- Fast search and sort capabilities
- Handles records up to 64,000 characters in length
- Organize files with up to 20 indexes
- Access up to four files simultaneously
- Cut, past and copy data to other files
- Change file definitions and format
- Create subsets of files
- Interfaces with **TextPro** files
- Complete built-in reporting capabilities
- Change setup to support virtually any printer
- Add header, footer and page number to reports
- Define printer masks for all reporting needs
- Send output to screen, printer, disk or modem
- Includes and supports RAM disk for high-speed 1040ST operation
- Capacities: max. 2 <u>billion</u> characters per file
  max. 64,000 records per file
  max. 64,000 characters per record
  max. fields: limited only by record size
  max. 32,000 text characters per field
  max. 20 index fields per file
- Index precision: 3 to 20 characters
- Numeric precision: to 15 digits
- Numeric range $\pm 10^{-308}$ ti $\pm 10^{308}$

Atari ST, 520ST, 1040ST, TOS, ST BASIC and ST LOGO are trademarks or registered trademarks of Atari Corp.
GEM is a registered trademark of Digital Research Inc.

Selected Abacus Products for the ATARI ST

PaintPro

Design and graphics software for the ST

PaintPro is a very friendly and very powerful package for drawing and design on the Atari ST computers that has many features other ST graphic programs don't have. Based on GEM™, **PaintPro** supports up to three active windows in all three resolutions—up to 640x400 or 640x800 (full page) on monochrome monitor, and 320 x 200 or 320 x 400 on a color monitor.

PaintPro's complete toolkit of functions includes text, fonts, brushes, spraypaint, pattern fills, boxes, circles and ellipses, copy, paste and zoom and others. Text can be typed in one of four directions—even upside down—and in one of six GEM fonts and eight sizes. **PaintPro** can even load pictures from "foreign" formats (ST LOGO, DEGAS, Neochrome and Doodle) for enhancement using **PaintPro**'s double-sized picture format. Hardcopy can be sent to most popular dot-matrix printers.

PaintPro Features :

- Works in all 3 resolutions (mono, low and medium)
- Four character modes (replace, transparent, inverse XOR)
- Four line thicknesses and user-definable line pattern
- Uses all standard ST fill patterns and user definable fill patterns
- Max. three windows (dependng on available memory)
- Resolution to 640 x400 or 640x800 pixels (mono version only)
- Up to six GDOS type fonts, in 8-, 9-, 10-, 14-, 16-, 18-, 24- and 36-point sizes
- Text can be printed in four directions
- Handles other GDOS compatible fonts, such as those in **PaintPro Library # 1**
- Blocks can be cut and pasted; mirrored horizontally and vertically; marked, saved in LOGO format, and recalled in LOGO
- Accepts **ST LOGO, DEGAS, Doodle & Neochrome** graphics
- Features help menus, full-screen display, and UNDO using the right mouse button
- Most dot-matrix printers can be easily adapted

PaintPro works with Atari ST systems with one or more single- or double-sided disk drives. Works with either monochrome or color ST monitors. Printer optional.

PaintPro   Suggested Retail Price: **$49.95**

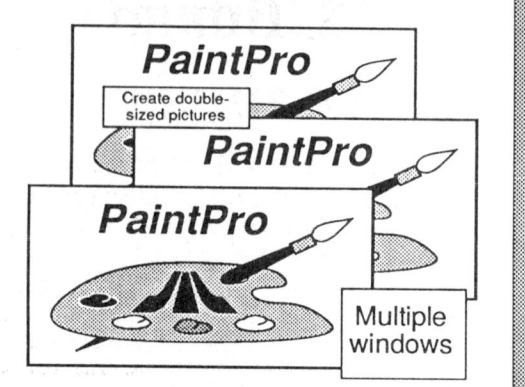

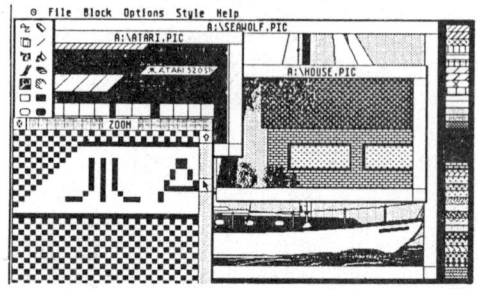

Selected Abacus Products for the

PCBoard Designer

Interactive CAD Package for printed circuit board layout on the Atari ST

PCBoard Designer is an interactive, computer-aided design package for creating electronic printed circuit boards. It drastically reduces the cost, time and tedium of making one or two-sided pc boards. The advanced features of **PCBoard Designer** can improve a designer's productivity ten-fold.

PCBoard Designer is easy to use. Design parameters are conveniently entered and modified at the computer. The user can position the components interactively by moving them on the screen using the mouse. This lets the user compare alternative component placement with no extra effort.

As the user position the components on the screen using the mouse, **PCBoard Designer** displays the new connections! Automatic routing is fast and precise.

The most powerful feature of **PCBoard Designer** is its fast automatic routing capability. Traces are automatically and precisely drawn on the screen. If the user changes the design, the traces can be immediately redrawn—this feature alone can save an enormous amount of time and money. In addition, the user has options of 45° or 90° angle traces, different trace widths, routing from pin to pin, pin to BUS, BUS to BUS, as well as two-sided boards. The rubberbanding feature lets you see the user-defined components during placement—and the user can reposition your components at any time during the design process.

PCBoard Designer prints the completed layout to any Epson/compatible dot matrix printer and Hewlett-Packard plotters at 2:1. The high-quality printout is camera-ready for final photo-etching. **PCBoard Designer** also prints the component layout, and lists every component and connection as well.

In conjuction with the Atari ST computer, **PCBoard Designer** is the most affordable PC board CAD package available. It boasts features that not available on systems costing thousands of dollars.

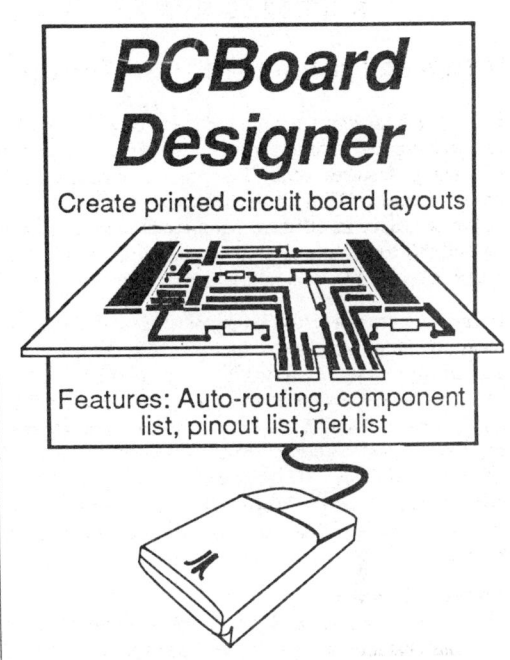

How PCBoard Designer works

There are basically four steps in creating a working pc board:

- **Specify the components:** For example, IC4 is an integrated circuit that fits in a 14-pin dual-in-line socket. You can also define custom component types, for example a 99-pin circular IC.

- **Specify the connections:** For example, pin 2 of integrated circuit IC4 is connected to lead 1 of transistor Q7. You can change the connections at any time.

- **Position the components:** Move the components to their desired position on the screen by using the Atari ST's mouse. You can reposition them at any time. **PCBoard Designer** automatically routes the connections when you're done.

- **Output the design:** The finished board can be printed on any Epson/compatible printer or Hewlett-Packard plotter. The printout is suitable for photoetching. You can also print the component layout (for silkscreening), the component list, and the list of connections.

Atari ST, 520ST, 1040ST, TOS, ST BASIC and ST LOGO are trademarks or registered trademarks of Atari Corp.
GEM is a registered trademark of Digital Research Inc.

Selected Abacus Products for the ATARI ST

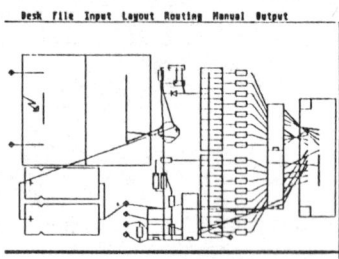

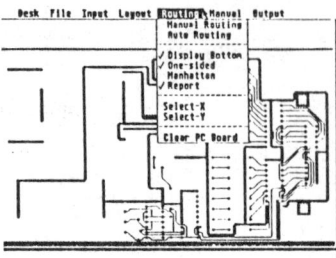

"I was thoroughly impressed... a powerful, multi-featured design tool that can be easily learned and used."

—Bill Marquardt
Input magazine

"What makes this program especially easy to use is that the components are drawn to scale on the screen. This comes in handy when it's time for the user to position the components.

"The author invested a lot of blood, sweat and tears writing this portion of the program. **PCBoard Designer** *has a wide selection of options here that allow for flexible design. Either all of the connections or an individual connection can be routed at the click of the mouse button.*

"One thing is clear, though: author Florian Sachse has produced a first-class software package. This program will undoubtedly be a godsend to the engineer and electronic hobbyist alike."

—DATA WELT Magazine
APRIL 1986

Abacus Software, Inc.
5370 52nd St. S.E.
Grand Rapids, MI 49508

(616) 698-0330

PCBoard Designer (continued)

PCBoard Designer Features:

- PC boards may be one-sided or two-sided
- Components are drawn to scale on the screen
- Custom components may be used
- Component positioning is flexible and interactive
- Components may be roatated in 90° increments
- Traces are drawn using sophisticated and fast automatic routing techniques—the user has the ability to make 45° and 90° angle traces, variable trace widths, pin to pin, pin to bus and bus to bus routing
- "Blockades" may be inserted onto the board to handle special cases
- Printout is high quality and suitable for photo-reproduction
- Features are clearly displayed and are selectable from the drop-down menus

Hardware Requirements:

Computer: Atari 520ST or 1040ST computer and monochrome monitor with one or more single-sided, double-sided, or hard disk drives.

Printers/Plotters: PCBoard Designer prints your completed layout to any Epson or Epson-compatible dot matrix printer at 2:1. Epson FX-80, FX-100, Toshiba, NEC P6 and P7 or compatible printersrequired for photo-ready traces. Also works on Hewlett/Packard plotters.

Package: Includes 100 page manual in 3-ring slipcase binder and program diskette.

Free phone support to registered users.

PCBoard Designer can dramatically improve design productivity by eliminating many redundant steps and time-consuming alterations. With all of its advanced time-saving capabilities, **PCBoard Designer** pays for itself after the first successfully designed board.

PCBoard Designer

Suggested Retail Price:
$195.00

Atari ST, 520ST, 1040ST, TOS, ST BASIC and ST LOGO are trademarks or registered trademarks of Atari Corp.
GEM is a registered trademark of Digital Research Inc.

Selected Abacus Products for the ATARI ST

PowerLedger ST
(formerly PowerPlan ST)

Spreadsheet/Graphics package for the Atari ST

"A superior spreadsheet program for weekend bookeeping to the heavyweight job costing applications, (Powerledger ST) is a definite winner."

—Judi Lambert
ST World

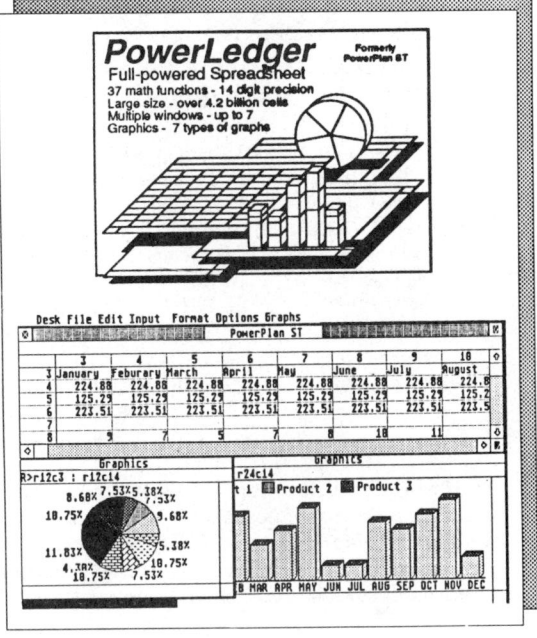

Ever since VisiCalc and Lotus 1-2-3 stormed the personal computer market, the computer has become an important planning tool. **PowerLedger ST** brings the power of electronic spreadsheets to the Atari ST line of computers—it lets the user quickly perform hundreds of calculations and "what-if" analyses for business applications, and crunch raw data into meaningful, comprehensible information, to keep track of budgets, expenses and statistics.

PowerLedger ST is a powerful analysis package that features a large spreadsheet (65,536 X 65,536 cells—over 4 <u>billion</u> data items). It also contains a built-in calculator, online notepad, and integrated graphics.

PowerLedger ST is also very easy to learn, since it uses the familiar GEM features built into the ST. And **PowerLedger ST** can use multiple windows—up to seven. Data from the spreadsheet can be graphically summarized in in pie charts, bar graphs and line charts, and displayed simultaneously with the spreadsheet. For example, one window can display part of the spreadsheet; a second window a different part; and a third window, a pie or bar chart of the data.

PowerLedger ST works hand-in-hand with our **DataTrieve** data management package and our **TextPro** wordprocessing package.

PowerLedger ST's extraordinary combination of data and graphic power, ease of use and low price makes it a perfect tool for every ST owner's financial planning needs.

PowerLedger ST works with Atari ST systems with one or more single- or double-sided disk drives. Works with either monochrome or color ST monitors. Works with most popular dot-matrix printers (optional).

PowerLedger ST Features:

- Familiar drop-down menus make PowerPlan easy to learn and use
- Large capacity spreadsheet serves all the user's analysis needs
- Convenient built-in notepad documents your important memos
- Flexible online calculator gives you access to quick computations
- Powerful options such as cut, copy and paste operations speeds the user'swork
- Integrated graphics summarize hundreds of data items
- Draws pie, bar, 3D bar, line and area charts automatically (7 chart types)
- Multiple windows emphasize the user's analyses
- Accepts information from DataTrieve, our database management software
- Passes data to **TextPro** wordprocessing package
- Capacities: maximum of 65,535 rows
  maximum of 65,535 columns
  variable column width
  numeric precision of 14 digits
  maximum value 1.797693×10^{308}
  minimum value 2.2×10^{-308}
  37 built-in functions

PowerLedger ST   Suggested Retail Price: **$79.95**

Atari ST, 520ST, 1040ST, TOS, ST BASIC and ST LOGO are trademarks or registered trademarks of Atari Corp.
GEM is a registered trademark of Digital Research Inc.

Selected Abacus Products for the ATARI ST

TextPro
Wordprocessing package for the Atari ST

"TextPro seems to be well thought out, easy, flexible anf fast. The program makes excellent use of the GEM interface and provides lots of small enhancements to make your work go more easily... if you have an ST and haven't moved up to a GEM word processor, pick up this one and become a text pro."

—John Kintz
ANTIC

"TextPro is the best wordprocessor available for the ST"

—Randy McSorley
Pacus Report

TextPro is a first-class word processor for the Atari ST that boasts dozens of features for the writer. It was designed by three writers to incorporate features that they wanted in a wordprocessor—the result is a superior package that suits the needs of all ST owners.

TextPro combines its "extra" features with easy operation, flexibility, and speed—but at a very reasonable price. The two-fingered typist will find **TextPro** to be a friendly, user-oriented program, with all the capabilities needed for fine writing and good-looking printouts. **Textpro** offers full-screen editing with mouse or keyboard shortcuts, as well as high-speed input, scrolling and editing. **TextPro** includes a number of easy to use formatting commands, fast and practical cursor positioning and multiple text styles.

Two of **TextPro**'s advanced features are automatic table of contents generation and index generation—capabilities usually found only on wordprocessing packages costing hundreds of dollars. **TextPro** can also print text horizontally (normal typewriter mode) or vertically (sideways). For that professional newsletter look, **TextPro** can print the text in columns—up to six columns per page in sideways mode.

The user can write form letters using the convenient Mail Merge option. **TextPro** also supports GEM-oriented fonts and type styles—text can be **bold**, underlined, *italic*, superscript, outlined, etc., and in a number of point sizes. **TextPro** even has advanced features for the programmer for development with its Non-document and C-sourcecode modes.

TextPro ST Features:

- Full screen editing with either mouse or keyboard
- Automatic index generation
- Automatic table of contents generation
- Up to 30 user-defined function keys, max. 160 characters per key
- Lines up to 180 characters using horizontal scrolling
- Automatic hyphenation
- Automatic wordwrap
- Variable number of tab stops
- Multiple-column output (maximum 5 columns)
- Sideways printing on Epson FX and compatibles
- Performs mail merge and document chaining
- Flexible and adaptable printer driver
- Supports RS-232 file transfer (computer-to-computer transfer possible)
- Detailed 65+ page manual

TextPro works with Atari ST systems with one or more single- or double-sided disk drives. Works with either monochrome or color ST monitors.

TexPro allows for flexible printer configurations with most popular dot-matrix printers.

TextPro   Suggested Retail Price: **$49.95**

Atari ST, 520ST, 1040ST, TOS, ST BASIC and ST LOGO are trademarks or registered trademarks of Atari Corp.
GEM is a registered trademark of Digital Research Inc.

ATARI ST REQUIRED READING

INTERNALS
Essential guide to learning the inside information of the ST. Detailed descriptions of sound & graphics chips, internal hardware, various ports, GEM. Commented BIOS listing. An indispensible reference for your library. 450pp. $19.95

GEM Programmer's Ref.
For serious programmers in need of detailed information on GEM. Written with an easy-to-understand format. All GEM examples are written in C and assembly. Required reading for the serious programmer. 450pp. $19.95

TRICKS & TIPS
Fantastic collection of programs and info for the ST. Complete programs include: super-fast RAM disk; time-saving printer spooler; color print hardcopy; plotter output hardcopy. Money saving tricks and tips. 200 pp. $19.95

GRAPHICS & SOUND
Detailed guide to understanding graphics & sound on the ST. 2D & 3D function plotters, Moiré patterns, various resolutions and graphic memory, fractals, waveform generation. Examples written in C, LOGO, BASIC and Modula2. $19.95

BASIC Training Guide
Indispensible handbook for beginning BASIC programmers. Learn fundamentals of programming. Flowcharting, numbering system, logical operators, program structures, bits & bytes, disk use, chapter quizzes. 200pp. $16.95

PRESENTING THE ST
Gives you an in-depth look at this sensational new computer. Discusses the architecture of the ST, working with GEM, the mouse, operating system, all the various interfaces, the 68000 chip and its instructions, LOGO. $16.95

MACHINE LANGUAGE
Program in the fastest language for your Atari ST. Learn the 68000 assembly language, its numbering system, use of registers, the structure & important details of the instruction set, and use of the internal system routines. 280pp $19.95

LOGO
Take control of your ATARI ST by learning LOGO—the easy-to-use, yet powerful language. Topics covered include structured programming, graphic movement, file handling and more. An excellent book for kids as well as adults. $19.95

PEEKS & POKES
Enhance your programs with the examples found within this book. Explores using the different languages BASIC, C, LOGO and machine language, using various interfaces, memory usage, reading and saving from and to disk, more. $16.95

BEGINNER'S GUIDE
Finally a book for those new to the ST wanting to understanding ST basics. Thoroughly understand your ST and its many devices. Learn the fundamentals of BASIC, LOGO and more. Complete with index, glossary and illustrations. +200pp $16.95

BASIC TO C
If you are already familiar with BASIC, learning C will be all that much easier. Shows the transition from a BASIC program, translated step by step, to the final C program. For all users interested in taking the next step. $19.95

The ATARI logo and ATARI ST are trademarks of Atari Corp.

Abacus Software

5370 52nd Street SE Grand Rapids, MI 49508 Phone (616) 698-0330

Optional diskettes are available for all book titles at **$14.95**
Call **now** for the name of your nearest dealer. Or order directly from ABACUS with your MasterCard, VISA, or Amex card. Add $4.00 per order for postage and handling. Foreign add $10.00 per book. **Other software and books coming soon.** Call or write for your **free** catalog. Dealer inquiries welcome—over 1400 dealers nationwide.

How to Order

Abacus 5370 52nd Street SE Grand Rapids, MI 49508

All of our ST products—applications and language software, and our acclaimed 14 volume **Atari ST Reference Library**—are available at more than 2000 dealers in the U.S. and Canada. To find out the location of the Abacus dealer nearest to you, call:

 **(616) 698-0330**
8:30 am-8:00 pm Eastern Standard Time

Or order from Abacus directly by phone with your credit card. We accept Mastercard, Visa and American Express.

Every one of our software packages is backed by the **Abacus 30-Day Guarantee**–if for any reason you're not satisfied by the software purchased directly from us, simply return the prooduct for a full refund of the purchase price.

Order Blank

Send your completed order blank to:
Abacus Software
5370 52nd Street SE
Grand Rapids, MI 49508

Your order will be shipped within 24 hours of our receiving it

Name:
Address:
City   State   Zip   Country
Phone: /

Qty	Name of product	Price
	Mich. residents add 4% sales tax	
	Shipping/Handling charge (Foreign Orders $12 per item)	$4.00
	Check/Money order TOTAL enclosed	

Credit Card#
Expiration date   Cardholder Signature

For extra-fast 24-hour shipment service, order by phone with your credit card

ATARI ST INTERNALS

This INTERNALS volume is a welcome addition to any ST programmer's library. Inside you'll find important hardware and programming information for your ST. Contains valuable information for the professional programmer and ST novice. Here is a short list of some of the things you can expect to read about:

- 68000 processor
- WD 1772 disk controller
- ACIA's 6850
- Centronics interface
- MIDI-interface
- GEMDOS
- Interrupt instructions
- BIOS listing
- Custom chips
- MFP 68901
- YM-2149 sound generator
- RS-232
- DMA controller
- BIOS & XBIOS
- Error codes
- Blitter chip

About the authors:
The authors, Klaus Gerits, Lothar Englisch and Rolf Bruckmann, are all part of the experienced Data Becker Product Development team, based in Duesseldorf, W. Germany. They are all best selling computer book authors and very knowledgable concerning the subjects presented in this book.

ISBN 0-916439-46-1

A Data Becker book pu

You Can Count On
Abacus